CHICANO ODYSSEY

TRAJECTORIES ACROSS A MILLENNIUM

CHICANO ODYSSEY

Trajectories Across a Millennium

Michael A. Mares, PhD

© 2025 by Michael A. Mares, PhD
All Rights Reserved
No part of this book may be reproduced in any form or by any electronic or mechanical means including information storage and retrieval systems without permission in writing from the publisher, except by a reviewer who may quote brief passages in a review.

Sunstone books may be purchased for educational, business, or sales promotional use. For information please write: Special Markets Department, Sunstone Press, P.O. Box 2321, Santa Fe, New Mexico 87504-2321.
Printed on acid-free paper
∞
eBook: 978-1-61139-768-0

Library of Congress Cataloging-in-Publication Data

Names: Mares, Michael A., 1945- author
Title: Chicano odyssey : trajectories across a millennium / Michael A. Mares, PhD.
Description: Santa Fe : Sunstone Press, [2025] | Summary: "The story of how Chicanos or Mexican American Indo-Hispanic mestizos, came to America more than five hundred years ago and are active contributors to the American future"-- Provided by publisher.
Identifiers: LCCN 2025033392 | ISBN 9781632937384 paperback | ISBN 9781632937537 hardcover | ISBN 9781611397680 epub
Subjects: LCSH: Martínez family | Myers family | Devine family | Gutiérrez family | Mexican Americans--New Mexico | Mexican Americans--Ethnic identity | Mexican Americans--Politics and government | Mexican Americans--Race identity | New Mexico--Genealogy
Classification: LCC F805.M5 M37 2025 | DDC 929.20973--dc23/eng/20250903
LC record available at https://lccn.loc.gov/2025033392

WWW.SUNSTONEPRESS.COM
SUNSTONE PRESS / POST OFFICE BOX 2321 / SANTA FE, NM 87504-2321 /USA
(505) 988-4418

1a: San Felipe Church in the early 1940s by Fred Geary. Woodblock print, permanent art collection, Kansas State University.

Acknowledgements

My wife, Lynn, read and edited the entire book and knew much of the story I was telling since she met me in 1960 and we married in 1966. John J. Aragon, an Old Town, Albuquerque, New Mexico Chicano, has known me since 1950—longer than any living person—and shared with me the grim educational experiences at San Felipe School. He read parts of the manuscript and made many helpful suggestions, especially by providing names of outstanding Chicanos who merited inclusion in my appendix of extraordinary Chicanos. Janalee Caldwell also read and commented on an early draft of the entire manuscript. Paul Handford provided some interesting citations for me to consider, proving that an Oxford education can be useful. My brother, Chris, reminded me of many of the odd characters in Old Town who are mentioned in the book. Douglas P. Reagan, a friend since 1966, read parts of the manuscript, made many suggestions and encouraged me to complete the book and get it published. My aunt Donna, widow of Christie Mares, made photographs and written documents available to me related to his military history and early life. His son, Danny, also assisted with aspects of gathering documents related to my Uncle Christie. Quinn Floch generously prepared the figures. I thank them all.

Contents

Preface » 15

1 / The National Medal » 17

2 / You Don't Look Chinese » 25

3 / What the Hell Am I? » 43

4 / Genetic Trails Across Time and Space » 45

5 / I'm Not Mexican, I'm Spanish » 67

6 / Oñate and the Conquistadors » 83

7 / Erasing the Conquistadors » 101

8 / Wars of Conquest » 121

9 / A Chicano Oasis » 139

10 / Child of No One » 145

11 / Chicano Childhood » 155

12 / Hard Times in Old Town » 175

13 / A Green Island in a Brown Sea » 183

14 / Chicanos in the Valley, Anglos in the Heights » 191

15 / Outhouses, Pachucos, Rock and Roll » 205

16 / Learning to Read and Calculate » 215

17 / San Felipe de Neri School » 223

18 / Altar Boy » 235

19 / Music and the Church » 243

20 / Family Gatherings, Playing in the Barrio » 257

21 / Sister Blandina and San Felipe School » 267

22 / A "Murder" by Nuns » 275

23 / Highway Laborer » 291

24 / Ranch Life During the Great Depression » 297

25 / New Bishop in Town » 307

26 / Wagon Mound » 313

27 / Tracks Across New Mexico » 323

28 / A Mexican Marine » 335

29 / "Time just gets away from us." » 357

30 / Notable Mexican Americans / Chicanos » 385

Readings » 431

For:

Juana Rebecca Gutierrez Devine. Grandma, 1874–1963

Maria Adelina Florencia Devine. Nina, 1902–1998

William Leslie Devine. Billy, 1904–1996

Tus vidas me salvaron.

September 9, 2022, Santa Fe, New Mexico. I arose before dawn and watched the giant orange full moon—the harvest moon—from my back patio in the foothills above Santa Fe as it was setting over the Jemez Mountains to the west, seeming to sink into the dark earth while falling from the star-filled sky. With binoculars, I was able to see Crater Alphonsus, a seventy-mile-wide crater named after Spanish King Alfonso of Castile, also known as Alfonso the Wise, an early astronomer. Alfonso was my twenty-third great grandfather. ¡Hola abuelo!

Preface

My maternal great great grandmother was born in Spain in 1814; my great grandmother was born in Mexico in 1831; my grandmother was born in the United States in 1874. They were not born hundreds of miles apart but each entered the world in the same small complex of adobe houses in Old Town, Albuquerque, New Mexico, which had passed from Spanish rule to Mexico and to the United States in the period from 1692–1850. (Chapter 9)

As I write these words in August, 2024, only a few months before the U.S. presidential election, it is clear Chicanos/Mexicans/Mestizos—even those with a long history in this country—are going to be persecuted in new ways should the Republican Project 2025 be put in place by a new administration. Among other things, the plan is extremely anti-immigration, especially for non-White people. It is designed to stop immigration completely across the Mexican border and to find all undocumented or marginally-documented immigrants already in the country, capture them, and deport them (with or without their families), including the ever-hopeful Dreamers. They'll disappear.

New Mexico's story is one of racial changes over time, but Chicanos who originally comprised the vast majority of New Mexico's people make up only about half the population of the state today. While the percentage of Chicanos has declined somewhat over the years, and while there have been economic and cultural impediments placed in the paths of Chicanos and Native Americans, there has been lots of intervening strife (but also some harmony among the ethnic groups over the years in New Mexico).

This book is my attempt to highlight parts of a complex single-family lineage in New Mexico, a lineage that can be followed into the dim mists of history. My grandparents were Mares, Martinez, Devine and Gutierrez. I traced some of them back through time across the ages. The easiest family to follow as far as genealogy is concerned is the Martinez family, which has left clear tracks back to medieval Spain and was examined by genealogists decades ago. Thus, I have concentrated on that group of ancestors and relatives. The Mares, Gutierrez, and Devine families are more difficult to trace back through time, so I have expended much less effort on those lineages. Regardless of which lineage I followed, however, members of my extended family have left a mark on the State of New Mexico as they lived their lives and, for that matter, left a mark on the Americas and the lands of their origin. My story also illustrates what it was like to grow up in New Mexico as a Chicano in the 1940s and 1950s, where cultures had clashed in the past, and where young people growing up in the mid-20th century had to overcome challenges that were echoes of those past conflicts.

Michael A. Mares, PhD
Santa Fe, New Mexico

I

THE NATIONAL MEDAL

May 8, 2014 in Washington, DC, was a beautifully sunny spring day. I had been flown to our nation's capital as a guest of the White House because my museum (the Sam Noble Oklahoma Museum of Natural History) had been selected as one of the top museums in the United States and was to receive the nation's highest honor for a museum, the National Medal for Museums and Libraries. I was the museum's director and had been the person responsible for the development, construction, and operation of the museum since the early 1980s. I was permitted to invite a guest to be part of the medal ceremony and chose Ernesto Vargas-Parra, a high school student who had won a prestigious Gates Scholarship to pay for his college expenses. He won in part because he had participated in one of the museum's innovative educational programs that dealt with discovering and studying fossils—ExplorOlogy®. Such programs help separate kids from the crowds of other applicants for scholarships or to enter universities. Our museum provided Oklahoma students, many of whom were from small towns in rural Oklahoma or have few educational resources in an impoverished state, the chance to do real field and laboratory science on vertebrate fossils with real scientists.

Ernesto is the son of Mexican migrant fruit pickers and had been born in the same Seattle-area hospital as my granddaughter because his parents were picking fruit in Washington at the time. (My younger son, an attorney and graduate of the University of Washington School of Law, was living in Seattle when his daughter was born. My late elder son was also there working as a Microsoft game software engineer.)

One of Ernesto's major high school educational accomplishments was being selected for, and completing, the museum's ExplorOlogy® program. The class studied fossils with museum curators who published their work regularly in major scientific journals. Some were leaders in their particular field of science. The students learned how to work and care for museum collections and then traveled with the actual field researchers to various localities in and out of Oklahoma. They were able to learn how paleontologists do their work and were members of research teams that discovered new fossils, species new to science that had never before been known about or seen. By having Ernesto attend the White House ceremony, I would underline how powerful the museum's fossil education program was in a state that offers few opportunities in science for high school students. The fact that he was a Chicano, son of Mexican migrant fruit pickers, just highlighted how effective the museum's outreach programs were at reaching students who normally would never have the opportunity to be included in such special educational programs.

Ernesto is intellectually gifted and motivated and was a star of the program. His visit to DC would give him a once-in-a-lifetime opportunity to see the White House and participate in the national medal ceremony. Ernesto and I were both excited to attend and neither of us had ever been to the White House. I thought how extraordinary that two Chicanos, one young and just starting out, and the other old and coming to the end of a long career, should both end up being honored together at the White House. What a country. [Note: On May 22, 2024, Ernesto Vargas-Parra successfully defended his PhD thesis on the evolution of fossil trilobites at the American Museum of Natural History in their program of Comparative Biology.]

The White House

My wife accompanied us to DC; she had actually been to the White House when she was in high school. She had been in the Civil Air Patrol cadet program and was selected as the top cadet for the State of New Mexico in 1962 when she was seventeen years old. This meant she flew on an Air Force C-47 (the kind of plane that carried U.S. paratroopers to jump behind the D-Day beaches at Normandy) from Albuquerque to Washington DC, with numerous stops along the way to pick up other cadets and to refuel. In Washington, she met President John F. Kennedy in the Rose Garden, shook his hand and chatted with him for a few seconds.

Though I have been to Washington, DC more than a hundred times over the years for science advisory business, museum work, as a member of the Fulbright Board of Directors, serving on various Smithsonian committees, working on several National Science Foundation committees, advising the Ford Foundation, lectures, tourism, even to testify before Congress about the importance of museums in American life, Lynn had been one-up on me for White House visits for a half century. A picture of her and John F. Kennedy shaking hands hangs above her desk. As we entered the White House she said, "I like to check up on the White House every fifty years or so to see how they're keeping it up."

The Ceremony

The museum medals were to be presented by First Lady Michelle Obama in the East Room, which is the room seen almost every day on TV with the gold curtains and brass fixtures. When we were there, large paintings of George and Martha Washington were hung behind the stage. Each awardee and their guest were given a chance to meet individually with Mrs. Obama for a chat and for a photo op before the ceremony.

Fig. 1b: Michelle Obama awarding the National Medal for Museums and Libraries to the author. Ernesto Vargas is the student from the museum program.

I had read about how people have ideas of things they want to say when they meet a really powerful or famous person and then clam up and stumble over their words. No one is immune. I was a glib museum director and professor and had lectured to thousands of people at a time at many universities and international conferences. I was sure that would not happen to me. I was wrong. I muttered some things to her that she barely heard, but she graciously responded to me in any case. If I ever meet her again, I will do better. I learned after Queen Elizabeth's death, as stories of her life came out, that when President Barack Obama first met the Queen he, too, became tongue tied. I understand completely, Mr. President.

I showed Mrs. Obama a picture of my baby granddaughter sitting on the floor watching President Obama's speech the night he was elected. I told her how important medical care was for us, especially to cover pre-existing conditions. Mrs. Obama said they were fighting for exactly that kind of care for the people of America, especially the children.

There were only ten museums and ten libraries being honored with the National Medal, out of one hundred fifty thousand such organizations in the country. Each museum director, or librarian, or other official, along with the guest they had brought, was asked to go up on the stage one at a time to meet with Mrs. Obama where she would make the presentations. The unique programs and accomplishments of each organization were described to the gathered crowd as the medal and plaque were awarded.

The room was full of supporters, reporters, politicians and other VIPs. Mrs. Obama, who is very tall, leaned down to me as the accomplishments of the Sam Noble Museum were being described and, remembering my garbled conversation earlier in the day, said, "When you go home, I want you to hug your granddaughter and tell her the hug came from me." When the Sam Noble Museum was introduced, Mrs. Obama talked about our fossil programs for school children and our Native American language programs, which were reaching thousands of Native people and their tribes, not only in Oklahoma, but across the United States, helping bring back languages nearly lost due to U.S. government policy against Native Americans.

The medal ceremony was broadcast on White House Television on the World Wide Web and museum staff members back in Norman, Oklahoma, who were an integral part of our success and, indeed, museum supporters around the world could watch it and cheer. When all of the medals had been presented and the photographs taken, we were told we could visit any parts of the White House open to the public and would gather for a reception in the state dining room later in the day.

We were given the run of many of the public rooms of the White House before and after the ceremony in the East Room. Michelle Obama noted at the start of the medal ceremony that the White House is, in effect, a museum. As we wandered through the many rooms, gawking at the items and artwork on display and marveling at the history of America's marvelous house, we came upon Aaron Schikler's painting of John F. Kennedy. This painting was always my favorite painting of Kennedy and is the one overseen by Jackie Kennedy, herself, eight years after Kennedy's assassination.

The painting shows Kennedy looking down, thinking deep thoughts, no doubt, and looking like a humble man. I always found the painting illustrated so many of Kennedy's qualities as perceived by us, the people of the United States. I took a photo of it and sent it to my son in Seattle. He responded immediately with, "Wow! You're there all right." And I was. Who would have imagined this when I began my life's journey so many decades earlier in the Chicano barrio at the heart of Albuquerque. I turned to my wife and said, "This is a long way from Old Town."

Fig. 2. Exterior of the San Felipe Church in Old Town, Albuquerque, New Mexico, ca. 1881. Center for Research, University Libraries, University of New Mexico.

Fig. 3. Great grandfather Juan Gutierrez (seated against fence) outside San Felipe Church where a funeral is underway, Old Town, Albuquerque, New Mexico, ca. 1890.

2

YOU DON'T LOOK CHINESE

I was interviewing for a position as assistant professor at the University of Pittsburgh in 1973 with my newly-minted PhD in zoology recently awarded by The University of Texas at Austin and was asked about my ethnic background. Such a question would not be asked today, of course, but a half century ago it was common to inquire. "I'm a Chicano," I said proudly. The man looked me over carefully and said, "Gee, you don't look Chinese." Lo these many years later, the United States is still struggling to understand its history as it pertains to minorities, especially Latinos (whatever those are) and as my genetic makeup will make clear, we Chicanos are composed of all races.

I consider myself Chicano, which I will define later. Other designations, such as Latino, Hispanic, Latin X, Mexican-American and others are often labels used to try to include anyone who speaks Spanish or has Spanish-speaking ancestors. People who are primarily Mexican, Puerto Rican, Cuban, South American, or have other ethnic origins, are often lumped together with Chicanos. However, we are very different, as will be shown.

The United States has been a nation with a predominantly White culture from the inception of the country on the east coast-largely by slave-holding Founding Fathers—and continuing through the 21st century, with bloody hiatuses for the Mexican War of the 1840s, the Civil War in the 1860s, and the Indian Wars West of the Mississippi from 1811–1924. Remarkably, the after-effects from all of these wars are still felt strongly today. A nation does not readily recover from a bloody war and America has never quite come to grips with minorities and how to deal with them, or with the people who were conquered. So many of America's modern problems can be traced to those three wars over the span of a century of the life of this young nation and ended more than a century ago. Thus, we still see challenges in dealing with Americans who are Black, Hispanic, and Native American—challenges that are the legacy of these wars that were so destructive to both the people who lost the war, as well as to those who won.

This is especially true in the former slave states, which are still dedicated to maintaining a dominant White culture and power structure; hence their efforts at redistricting and impeding access to voting by minorities and denying the full benefits of being U.S. citizens to Americans of color. In those former slave states and in some other deeply red states, they do not want Blacks voting. Period. And in Texas, they don't want either Blacks or Mexicans voting. ¡Caramba!

Native Americans

Indians have struggled to attain full citizenship since they were conquered in the Indian Wars, which lasted for over a century. The Dawes Act of 1887 was designed to assimilate Native peoples into American society, but it mainly functioned to steal their lands, eliminate their languages, and destroy their cultures. Only in 1924 did the Fifteenth Amendment grant the right to vote to Indians, but it took another forty years for all states to approve the amendment. Arizona did not allow Indian voting until 1948. New Mexico, which today has almost a quarter of a million Indians that make up more than ten percent of the state's population, did not permit Indian voting until the summer of my third year (1948). After the 1924 amendment, only two states remained to grant Indian voting rights: Maine and Utah. (Rollings, 2004) Maine gave in on

Indian voting rights in 1954, which left Utah as the last holdout. A court case that challenged Utah's residency requirements for voting—the last hope of Whites controlling Indian voting rights anywhere in the United States—was, surprisingly, upheld by the Utah Supreme Court, but under pressure from the U.S. Supreme Court, the residency laws were changed in Utah in 1957.

New Mexico Senator Joseph "Little Joe" Montoya, who had been an honorable liberal Chicano member of the Senate and served on the Watergate Committee, tried to deny voting rights to Indians in New Mexico in 1962 because he had lost his bid for Lieutenant Governor of New Mexico based on the votes of Navajos voting for his political rival, Tom Bolack. He argued the Indian votes should not be counted. The state court ruled Indians were part of the State of New Mexico and had the right to vote and have their votes counted. Ironically, Little Joe's Indian roots were deep, like members of other founding families of New Mexico, whereas his opponent Bolack was an Anglo oilman from Kansas. Little Joe voted against his own people.

The White power structure in many western states did not give up trying to limit voting rights for Indians and others. Through refusing to print ballots in Native languages, not placing polling places on reservations, requiring literacy tests and poll taxes, and by other nefarious mechanisms, people were still being kept from voting even after the passage of the Equal Rights Amendment. The Voting Rights Act of 1965 and related legislation in the seventies and eighties finally made it possible for Indians and others to vote more easily. (Library of Congress, 2023)

Texas has had trouble with Mexico since the Texas Revolution of 1835–1836 when the *Texians* stole Texas from the Mexicans because they wanted Texas to be a new slave nation and Mexico would not permit it. (Burrough *et al.*, 2021) In the Southwest, where peoples' memories are long, the results of the Mexican War (ended by the Treaty of Guadalupe Hidalgo) reverberate still today. American society continues to be challenged by minorities and the social upheavals from both wars. The reddest states in the Union have engaged in activities against Blacks and Chicanos for more than a century and a half and show no signs of stopping in the 21st century, but, as Bob Dylan sang, "The times they are a changing."

Demographics of immigration, lifespan, reproduction, and other qualities of society make a shift in the country from a majority-White nation to a White-minority nation inevitable by the mid-21st century, barring massive social changes such as deportations of millions, a civil war, a world war, or other major societal cataclysms. The end of slavery is marked by African Americans who celebrate Juneteenth as the actual end to slavery, marking the date federal troops arrived in Galveston, Texas (Texas again) on June 19, 1866, to inform the population the Emancipation Proclamation had eliminated slavery throughout the nation, including Texas, much to its chagrin. But prejudice and active efforts to limit voting by Blacks continue unabated.

Mexican and other Hispanic immigrants are currently flooding into the United States and within a few decades will be voting citizens. Moreover, as Donald Trump noted, these people are breeders. My great great grandmother, María del Carmen Mestas "Carmel" Sanchez, gave birth to twenty-five children in the 1820s and 1830s, though seventeen were stillborn. (There was no medical care in those days on the frontier.) My great grandfather, Don Pedro Martinez, had twenty-one children with two wives, one of whom (my great grandmother) died in childbirth with her fourteenth pregnancy.

In the 21st century, the White citizens of the United States have reduced their reproductive rate to the lowest level in decades. This is the final horror being confronted by the former slave states. It is a horror in the deep red states that supported Donald Trump and his thin veneer of racism and White supremacy. Their time is passing and they can neither come to grips with this fact, nor delay the inevitable. They live in fear, whether or not they are conscious of it.

Chicanos in a Changing United States

In 2022, the politically far right has come to embrace Replacement Theory, an idea that Whites are victims of some sort of minority, liberal, feminist, and Democratic cabal to increase the numbers of minorities and decrease the percentage of Whites in the U.S. population—dooming them to minority status forever. These ideas are not limited to the United States; they are global in scope and very popular with European Nazis. Ironically, as far as the U.S is concerned, those espousing the ideas are correct, but for the wrong reasons. They are presciently seeing the future, but they are not grasping the causes of this societal shift. They wish to cast themselves as victims, but they are not. They are simply part of a changing demographic taking place with each passing year. Demographics are a biological mathematical phenomenon; there are no victims involved.

They can try to extend their time in power using subterfuges, such as gerrymandering, passing voting laws that eliminate minority votes, scheming to deny Americans their vote in fair elections, building border walls, attempting desperately to stop immigration from Brown and Black people, and keeping minorities out of any positions of power or influence. That is like trying to fight the effects of global warming and the rising ocean tides by building walls along the beaches. It is a stopgap measure at best. It may work for a few years, or even a few decades, but inevitably it will fail at marginalizing minorities. "Just as sure as the turning of the earth," as Ethan Edwards put it in *The Searchers*, they will be the minority.

The late Samuel P. Huntington of Harvard University, influential professor and advisor to Jimmy Carter, as well as to the apartheid president of South Africa, Pieter Botha, and his murderous security service bureau (CCB), was appalled that Hispanic immigrants were being permitted into the United States or being tolerated when they entered illegally. I will quote him extensively since his ideas were important to the immigrant problem as it developed.

The persistent inflow of Hispanic immigrants threatens to divide the United States into two peoples, two cultures, and two languages. Unlike past immigrant groups, Mexicans and other Latinos have not assimilated into mainstream U.S. culture, forming instead their own political and linguistic enclaves—from Los Angeles to Miami—and rejecting the Anglo-Protestant values that built the American dream. The United States ignores this challenge at its peril.

Huntington 2004

Huntington may have done good work in his field, but his racial views were not part of the good work. There are more than 400 languages spoken in the United States (translatorswithoutborders.org); recently New York City was estimated to have more than six hundred languages represented among its citizens and perhaps as many as eight hundred. In case anyone was unclear on his meaning, Huntington continued,

> America was created by 17th- and 18th-century settlers who were overwhelmingly white, British, and Protestant....By the latter years of the 19th century, however, the ethnic component had been broadened to include Germans, Irish, and Scandinavians, and the United States' religious identity was being redefined more broadly from Protestant to Christian.... Would the United States be the country that it has been and that it largely remains today if it had been settled in the 17th- and 18th- centuries not by British Protestants but by French, Spanish, or Portuguese Catholics? The answer is clearly no. It would not be the United States; it would be Quebec, Mexico, or Brazil.

Huntington argued in various books and articles that America had to keep Brown people out of the country to avoid mongrelisation, and at the root of much racism is the fact that mestizos are a mix of races. (Davis-Undiano, 2017) Huntington continued,

Americans' idea of immigration is often symbolized by the Statue of Liberty, Ellis Island, and, more recently perhaps, New York's John F. Kennedy Airport. In other words, immigrants arrive in the United States after crossing several thousand miles of ocean. U.S. attitudes toward immigrants and U.S. immigration policies are shaped by such images. These assumptions and policies, however, have little or no relevance for Mexican immigration.

Mongrels, Mongrels, Mongrels

The American Southwest was taken by the United States government in an illegal war with Mexico. At the time, the U.S. government considered annexing all of Mexico, but was scared off by the Indo-Hispanic nature of the people of Mexico: Way too Brown and too difficult to control. These fears are articulated by Huntington, and later Trump and, for that matter, by the Ku Klux Klan, neo-Nazis, Qanon and other White supremacist groups rearing their heads in public these days after hiding under metaphorical rocks for decades. Racists live in absolute terror at the loss of the perceived whiteness of America. Maybe if they had something more to offer America other than the color of their skin—educational attainments or major accomplishments, perhaps—they might feel less excluded from the rich tapestry of culture and peoples that today is the United States.

Huntington's extensive body of work wringing his hands over Hispanics has been effectively criticized by a number of Chicano writers. Murillo (2013), for example, notes:

> Huntington's text alienates the Hispanic component of United States culture. 'The Hispanic Challenge' is an exercise in deceptive perspectivism, due in no small part to his homogeneous characterization of 'American' culture and xenophobic caricaturist synthesis of what he conflates as the Hispanic/Mexican populace in the United States. In this respect, Huntington is straightforward, the Hispanic/Mexican boom, since for Huntington there is no

cultural difference between the two, comprises a populace of educational, linguistic, economic and political backwardness which will corrode true 'American' culture.

Huntington feared Chicano language (with its *mas o menos* Spanish or Spanglish), community (stubborn refusal to assimilate), and work ethic (lazy Mexicans from the Land of *Mañana*). Perhaps he was influenced by Peggy Lee's popular 1947 song, "*Mañana*," sung with a very thick fake Mexican accent. ["The weendow she is broken and the rain is comin' in, but if we wait a day or two the rain may go away, and we don't need a weendow on such a sunny day. Oba! Oba!"] People were less sensitive in those days to such put-downs of an entire culture. We laughed along with the rest of America at her song, as did many people throughout Latin America. Parents would tell their kids, don't wait till *mañana* to do your chores like that song says. But we knew the song was not true. Everyone we knew worked all the time. Working hard is not enough, however. Huntington believed Mexican Americans could only be part of the Anglo Protestant Society if they *dreamed in English*. He felt patriotism drove him to feel this way. (Lozada, 2017)

Which Europeans Arrived First?

I do not wish to use a dead man's racist thinking as a straw man to support arguments of Chicano participation in North American life. However, before there was an Internet, Huntington was an important force and influencer of social policy in many areas, including immigration from Latin America. As will be made clear, my family extends far back through time and includes genes from many cultural groups. On the Native side, we arrived in the New World more than thirty thousand years ago, thirty millennia before the United States was even an idea in some brilliant slaveholders' brains.

If Huntington wished to argue European culture was brought to North America by White people on the Mayflower, well.... Centuries before the *Mayflower* landed at Plymouth Rock, itself as phony as Ireland's Blarney Stone, Kanellos (2002) noted,

Western culture was introduced to the lands that would become the United States, not by white northern Europeans, but by Hispanic peoples: Spaniards, Hispanicized Africans and Amerindians, mestizos, and mulattos.

The making of the historic cultural stew had begun almost a century before the sails of the approaching *Mayflower* could been seen from the shores of northeastern North America.

My late brother and scholar, E. A. "Tony" Mares, PhD, responded to Huntington's views on Chicanos not being part of U.S. culture (Mares, E.A., 2009a, in Montiel *et al.*, 2009):

The ethnocentrism and cultural provincialism of Huntington's remarks are truly stunning. We do not see ourselves or our views as a threat to any culture's way of life. Yet there are several questions we need to deal with: Are Hispanics part of Western civilization and to what extent? How do the members of this complex culture relate to the processes of self and group identity, community, the nation-state, and globalization?

Other Chicanos also responded to Huntington's writings, e.g., Curzio and Valdés-Ugalde (2004: 24) who noted, "Huntington's ideas demonstrate above all a kind of illustrated xenophobia that we had not seen in his work and that has surprised analysts." They note that Huntington is putting forth ideas of a colonial religion, touting America's putative nativist exceptionalism, recommending it must isolate Chicanos who have different ideas from White society and "freedom for all" does not actually include "all." In other words, it includes us gringos, but not Chicanos.

The *Mayflower* Finally Arrives

By the time the storied founding ship *Mayflower* arrived in 1620 in what was to become (one hundred fifty-six years later) the United States of America, the Southwest and most of the Americas had been conquered for Spain (and Portugal) and Catholicism for more than a hundred years, and the city of Santa Fe had been operating as the capital of those new Spanish territories for more than a decade. The Spanish territories were larger than the entire nation of Spain and twice as large as England.

Conquistadors arrived in the New World in 1492 in the form of the Italian, Christopher Columbus, who claimed the new lands for Spain. My distant grandfather fought alongside Cortés as he conquered the Aztec Empire in 1521. Cortés's lieutenant, Vasco Nuñez de Balboa, after long and costly battles across Panama, was the first European to see, wade into, and claim for Spain, the Pacific Ocean in 1513—sixty-seven years before Sir Francis Drake became the first Englishman to sail that vast ocean. It is not Hispanics who were the latecomers to this "new" land.

A New *Reconquista*

In 2017, Carlos Lozada, writing in the *Washington Post*, noted Huntington had written:

> Mexican immigration is leading toward the demographic *Reconquista* of areas Americans took from Mexico by force in the 1830s and 1840s ... stating that the United States is experiencing an 'illegal demographic invasion.'

Apparently, perhaps Huntington's ideas were in line with the thinking regarding immigration and foreign cultures encouraged by politicians in 2025.

The term *Reconquista* originally referred to the retaking of Spain and adjoining countries by the Catholic armies of the Iberian Peninsula. They conquered the Moors, whose expulsion after an almost eight-hundred-year war led directly to Spain's sending Christopher Columbus in search of a new route to Cathay, finding instead the New World. So, Catholics of that day reconquered their original lands and expelled the Moors, who were the invaders. That was the original *Reconquista*.

There is another use for the term *Reconquista*, and that is in regard to Spain's retaking New Mexico after the Pueblo uprising of 1680 had expelled the Spanish to Mexico. Conquistadors reclaimed the territory after only twelve years with New Mexico Governor Diego de Vargas leading a successful *Reconquista* of New Mexico territory. In this case *Reconquista* is used to describe the re-taking of land after the inhabitants of the land (the original conquerors in the case of New Mexico) had been driven out by warriors gathered from the original inhabitants (the Native peoples).

Chicano Homeland

There is one sense in which Huntington's use of the term *Reconquista* fits and that is the sense used by Chicanos in the American Southwest to support splitting off the lands illegally taken from Mexico by the United States. These actions led to poverty and social unrest across that vast area in the United States and Mexico. (Associated Press, 2000; Federation for American Immigration Reform, 2022; Truxillo, 2000) One proffered solution was La República del Norte, a reunification and nationalization of the lands that had been taken illegally by the United States in the Intervention of the United States against Mexico, known in the United States as the Mexican War.

Why would any Chicanos—even admittedly a fringe secessionist group—consider breaking away from the United States? Could it be they have been mistreated by the larger White society that listens to people like Huntington. Perhaps the hostile continuing racism of many

Anglos against the Chicanos is to blame. Racial purity is an ugly thing to talk about, but it continues to rear its dreadful head.

Rhapsodizing Over Dictators

In July 2022, Victor Orban, Prime Minister (and dictator) of Hungary, finally came out and clarified any doubts people might have had as to his racist beliefs. He referred positively to a racist book published in the early 1970s, *Camp of the Saints* by Jean Raspail, a travel writer who wrote the novel predicting how immigration—in the novel's case by refugees from India—irrevocably changed European society for the worse (at least as far as Raspail had come to know it and love it). The novel influenced many racists around the globe.

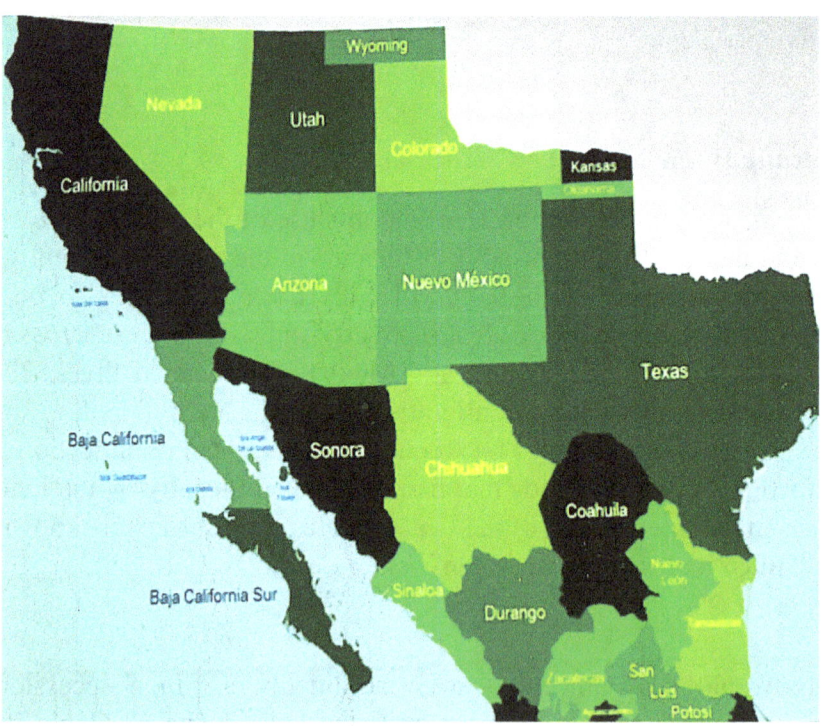

Fig. 4. Proposed new nation: La República del Norte, after a secession and reordering of states taken by the United States as illegally conquered territories of the Southwest and Mexico. Wiki commons.

Legendary Chicanos

Many mestizo Chicanos were grateful to be Americans. Perhaps Maximiliano Luna, a young Republican businessman, politician and soldier from Los Lunas, New Mexico, would be a good one. His name is the first listed on the Rough Riders Memorial, even though he died in the Philippines during the Philippines Campaign and not in Cuba. It was placed there at the request of Theodore Roosevelt, himself, for one of his four heroic captains in the Rough Riders who was also his translator in the Cuban campaign. Think Battle of San Juan Hill. Another possibility is Danny Fernandez, remarkably from the same small hometown as Maximiliano Luna. He won the Medal of Honor in Vietnam by throwing himself on a grenade and saving his men.

There are so many others from whom to choose, including Joe Pantaleón Martinez of Taos, New Mexico, who was the first Chicano to receive the Medal of Honor for bravery in combat *on American soil*, against the Japanese in Alaska's Aleutian Islands. He single-handedly killed five Japanese machine gunners, freeing his men to complete the assault and taking a bullet in the head in the process. There was a Navy ship named after him, the *USS Private Joe P. Martinez*.

Ranger Sergeant Leroy A. Petry (Tapia) from Santa Fe, New Mexico had eight deployments (two to Iraq, six to Afghanistan) and won the Medal of Honor in Afghanistan for engaging the enemy while they attacked his men with rifle fire and grenades. Although wounded, he picked up one of the enemy grenades and tossed it away. It detonated, blowing off his hand and part of his arm. He tied off the stump and, under fire, directed a rescue squad to find and help his men. In addition to the Congressional Medal of Honor, he won many decorations, including a Purple Heart and two Bronze Star Medals.

Richard Edward Cavazos is another to consider. He was the first Chicano to become a four-star general. In the Korean War, he led three assaults against the enemy while taking heavy fire. After his men were ordered to withdraw, he stayed, searching for wounded and carrying them back to the U.S. lines. He saved five men that way, while being badly wounded himself. He snagged the Distinguished Service Cross for his actions, along with a Silver Star Medal, five Bronze Star Medals with valor, and the Purple Heart. Fort Hood, in Texas, originally named in honor of the traitor General John Bell Hood who rushed to uphold slavery and fight for Texas when the Civil War began, has been renamed Fort Cavazos for the illustrious Chicano soldier.

Of course, there are those eighteen Hispanics who were awarded the Medal of Honor by President Barack Obama at the White House in the largest ceremony ever held for Medal of Honor recipients. It seems Chicanos, African Americans, and Jews had somehow been given lesser medals for their heroism, which was actually at a level to merit the Medal of Honor.

Demographics is Mathematics

I was trained as a population ecologist. Knowing how to read population demographic charts and tables makes it simple to see the truth of what the demographics of the United States will be in thirty years. This is not prognostication; it is mathematics. It is how rockets are sent to the moon or asteroids are hit in mid-flight while almost seven million miles from Earth by a rocket fired ten months earlier. Math. Demography is destiny. The minorities of today will become the majority of tomorrow and, as voting impediments to minorities are removed, either through new laws or by force, the nation will be very different by the end of this century as Whites become a minority group as far into the future as we can see today, and probably forever. Like it or not, that is the way it is going to be and absolutely no one can do anything about it.

It may not just be the Chicanos who are making life difficult in America. Will the present-day minorities turn the tables on the present-day majority and make it hard for them to vote, receive healthcare, get a good education, and so on? Hard to say. One of Lao Tzu's famous quotations is: "Those who have knowledge, don't predict. Those who predict, don't have knowledge." Since I agree with the futility of foretelling the future (recall my comments on the future racial makeup of the United States are not predictions, they are simply mathematical projections), I can only hope such reciprocity will not take place, that people are better than that, but it is something for the current ruling majority to keep in mind.

Consider the findings of Jeffrey Passel and D'Vera Cohn (2008) for the Pew Research Center examining U.S. population projections from 2005 through 2050. Their census data show the remarkable changes that will occur in the United States over a very short span of time. (Table 1) Between 2005 and 2050 (and we are already halfway through that time span), the percentage of White Americans declined to forty-seven percent, down from sixty-seven percent in just forty-five years. I am seventy-nine years old as I write these words and forty-five years seems like a very short span of time to me. Forty-five years ago, Ronald Reagan began a second term in 1984 and Steve Jobs launched the Macintosh computer. Forty-five years is not a very long time in the life of a nation or even in the lives of people. Interestingly, these demographic transitions will occur at different times for different age groups (which follows from the mathematics of population demographic analysis). Younger Whites are already in the minority and each age group will take its turn moving into minority status in the coming decades.

	2005	2050
Population (in millions)	**296**	**438**
Share of total		
Foreign born	12%	19%
Racial/Ethnic Groups		
White	67%	47%
Hispanic	14%	29%
Black	13%	13%
Asian	5%	9%
Age Groups		
Children (17 and younger)	25%	23%
Working age (18-64)	63%	58%
Elderly (65+)	12%	19%
All races modified. Not Hispanic, American Indian/Alaska Native not shown.		

Table 1. U.S. Population, Actual and Projected 2005–2050 (Pew Research Center, 2008)

Thus, just over twenty years from now, the racial makeup of the U.S. will be quite different from what it is today (Table 2, Table 3) and the differences will only get more pronounced with each passing decade. My advice to the White power structure: Start supporting minorities today because tomorrow *you* will be the minority and, God forbid, the new majority may decide to act like you have acted over these many generations. They may use your behavior as the model for dealing with the new minority (i.e., you).

Year	Age
2020	under 18
2027	18-29
2033	30-39
2041	40-49
2050	50-59
after 2050	60+

Table 2. Year when Whites become minority by age group

Race	Percent of population
White	49.7 %
Hispanic	24.6%
Black	13.1%
Asian	7.9%
Multiracial	3.8%
Other	0.9%

Table 3. Racial profile of the U.S. population in 2045 (Metropolitan Policy Program at Brookings. W. H. Frey analysis of U.S. Census population census projections, 2018.)

Perhaps we will all follow gentle and genial Barack Obama's counsel: "I see what's possible when we recognize that we are one American family, all deserving of equal treatment." I hope so, but why do I feel it is not as simple as those fine words suggest? I think that America is coarser now than President Obama implied. Perhaps it is history that I am hearing, and we Chicanos are steeped in the mixed history of the American Southwest and Mexico, where cross-cultural strife has been a constant for centuries. It continues today.

What Are Chicanos Anyway?

People have trouble defining Chicanos. E. A. "Tony" Mares (the late Chicano poet and historian) took a shot at giving a Hispanic scholar's view of this complex community of inhabitants of the Southwest:

> I use the terms Chicano, Mexican American, and Indohispanic interchangeably to refer to Mexican Americans who, with respect to their individual or communal identity (to the extent they still have one), form part of a spectrum of people. At one extreme on the spectrum are persons and communities who see themselves as indigenous, or fantasize themselves as such. At the other extreme are those who fantasize themselves as pure Spanish, whatever that is, or who think of themselves as Spanish American. My favorite term for those Hispanos who shared cultural traits with indigenous communities is Indohispanic, because I cannot think of a clearer or more inclusive term to convey the breadth and depth of this cultural complex. (Mares, E. A., 2009b: 138)

Chicanos always challenge people to define them (e.g., see Salazar, R. 1970, the first Chicano reporter for the *Los Angeles Times* who was killed by police at a Vietnam War protest). Another definition of Chicano is the following: "A Chicano is a Mexican American with a non-Anglo image of himself." (Salazar, 1970), but see also, Hernandez (2020). One of the best definitions of Chicano was provided by the Chicano comedian Cheech Marin (2012):

> What is a Chicano? Who the hell knows? To me, you have to declare yourself a Chicano in order to be a Chicano. That makes a Chicano a Mexican American with a defiant political attitude that centers on his or her right to self-definition. I'm a Chicano because I say I am....But no Chicano will agree with me because one of the characteristics of being Chicano is you don't agree with anybody, or anything. And certainly not another Chicano. We are the only tribe that has all chiefs and no Indians.

Truer words were never spoken.

3

WHAT THE HELL AM I?

Genetic Analysis

New Mexican roots for more than four centuries, Native American for millennia, Aztec, Mayan, Mexican, Central American, Sephardic Jew, Ashkenazi Jew, Spanish, Cuban, Portuguese, Irish, French, Basque, Sardinian, German, Scandinavian, Chinese, Filipino, Austronesian, Japanese, Korean, Cypriot, North African, Sub-Saharan African, Ghanaian, Liberian, Sierra Leonean, Angolan, Congolese, Senegambian, Guinean, Nigerian, Sri Lankan, Pakistani, Indian, Gujarati Patidar, and a dollop of Neanderthal.

What am I? I am a Chicano. I am the United Nations. I am humanity. I am the melting pot. "Hispanics" is far too simple a term to capture the rich and complex genetic history of most New Mexican Chicanos. LatinX? Forget it.

Complexity related to language and culture of countries in the Americas makes combining them difficult. The term Hispanic is widely used these days to include many Spanish speaking peoples, but Chicanos are not Puerto Ricans, Cubans, South Americans, or other cultures of the Caribbean islands. While it is thought that language unites them, they are actually quite different one from another in their politics, behavior, history, and culture. Latino is an even less descriptive term, for it includes people from Latin America, such as Portuguese-speaking Brazilians. Chicanos are the mestizo mix of the genes of the Iberian Peninsula since before the year 1,000 CE, as well as the genes of the Native peoples of the New World, and the genes of the Spanish conquistadors and their often mestizo offspring. Chicanos do not fit easily into categories. They are, by their genetics and belief system, music, food, family life and overall behavior, different.

4

Genetic Trails

Kings, Soldiers, Natives

The old families of New Mexico have left tracks extending back through time, crossing continents and millennia carrying the genetic traces of much of humankind. (Table 4, Table 5) Among my direct ancestors are kings and queens of Spain, France, Portugal, Germany, and England. Many of my ancestors were soldiers of one type or another. Some were kings, some were foot soldiers to conquistadors, and some, perhaps most, were villains or peons, but their tracks are harder to find. King Alfonso X of Castile, b. 1221, my twenty-third great grandfather, was a brilliant scientist and intellectual and has a crater on the Moon named in his honor. His father was a saint: King Ferdinand of Castile, b. 1199–1201, my twenty-fourth great grandfather, who was canonized as Saint Ferdinand, or San Fernando in 1671 and known today in part by the city and valley in California and many other places that bear his name. There is a pope in my familial lineage, my very distant uncle, Pope Callixtus II (1065–1124). He issued the papal document (*Sicut Judaeis*) that forbade Catholics from forcing Jews to convert and stealing their land and property; he also protected the sanctity of Jewish cemeteries.

Fig. 5. King Alfonso X of Castile, Alfonso the Wise (1199/1252–1284); moon crater named in his honor; my twenty-third great grandfather.

Fig. 6. Tomb of San Fernando, King Ferdinand III of Castile, in Seville Cathedral, 1199/1201–1252. (My twenty-fourth great grandfather is supposedly uncorrupted.)

Some of my ancestors were native people in the Americas. Though their genealogical records are almost non-existent, their genetic contributions are clear. (I am twenty-one percent Native American.) In addition to the notable ancestors discussed above, my ancestors have also been slaves (held by Natives) and slave holders (of Natives). As a child, I used to listen to my TV-hero, Roy Rogers, sing the song, "The San Fernando Valley," and also watched the eponymous film starring Rogers. (Rogers, 1944) I had no idea the saint he was singing about was one of my distant grandfathers. Centuries later my sixteenth great grandfather, Pedro Martin Serrano Sandoval, b. 1465, was a soldier for Queen Isabella and King Ferdinand. He played a role in helping Spain run the Moors out of Europe and by so doing freed up the rulers of Spain to form the Spanish nation and to send Christopher Columbus on his mission of discovery, a mission that, for better or worse, changed the world. Martín Serrano's son, Capitán Hernán Martín Serrano II, was born in Zacatecas, Mexico in 1548 and became a conquistador sergeant in Oñate's army. He was accompanied by his wife, Juana Rodriguez. They became one of the earliest families to found the new city of Santa Fe in 1609.

There are Moors in my lineage, as well as Sephardic Jews, surely leading to some internal conflict in my family, if not within our own psyches. My ancestors helped Spain conquer Puerto Rico; my thirteenth great grandfather, Hernando Martin-Serrano I de Molina, b. 1500, sailed with Ponce de Leon to Puerto Rico. He then fought alongside Hernán Cortés to subdue the Aztecs and, as the first blacksmith in the New World, this distant great grandfather made the chains and the cage that imprisoned Moctezuma, thus initiating, actually and metaphorically, the Conquest of the Americas.

Renaud 1 of Burgundy* (990)	Adelaide of Normandy* (1002)
William I of Burgundy, Count* (1020)	Countess Stephanie* (1035)
Raymond of Burgundy, Count of Galicia*(1070)	Queen Urraca the Bold* (1080)
Emperor of All Spain, Alfonso VII* (1105)	Queen Berengaria of Barcelona* (1116)
King Ferdinand II* (1137)	Queen Urraca of Portugal* (1148)
King Alfonso IX of Leon* (1171)	Queen Elisabeth of Swabia (1205)
King Ferdinand of Castile* (1201) [Saint]	Queen Beatrice of Swabia* (1198)
Alfonso X, King of Castile* (1221)	Queen Violant of Aragon* (1236)
Sancho, King of Castile* (1258)	Queen Maria de Molina* (1265)
Prince Pedro Sanchez de Aranda y Castile* (1290)	Maria Jaimez of Aragon (1299)
Juan Sanchez de Aranda (1313)	Unknown
Pedro Fernandez de Aranda Sanchez (1340)	Maria Juana Sanchez (1349)
Señor de la Casa Aranda, Juan Fernandez (1370)	Urraca Alfonso de Porras (1379)
Pedro Fernandez de Aranda (1400)	Maria Garcia de Escamilla (1400)
Jose Fernando de Aranda (1440)	Catalina Serrano (1444)
Pedro Serrano Sandoval (1454)	Catalina Fernandez (1480)
Hernando Martin-Serrano I de Molina (1499)	Unknown
Capitán Hernán Martin Serrano II (1556)	Ines (1586)

Table 4. The first half millennium of my direct family lineage, mostly through the Martinez family (* denotes royalty). Genealogical connections were obtained from many published genealogy web sites as well as my own research. Most royalty have been well researched by genealogists and have individual websites with family relationships illustrated.

Cortés was a tough leader. It had been a hard trip for him and his men, fraught with dangers crossing the Atlantic to the New World. They had lost the spirit of exploration to continue on with him and head inland. He solved the problem by burning ten of his eleven ships. There was no going back and his men fell into line and proceeded to conquer the Aztecs. I can imagine my thirteenth great grandfather watching those ships burn. Life as they knew it was suddenly different due to Cortés' actions. They were now on their own in this unknown New World.

Such stories could be told by many people, perhaps, but this is about my family and our story, and I will tell it. I don't think anyone in my family knows it. Most of those who might have cared about this history are dead and the new generations could not care less about extinct ancestors, or even how they came to be who they are. Maybe they will care when they are older. I think it is interesting to see how a nation, a territory and a state were influenced by various members of a familial lineage, even if the tracks of the family as they extend back through time are hard to discern. E. A. "Tony" Mares described the situation:

> Grieve if you must, *hermano*.
> We will never see the footprints
> we leave behind in the dust.
> Ahead is the windswept trail
> we barely see as it disappears.

(Mares, E. A., 2010)

Cultural Mixing in Deep Time

Perhaps thirty millennia ago, Native peoples colonized the New World. It was a long-distance march across Asia and the Bering Strait into a land whose most unusual trait was an absolute lack of human beings—the last and only place on earth without them. The colonists walked or used boats of some type—there were no horses or other means of conveyance so long ago. (Wade, 2017) The wheel was not invented in the New World and, in any case, was not invented in the Old World until 4500 BCE. The migration to North America took place long before then. There were many colonization events that occurred after people first reached the Americas, often with multiple Native languages being involved or developing among the various groups.

Capitán Luis Martin Serrano I (1594)	Catalina de Salazar Diaz (1604)
Aférez Pedro Martin Serrano y Salazar (1635)	Juana Apalonia de Arguello (1648)
Francisco "El Ciego" Martin Serrano (1680)	Maria Casilda Contreras (1684)
Antonio Martin Serrano (1706)	Maria Catalina Villalpando (1704)
Mario Cayetano Martin Serrano (1735)	Maria Juana de Tapia (1727)
Jose Francisco Martin (1765)	Maria Tomasa Sanchez (1778)
Jose Felipe Martin (1811)	Maria Marcela Vigil
Don Antonio Severino Martinez (1761)	Maria del Carmel Santistevan
Jose Santiago Martinez (1806)	Maria Dominga de la Luz Lucero
Pablo Martinez (1833)	Libradita Romero
Don Pedro Martinez (1861)	Simonita Lucero
Alice Martinez de Mares (1891)	Eduardo Severino Mares
Ernesto Gustavo Mares (1914)	Rebecca Gabriela Devine (1916)
Michael Allen Mares (1945)	Lynn Brusin Mares (1945)

Table 5. The second half millennium of author's direct family lineage, mostly through the Martinez family.

Eventually, the newcomers colonized the entire North American continent and continued southward into the Caribbean and on into Central and South America. In a way they repeated the patterns of colonization of the North and South American continents by mammals after the ancestral New World mammals had reached North America from Eurasia, but the colonization events of mammals occurred millions of years earlier than those of humans. The patterns were similar, however, as the mammals, too, moved from Eurasia across North America and into Central and South America over the newly formed Panama Land Bridge three million years ago, where they underwent a flowering of evolution into many new types of mammals. (Mares, M.A., 1985)

The precise time frames for the multiple colonizations of the Americas by people are not known, but a great deal of data from artifacts, archeological specimens, genes, and other research chronicles the remarkable migration of various groups of people into an uninhabited land. The original immigrants dispersed into the vast array of habitats they encountered as they moved eastward and southward across the breadth of the continent, from the Arctic tundra and taiga forests, and then south through cool rain forests, redwoods, coastal habitats, the complex vegetation of California, and into deserts, mountains, grasslands, and the dense deciduous and coniferous forests and swamplands of the eastern United States. They had encountered two entire continents that had never been colonized by people. They occupied the diverse landscapes over millennia, and they diversified into many tribes, developing a host of languages and cultures.

The time of colonization of the Americas has been controversial for decades. However, one of the curators at the Sam Noble Oklahoma Museum of Natural History, Don Wyckoff, PhD, discovered an extinct bison in Oklahoma found with stone tools and was dated at about thirty thousand years before the present ("bp"). The museum had covered the costs of carbon-dating the specimens and so the fossil and accompanying tools became part of the museum's permanent opening day exhibits. The site, known as the Burnham site, was not immediately accepted by many anthropologists when published because they were fixated on the Clovis Culture of thirteen thousand years bp as the time of colonization of the Western Hemisphere. Indeed, today the Burnham site is still controversial with suggestions the artifacts could have moved due to soil/water movements over the millennia so they are not presenting an accurate depiction of their depositional state at the time they were first buried. (*Encyclopedia of Oklahoma History and Culture*) Neither hypothesis has been proven, however. The Clovis hypothesis of the earliest Americans has been sunk by recent research findings. People were in the Americas long before the Clovis people.

Peopling the Americas

Recent research utilizing Native American DNA and other methodologies has found colonization of the Americas actually occurred in three waves thousands of years apart. (Rasmussen *et al.*, 2010; Handwerk, 2023; Price, 2023) While most of today's Native Americans descended from migrants who entered the New World about fifteen thousand years ago in the First American Wave (Reich, 2012; Potter *et al.*, 2018), significant portions of the Native genome reflect different colonization events

(Rincon, 2004), with research suggesting the first colonists came from Australia and were not Native Americans at all. (Skoglund *et al.*, 2015) Moreover, new genetic research published in 2020 (Becerra-Valdivia and Higham, 2020) suggests humans were in the New World as long ago as thirty thousand years bp and their presence coincided with many extinctions of the mammalian megafauna of the time (suggested earlier as the Pleistocene Overkill Hypothesis. (Martin, 1973) They note their data effectively refute the Clovis first hypothesis.

At the time of the Conquest in 1492 CE almost three hundred different languages characterized the lands north of present-day Mexico, with many more arising southward through Mexico, Central America and South America. Nearly two thousand native languages developed in the Western Hemisphere divided among perhaps one hundred million people; it was a veritable stew of native languages and tribes, but the clock was ticking and enormous changes were about to occur.

After a hiatus of thirty thousand years while living in the Americas, the colonizing tribes were about to encounter their first European languages with the arrival of the conquistadors in 1519 in the form of Hernán Cortés de Monroy y Pizarro Altamirano, who conquered the Aztec Empire. Is it any wonder over time the American continent would become a farrago of different racial histories, languages, and genetic identities? Europeans who were early colonists (by modern standards) became a part of the racial and linguistic mixing. Many of these groups were ancestral to the original inhabitants and colonists of what became New Mexico. Hundreds and more likely thousands of them were my ancestors.

A Vital Collaborator

One of Cortés' great collaborators in his conquest of the Aztecs was an Indian Aztec slave, popularly known as La Malinche (Malitzen) who, as the daughter of an Aztec chief, had been educated and spoke several native languages. (Farah, 2019) She had been sold into slavery by her mother after her father died and her mother had remarried. Eventually she was sold to a Mayan Cacique in Tabasco where she was one more slave among many. When the conquistadors arrived, the Cacique gave her to Cortés as a gift of honor. The gift ended up affecting the fate of Mexico and the New World. La Malinche was highly intelligent and ended up acting as Cortés' advisor, translator, guide and mistress. (Candelaria, 1980)

Wherever Cortés went, Doña Marina (La Malinche's Spanish honorific name) went too, and was actively involved in contact and context of how other tribes and peoples were treated by Cortés and how they treated him. Twice she sniffed out plots to kill Cortés and saved him and his men from attacks, actions that led some to dub her the greatest villainess in Mexican history. In fact, when Cortés avoided a trap set by Montezuma in Cholula, the natives were convinced a special mystical ability protected Cortés. That mystically talented friend was La Malinche, who has been considered to be the first Mexican American. (Valdéz, 1971) At times she acted as Cortés's spy among the many Indian tribes of Mexico from the Yucatán Peninsula to the Valley of Mexico.

Fig. 7. La Malinche, by Ramón Canto, 1883, Mexican. La Salle University Art Museum Collection, 16-LA-106.

La Malinche is hated by many modern Mexicans but was likely beloved by the Aztecs of the time, not only as a former Aztec princess for all practical purposes, but for her wide-ranging abilities in many fields. She was able to act while being close to the powerful conquistadors and became especially close to their leader, Cortés. Some credit her with being Cortés's lover and the mother of his child, the first Chicano born in the New World: Martín Cortés el Mestizo. She lived to the age of twenty-nine, dying of smallpox in 1529 in Mexico City. Cortés had no other male issue, so he had Pope Clement VII recognize the legitimacy of Martín in a papal bull. Martín was educated in Spain and became a Knight of the Order of Santiago, the highest level of achievement for a Spanish knight. (Ackermann, 1826)

Influences on New World Cultures

Manuel Gonzales, in his 1999 book, *Mexicanos: A History of Mexicans in the United States*, notes the complex mix of peoples and cultures in Spain that would influence, sometimes centuries into the future, the people of New Mexico who had Spanish roots. After the Upper Paleolithic, Gonzales (1999: 10) notes:

> The following millennia are shrouded in mystery but the Iberian Peninsula, a natural bridge between two continents, must have attracted a variety of people. Among them were Iberians, 'dwellers along the Ebro River,' as they came to be called by the Greeks. Basques, whose origins are still much debated; Celts, who dominated the region in the period 900 B.C.-650 B.C.; Phoenicians, contemporaries of the Celts...and Greeks, who came at around 600 B.C. to settle the coastal areas.... Undoubtedly...the most Influential of the ancient peoples to arrive were the Romans.

The Roman legions took over Hispania (their name for the land that would become Spain) in 202 BCE. Half a millennium later, in the 3rd century CE, Christianity swept across the region, soon to be overrun by the various tribes and armies of German Vandals, including the Ostrogoths and Visigoths (barbarians), who extended their control from Spain through Italy, to North Africa, sacking Rome in 455 CE. Eventually, the Roman Emperor, Justinian the Great, drove the Vandals out of the region in 534 CE. (*See also* Adams, 2006)

My maternal grandmother's maiden name was Gutierrez, which has its roots in the Visigoth culture that overran Spain. These were not periods of constant war as it may appear in a short overview. There were centuries when the major cultural opponents lived in relative peace. No doubt social interactions of one type or another occurred with mating being widespread across cultures and the gene pool becoming mixed to include everyone in that diverse human population.

Muslims and the *Reconquista*

In 711 CE, the Muslim army led by a Berber general, Tariq ibn-Ziyad, swept northward driving the Goths out of the Iberian Peninsula and placing most of Hispania under Islamic rule. Muslim rule extended across much of Spain for the next seven hundred eighty-one years and was relatively peaceful (with occasional uprisings and battles in various cities occurring after long periods of relative tranquility), while also contributing greatly to science, literature, the arts, architecture, and other flowerings of culture characteristic of a rich multi-cultural and multi-religious society. Gradually, Catholic kingdoms in northern Spain united to conquer the Muslims across Spain (in a series of battles termed the *Reconquista*). The battles took place over four centuries (1085–1492), with the final defeat of the Muslims occurring at Granada.

The conquest of the Moors left Queen Isabella I and her husband, King Ferdinand, as rulers of the Spanish Empire. As Catholics reigned supreme, Jews and Muslims were forced to either convert or emigrate. My genes tell me my lineage was both Jewish and Muslim, as well a host of other groups, so I assume we ended up in the New World in part to escape the Inquisition and the general atmosphere of religious intolerance, often at the point of a sword. However, some of my direct ancestors in Hispania had been kings, queens, princes, and counts, and had participated in the *Reconquista* and many other battles between and among themselves and the many conquerors of the Iberian Peninsula (the older versions of conquistadors), for more than a millennium. War, not peace, is the human condition. Peace is an exceedingly rare anomaly.

Subduing Primitive People

The date 1492 had major ramifications in history, and not only for being the period when the Muslims were driven out of Spain once and for all and Spain returned to Catholic rule. It was also the year the Spanish monarchs sent the Italian explorer Christopher Columbus to find a new route to China (Cathay) and India and bring riches to Spain, while enhancing Spain's standing among the explorer seafaring nations, such as Portugal and England. He did not reach either China or India, which he never realized in his lifetime. (Morgan, 2009) The new continent he encountered, peopled by millions of natives (Indios, he called them, thinking he had reached India) would eventually be claimed by Spain and explored and conquered by its conquistadors.

The militarily sophisticated Europeans, experienced warriors all, were about to meet stone-age people having little or no metal, no gunpowder, no cannons, no horses, no war dogs (the only dogs they had were tiny Chihuahua-like dogs and were raised primarily for food), no military capabilities other than wooden spears, knives, bows and arrows, wooden clubs, rocks and slings. The Indians were doomed from the outset, but did not know it. It would have been far better for all of them had they surrendered.

Shortly before his death, the physicist, Stephen Hawking, in working with a team to establish Breakthrough Listen, a new effort to search for intelligent life throughout the universe, warned against trying to make contact with an alien civilization. He likely considered the history of the conquistadors and the Native Americans when he noted, "We don't know much about aliens, but we know about humans. If you look at history, contact between...civilizations with advanced versus primitive technologies have gone badly for the less advanced. (Cofield, 2015, Space.com. July 21)

Deaths From Many Causes

Diseases (smallpox and others) were likely the main cause of death for tens of millions of Native people in both North and South America, but certainly many hundreds of thousands, if not a million or more, were killed in battle or slaughtered by the conquistadors and other invaders. Most of the deaths could have been avoided, even if their lives would have been spent in suffering and slavery, had they elected not to fight the Spanish. Of course, they could not know the passage of time would ultimately change the world, but there would be many more Native Americans alive today had they recognized the hopelessness of their military situation and given up their arms. That is seldom how history works, however; maybe it never works that way.

Columbus could be considered the first conquistador and, as with those who came later, not all his actions were admirable, but few important historic figures throughout humanity's long and bloody span would be considered admirable in today's retrospective world. The history of humanity is the history of mass slaughter of millions of people, if not a billion or more, by armies, tribes, naval forces, religious fanatics, intolerance, and an innate human viciousness that has transformed the world into the bloody globe we inhabit today.

We like to frighten ourselves with stories of monsters who slaughter humans, but it is human beings who are the real monsters in the world, almost since they became bipedal, picked up a rock, gathered into groups, and started cracking heads. We have killed each other and everything else in nature and, with current trends affecting the loss of diversity across the globe through habitat destruction, climate change, and expanding global pollution of all types, we may eventually kill everything on the planet. What other monster could do that? *Tyrannosaurus rex* was a piker as far as monsters go, ditto any lions, tigers or bears. Humans are the most perfect monsters that ever evolved. We are capable of destroying everything on the planet and seem to be incapable of modifying our destructive behavior, even if it destroys us all in a final apocalypse. We even delude ourselves into thinking we are actually noble creatures, the pinnacle of evolution (or creation).

There are a few good guys in history, but not many. The march of humanity across time mainly includes conquerors who have left their mark on the world of the past as well as on the present world we inhabit. The conquered themselves were likely merciless conquerors during their lives before external threats arrived in their world in the form of much more powerful adversaries. Countries have formed, disappeared, and re-formed, waxed, waned and disappeared again. The world has always been a tough place and it is the strong and often cruel leaders who have made the world what it is today, as far as national boundaries, genetic diversity, and cultural development are concerned. The conquistadors, by definition, were in the New World to conquer its inhabitants and take control of a massive territory, whether the natives agreed with this plan or not. Attempting to attach modern mores to historical figures is a hopelessly silly task.

The Spanish had modern (for that time) European weaponry and centuries of experience with large battles between armies: the stone-age Native peoples had none of these. The Spanish had steel, gunpowder, cannons, armor, military strategy, crossbows, war dogs, horses, the wheel, and other battlefield weapons. The outcome of the war was a foregone conclusion before it ever began. Indeed, it was over before the Spanish set sail for the New World. Spain would win; the Native peoples would lose anywhere and anytime they battled the invading armies. It was only a matter of time and a question of how brutal the conquistadors decided to be. By and large, they were very brutal, as is the nature of war everywhere across the millennia. No one at the time could have guessed breeding with the conquerors permitted the Native lineages to continue far into the future as part of the mestizo genomes, long after many of the "pure" Native peoples had disappeared and the conquistadors were long gone. In some sense, this could be considered a victory for the Natives. They are still here in one form or another, not only as Native people, but as part of the DNA of every mestizo and surviving Native American.

Bishop Las Casas

Bishop Bartolomé de las Casas arrived in Hispaniola from Spain in 1502 as a layman who had been rewarded with land and Indian slaves for his efforts in the Spanish Army in Spain. He took part in a failed experiment at developing a new town, for which he was a landowner who also owned the resident Indians. In Spain, before leaving for America, he had entered the academy of the cathedral in Seville, where he studied Latin. After arriving in America, his studies continued and he became the first priest to take Holy Orders in the New World. He tried to evangelize his Indians living on his properties but was driven away by both the other Spanish landholders and slaveowners and by the Indians themselves who launched attacks against him. (*See* Digital History, 2021; Friede and Keen, 1971)

Fig. 8. Bishop Bartolomé de las Casas. Wikipedia Commons.

In 1514 he had an awakening on the evils of slavery and gave his land and slaves back to the governor. He returned to Spain to encourage King Charles I to issue rules for better treatment of Indians in the New World. He then traveled back to America and over time became the Bishop of Chiapas. His efforts at seeking better treatment for the Indians were rewarded when he received an official appointment with the title Protector of the Indians. He then famously wrote about the atrocities committed against indigenous people by the Spanish colonizers, noting "...the Spanish have destroyed such an infinitie of soules" searching for gold. (Morgan, 2009) The atrocities to which he bore witness, if true as he described them, were horrible but not unusual throughout the sordid history of human hostilities.

Throughout history there are literally too many examples of horrific atrocities to count, but a few comments on the Japanese in World War II should suffice to illustrate the viciousness that resides within the people of almost all countries, especially those at war—even modern and highly cultured societies like Japan. Like the early Spanish with the Indians in the New World, the Japanese did not consider the Chinese to be fully human. During World War II, the Japanese attacked China and murdered thirty million civilians, burying prisoners alive, laying waste to millions following Emperor Hirohito's "kill all, burn all, loot all" mandate. Prisoners were frozen bit by bit and the frozen parts cut off without anesthesia until only a living torso and head remained. The torso and head were then used in disease research.

The crew of an American B-29 bomber that crash landed in Japan were dissected alive in a medical school's anatomy class. Acts of cannibalism of prisoners who were still alive were not uncommon. (Blumenthal, 1999; U.S. National Archives, 2016; Shelton and Adelman, eds., 2005) Japanese soldiers would take little babies away from women and toss them into the air, catching them on their bayonets in front of their mothers. (Warner, 1945) And all this occurred in the middle of the 20th century, five hundred years after the time of the conquistadors. As Ed Harris' character, William Parcher, noted in the film "A Beautiful Mind," "Man is capable of as much atrocity as he has imagination."

War Dogs and Elephants

Indians, who were thought not to be human by many Spaniards, were roasted alive, ripped apart and fed to dogs. (The conquistadors were known to feed their enemies, alive or dead, to their giant fighting dogs of war.) Indians had their babies ripped apart or cooked on a grill, their chiefs roasted over slow fires, and were tortured and murdered in other ways that almost defy comprehension. Sport hunts were set up by the Spanish to hunt native men, women, and children with their war dogs, which would rip the people to shreds and then proceed to eat them. The conquistadors believed encouraging the war dogs to eat their enemies made the dogs fight more aggressively in battle.

Fig. 9. War dogs of the Spanish Conquistadors, 1598, engraving by Theodor de Bry depicting a Spaniard feeding slain indigenous women and children to his dogs.

War dogs were the super weapon of the conquistadors against the Indians. In battle, the object is to kill the enemy, no matter how, and the more you kill, the faster you win the war and the fewer men you lose. If one has a superior weapon, one uses it to conquer the enemy—and conquer means kill. There is no nice way to kill an enemy. In 1945, the

United States used nuclear weapons against the Japanese to kill more than seventy thousand people in the blink of an eye and hundreds of thousands more through the toxic effects of radiation. As early as 280 BCE, the Greeks used war elephants against the Roman legions. Rome, having no defense against the massive beasts, was routed and its soldiers slaughtered. Within a year, the Romans had learned elephants were inordinately afraid of pigs and fire, so they set pigs on fire and drove the squealing and screaming flaming animals toward the elephants, which gave up the fight immediately, running away in panic. The super weapon of the Greeks had been neutralized by flaming pigs. Rome began using war elephants as well. War elephants were used regularly in battle for decades.

Treatment of Native People

Several scholars feel Las Casas far overstated the lurid descriptions of torture and mutilation of Natives by the Spanish in order to get the attention of the Spanish royalty to pass laws to protect Indians. (Cervantes, 2020) He was, after all, the only highly educated person bearing witness to such atrocities. His inflammatory exaggerations (Allen, 2010) presented very one-sided descriptions of the goodness of the natives and the inhumanity of the Spaniards. His publications also aided Spain's rivals (England, France, The Netherlands and others) in the propaganda war, making Spain look like a cruel kingdom that mercilessly destroyed indigenous people.

In the 1500s, European nations and kingdoms jockeyed for hegemony in the world, especially on the high seas. Spain's colonization and annexation of the Americas added greatly to its power and prestige among Europe's ruling powers. Spain's enemies developed The Black Legend (the fake news of its day highlighting imaginary or exaggerated stories of Spanish cruelty to native peoples) to destroy Spain's reputation in the world. Bishop Bartolomé's report on the treatment of Indians was fodder for Spain's enemies and competitors. It was true, however, Indians in the New World were dying from being killed by the conquistadors, especially by diseases brought from Europe to the New World. Diseases were the invisible weapon to which the natives had little resistance. Indians perished by the millions. Most of the other empires had false or exaggerated black legends spread about them during their peak time of power by other empires or wannabe empires in order to weaken them and strengthen their enemies. Fake news is not a modern invention.

The Las Casas report played into the hands of those rulers who wished to have some sort of control put on Spain to limit its actions in the New World and thereby strengthen their own positions among world powers so they could take the land Spain was after instead of allowing Spain to take it. For example, William of Orange (1533–1584), Prince of the Netherlands, noted Spain: "...committed such horrible excesses that all the barbarities, cruelties and tyrannies ever perpetrated before are only games in comparison to what happened to the poor Indians." (Digital History, 2021)

Of course, William of Orange and The Netherlands were breaking away from Spanish control on religious grounds, not wishing to recognize Roman Catholicism and having their own several brands of Protestantism replace Catholicism, so his judgment of the Spanish Nation and its conquistador activities in the New World are suspect. Propaganda (the fake news of that era) was published against Spain during the Hispano Dutch War (the Eighty Years War of 1566–1648, including the Thirty Years War) and the Anglo-Spanish War (1585–1604). The wars involved much of the known world, including the Caribbean, Europe and South America. Prince William was assassinated in 1584 by a Frenchman, Balthasar Gérard, a follower of Philip II who felt William had betrayed both the Spanish King and the Catholic Church.

Nevertheless, Las Casas brought these inhuman tortures (real, exaggerated or invented) to the attention of the King of Spain, who passed new laws dealing with Indians and other subjects of Spain in the New World and their treatment by conquistadors. Bartolomé de Las Casas particularly lamented the atrocities of those who came after Columbus (though Columbus and his men were also quite cruel to most natives). At one point, Casas recommended that African and white slaves (with which he was familiar in Spain) be used in the Caribbean, rather than Native slaves. In later life he changed his mind on the morality of slavery altogether, coming to the conclusion all slavery was wrong, no matter the race of people involved.

Spain's conquest of the Indians in the New World led to major discussions on the treatment of the Indians. Many people felt Indians were subhumans and did not require the kind of treatment given to human beings in similar circumstances. Cabeza de Vaca, however, on his travels through Florida in the 1530s came to the conclusion the Indians were humans and moreover they had a dark side of cruelty, noting if we want to convert them, we need to treat them well. Other writers of the time noted Indians were as cruel as Spaniards. (Léry, 1992) The Laws of Burgos (1512) dealt with the welfare of the Native peoples, but Casas highlighted the maltreatment of Indians during and after the time of Columbus and pointed to the fact that more laws were needed.

Laws of the Indies

The Laws of the Indies passed in Spain dealt with such issues and attempted to control the conquistadors. Debates were held on what the rights of conquered people should be. (Valladolid Debate of 1551/52; Dumont, 1997) The Laws of the Indies included plans for how Indians should be treated and how settlements and cities should be developed in the New World. It noted the size of plots of land that should be set aside for farming by Indians, including corn, wheat, barley, and other crops, as well as planting and cutting of forests by Indians. There were one hundred forty-eight rules on settlement design, including placement and size of the central plaza, the size and orientation of streets that delimited the plaza, placement of hospitals and churches, and other plans that have been followed in much of the world for hundreds of years and can be seen in many towns and cities even to the present day.

After returning to Spain and becoming a member of the court, Las Casas defended Indian issues, even arguing against some of the prevailing feelings that Indians were less than human and thus required Spanish overseers. Such thinking was not limited to Spain. The Constitution of the United States recognized slaves as sixty percent of a free person in determining congressional representation, almost two centuries after Las Casas was beginning his efforts to protect Native Americans and argue against all kinds of slavery. (Indians were not really included in the Constitution and were not U.S. citizens recognized by law until 1924—and even then, they could not vote.)

Las Casas, who had been accused of treason by his enemies for promoting the cause of the Indians against Spain's domination, maintained Indians were fully human and must not be conquered and turned into slaves. After his death, he was vilified for centuries for saying the Spanish were far less than perfect and their treatment of the Natives had been unjust. He was branded a traitor and a madman, and blamed for the slave trade from Africa, though he had come to realize while still a young man how wrong slavery was for all people.

Later scholars believed Las Casas was the first person to espouse liberation theology, strongly promoting the liberation of oppressed people. Over time, he has come to be viewed as a giant of human rights and an important voice railing against the immorality of colonization of the New World, but always with the caution that he may have greatly exaggerated what he witnessed in order to impress the Spanish rulers with the cruelty underway in their name, and the need for more restrictive laws against the maltreatment of Indians.

In recognition of his efforts on Indian rights, there is an effort underway by his Dominican order to elevate him to sainthood in the Catholic Church as the servant of God, though he remains controversial and canonization has not yet taken place. The Church moves slowly in such matters and it has only been four hundred years or so since Las Casas died, so his status is as yet unresolved.

Warring Armies and Tribes

Conquering armies always leave their genes in the gene pool of the conquered. Rape-and-pillage was not just a colorful phrase to describe the behavior of conquering soldiers, which is why Genghis Kahn's genes are represented in sixteen million people living today. (Mayell, 2003; Zerjal *et al.*, 2003; Callaway, 2015) The people of Spain at the time of the *Reconquista* and the beginning of the Age of Exploration were already a grand mix of genetic information from numerous cultures and places in Europe and Africa. After Columbus returned from his first voyage and described what he had found, the Catholic monarchs were excited about converting the heathen and bringing the true religion of Catholicism to the technologically primitive people of the newly discovered lands. This would require small armies of conquistadors, many soldiers, adventurers, and explorers, and eventually friars, to bring enlightenment to the so-called New World, as well as colonists to build towns in the new lands.

The stage was set. The Spanish explorers, conquerors and priests would interact with the Native peoples, including having children, one way or another. Spain claimed much of the western parts of North America and most of Central and South America. Spain's complex cultural and genetic prehistory had landed in the New World and was heading toward New Mexico. (Truxillo, 2001) These were my progenitors: Spanish, Visigoths, Ostrogoths, Muslims, Jews, Greeks, Romans and the entire cultural amalgam developed in and around the Iberian Peninsula. They had traveled through time and across space with all of their inherited social, military and genetic complexity to meet, subdue and mate with the stone-age native peoples of the New World—also my people.

5

I'm Not Mexican; I'm Spanish

Despite the huffing and puffing for status among the economically disadvantaged people having Hispanic roots in New Mexico in the mid-20th century, the longer a family had been in New Mexico, the more complex were its racial origins. Most Chicanos were proud to be descended from conquistadors. When I was a child, logic suggested the longer a person's family had inhabited the state, the closer they would be to the conquistadors from Spain and the larger their allotment of "pure" Spanish blood. Logical thinking, but wrong. Totally wrong. It took scientific research to clear up this historical misunderstanding, but matters were not really cleared up, as far as genetics goes, until the 21st century. It turned out the homespun logic about purity of blood was incorrect. Genes do not work that way.

Spain had instituted a *casta* (caste) system in the Americas to systematize, categorize, and even stigmatize the racial mixing of inhabitants of the New World and compare them to the "pure blood" Spanish. (Davis-Undiano, 2017) With the different *casta* categories, people knew their place and were assigned roles in society based on supposed purity of blood, or degree of racial mixing. Skin color was a major factor in such considerations. The Spanish were the first, or among the first, people to develop racial stereotypes and to apply them to the racial mixing occurring across the new lands of Spain.

Quijano (2000) had suggested the Spanish actually invented racism because of miscegenation in the Americas. (Davis-Undiano, 2017) Certainly, Spanish ships brought the first Africans to the New World, most of them as slaves. However, Spain was never a major slave trading country. Portugal transported 3.9 million slaves from 1524–1866, with most going to Brazil. England was a close second in slave trading with 3.1 million, most destined for the Caribbean. France, (1.3 million) and the Netherlands (six hundred thousand), all ranked ahead of Spain, with its five hundred sixty-eight thousand slaves transported to the New World (Buchholz, 2020), a mere fourteen percent of the British total and only six percent of the total slave trade.

As genetics research would eventually make clear, almost no one was pure anything if Hispanic genes were involved. (Recall the many peoples of the medieval Iberian Peninsula, interbreeding for a millennium or more.) In fact, as *23 and Me*, the genetics ancestry-tracking site noted:

> There is a wide range of human diversity in the world, and sometimes our algorithm is unable to match a region of your DNA to a specific population with confidence. Individuals whose ancestors came from multiple continents and who mixed many generations ago typically see more "unassigned" ancestry in the Ancestry Composition. Individuals whose ancestors came from just one continent (or individuals whose ancestors intermixed more recently) typically see less "unassigned" ancestry.

My wife and I are perfect examples of the genetic extremes of immigrant progeny. Her ancestry is fifty percent Finnish and fifty percent Irish. White. Not so for New Mexicans going back through time. We are a mongrel mix of all cultures: mestizos writ large. My best man, who also went to school with me at San Felipe School in Albuquerque and who is also a mongrel Chicano, married a Vietnamese woman he met while in the Army during the Viet Nam War. Unlike our global mix of genes, her ancestry is one hundred percent Vietnamese, pure Vietnamese on both sides of her family.

Whatever their perceived superiority or inferiority, almost all "Spanish" or Mexicans were poor, so there was little economic advantage to being one or the other. Many, if not most, of the original Spanish landholders who had been gifted land by the King of Spain when New Spain (New Mexico) belonged to Spain, had lost their lands in various nefarious deals involving Anglos ending up with their ranches. They went from landed gentry to poor Mexicans in short order. Only remembered dreams of past glories remained.

Whose Land Is It Anyway?

My dad grew up in Wagon Mound, New Mexico, on his uncle's ranch. His uncle had raised my grandmother, his niece, so he was sort of a grandfather/granduncle to my dad and his siblings. The ranch was fifty-five thousand acres in size and included long stretches of the Canadian River, with mule deer, elk, bighorn sheep, pronghorn, bears, wolves, pumas, bobcats and other wildlife. Its habitats ranged from ponderosa pine to piñon pine/juniper forests, rocky cliffs, grasslands, canyonlands, cactus flats, rivers and streams. Other members of his mother's family (the Martinezes, a founding family of New Mexico and one of the major genealogical lineages I followed) had other ranches. Having entered as conquistadors, they basically controlled much of northern and northeastern New Mexico: as far west as Taos and Abiquiu, as far north as the Colorado line and as far east as Oklahoma and Texas. Scattered here and there were a few smaller (but not small) Mares ranches, especially in the mountains above Taos and near Mora. Over the years, almost all of the land was lost by the families that had originally held royal land grants.

I wished many times that the ranch on which my father had grown up still belonged to the family. The land, of course, was largely taken from the Indians, but there was a lot of land and not that many Indians after the Conquest and they were no match for the Spanish conquistadors in any case. Though the various branches of the family were the owners of much of northern New Mexico in the 1700s and 1800s, through a variety of nefarious transactions most of the Hispanic landowners were eased off their lands, their vast ranches taken over by moneyed and politically astute Anglos, and the former landowners relegated to small parcels of farmland or to no land at all. This was the same thing that had happened to the Indians, but this time the force used was the law, not armed soldiers. Padre Martinez of Taos fought against removal of the land from mestizo settlers, but to no avail. His stand against the practice only made him more enemies among the soon-to-be ruling class.

In northern New Mexico, this remains a sensitive issue to this day, and it is not uncommon for Anglos to feel unwelcome in a state that is now largely owned and run by them. Such historically-based racial tensions may appear suddenly in cities such as Santa Fe, where native Santa Fesinos have been swept out of town before a flood of folks with a lot of money. Without the Indians and Chicanos, Santa Fe, rather than being the "city different," would in fact be the city little different from other overpriced towns scattered around the country that serve as summer or winter playgrounds for the wealthy.

In the general Santa Fe area there are, or were until recently, a number of famous residents. Santa Fe has become a magnet for famous people. The small wealthy mountain town with its ethnic flavor is a magnet for the rich and famous.

Chicanos have and continue to contribute to American society, making it richer and more complex, from the arts and sciences to music and the culinary fare that today characterizes multicultural America.

Let's Hear It for Slavery

Imagine there was a superpower in the world whose leader wanted to spread slavery and also wanted to illegally obtain more territory to expand his nation westward, a la Hitler's Lebensraum in the 1930s and 1940s. Let's call it Manifest Destiny. The leader had the army, the means, and a nation that was much weaker against which he could declare an illegal war and march into their country killing and destroying as many people as possible. He would take their nation by force and slaughter. His nation was much larger and his army much more powerful, better equipped, highly trained, and larger as well. His country had better weaponry, ships, and an overriding vision of extending the nation westward.

The United States of America in 1846 with the slave-owning racist James K. Polk as President, first signed a bill begun by President John Tyler and sneaked it through the Senate and annexed slave-owning Texas as the fifteenth slave-owning state in the Union in 1845, and then looked with hungry eyes toward Mexico, an unstable non-slave country ripe for the taking.

The land of the Southwest, and maybe Mexico as well, was much too large for Mexico to defend successfully, which is the same problem Spain faced defending its New World territories. The U.S. could take the land easily; it only needed an excuse for war. It happened in 1847 when a troop of U.S. soldiers set a trap for the Mexicans and some U.S. soldiers were attacked and killed. Many members of Congress did not believe Polk about the attack, including Abraham Lincoln, who introduced eight bills requiring proof of the battlefield assertions and their veracity. Many members felt it was a setup by Polk's generals to provide an excuse for war. Like so many wars of the United States throughout its history, it was a made-up war. Polk accused his detractors of treason.

An Unjust War

Polk and his generals chose a strip of disputed land along the Nueces River (located today in Texas) to initiate their plan. Did it belong to Mexico or to the United States? No one could say with certainty; national boundaries were murky in those days. (New Mexico territory, for example, at one time extended northward to Alaska.) Both nations claimed it, but it was easy to get the Mexicans to attack a small troop of cavalry and kill U.S. soldiers. War followed. The trap had been set and the Mexican troops had fallen into it in 1846. Mexico was invaded in 1847. Ulysses S. Grant called it "One of the most unjust [wars] ever waged by a stronger against a weaker nation." (Pimentel, 2020) Abraham Lincoln noted,

> It was outright theft, built on a foundation of racism and imperialism.... I see no need to ascribe greatness to this particular means to an end, no more than white privilege gives anyone license to ignore the racial history upon which our country is built.

(Pimentel, 2020) Mexico never declared war against the U.S. in this war for Manifest Destiny. It was entirely a U.S. operation.

Fig. 10. "Battle of Churubusco—Fought near the city of Mexico 20th of August 1847 / J. Cameron." Hand tinted lithograph.

Surprisingly, Mexico fought bravely, but a U.S. victory was inevitable. The U.S. won all major battles and ended up stealing a half million square miles of territory from Mexico, including New Mexico, California, parts of Utah, Arizona, parts of Colorado and parts of Texas. This was more than twice the size of Spain and France combined. General Winfield Scott attacked Mexico City in 1847, including Chapultepec Castle, a military academy for boys. U.S. forces slaughtered young cadets, martyrs who came to be known as *Los Niños Héroes* (the Boy Heroes). After Mexico City was taken by U.S. troops, Mexico surrendered. Peace negotiations followed and the infamous Treaty of Guadalupe Hidalgo was signed and approved on July 4, 1848. The treaty mentioned Mexican lands in the new U.S. territory:

ARTICLE VIII

Mexicans now established in territories previously belonging to Mexico, and which remain for the future within the limits of the United States, as defined by the present treaty, shall be free to continue where they now reside, or to remove at any time to the Mexican Republic, retaining the property which they possess in the said territories, or disposing thereof, and removing the proceeds wherever they please, without their being subjected, on this account, to any contribution, tax, or charge whatever.

Those who shall prefer to remain in the said territories may either retain the title and rights of Mexican citizens or acquire those of citizens of the United States. But they shall be under the obligation to make their election within one year from the date of the exchange of ratifications of this treaty; and those who shall remain in the said territories after the expiration of that year, without having declared their intention to retain the character of Mexicans, shall be considered to have elected to become citizens of the United States.

In the said territories, property of every kind, now belonging to Mexicans not established there, shall be inviolably respected. The present owners, the heirs of these, and all Mexicans who may hereafter acquire said property by contract shall enjoy with respect to it guarantees equally ample as if the same belonged to citizens.

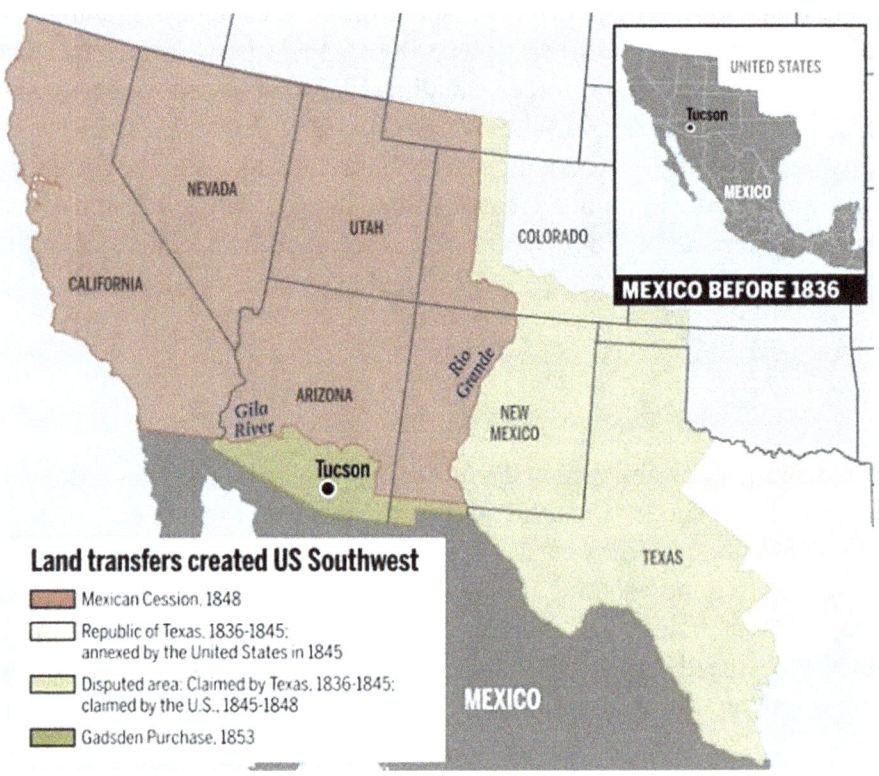

Fig. 11. Land transfers from Mexico to the U.S. creating the American Southwest.

Scalpers Everywhere

Alas, the land agreements in this treaty were not followed as Mexican lands were just too extensive and valuable to leave in the hands of swarthy Mexican mestizos. Mexicans had good reason to be suspicious of these agreements. Only ten years earlier Texas rangers had swarmed into New Mexico's Hidalgo County (following a law passed in neighboring Sonora, Mexico) and begun killing and scalping Indians whose scalps were worth about one American silver dollar apiece. Those scalped included men, women, and children, sometimes scalped alive. (*The Scalp Industry*, University of Virginia) Chihuahua offered one hundred dollars for the scalps of braves and fifty dollars for squaws, with lesser amounts for children.

As the value of scalps increased, some Indians, desperate for money, began scalping their comrades. It was only a matter of time until Mexican scalps which, truth be told, were difficult to distinguish from Indian scalps in any case due to the fact these were Chicanos (Coyote mongrels to the scalpers). They were also worth one hundred dollars, so it was time to kill Mexicans wherever they could be found. After the treaty, scalp-hunting took place on an expanded level. (Chamberlain, 1850, 1956) One raid in the Big Bend of Texas led to two hundred fifty scalps being taken.

Scalps soon became so valuable that scalpers began scalping other scalpers. With this kind of business plan, their days were numbered and they began to disappear from the dangerous Southwest. Scalping laws remained the law of the land until 1880. My grandmother, Rebecca Gutierrez, was born in 1874. On her sixth birthday in January, 1880, the future wife and daughter-in-law of military men, could no longer be legally scalped.

Still, while scalps were worth a lot of money, scalping was merely a distraction. The real treasure of the Mexicans was not the hair on their head, but their land, documented and approved in the treaty of Guadalupe Hidalgo. Ways were devised to "legally" transfer the land from Mexican grant holders to Anglos. Even saintly Sister Blandina commented on crooked land deals after being in New Mexico for a couple of years:

> I am going to make a further prediction. The 'land-grabbers' will do tremendous havoc among our native population, both spiritually and financially.... Progress will come, I do not doubt, but spiritual death will also come. And 'what doth it profit a man if he gain the whole world and lose his own soul?' (Segale, 1948: 188)

This is still a sore point in northern New Mexico, where the wealthy landholders were transformed into the impoverished classes seemingly in the blink of an eye, though it actually took many decades.

Fig. 12. A group of Crow Indians who were killed and scalped in 1874. Wikimedia Commons.

This Used to Be Our Land

Once, on a hunting trip with my dad when I was fourteen, we had hunted for deer in the prairies and canyons near Wagon Mound, where all the lands originated with Spanish land grants. It was a tough year for deer and we had seen nothing after two hard days of hiking the rocky, pine canyons for many miles. We decided to hunt in the mountains further west. "I know a place we can try," my dad said. "It's on the road to Ocaté. It used to be a family ranch."

At a small cafe, we encountered some Indian friends of my father who had been doing some powerful hunting and some powerful drinking as well. There were six of them in a car and a pickup and they had killed a bear, two huge buck deer and two turkeys. The bear was strapped to the automobile's roof and its blood ran down the windows. A turkey dangled from the car's door handle, with two bucks and the other turkey in the truck bed. It had, indeed, been a memorable hunt, but they wanted to bag another deer.

Each Navajo wore a brightly red or yellow checked wool jacket and had bandoliers wound around his neck and down the chest, like Pancho Villa. One of them even wore an old .44 in a holster, like a turn-of-the-century gunslinger. The car overflowed with high-powered rifles. They said they knew a good place to hunt and invited us to join them. They had been far more successful than we, so we followed their bloody vehicles as they raced westward over the gravel road.

We drove perhaps thirty miles or so and my dad slowed down and said, indicating a large ranch, "This used to be one of our family's ranches. It always had good hunting." The Indians got out of their vehicles with rifles, pistols and knives bristling. There was perhaps a mile or more of fall pale-yellow desert grassland along the fence leading to low hills, with a dark green blanket of piñon pine forests in the distance. Here and there a few tall ponderosa pines could be seen towering over the piñon and juniper trees.

"Let's go to those hills," my dad said, "there ought to be deer there."

Did I mention my dad was five foot six inches and I was five seven? The six Indians were all over six feet tall and looked remarkably fit and tough. The ranch had a gate that was unlocked, but uninvitingly closed. We stopped to open the gate. All eight of us were armed with high-powered rifles, knives, and other assorted weaponry. As we opened the gate, a Gringo foreman raced his pickup toward us. He slid to a stop and got out of the truck, leaving the headlights on. He was wearing a revolver in a holster at his side. As he approached, he snarled at us to get off the ranch. Hunting was not allowed. As he put it (I use quotation marks to give the flavor of the conversation as I remember it):

"You boys get the hell out of here." I may have only been fourteen, but I knew this fellow was making a serious mistake. Not only had the Indians been drinking, they had also been killing things all day. Although my dad and I were ready to move on to look for another spot, the Indians took umbrage at both the foreman's tone and his message. They asked again, very nicely, if they could hunt on the ranch for a few hours.

"Hell no," was the reply to one of the most successful and best-armed Indian hunting parties since the days of Crazy Horse. My dad said he actually knew the ranch quite well, as a relative of his used to own it many years ago. "It was in our family." "I don't care who the hell owned it," said the foreman. "You boys aren't going to hunt here."

His unreasonably aggressive tone bothered all of us, none more so than the Indians. Without speaking to one another they came to a group decision. "We owned this land long before you did and long before his family did" (nodding toward my dad). "And we are going to hunt here today." This was said quietly—so quietly that the slamming of live rounds into the chambers of their rifles was louder than the crack of a rifle. It appeared they were going to kill the ranch hand, and I think all of us, including the rancher, realized it at the same instant. His eyes grew wide. His pickup truck offered no protection and he was a long way from the ranch house, several miles to the north.

His hand began to move down toward his pistol, but his pathetic six-shooter was no match for a squad of angry, inebriated Indians armed to the teeth. One could almost see his thinking reflected in the movement of the hand as it continued to reach slowly for his pistol. If he screwed this up, he might end up on the roof of the car with the bear. We all watched the cautious progress of the hand toward the gun. Then it recoiled like a spider encountering a hot plate, cautiously crawling back up toward the man's belt. He had realized his pistol could not help him.

His intimidating manner was going to do no good with this group. They could not be intimidated.

He was all alone and had stupidly confronted a small militia of angry hunters having centuries of racial inequities, land schemes, scalping, and unfairly induced poverty buried within. He was about to give his life in defense of a ruminant that, I am sure, he hunted regularly and did not give a rat's ass about in any case. We were just people to keep off the ranch and to show who was boss. Indians and Chicanos? All the better, but now it was blowing up in his face. As the tension built, I could see the foreman decide to live, to see his family again, to see the New Mexico sun rise above the golden grasslands and the dark green hills.

> "Hey boys," he said, "there's no reason to get all upset. The boss told me not to let anyone on the ranch, but, hey, I think it would be all right if you hunted here for a while. In fact, I know a good spot for hunting. Why don't y'all follow me? I don't know what I was thinking. Hehe." Smiling like the Cheshire Cat, he said, "You can stay as long as you like. Just be sure to close the gate when you leave."

He took us to the forested hills we could see in the distance. As we got out of our vehicles, he floored the gas on his pickup truck and headed away, wheels spinning in a cloud of dust to some distant ranch house and, I am sure, a triple shot of whiskey. He had almost died and he knew it. We all knew it. The bad part of this otherwise uplifting story is we hunted all afternoon and never saw a deer, a bear, a turkey or even a squirrel, but it was a victorious hunt nonetheless.

A Cautionary Hunting Tale

Crazy things can happen on hunts when men are armed and thrown back into their more feral lives. A family friend, who was a plumber by trade, was also a war hero and a Chicano. He was a combat veteran of World War II and had been shot up by the Germans. The top of his head had been blown off so his brains were visible and he was also shot in the abdomen. The wound in his head had been repaired with a "silver plate" (probably tantalum). It looked like he was a goner to his buddies, but he was tough. He was taken to a medical unit and eventually sent to a hospital in France.

After a long convalescence, he returned to New Mexico with a chest full of medals. "You know," he said, "I heard someone say when you get shot it doesn't hurt, it only hurts later. Well, I can tell you that's a bunch of bullshit. When I was wounded, there was more pain than I had ever felt in my life." Remarkably, he not only survived his wounds, but came home to found and run a small plumbing company.

Curiously, in telling us to be careful when we hunted, he related the time he had gone deer hunting in New Mexico and, having been shot in combat before, was very careful to always wear a fluorescent orange jacket and matching hat so he would not be shot by accident. One morning, while deer hunting, he heard a bullet whiz over his head. He crouched down and tried to figure out who was shooting. He saw a man raising his rifle while looking at him through a scope, so he waved his arms and yelled at him not to shoot. The man shot him anyway with a high-powered deer rifle. It blew out his lung and, incredibly and against all odds, the crusty old veteran survived again. The man who shot him was a military officer. He was questioned by police and swore he was certain that the man clad in orange from head to toe and yelling at him was a deer. You never know about people, even trained people. Buck fever, I guess.

He told us another story. He and two guys decided to go deer hunting in the mountains of New Mexico. He did not know the two men very well, but they had met somewhere and decided to put together a deer hunt. As frequently happens in New Mexico, they saw few deer and killed none. The area was, however, chock-a-block with squirrels. Unfortunately, it was not squirrel hunting season and they did not have a squirrel license. Did that stop them? No. They shot a bunch of squirrels anyway, then got nervous because squirrels were illegal to hunt at that place and time. They decided to hide the dead bushy-tailed rodents in the hubcaps of their truck.

They were sitting around the camp when they heard a vehicle coming slowly toward them. Though they appeared to be in the middle of nowhere, it was following their tracks right toward their camp. As luck would have it, it was a game warden. The warden chatted with them and asked if they had gotten any deer. Nope, hunting was lousy. "How about squirrels?" he asked. "Oh no, we haven't hunted squirrels. They're out of season." The game warden walked around their camp, then went over to their truck, which was parked a short distance away. He asked, "Mind if I look around?" "Help yourself."

As he headed for the truck one of the men said, "If he finds the squirrels, let's kill him. We can hide his truck and bury him here. No one will ever know." The second man thought it over and said, "Okay, I'm in." My dad's war-hero plumber friend said, "Are you guys crazy? For squirrels? I won't do it. I've killed men before; you haven't. Leave the warden alone." If they were not all together in the proposed conspiratorial plot, they could not do the crime. Of course, the experienced warden found the squirrels in a trice, since small game are often hidden in hubcaps. He confiscated their guns, gave them a ticket and a summons and told them to come to the wildlife offices later that week. He never knew how close he had come to dying that day, saved by a tough, old, wounded veteran with integrity.

6

Oñate and the Conquistadors

Don Diego De Vargas, born in the late 17th century, was a conquistador, but Juan de Oñate y Salazar is considered by some to be the last conquistador, perhaps because his deeds were more cringeworthy. Oñate founded Santa Fe Province as a part of New Spain in 1610 and appointed himself governor. He established a settlement just north of the present city of Santa Fe. The modern site for the city of Santa Fe was established by New Mexico's second governor, Don Pedro de Peralta, in 1607. Peralta also gave Santa Fe a new name, La Villa Real de la Santa Fe de San Francisco de Asís. It was and still is the capital city of New Mexico, the oldest capital city in the United States, and the oldest European community west of the Mississippi, as well as the highest elevation capital city in the country.

Oñate

Oñate, who had been born in the New World in Zacatecas in 1550, was a cruel conqueror, although whether he was more cruel than earlier conquistadors or, for that matter many Native Americans, is unclear. He was, however, held to a higher standard than earlier conquistadors, because Spain had enacted the Order on New Discoveries in 1573. This law required charitable treatment of Native peoples who were potential converts to Catholicism, thanks to the efforts of the Franciscan Friars. There were exceptions in the case of self-defense or in cases where Indians who had agreed to submit to Spanish rule later rebelled. (Simmons, 1991) In that case, the charitable treatment generally demanded of a conquistador was no longer required. My Spanish ancestors rode with both Oñate and De Vargas, and some stayed on in New Mexico to become some of the first families in the territory. For better or worse, they are a part of this history.

Oñate traveled through much of the Southwest on journeys of discovery. (See Simmons, 1991) He encountered the Sky City of Acoma in New Mexico (which Coronado had encountered one hundred fifty years earlier). The Acoma people had inhabited their pueblo situated atop an extraordinarily inaccessible four-hundred-foot-high mesa for at least a thousand years, and perhaps as many as two thousand years. Acoma still holds the record for the longest continually inhabited city in the United States. Oñate hoped to have a peaceful relationship with the Acoma. However, there were two groups of Acoma in the pueblo; one felt the Spaniards would respond to peaceful interactions and one wanted war with the Spaniards. They clearly were unaware of the disparity in armaments between the two groups and the fighting ability of the Spanish. For all practical purposes the Spaniards were the Supermen of their day. Oñate negotiated with the peaceful Acoma and then rode off to contact other pueblos. Everything seemed to be fine when he left.

The Acoma Assault Oñate's Soldiers

While Oñate was gone, he left thirty-one of his soldiers behind to negotiate trade deals with the Acoma. However, shortly after he left, the warlike branch of the Acoma assumed power within the tribe and attacked the Spaniards without warning. One of those murdered was Juan de Zaldívar, Oñate's nephew, to whom he was very close. Oñate learned about the massacre and was shocked to hear that his men, who were there on a peaceful mission, were beaten to death and literally torn to pieces. He returned to Santa Fe, where the families of the slaughtered men were devastated by the news of the killings. They cried out for revenge on the Acoma by Governor Oñate and his troops. As George Bush said after the people of the United States were clamoring for revenge against the 911 attackers: "I can hear you....The rest of the world hears you...and the people who knocked these buildings down will hear all of us soon." (Gregg, N.D.) They did, and more than two hundred thousand civilians in Iraq would die from the actions of coalition forces (Watson Institute, 2021), though Iraq was not complicit in the 911 attack. Throughout history most leaders will respond to the cries of their people for revenge after an unprovoked attack, e.g., witness the response of the United States to Japan's sneak attack on Pearl Harbor on December 7, 1941. The response to that attack ended in 1945 with the first use of the Atomic Bomb and war deaths of more than three million Japanese.

Fig. 13. Sky City of Acoma atop a four-hundred-foot rocky mesa with sheer rock cliffs. Marshall Henrie in Wikipedia Creative Commons.

Fig. 14. Juan de Oñate sketch.

As Governor of New Mexico, Oñate had to consider the safety of his people, as well as the future of Spanish rule in the Territory. He was under strict orders from Spain not to engage in conflict with the Indians, yet he faced an uprising that, were it not put down, could mean the end of Spanish rule in New Mexico Territory, as other pueblos would feel empowered to slaughter the relatively small number of colonists in New Mexico. In addition, the spirit of the people and the morale of his men demanded vengeance for the deaths of their family members and friends. What would you do, inhabitants of the 21st century, if you were in his position and shouldering his responsibilities? Walk away? Somehow, I doubt that would be your response to having your loved ones torn to pieces and tossed off a four-hundred-foot cliff.

Just after Christmas Day, 1598 (the small colony's first Christmas in New Mexico, marked by grieving), the Governor called all of the clergy together for a meeting and asked them the following:

Don Juan de Oñate, Governor, Captain General, and Adelantado of the provinces of New Mexico requests an opinion as to what conditions are necessary in order to wage a just war (against these Indians). In the event of such a war, what steps may be taken against those warred upon and against their possessions?

In effect, he wanted to know, given the strictures placed on him by Spain and the Church, did he as governor have a legal and moral right to attack the Acoma and, moreover, what would be a fitting punishment for the Indians who carried out the surprise massacre?

A two-week judicial proceeding was undertaken for testimony and other evidence. (Simmons, 1991) His officers recommended leveling Acoma pueblo because if they failed to do so it would be open season on Spaniards by all the Pueblos in the territory and the colonists would lose their very tenuous foothold in New Mexico. (Jones, 1966) Their future and the future of their descendants in this new land were at stake. Some of Oñate's soldiers had been tossed alive from the mesa to die shattered on the rocks below. Remarkably, one soldier, Juan de Olague, had leaped over the cliff edge in search of a quick death rather than being beaten to death by warclubs and then ripped to pieces. He survived the fall when he landed in a sand dune. As might be expected, Olague felt the Acoma were especially treacherous and needed punishing.

The final people to give testimony were the friars, speaking for the Church and its rules. They found, officially, that Oñate was the legitimate ruler of New Mexico, as recognized by the King of Spain, and the Indians of Acoma had sworn fealty to Spanish rule and Spanish law. The Indians subsequently had broken Spanish law to launch a surprise attack on peaceful soldiers. Oñate was free to exact revenge as far as the Church was concerned. What would you have done with your 21st century conscience if you had the responsibilities and duties of Oñate? Let New Mexico revert to the Indians and return to Mexico? Why do I doubt you would have chosen that path, especially after dedicating your life and fortune to tame the new land and make a new life for yourself and your family, not to mention your duty to Spain and the King?

After the court hearing and still looking for guidance, Oñate called his men together in a large public meeting to discuss the findings of the court and ask for their opinion. A general consensus was if the Acoma were not brought to justice, the Spanish families in New Mexico would have to abandon the Territory, for no one would be safe if the Spanish did not respond to the attack. The Indians would rip them apart, literally, rape the women and kidnap the children. After weighing all sides in the matter, Oñate declared "war by blood and fire" on the Acoma (a traditional saying in Spain before combat).

Oñate was asked by the people not to lead his troops into battle at Acoma personally. Even Coronado's Captain, Hernando de Alvarado, in 1540, one hundred and fifty years before Oñate's time, noted Acoma was one of the strongest pueblos he had ever seen. Coronado and his men felt Acoma Pueblo, the Sky City, could not be taken by military troops and was unassailable. (Minge, 2002) If Oñate's army lost to the Acoma—a tribe that had never been conquered by a warring foe and whose pueblo had never been breached—Oñate would be needed to lead the retreat of the Spaniards back to Mexico before the Pueblos rose up against the colonists in New Mexico and slaughtered them all.

Battle of Acoma

Oñate reluctantly sent part of his small army to Acoma, with his young nephew, Sargento Mayor Vicente de Zaldívar, in charge. Vicente was the brother of Oñate's murdered nephew. He was under orders to demand the Acoma tribe surrender to Spanish rule peacefully. Barring that, Zaldívar would assault and punish the Acoma. Oñate would be more than one hundred twenty miles away (at least four days journey on horseback) if and when the pueblo of Acoma was assaulted. He would know nothing about the assault or its outcome. He told his nephew if the Acoma gave up the warriors who had murdered his soldiers and agreed to submit to Spanish rule once again there would be no battle. He admonished his nephew if he did have to attack the pueblo he was to use "clemency" rather than "severity."

Acoma could only be accessed by climbing the cliffs using precarious handholds in the rock. (There was no road or track onto the mesa until more than three centuries later when a Hollywood movie company filming a silent film titled "Redskin" was shot on the mesa in 1929; the road they built was later improved by John Ford, while making several John Wayne westerns. It remains the only road that accesses the Sky City today.)

As ordered, in the winter of 1599, the Spaniards asked the Indians to surrender to Spanish rule and turn over those who had attacked and killed the soldiers. More than a thousand Acoma warriors responded with arrows, stones, large chunks of ice, and other heavy things being thrown off the high cliffs in an attempt to kill the small group of Spanish soldiers far below. Zaldívar had only seventy men. The Acoma let them know after they wiped out this small troop of Spaniards, which they ridiculed, they would proceed to kill all Spanish in New Mexico.

The Sky City did indeed appear impregnable to the Spanish soldiers. Grave doubts arose among Zaldívar's men, seeing how few they were in number, how large the enemy force was and how impenetrable was the mesa. Zaldívar was able to rally their morale with a fiery speech to boost their spirits and instill courage. The honor of Spain and the future of New Mexico were at stake, as well as the men's personal honor. They were Spaniards. Zaldívar devised a strategic plan for taking the mesa. He would initiate a full-frontal assault at the base of the mesa with his men attempting to climb up the main trail that used the handholds made by the Indians (an assault that likely would fail), but in a bold move, he himself would lead eleven men on a sneak attack from the opposite side of the mesa while the main assault was underway. With hundreds of Indians distracted by the diversionary assault, Zaldívar and his small group of men climbed the mesa unopposed. When they reached the top, they were spotted by the Indians and about four hundred warriors attacked the eleven men. Remarkably, the tiny group of desperate Spaniards held out until nightfall in fierce hand-to-hand combat, backed against the cliff edge.

Some reinforcements arrived in the early morning and Zaldívar had them bring ropes to haul two of the cannons Oñate had brought from Mexico up to the top of the mesa. The effectiveness of the cannons is described in a firsthand account by Gaspar Pérez de Villagrá, the legal officer for the Oñate expedition, who accompanied Oñate's army. (Villagrá, 1610a, b):

> Firing the cannons' two hundred spikes each, the Spanish began to cut down many of the warriors that were fighting them and level the houses of the pueblo, eventually setting some on fire. A strong wind began to whip the fire from house to house and the pine logs began to flame. The Indians, seeing they were lost, began to kill one another or burn alive in the houses rather than surrender.

Death Before Surrender

The Acoma had an understanding among themselves that they would never surrender if they were being conquered. They would die instead. Villagrá reported:

> Seeing themselves now conquered, 'began to kill Each other, and did so in such fashion That sons from fathers, fathers from their loved children, Took life away, and further, more than this, Others in groups did give aid to the fire So that it might leap up with more vigor, Consume the pueblo, and destroy it all. (Villagrá, 1610 a, b, verses 250-255)

Many jumped to their deaths from the cliffs. Many centuries later on the island of Saipan in the Marianas (where my uncle Christie Mares fought and was wounded), more than a thousand Japanese civilians also chose suicide over surrender; parents tossed babies and young children to their deaths over high cliffs and then jumped after them. (Critical Past, Marines on Saipan, 1944) After three days of fighting, the surviving Indians surrendered. As many as eight hundred Acoma (five hundred warriors, three hundred women and children) died before hostilities ended—many by their own hand. The Indians said they knew they had lost when a Spanish warrior on a white horse with a flaming sword in his hand and a beautiful woman walking next to him appeared in the clouds of smoke from the burning village. Always the scientist, I consider this a good example of pareidolia, like the demon in the World Trade Center's smoke clouds (*SF Gate News*, 2001), but the Indians had no doubt it was an omen of a Spanish victory and it frightened them sufficiently that they subsequently surrendered.

The Spanish agreed their victory was a miracle, given the fact they were outnumbered fifteen to one and only lost one soldier (due to friendly fire). As to the vision of the ghostly Spanish knight, the Spaniards were certain it was an appearance of Santiago Matamoros, or Saint James the Moor Slayer (859 CE), one of the original apostles and the brother of Saint John the Apostle. Santiago Matamoros (at least in myth and lore) was the Apostle James come back as one of the greatest Spanish warriors who ever lived. He became the patron saint of Spain at one time. Though long dead, he was said to appear riding a white horse with a blazing sword in his hand when important battles were underway, exactly what the Acoma described.

Fig. 15. Santiago defeating the Moors, by Giovanni Battista Tiepolo, 1749–1750.

Santiago had appeared at a number of battles in the Middle Ages, including those of the *Reconquista*, and was reputed to have been a part of the massive Battle of Guadalajara, Mexico in the Mixton War, as well as a later battle in the mountains above Guadalajara. (Simmons, 1991) Zaldívar and his troops believed the woman was the Blessed Virgin, giving her blessing to the Spanish soldiers and assuring their victory over the heathen.

Trial, Verdict, Punishment

The five hundred Acoma survivors were mostly women and children. Zaldívar led the captives toward San Juan Pueblo. Oñate, meanwhile, after quelling a minor assault from a group of Pueblos, gathered his soldiers and, still having no news from Acoma, headed for Santo Domingo Pueblo, which was on the trail to Acoma. There he met up with Zaldívar and his small group of soldiers returning with the captives. Oñate wanted to make examples of the Indian prisoners so other Indians would be reluctant to turn against Spanish rule in the future. He held a formal trial that began that very day in Santo Domingo. Oñate appointed one of his men to act as defense counsel.

The trial lasted for three days with the defense pleading for mercy because the Indians were uncivilized and didn't know any better. They were found guilty, of course, but none was sentenced to death, which might have been the expected outcome of the trial considering they had murdered soldiers in a surprise attack. Punishment was meted out, however. Men over twenty-five years old had part of their foot amputated. In some accounts, the toes of one foot, or the front part of the foot, rather than the entire foot, were amputated; in other accounts the right hand was amputated. The facts, whatever they may be, are lost in the mists of history, but since Oñate wanted to use the defeated Indians as slaves, it makes sense that the toes were removed rather than the foot, an account supported by Oñate's own personal journal, where the *puntas de pies* (tips of the foot) were removed. A footless slave in the 1600s had little value. Boys and men from ten to twenty-five were sentenced to twenty years of servitude, as were women over twelve years of age.

Amputation had been a standard punishment for a variety of crimes in the Middle East, Spain, among pre-contact Peruvian Indians (Lastres, 1943; Verano *et al.*, 2000; Fernandes *et al.*, 2017) and other places in the world since at least 1500 BCE and was common in Moorish Spain. In fact, it was part of Hammurabi's Code in 1750 BCE as a legal act of punishment. (Kirkup, 2007; Mavroforou *et al.*, 2014) These were barbaric times around the world, whether one belonged to advanced societies, such as the Spanish or stone-age people such as Native Americans. (Gates and Marafioti, eds., 2014) As Bernard Bailyn (2013) noted:

> Among the Powhatans of the Virginian plain, battling furiously against or as allies of a would-be native overlord, and among the aggressive Iroquois and their Huron and Algonquian victims in upcountry New York and the eastern Great Lakes, warfare, with all its personal horrors, was commonplace. Raiding parties, seeking revenge, tribute, or restitution, devastated whole villages, pillaging stores of food, destroying crops and habitations, butchering the wounded, and carrying off the women, children, and defeated warriors. The women and children who survived were often adopted as replacements for the victors' recently deceased kinfolk, but the captured warriors were brought home as trophies, along with severed hands, feet, and heads. Beaten continuously, the prisoners were often maimed—fingers chopped or bitten off to incapacitate them for further warfare, backs and shoulders slashed, then systematically tortured, by women gashing their bodies and tearing off strips of flesh, by children scorching the most sensitive parts of the immobilized bodies with red-hot coals—while judgment was passed on whether they would live as dependents, in effect as slaves, or die.... If condemned, they would most likely be burned to death after disembowelment, some parts of their bodies having been eaten and their blood drunk in celebration by their captors.

Thus, Oñate's ordering the partial amputations for the men of Acoma may not have been uncommon by the standards of his time. Amputations, and beheadings for that matter, are still common in certain parts of the world under Sharia Law (Pannier, 2008) or by the standards of the Native Americans themselves. Nonetheless, Oñate was charged by the King of Spain with unnecessary cruelty to natives, as well as to his own Spaniards. Eventually the charges were dismissed. Their dismissal was not necessarily reflective of his actual brutality, but because he had returned to Mexico to replenish the fortune he had lost in paying for his unsuccessful colonization, exploitation, and pacification of the territory (by the standards of other conquistadors). When he was wealthy once again, his family connections and a new Spanish king overturned his twelve convictions out of the thirty charges for which he had originally been tried. He had been found not guilty on eighteen charges in his original trial. (Carlson, 2008) The overturning of charges for which he had been convicted occurred fourteen years after Oñate had left New Mexico, never to return. In fact, Oñate spent only eight years in New Mexico before being recalled to Mexico.

Some of my paternal grandmother's Martinez ancestors (including my twelfth great grandfather, Capitán Luis Martin Serrano II) were part of Oñate's army and stayed on in Santa Fe and northern New Mexico to make their lives after Oñate left, which is how I happened to come along so many centuries later. Given America's latest attempt to revise everything in its past, Oñate, once considered a hero by New Mexicans for having helped open and settle New Mexico, is now considered a villain by many, especially Native people, and his statues are occasionally destroyed, or his foot on the statue may be cut off. These are bloodless amputations, but their symbology is clear, even if it may not be correct.

Global Slaughters Across Time

Discussing Oñate during the current cancel culture movement elicits anger from some people, whether one is for or against the opening of the Southwest, or the domination and subjugation of the Natives, or the development of the United States as a nation. I have direct ancestors who were part of Oñate's expeditionary force and I number many ancestors among the Indians he exploited, and even among the U.S. Cavalry that fought the Indian Wars. It is difficult to take sides in the argument as to the morality of those actions in those long-ago times when considering the broad sweep of history. Context must be given consideration. As Buddha noted: "Suffering is wishing things were other than they are."

The Spaniards slaughtered many Native Americans, as did the French, English, Portuguese and Americans, but the Native peoples also slaughtered themselves in many major battles, especially in the Southwest in wars between nomadic tribes, Pueblos and seminomadic tribes. In a sense, they fought forever-wars for centuries, just as the peoples of the Iberian Peninsula had been fighting for a millennium. (Masich, 2017, Minnesota Historical Society, N.D.) Wars among native peoples characterized not only North America, but Central and South America, too. Pre-Columbian tribes throughout the Americas practiced ritual human sacrifice with torture, often with still-beating hearts removed from the person being killed. (Schüren and Gabbert, 2020)

Genetics research, while shedding much light on relationships and ancestral history, can confound people who either have not had their genes analyzed, or who disbelieve science if it challenges their fundamental ideas as to who they are, something that is unfortunately common in America today. However strongly we wish the past had unspooled in a different way, we are unable to describe how it should have developed along different paths. We cannot describe what the world would be like today had our woke ideas been implemented during the time periods under consideration. To think today's ideas could be applied *post hoc* is silly. The past remains immutable, absent more first-hand information and documentation to understand it better.

The Encyclopedia of Indian Wars by Gregory Michno estimates over a forty-year period in the Indian Wars (1850–1890), there were over six hundred fights between the Army, civilians and Indians. There were more than twenty-one thousand casualties, dead and injured. Army and civilian casualties totaled six thousand plus (thirty-one percent) and Indian casualties were over fourteen thousand (sixty-nine percent). Deaths were probably one-third of these totals or slightly higher. For perspective, during the year following the October 7, 2023 attack on Israel by Hamas, when Israel launched a war against Hamas in Gaza and elsewhere, more than forty thousand people died of war-related assaults against civilians and terrorists. Weapons have greatly increased in lethality over the intervening centuries.

What countries and societies throughout history have not been steeped in war and slaughter? I am at a loss to name even one, other than San Marino, which is an old but tiny country of twenty-five square miles taking up a very small patch of what would otherwise be northern Italy. It is about sixty percent the size of Disneyworld. Other than that, all countries have been warring nations throughout history, including the tiny Vatican state (one-eighth the size of Central Park). When the September 11, 2001, attacks occurred, almost three thousand civilians were killed. That new record for civilian deaths in the United States surpassed the previous record for America: the eight hundred German immigrants slaughtered in the town of New Ulm, Minnesota in a surprise attack by Dakota Indians in 1862, one hundred thirty-nine years before 9/11. (Steil and Post, 2002)

We are all descendants of highly flawed and warlike people and no one's hands are clean. As my late colleague, Paul Colinvaux, noted (1980),

> The actual record of human affairs is a tale of battles and rebellion, conquest, and trade, colonies, tyranny, liberation and empire. The nations come and go fighting, and the focus of power shifts from one nation to another. History repeats itself as an emergent people expands against its neighbors, lives on in splendour and freedom for a time, and then slides away into ignominious eclipse.

We may feel good ascribing revisionist thinking to the battles between conquistadors and Indians, or to the U.S. Cavalry and its battles with Indians or Mexicans, or to the U.S. Army's war with Mexico, but history and its facts are stubborn things. I had ancestors and relatives in each of those wars. The world we inhabit today is a result of those earlier conflicts, as are the lives we lead.

As I write these words, the Tigray War rages in Ethiopia, with up to a half million deaths. The Iran-Iraq War of the 1980s had more than a million casualties apportioned between both warring powers. At the end of the 20th century and into the 21st century, the Second Congo War with the Rwandan Genocide ended in 2008 resulted in 5.4 million deaths. The ongoing Syrian Civil War has resulted in a minimum of six hundred thousand deaths of male combatants and uncounted civilian deaths. Putin wages war in Ukraine at the close of the year 2024 and thus far there have been at least five hundred thousand casualties.

As morally superior and comfortable armchair observers for whom time and context have no meaning, one can criticize everything from the conquistadors' treatment of Indians to the morality or immorality of the U.S. Cavalry fighting Native peoples across the western United States (which, along with the Mexican War, actually led to the formation of the United States as we know it). What are you doing to stop the slaughters in real time that are occurring as I write? History tells us there is no way to stop humanity's urge to slaughter one another, whether for religion, money, lust, love, food, minerals, natural resources, power, land, greed, or ideology. Cutting the foot off a statue or protesting some monument with a small crowd of other powerless people is a pathetic way to rewrite history while ignoring the ongoing human crises that surround us across the globe today and threaten our own existence.

Fig. 16. Master Sergeant John Devine, 1st Cavalry Dragoons, my great grandfather.

At the end of the film, "She Wore a Yellow Ribbon," the cavalry regiment rides out again after a number of major Indian battles had been fought, including the Custer massacre. The narrator notes:

> So here they are: the dog-faced soldiers, the regulars, the fifty-cents-a-day professionals... riding the outposts of a nation. From Fort Reno to Fort Apache—from Sheridan to Stock—they were all the same: men in dirty-shirt blue and only a cold page in the history books to mark their passing. But wherever they rode—and whatever they fought for—that place became the United States.

My great grandfather, Master Sergeant John Devine, from Armagh, Northern Ireland, was a dragoon in the US 1st Cavalry Regiment across the western territories of the United States and into Mexico. He survived the war and was recognized as a hero during military celebrations on Veteran's Day in Albuquerque, New Mexico, where he retired. Most successful countries today were born in fire, matured in flames, and became nations only after wars of slaughter on a grand scale. War, not peace, is the way of humanity and it has always been that way.

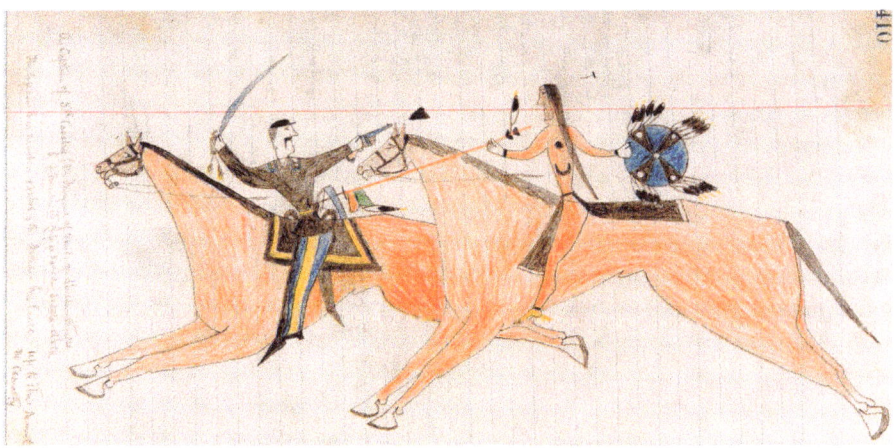

Fig. 17. Ledger art, Indian and cavalryman fighting. Sam Noble Museum ethnology collection.

Fig. 18. Subaltern of the 1st Regiment of Dragoons (right foreground); ordnance sergeant (left foreground) of which there was one on every Army post (including my great grandfather who was also an ordinance sergeant.) Wikimedia, public domain.

7

Erasing the Conquistadors

Clans seek their superiority. My mother always referred to my dad's origins as being one of the "mountain people." "Those mountain people marry their cousins and nieces and uncles." Curiously, my paternal grandmother, Alice Martinez, did marry her stepuncle (whatever that is), Eduardo Mares. *Y es así.* My mother's people, besides being half Irish, were from the New Mexico lowlands, hence less Indian they thought. When one is near the bottom of the economic hierarchy there is some comfort to be had by knowing that others are even further down the ladder. "We may not have much, but at least we're not as bad off as those poor Indians." Schadenfreude.

These differences surface periodically during centenary or other celebrations marking the founding of various towns and cities in New Mexico. Some families would radiate a superior air over the perceived more mestizo mix of Indians and Mexicans, often demonstrated by gradations of skin color from very light to very dark. They did not know, or did not want to know, that they were all mestizos (remember the *casta* system). In fact, an unwritten *casta* system existed among the old-line New Mexico families for centuries.

Statue Wars

In June, 2020, the Albuquerque Museum in Old Town—built on my old baseball field—had a small mob of about three hundred people (greater Albuquerque's population is one million) protesting the presence of bronze statues on museum property. The statues celebrated the arrival of Juan de Oñate in New Mexico, with soldiers, settlers, wagons, and livestock depicted in 33 life-size statues in the art piece titled *"La Jornada,"* "The Journey." (Romero, S., 2020) A group of Indians and some Hispanics and Anglos gathered to protest the statue's being exhibited at the city museum—not only exhibited, but being the centerpiece of the outdoor art on the museum's grounds. The large piece welcomed visitors to the museum and invited them to walk among the conquistadors—art interacting with and educating visitors. It is a remarkable tribute in bronze to an epic moment in New Mexico's history. Almost everyone loved it. Almost.

Members of the right-wing New Mexico Militia, along with some Chicanos and some Anglos, showed up to defend the statue from a crowd of protestors. As George Carlin said, "Something is wrong here." Chicanos, Anglos, and Indians were protesting the statue's existence and demanding its removal, and the racist right-wingers (mostly Anglos) and a few Chicanos were defending the statue. The protest was descending into farce.

Fig. 19. Oñate statue in Rio Arriba, New Mexico. Wikimedia.

To make the protest more interesting, the bronze foot that had been cut off of another Oñate statue years earlier in a small town in northern New Mexico and had been missing ever since showed up at the rally, being carried by three masked men. One of the men carrying the bronze foot turned out to be Brian Hardgroove, bass player for the hip hop group, Public Enemy (Rock and Roll Hall of Fame inductees). He said carrying the missing foot "...is a powerful act of resistance" and supported solidarity between African Americans and Native Americans. One Anglo protestor was shot by a Chicano protestor, who himself had once been a candidate for city council. *¡Ay Dios!*

A riot was forming when police finally arrived in full riot gear to calm things down. (KOAT-TV, Albuquerque, June17, 2020) Using rubber bullets and tear gas, the police finally got things under control. The Mayor of Albuquerque, doing his best imitation of Bravely Bold Sir Robin in "Monty Python and the Holy Grail," announced the statue of Oñate would be removed. As *The New York Times* (Romero, S., 2018) put it:

The agitation against honoring Oñate reflects a tension that has long festered between Native Americans and Hispanics over Spain's conquest more than four centuries ago, with protests this year over police violence unleashing a broader questioning of race relations in this part of the West.

Political Correctness and History

The political correctness of recent years has magnified the differences among ethnic groups (and even differences within ethnic groups) by casting blame back hundreds of years with cross-century shaming, applying 21st century wokeness (mainly in the United States) to historical figures that have been gone from the scene for centuries. Those being disparaged may have acted within the dictates of their moment in history, or the mandates of their rulers, or the orders of the Church. We cannot judge what we might have done had we been in their place, living in the world they inhabited, and knowing only what they knew. They had responsibilities and duties to the soldiers and civilians they led. The role of leader is always challenging, but it is more difficult to be a leader in a hostile environment where a wrong decision can lead to the death of your soldiers or the civilians you have been ordered to protect, or the loss of the territory you have conquered at great cost for king and country, with a resulting slaughter of your own people.

Presentism

We may think today's world with its mores and "modern" views of race, ethnicity, and justice, can be used to explain the actions of those who lived long ago, but things just do not work that way. The world of the 16th century is not and cannot be interpreted as if it were an earlier version of the 21st century, with the same prevailing views of justice, morality, and behavior that operate today in the United States (if they do in fact operate in this country beyond a relatively small group of people). The world is not now and never was how the cultural dreamers perceive it. More than 230 million people died in wars in the 20th century, a number that is half the entire population of the world in the year 1500.

Historians have a word for this kind of thinking—presentism—which means interpreting the past based on modern ideas, ethics, sensitivities, sensibilities and societal views that have no place in the time period being discussed by present-day people. As Barbour (2002: 117) noted:

> Present-minded analysis is fundamentally ahistorical, for it refuses to deal with the past as it was. Measuring the past with an anachronistic yardstick encourages careless reasoning, and it ignores the contextual framework without which the past becomes incomprehensible.

Alas, in our modern world, ignorance has become a virtue, and the greater the ignorance, the greater the propensity to run for political office, start a podcast, opine on anything and everything, become an influencer armed with nothing but opinions and a computer, and connect with people holding similar views—people trapped in their computers and social media. Water seeks its own level as do those who have little information but nevertheless delight in possessing and using a big Internet idea amplifier. Sometimes I feel I am living in the movie "Idiocracy." It is a frightening feeling indeed for a university professor and a scientist.

Defiling a statue does not improve the cultural situation of anyone, though it may make a few ideologues feel better or boost the ego of those who have little or no real power, but can express their unhappiness publicly by attacking statues and fomenting some minor chaos.

There are often public arguments in the local papers or at meetings and other gatherings of the various cultural groups that make up the people of New Mexico, today and in the past. Today, however, the Internet has placed a global bullhorn in the hands of every person who holds an opinion on anything, right or wrong, informed or ignorant, profound or unhinged.

Organizing *Locos*

At one time, every small town had a few mentally challenged people who were isolated from the larger society because they held weird or even insane views. In Argentina they called them *los loquitos* (crazy ones), but they were viewed affectionately as benign curiosities; there was no danger of their meeting others of their ilk and forming larger groups of *loquitos*, although Argentina's recent presidential election may be showing the rise of the *loquitos*, including President Javier Milei, whose principal advisers are a group of cloned dogs. Today, however, in my opinion, all one needs to do is put their views on the web and they can find other *locos* who share their crazy beliefs, for good or ill. Organizations such as museums, universities, or municipal or state governments tremble at negative publicity of any kind by anyone who is aggrieved, even if it is coming from a very small subset of society and even if it is outrageous. In today's world, almost everyone is an aggrieved, forlorn victim of societies past and present.

This allows relatively small groups of passionately committed people to paralyze cowardly bureaucrats with fear—a basic go-to instinct for bureaucrats. Seldom is anything said or published about Chicanos, Indians, or conquistadors that can then be discussed rationally by members of any of the groups holding any particular opinion. Reasoned discourse, respect and even an understanding of history, are lacking. Too often, we flail away in ignorance, anger, and fear. We eschew true scholarship and do not want to spend the significant amount of time it takes to really understand the issues. Rather, we use emotions and garbled information filtered through people expressing their opinions on some website or social-media platform, people who are remarkably truth- and information- challenged. It is so much easier to spout uninformed opinions than to take the time to research and understand an issue. It is also a recipe for societal disaster and the antithesis of scholarship.

Santa Fe Monuments

New Mexico's capital city of Santa Fe has become a hotbed of cultural strife for recent celebrations such as the Santa Fe Fiesta, which was established in 1712 by Governor Marqués de La Peñuela, eight years after Conquistador Don Diego De Vargas' death. Over the intervening centuries, the fiesta has adhered to its religious underpinnings and its message of celebrating the peaceful re-taking of the city by De Vargas. The fiesta grew and developed a number of ancillary celebrations over time, but the reenactment of De Vargas's peaceful *entrada* has been a continuing part of the celebration for centuries.

Just after the Civil War, which was fought across New Mexico (Kerby, 1958), a monument was erected in the central plaza of Santa Fe. It was called the Soldiers' Monument, a thirty-three-foot-tall stone cenotaph, comprised of a twenty-three-foot-tall obelisk on a ten-foot-tall pedestal. There were four marble panels on the pedestal, three honoring Union Soldiers, and the fourth honoring U.S. soldiers who died fighting the "savage Indians."

The second panel honored the heroes of the Battle of Valverde, a battle in which at least two of my ancestors fought (my great granduncle Vicente Mares and my great great grandfather, Sergeant Pablo Martinez), and which the Union lost. Many people felt New Mexicans were not sufficiently supportive of the Union forces in the Civil War due to the fact that the northern army had taken New Mexico by force in the Mexican War and now governed New Mexico. There were serious doubts about the loyalty of New Mexicans. The third panel honored the heroes of the Battle of Glorieta, where the South was soundly defeated.

Fig. 20. Battle of Glorieta Pass, New Mexico, 1862. Roy Anderson, National Park Service. Wikipedia.

The head of the plaza monument committee was Judge John P. Slough, Chief Justice of New Mexico Territory who had been the commander of the Union forces at the Battle of Glorieta, the decisive battle of the Civil War in New Mexico. He was murdered by a political rival shortly after laying the cornerstone of the monument. Slough was an obscene man who loved to fight. He was shot by a New Mexico state legislator who was found not guilty due to self-defense. The Territorial Legislature in response then insisted the soldiers who had died in the (ongoing) Indian Wars be honored, along with those who participated in the recently-ended Civil War battles in New Mexico. The legislature passed a law dictating the text of the fourth panel just as the monument was being finalized; it was in the legislature that the term "savage Indians" originated.

The term "rebel" was used to describe the Confederate soldiers who tried to conquer New Mexico Territory (and failed). Most were Texans and, in the 1930s during the Great Depression, in a remarkable display of chutzpah, a group of Texans tried to have the monument removed because it used the word "rebels." Here I agree with them; the word "traitors" would have been more precise. Their entreaty went nowhere. There were periodic attempts to modify, replace, or remove the obelisk over the years. Indians strongly objected to the word "savage", but basically the monument stood undisturbed for one hundred six years.

Fig. 21. Recently-completed Soldier's Monument on the Santa Fe Plaza (about 1869). Photograph by Nicholas Brown, Courtesy of the Palace of the Governors Photo Archives, Negative Number 011252.

In 1973, AIM, the militant American Indian Movement group, demanded the monument be removed or the wording changed. In response, an explanatory plaque was added to appease the various aggrieved parties. The plaque tried to clarify why the historical monument should be left in its original form. The words are worth considering in this discussion about cultural clashes in New Mexico:

Monument texts reflect the character of the times in which they are written and the temper of those who wrote them. This monument was dedicated in 1868 near the close of a period of intense strife which pitted northerner against southerner, Indian against white, Indian against Indian. Thus, we see on this monument, as in other records, the use of such terms as 'savage' and 'rebel'. Attitudes change and prejudices hopefully dissolve.

Attacking Statues and Monuments

In 1974, someone chiseled off the word "savage" from the fourth panel. The Anglo State Historian said it most likely was an Anglo, since Indians did not destroy property. Curiously, when "savage" is used as an adjective, as it was on the plaque, it means fierce, violent, and uncontrolled. To me, those do not seem like pejoratives for people acting in the heat of a pitched battle defending their people, their lands and their way of life. On the contrary, it is what might be expected of any warriors engaged in desperate fights to the death anywhere on earth. On the other hand, if "savage" is used as a noun, it means a brutal or vicious person, a barbarian, demon, or monster. Such was not its use on the fourth panel.

How it is used makes a big difference with that particular word, but I am entering territory where the reasoned discussion of grammar has no place, so I will move on. In any case, in the late 1900s and early 2000s, "savage Indians" turned out to be a poor choice of words, though I doubt any of the people involved in making and dedicating the monument in 1868 could have foreseen the problems that would arise in the distant future from their choice of words. Not only do we generally not think that far into the future, but there is no reason to do so. The future remains the undiscovered country. The monument was designed to honor, not disparage, but of course that was more than one hundred fifty years ago. Times change, but history does not change without new data.

Alas, the noble sentiments on the explanatory plaque might have gathered some support among reasonable people in the seventies, but not a half century later in the woke 21st century, where everyone is aggrieved over something, even if it happened centuries earlier and one did not have a dog, or even a war dog, in the fight. In 2020, the monument again appeared in the crosshairs of several small activist groups seeking to have it removed, including the NDN Collective, an indigenous activist group "committed to creating a world that is more just and equitable for all people and the planet."

Crowds of protestors gathered in the plaza to discuss the monument problem. The monument was defaced again and it was clear a very small group of protestors wanted it gone. In October, 2020, some attacked the monument with ropes and tools and knocked parts of it down. There were groups in Santa Fe that defended historical monuments and other groups that felt all monuments were bad. Shortly after the monument was toppled, two Anglo men were arrested for the crime. The monument was removed and a decision as to what is to become of it is pending at the time of the publication of this book. (*Attanasio and Fonseca, 2020)*

On March 15, 2023, a plan was put forth to rebuild the original monument in the plaza, but a crowd of people had strong feelings against the plan, citing the long-simmering arguments of racism against Native Americans and other concerns discussed years before. (Gilmore, 2023) The proposed monument development program was removed from consideration once again, with a plan to revisit the whole question of a monument in the plaza at some time in the future when emotions may have cooled.

Monument controversies have not disappeared from Santa Fe. On Indigenous Peoples Day in Santa Fe, October 10, 2022, another small protest march (fewer than one hundred people from greater Santa Fe's one hundred fifty thousand population) was picked up by the local media and made to seem much larger than it actually was. There is often not a lot going on in small town Santa Fe. The crowd of mostly Native

Americans decided to deface the Kit Carson monument near the Federal Courthouse, a short walk from the central plaza, while pointing out Carson had forced the Pueblo Indians to undertake the three-hundred-mile Long Walk of 1864 during which many Navajos died. Their thinking is somewhat garbled.

Kit Carson

There are a lot of things to dislike about Kit Carson. He hated my distant uncle, the Taos priest, Padre Martinez, who was highly educated and did not back down from anyone, including Kit Carson. In fact, Martinez performed the marriage ceremony between the thirty-three-year-old Kit and his beautiful fifteen-year-old mestiza wife, Josefa Jaramillo. She was likely his third wife. Carson was illiterate and it must have galled him to see this erudite mestizo priest being held in such high regard throughout northern New Mexico, while many viewed Carson as an illiterate bumpkin.

Fig. 22. Kit Carson circa 1860. Wikipedia. Mathew Brady or Levin C. Handy; United States Library of Congress, Prints and Photographs division.

Barbour (2002) suggests Carson did not hate Indians. However, there is good evidence Carson not only hated many tribes, but slaughtered women and children regularly in the Northwest and in California. (O'Brien, 2022) Carson fought with Indians, killing perhaps two dozen in battle or other altercations, and excluding the massacres that may have involved more than seven hundred dead. As the world's premiere warrior nation, we have learned one does not have to hate your enemy in order to kill them; it is part of the nature of warfare. John McCain referred to his captors who used inhumane and unremitting torture and murder for years, as "gooks." He made it clear he did not refer to all Vietnamese in that way but would hate his captors for as long as he lived. (Stanley-Becker, 2018) McCain later apologized for the slur (his apology obviously influenced by politics). As Senator Bob Dole, a Medal of Honor winner himself from World War II noted, "You spend five years in a box, and you're entitled to speak your mind." (Stanley-Becker, 2018)

Carson had abiding friendships with some Indians and married at least two Indian women, with one of whom he had a child. As a mountain man these kinds of things were typical behavior, since the fur trappers had to deal with many different Indian tribes and traveled widely for pelts, sometimes for years, among the Indian nations of the West. As a soldier, however, he was considered an excellent warrior. Carson was required to follow orders and it was in following orders that his reputation today has suffered, especially among Native peoples.

The Long Walk of the Navajo

The warlike Navajos in the middle decades of the 19th century threatened much of New Mexico, including White and Hispanic settlers, as well as other Indian tribes, and some in the White power structure felt the Navajos, as a tribe, should be exterminated, which says a great deal about how Whites viewed the warlike tribes. Pressure was building to wipe them out but others did not support this idea. In an attempt to remove the threat of the Navajos without having to kill them all, a plan was devised by General Edward Canby in 1861 (with the Civil War and Indian War raging in the United States and in New Mexico Territory) to move all the Navajo people (perhaps nine thousand of them) from their homeland in northwestern New Mexico to Bosque Redondo in southeast New Mexico where they would be more isolated and less of a danger to other tribes, to whites, and to Hispanics.

It was Canby who commanded the Department of New Mexico military forces and was victorious over the South at the Battle of Glorieta, sending the Confederate forces back to Texas. (Alberts, 1998) Canby was replaced by General. James H. Carleton in 1862. Carleton had been in the 1st U.S. Dragoons (my great grandfather's regiment) in Indian battles across the West. Carleton established Fort Sumner to house the Navajos so the Army would capture and transport them to the southern part of the territory. Carleton called the Navajos a great evil since they killed Whites, Mexicans and other Indians. Carleton then ordered Colonel Kit Carson to travel to the heart of the Navajo nation and receive the surrender of the Navajos.

When Carson arrived, there were no Navajos waiting to surrender; they had fled to the deserts in the territories of other Indian peoples, like the Chiricahua Apaches and Utes. Carson instituted a policy of destroying all food and other goods in the Navajo territory to force them to surrender so they could eventually be removed to a new area where they would not pose any more threats and where they would not have to be exterminated.

Fig. 23. Long walk of the Navajo, 1864. U.S. National Archives photograph.

Eventually, other Indian tribes helped the U.S. Army and Carson capture the Navajos and forced them to walk to their new home in eastern New Mexico. The deaths and inhumanity of The Long Walk led modern-day Native Americans to argue that having the statue of Kit Carson in Santa Fe was like having a statue of Hitler in the city, but Carson was no Hitler and it is a false and hyperbolic comparison. Christopher Houston Carson had undertaken a scorched earth policy against the Navajo, killing their livestock and burning their villages until starvation was rampant, in order to get them to surrender. This has been done many times in warfare in many countries across the centuries, including in the United States by U.S. Forces of the Army of the North in the Civil War in the South and in the Viet Nam War. In 1864, Carson and his men forced thousands of Navajos to march across the desert to the Bosque Redondo, an Indian reservation near Fort Sumner, three hundred miles distant with the loss of more than three hundred Navajos along the way.

During the Long Walk of the Navajo, they walked in perhaps fifty-three different groups, so Carson did not lead them all, though he was ordered to oversee the removal. In some respects, the Long Walk recalled the Trail of Tears of the Eastern United States, but on a greatly reduced scale, and also presaged the Bataan Death March of U.S. prisoners under the Japanese in 1942, but again at a much smaller scale. During the Trail of Tears (1830–50), a landgrab of Indian lands led to forced removal of the five civilized tribes from the eastern U.S. to Oklahoma, relocated a hundred thousand Indians and led to the deaths of fifteen thousand on the journey. Many have argued the Trail of Tears was a genocidal act. In the infamous Bataan Death March, Japanese actions led to the deaths of eighteen thousand U.S. soldiers. So by other death-march standards in history, the march overseen by Colonel Carson cost relatively few Indian lives. Shortly after the Navajo were relocated in 1864, they were allowed to walk home to their ancestral lands inside the four sacred mountains in the Four Corners area, now known as the Navajo Nation.

The illiterate Carson feuded with my highly-educated great great grand uncle Padre Martinez, so he was not a friend of the family, though some of my family members had fought alongside him in support of the United States during the Civil War in New Mexico. He was a good soldier, as everyone agreed, but the diminutive five foot four Carson was not physically intimidating, though he had a hair-trigger personality that could suddenly erupt in violence. Carson was also a good scout, scouting for the Fremont Expedition that explored the far west including Utah, Oregon and California, where the expedition almost froze to death in a snowstorm near where the Donner Party would resort to cannibalism and die some years later. It was Kit Carson who led them out of the blizzard, mostly naked, worn down, starving, and eating salted dog skins—but alive. Carson City, Nevada is named in his honor for his work as a scout.

Everyone who knew Kit said he was very lucky, getting into danger and then somehow finding a way out. (Sides, 2006) He was always courageous and willing to fight Indians or others when he felt they had done wrong, or sometimes just for being Indians. Now the brave Kit Carson of history was coming into the crosshairs of the woke crowd in Santa Fe. But he was not there to defend himself; he had died in 1868 in Taos, the same year the Plaza Monument had been erected in Santa Fe.

There is no doubt tensions related to this or that monument will continue to appear in the years to come and not only in Santa Fe, but throughout New Mexico. Spaniards, Mexicans, Gringos, and even Indians can find themselves the targets of political correctness and wokeness run amuck. We have become that kind of country. Is there a difference between monuments honoring Civil War soldiers, who betrayed their country and fought to maintain slavery in the rebel states and those honoring conquistadors? Perhaps. Context is always important, at least to those who do not engage in presentism.

Most Civil War monuments are in the South and the borderlands of the South (e.g., Washington, DC), although the Southern Poverty Law Center noted more than seven hundred such monuments are scattered among thirty-one states and the District of Columbia. Most Americans are unaware that the majority of the Civil War's monuments were not built in the war's immediate aftermath—in contrast to the Santa Fe monument built as the Civil War ended and while the Indian wars were still underway. Rather, most Civil War monuments were built from 1890 to as recently as the 1950s. Most monuments were advocated by the United Daughters of the Confederacy, a group cozy with the Ku Klux Klan and one that worked to keep alive the Lost Cause explanation for the Civil War: It was states' rights, not slavery. It was never slavery. The North was just too powerful. Many people, especially southerners, still believe this.

Barbarians?

The Indian Wars were still underway when the Santa Fe monument was dedicated. Dedication took place eight years before General Custer and his men were slaughtered at the Little Bighorn. After the 7th Cavalry was wiped out (at least Custer's contingent), the Indians proceeded to mutilate the bodies, beheading them, mutilating genitals, disemboweling them and generally destroying the corpses. A number of Indian tribes practiced mutilating their enemies after they had killed them because they believed it rendered them helpless in the afterlife. A group of Indian women demanded Custer's body be turned over to them, saying he was a relative. He was not. After they had his body, they pushed long sewing awls into his skull through his ears, because he apparently had not heard the chiefs when he smoked a peace pipe with them and promised not to go to war against the Cheyenne. (Sagan, 2017)

The women also said Custer had raped a Cheyenne woman after the battle of the Washita River in 1868, when the 7th Cavalry attacked Black Kettle's southern Cheyenne in Oklahoma, although other information suggests Custer had married the woman, Princess Monahsetah. (Kelly-Custer, 2008) However, the historian Stephen Ambrose (1975) flatly dismissed rape or "marriage." The author of the book about Princess Monahsetah is supposedly the great great granddaughter of General George Armstrong Custer and Princess Monahsetah. Ambrose reports Custer as being sterile and so could father no children. Whatever the truth might have been, after the Little Bighorn battle, as an act of revenge, the women pushed an arrow up Custer's penis. (Sagan, 2017)

Does that make them savages or barbarians? They were warriors and tribal members carrying out the violent actions expected of them at that time by their own people, just as many eastern tribes engaged in extensive torture of captives before killing them. (Knowles1940) But if you were a soldier in the 7th Cavalry or a family member of a cavalryman or someone related to the many people slaughtered by marauding war parties and scalpers across the West, and all that stood between you and a frightful death was the U.S. Cavalry, you might think differently. Wouldn't you?

Fig. 24. Vicente Mares, my great great uncle, 1865 after the Battle of Valverde.

8

WARS OF CONQUEST

The Conquistadors

"They open their breasts, while they are alive, and take out the hearts and entrails, and burn the said entrails and hearts before the idols, offering that smoke in sacrifice to them." (H. Cortés)

After Columbus blundered into the New World, Spanish colonization continued throughout the new territories. Nevertheless, with the passage of time the Spanish (Galicians as they called themselves) found they had a somewhat tenuous hold on the vast Spanish empire in the New World north of present-day Mexico. They had to subjugate the Native peoples across an area much larger than present-day New Mexico, which is the fifth largest state in the union today and covers almost one hundred twenty-two thousand square miles. Indeed, Santa Fe Province alone at that time was larger than all of current New Mexico (and included parts of what became Arizona, Utah, Texas, Colorado, Kansas and Oklahoma). New Mexico Territory of the 1600s was larger than all of Spain. The Spaniards had a total of only twenty-eight hundred soldiers and their few Indian supporters across a vast land with its thousands of pueblos and tribes. Moreover, they were hardly building on the goodwill of earlier conquistadors. Coronado and his men had spent two years in the pueblo territories in 1540–1542, during which time they destroyed a dozen Pueblo villages. When Coronado left central Mexico for New

Mexico, the next conquistador in line was Nuño Beltrán de Guzmán, who had been fighting in central and northwestern Mexico from 1529–1542.

Beltrán de Guzmán may have been the cruelest of all the conquistadors, killing, torturing and enslaving many thousands of Caxcanes. The Caxcanes struck back, roasting and eating Spaniards. The battles in the northwest became known as the Mixton War of 1540–1542, with fighting in and around Guadalajara. (Schmal, 2004) The Spanish were losing their major assault on the Indians due to a massive fifteen-thousand warrior army of Caxcanes. Eventually, reinforcements came from Mexico City with four hundred fifty Spaniards leading an army of as many as sixty thousand Aztec warriors and other native groups in massive battles. Thousands of Caxcanes fell to this armed force; then many of the surviving women and children were fed to dogs in a horrific slaughter. The Mixton War gradually became the Chichimeca War, which lasted forty years and led to the deaths of even more Indians and Spanish.

The very term "conquistador" refers to conquering armies subjugating people in the new territories for gold, God and king, in that order. Their job was to take and hold territory, convert people to Catholicism and subjugate millions of people to Spanish rule, while also taking any treasure they could find, especially gold (real—which they took, or imagined—which they searched for constantly). Eventually, the Spanish gold seekers searching throughout the New World took gold back to Spain worth more than eleven billion in today's dollars, as well as silver valued at half a billion in today's dollars. Very little gold or silver came out of New Mexico, however, despite the myth of the Seven Cities of Gold. The conquistadors wanted gold, but the Franciscan friars, especially those accompanying the later conquistadors, wanted souls to save. Gold or souls—each was viewed as a treasure by one or the other of the two groups of Spaniards, soldiers and priests. The Acoma rebellion was the first of the warning bells ringing to indicate all was not well with the subjugated Indians in New Mexico.

Natives Rebel

The Native people did not wish to be Catholics, domestics, servants, slaves or anything else that bespoke of Spanish domination. They did not want to turn over part of their crops or water to the conquerors, nor did they wish to give up their land. The Spanish received some support, however grudgingly, from those Pueblos that had been converted to Catholicism. Those Pueblo Indians often became part of the armies of the Spanish and assisted in slaving raids against non-Pueblo cultures. They had been warring with them for centuries in any case.

The Pueblos became increasingly more public in practicing their religion. The fealty to their Native religions irritated the Spanish, especially their priests. Pueblo medicine men were the leaders in the movement to maintain their traditional religion and not follow the newfangled and foreign Catholicism. Their religions were far older than Catholicism. In 1675 the unhappiness of the Spanish against Native religions led to Pueblo medicine men being captured or killed. When that occurred, the warriors from San Juan Pueblo went to the governor's home and threatened to kill him and his family if he did not release the remaining medicine men. Wisely, he complied. One of the medicine men released was Po'pay.

Escalating tensions set the stage for the Pueblo Rebellion of 1680. My ninth great grandfather, Francisco "El Ciego" Martin Serrano, was born in New Mexico during the rebellion and was spirited away to Mexico as an infant with the other refugees, only to return to New Mexico years later as a soldier in Conquistador Don Diego De Vargas's army. E. A. "Tony" Mares, in commenting on his epic poem about Po'pay, "Once a Man Knew His Name" (Anaya, 1987), noted:

> Po'pay was one of not only New Mexico's, but the United States' great unsung heroes. He was the leader of the first successful uprising against colonization, anywhere in the world, and for that alone I think he deserves great respect.

Today, Po'pay's statue stands in Statuary Hall at the U.S. Capitol. (Mares, E. A., 2009b)

Fig. 25. Po'pay's statue in Statuary Hall, U.S. Capitol.

Almost two centuries after Columbus had arrived in the New World and a bit over a century since Coronado had traveled through New Mexico Territory, the Pueblo Indians revolted against their Spanish overlords in New Mexico. (There had been earlier revolts in Mexico.) The Pueblo Revolt followed a long period of poor treatment of the Indians by the Spanish. Some of the access to water the Pueblos had for their crops and for the survival of the Indians themselves in this parched land was required to be transferred to Spanish farmers.

Regulations of the conquerors required the Pueblos to labor for the Spanish and to give them part of their crops, functioning basically as a tax. Additionally, the Pueblos continued to be extremely unhappy with the efforts of the Spanish to limit their native religious activities. Eventually their Kachina dances were banned, as was the use of peyote. Their carved Kachina effigies and masks were also destroyed. Po'pay decided to overthrow Spanish rule in the territory and set about gathering support from all the Pueblos near Taos and beyond. Zuni, Hopi, Northern Tiwa, Tewa, Tano, Pecos and almost forty other Pueblos agreed to support Po'pay's plan of rebellion.

In 1680, only about twenty-four hundred Spanish and mestizos lived in the region from Santa Fe to Taos and the surrounding areas. Santa Fe itself, the largest town, had fewer than two hundred armed men. The revolt began August 10 in settlements in northern New Mexico and around Santa Fe and, within a short time, four hundred settlers had been butchered, including women and children. Twenty-one of thirty-three Franciscan missionaries were also murdered, their bodies mutilated beyond recognition and their churches burned. The slaughter of almost five hundred Spanish settlers stood for two centuries as the largest civilian mass murder in North America (only to be surpassed by the carnage when the Dakota murdered German immigrants in a surprise attack in Minnesota in 1862), followed by the 9/11 slaughter of innocents in the Twin Towers.

Fig. 26. The Pueblo Revolt of 1680, detail from mural. U.S. Courthouse, Albuquerque, New Mexico. Wikipedia.

In Santa Fe, Governor Otermín led a counterattack from the Palace of the Governors and drove the Pueblos out of the city. (Sanchez *et al.*, 2013) That gave him and the remaining people (and their Native American slaves) a chance to escape from Santa Fe to Guadalupe del Paso (today's Juarez, Mexico, which was then a part of New Mexico), a distance of over three hundred forty miles on horseback, in oxcarts and on foot. On this long, slow retreat through Bernalillo, Albuquerque, Isleta and Socorro, the Pueblos did not attack the Spaniards. After the retreat, Po'pay ordered all vestiges of Spanish and Catholic rule, including Spanish crops, be destroyed. Each Pueblo was autonomous, so many pueblos did not follow his orders, especially the order to destroy crops in a land where food was always scarce.

The good times Po'pay had promised would follow by erasing all Spanish traces in New Mexico never materialized. Following what was the first incidence of cancel culture in the New World—wiping out Spanish culture—the drought continued, crops failed and raids by nomadic tribes increased, in part because the Spanish were gone. Eventually, Po'pay was removed as a leader of the Puebloans. New Mexico, a dry and impoverished land, then as now, had proven impossible to tame for the Spanish. The gold, silver and the rich cities Coronado and Oñate imagined were merely fevered dreams that never came true but always lured the dreamers over the next hill—to continue their search for riches and souls.

Don Diego de Vargas

Don Diego de Vargas Zapata y Lujan Ponce de Leon was named governor of New Mexico in 1688, while the Spanish were in exile in El Paso. The French were claiming new lands in North America that France received from Spain, including what later became the Louisiana Purchase, and it was with some urgency that De Vargas was sent to reclaim Santa Fe and the New Mexico Territory for Spain. De Vargas has been called the Peaceful Conquistador. (Buchanan, 2016) In August, 1692, he led a small force of fewer than a hundred soldiers to Santa Fe and retook the city peacefully. The bloodless re-conquest led some years later to the establishment of the multicultural Santa Fe Fiesta to mark the peaceful return of the Spanish to New Mexico. The Fiesta has been celebrated each year since 1712.

Fig. 27. Oil on canvas portrait Diego de Vargas by Julio Barrera, date unknown. Palace of the Governors, Santa Fe.

My uncle, Johnny Valdes, who descended from one of the founding families of New Mexico, was very involved in the Santa Fe Fiesta, having played the role of De Vargas in the 1943 reenactment of De Vargas' peacefully taking Santa Fe. He was the first president of Los Caballeros de Vargas and served on the Fiesta Council for decades. He even coauthored the official Santa Fe Fiesta song, "Fiestas de Santa Fe." Ultimately, he was responsible for bringing mariachis and their unique style of music to the Fiesta, having once been a mariachi himself. He thus elevated the celebratory nature of the Fiesta and including the singular musical style of Mexican mestizos with roots extending back through time to Hernán Cortés, the French conquerors of Mexico, black slaves and Native peoples. If ever a genre of music represented a group of mestizos, it is mariachi music. On my grandmother Alice's one hundredth birthday, Johnny brought mariachis to her room to serenade her with the traditional Mexican birthday song, *Las Mañanitas*. Johnny died in 1994, after a half century of Fiesta activities and, thankfully, before he could experience the changes in the Fiesta due to revisions to the De Vargas story and the changing views of the Conquest. The headline in the *Santa Fe New Mexican* announcing his demise referred to him simply as Mr. Santa Fe Fiesta.

Statues of the Virgin

Political correctness caught up with La Conquistadora, the statue of the Madonna and child carried by De Vargas for spiritual assistance in conquering the Indians (hence the statue's name). It recently had its name changed to Our Lady of Peace (changed in 1992, three hundred years after De Vargas first marched into Santa Fe with the statue that supposedly protected the conquistadors). It is also known, paradoxically, as Our Lady of Conquering Love.

Fig. 28. La Conquistadora statuette in the Santa Fe Cathedral. Wikipedia.

It was common for Spanish soldiers and conquistadors wherever they fought to carry a statue of the Virgin as a protectress, or amulet, to help them in battle. They carried statues throughout the Americas. I once attended a celebration of Argentine history and folklore music in Mendoza, Argentina, where all the original statuettes of the Virgin Mary that had accompanied the soldiers into the many early battles in Argentina's own conquest and development as a country, had been gathered together to venerate the Blessed Virgin. They honored the soldiers/conquerors (of generally indigenous people) who had thus "brought enlightenment" to Argentina—much as the Spanish had "pacified" Mexico and North America.

It was an impressive ceremony and included Nuestra Señora de Lujan (patron saint of Argentina), La Virgen del Milagro (Salta Province, Argentina), La Virgen del Valle (Catamarca Province, Argentina) and La Virgen del Carmen de Cuyo (Mendoza Province). This latter icon had first been dedicated by the Liberator, General San Martín, himself, considered the George Washington of Argentina and neighboring parts of South America. Each statuette was carried by a troop of soldiers. Throughout history, Spanish soldiers have looked to the Virgin for success in battle and that was certainly true in Argentina, in Mexico, as well as in the American Southwest.

In recent years (but beginning with the three hundredth celebration in 1992 of the founding of Santa Fe), the Fiesta has come under criticism because, though De Vargas's taking of the city (and territory) was initially done without bloodshed, the Indians under Spanish rule once again were subjected to indignities and suffering. De Vargas, peaceful though he wished to be, had to retake Taos Pueblo, as well as Acoma's Sky City and Zuni pueblos. De Vargas was highly effective at retaking the New Mexico Territory. As Athearn noted:

> In a period of five months Vargas, seemingly, had recovered the whole of New Mexico. He reduced the Indians, and prepared them for their return to Christian practices. He had formally reclaimed

New Mexico for the Spanish empire, without costing the King a single peso. Seventy-four Spanish captives held by the natives were released and 2,214 Indians were baptized by the Franciscans who travelled with the expedition. The stage was now set for phase two of Vargas' plan: the recolonization of New Mexico. (*Vargas Journal*, Espinosa, 1942), (Athearn, 1989; *see also* Athearn, 1979)

Acoma was again difficult to capture, but after several weeks the Spanish were in control, as before. Not all pueblos surrendered peacefully to De Vargas. By the time he returned to Santa Fe from his pueblo tour (and a 1693 visit to El Paso to expand his forces and increase the number of immigrants), he had to fight his way back into the city of Santa Fe. Four pueblos supported the Spanish, but most did not. After retaking Santa Fe, De Vargas had seventy Pueblo men executed for murdering Spanish civilians and took their children and women as servants for the colonists. Again, this was done to punish the murderers and encourage other Indian pueblos in New Mexico to be hesitant about attacking Spaniards. (Espinosa, 1942)

Battles with the Pueblos extended to near the end of the century, when De Vargas was replaced by a new Governor, Rodriquez Cubero, who promptly had De Vargas jailed and sent to Mexico for trial. (Most conquistadors ended up getting arrested, including Christopher Columbus; it was par for the course). After De Vargas was found not guilty in 1703, he received a new title, Marqués de la Nava de Barcinas, a promotion and an official recognition of his successful and significant accomplishments in New Mexico from the viewpoint of the Spanish Crown. He was also reappointed Governor of Santa Fe. Shortly thereafter, however, leading his men in an attempt to protect peaceful Indians from Apache raiders who were attacking the Pueblos, he was taken ill and died at the age of sixty-two in the town of Bernalillo, just north of Albuquerque. He was buried in the mission church in Santa Fe.

Before the age of the conquistadors, wars among Indian tribes were common throughout New Mexico. Pueblo Indians were attacked by seminomadic tribes (e.g., Apaches, Navajos) seeking food and material goods as booty. Pueblos would go to war with each other periodically. Pueblos and marauding tribes captured each other's women and children and wars of revenge would follow. They were wars of Stone-Age peoples. Everything moved on foot or, occasionally, by boats (but there was precious little water in arid New Mexico for boats, or even canoes). There were no horses or domestic livestock until these were brought into the New World by the conquistadors.

During the five hundred years or so before the Conquest, the lands that would become Spain were also involved in continuous bloody warfare as kings, princes and generals led armies against one another. The warring Native peoples of New Mexico were going to clash with the warring invaders from Spain. It was inevitable. The Spaniards sported the latest in weaponry and armor developed over a thousand years of warfare. The outcome of almost all the upcoming battles was easy to predict before they ever took place. In a conflict between modern 17th century warriors versus Stone-Age people, modern would always win.

Wars and More Wars

Although it is not generally well known, the American Civil War extended throughout much of New Mexico in 1861–1862. My family had men who fought on the side of the North, even though they were against the North's having taken New Mexico from Mexico by force. The Indian Wars also continued unabated. My Irish great grandfather, John Devine, from Armagh, Northern Ireland, was a master sergeant in the U.S. Cavalry Dragoons about the time of the Civil War and fought in the Indian wars across the West and in the Mexican War. He was also in the U.S. 8th Infantry.

The births of my great grandparents, John and Carmelita Devine's, seven children provide a good illustration of many U.S. Cavalry postings and forts across the map of the nation during this time of conflict in the Indian Wars, the Mexican War and the U.S. Civil War. Their first child,

Marie Gabriela, was born in April, 1855 at Fort Thorn, New Mexico, a fort situated on the west bank of the Rio Grande near what is today the desert scrubland near Hatch, New Mexico, the *chile* capital of the world. Fort Thorn had been established in 1853 to protect settlers from attacks by marauding Apaches and outlaw raids. Fort Thorn had the 3rd Infantry Regiment and the 1st United States Dragoons, my great grandfather's regiment.

By 1860, my great grandfather had been transferred to Fort Walla Walla, Washington Territory, a distance of fourteen hundred miles from Fort Thorn, where Simon was born in January. Fort Walla Walla had been established in the early 1800s but had been destroyed and rebuilt several times due to fires set by attacking Indian war parties. By 1860, the fort mainly provided protection to miners and settlers from roving bands of Indians.

In 1862, the dragoons traveled more than two thousand six hundred miles to Washington, DC. John Junior was born April, 1862 at Fort Lincoln, District of Columbia, as was James (my grandfather) in 1864. Fort Lincoln was designed to protect the U.S. Capital from rebel soldiers. Two-year-old John Junior died there before their next posting.

The second John Devine Junior in the family was named after his father and his deceased brother. He was born in 1866 at Ash Barracks (Fort Negley), Nashville, Tennessee, more than six hundred fifty miles west of Washington, DC. Fort Negley was the most heavily fortified fort in the U.S. Army, second only to Fort Lincoln. It was largely built by thousands of runaway slaves and free blacks and was almost impregnable from rebel army attacks during the Civil War (1861–1865).

Sergeant Devine's sixth child, Robert, was born in July, 1870 at Fort D. A. Russell, Wyoming Territory, twelve hundred miles distant from Nashville. The fort was home not only to the 1st Dragoon Cavalry, but also to the Buffalo Soldiers—African American Cavalry soldiers.

By the time my great grandfather arrived in Wyoming, there were few hostile Indians remaining near the fort. The troops were mainly used to protect the railroad and the railroad workers, as well as immigrants and travelers moving through the area, from roving Indians and bandits. The Golden Spike Ceremony celebrating the connecting of the railroads across America had taken place only a year before my great grandfather arrived at the fort.

Their last child, Charlie, was born in 1872 at Camp Bowie, Apache Pass, Arizona Territory. The mountains where Cochise found protection are known as the Dragoon Mountains where he hid out while the Army attempted unsuccessfully to capture him. Family lore (which is often incorrect) holds my great grandfather was captured by Cochise in the Dragoon Mountains. Cochise took his horse but left his rifle and sword and let him walk out of the desert and back to the fort. I have his sword and when I was a child, I always tried to remove it from the steel scabbard and swing it around. It was too heavy for me. Even as an adult, I am unable to wield the sword easily. Clearly, cavalrymen of yesteryear were much tougher than modern faculty members, even those who had been pick-and-shovel laborers in their youth.

End of the Mexican War

The taking of Texas, California, New Mexico and other territories in the Mexican War and the Treaty of Guadalupe Hidalgo in 1848 (only thirteen years before the Civil War began) established the Rio Grande (the Río Bravo) as the border between the U.S. and Mexico. Fifty-five percent of Mexico's territory was ceded to the United States with this treaty, making the war one of the greatest land grabs in history. The peace treaty in part helped lead to the American Civil War, since Texas was not permitted to remain a part of Mexico due to its support of slavery (which Mexico had outlawed in 1829—thirty-six years before the American Civil War put an end to the odious practice in the United States.)

The Treaty of Guadalupe Hidalgo was negotiated by the State Department's Nicholas Trist against the wishes of President Polk, who ordered him not to negotiate the treaty. Trist did so anyway (no email in those days and no telegraph in the West) and Polk's hand was forced. Polk presented it to the Senate and it was ratified in a mixed vote. In the original form of the bill, the United States agreed to respect the original Spanish land grants. That was stripped out of the final bill, leading to difficult times ahead for land-grant holders in New Mexico Territory, which included Arizona and parts of what would become several other states. The landed people (largely Spanish and Mexicans, including many of my ancestors) were going to become landless, inevitably, moving from rich to poor with the stroke of a pen. Due to the changing demographics of the United States, the pendulum is now swinging back on ethnic composition in New Mexico and Whites in the near future are in for as big a shock as my relatives who lost title to their ranches after the Mexican War.

Civil War in New Mexico

There is a family photo of Colonel Vicente Mares in his Union uniform. Lean, dark-haired, mustachioed and handsome, he had fought in the Battle of Valverde with Kit Carson and the New Mexico Volunteers. My great great grandfather, Pablo Martinez, was a sergeant in the New Mexico Volunteers and also fought in that same battle, although whether or not they knew one another I do not know. Although my family was represented in New Mexico's Civil War battles, many New Mexicans did not join in the conflict. They were still angered at having their territory ripped from Mexico in the illegal Mexican War only twelve years earlier, with the subsequent loss of their land rights. Interestingly, Abraham Lincoln was one of the congressmen who opposed the Mexican War, saying it was the "sheerest deception" by President Polk to provoke both countries into war and steal another piece of territory upholding the credo of Manifest Destiny. (Lincoln 1848)

The bottom line was the United States was a cruel slave-holding nation accustomed to stealing territory through unjust wars. Mexico, to its great credit, had outlawed slavery, which led Texas to start a war with Mexico over the issue. The *Texians* said they fought for freedom, but the freedom they desired so desperately was the freedom to own slaves. Of course, Mexican corruption was and still is notorious, so government instability seemed to be more common south of the border. Still, Mexico post-revolution was a very young country. New Mexico Territory had been part of Mexico for only a quarter of a century before it was stolen from Mexico by the United States. New Mexico had maintained allegiance to Spain for over two centuries before the Mexican Revolution threw off the Spanish yoke. So, as a new territory of the United States, New Mexico was far more Spanish and Mexican than it was American.

The New Mexico Civil War campaign extended from southern New Mexico near present-day Elephant Butte Reservoir, through Albuquerque and Santa Fe to as far north as Glorieta Pass near the Colorado border. The Southern Army (consisting mainly of Texans) was defeated (a presage to the end of the Civil War itself) and the New Mexico campaign ended. Some authors referred to the battle of Glorieta Pass where the Texans were badly beaten as the Gettysburg of the West. (National Guard Military)

Eventually, the mostly Texas Confederates dropped their bizarrely ambitious plan to capture Santa Fe and all of New Mexico and then, after wiping out the mestizos, move on to capture all of California. Slavery everywhere. They had big dreams indeed but after losing the final battle at Glorieta Pass, they retreated into Arizona licking their wounds and then slunk back to Texas from whence they had emerged. Such is the background of New Mexico history in the hurricane winds of change in the mid-19th century.

The feeling of mestizos' not being supportive of the United States would reverberate all the way to the Spanish American War of 1898, fully fifty years after the Treaty of Guadalupe Hidalgo was signed. Many Anglos felt Hispanics could not be counted on to support the United States in a war. They also felt this belief in a lack of support from Chicano New

Mexicans, whether true of not, could delay statehood for New Mexico Territory, something they wanted very badly. There was a great deal of money to be made with statehood—especially for the Anglos. The pressure to support the nation in war led many Chicanos to try to prove themselves good citizens by signing up to ride with Teddy Roosevelt's Rough Riders to prosecute the Spanish American War in 1898 and invade Cuba (another questionable American War). In all, more than a third of the famed Rough Riders were New Mexicans. (Melzer, 2017)

9

A Chicano Oasis

City in the Valley

I was raised in Old Town, the original heart of Albuquerque (called Alburquerque with an extra "r" at the time of its founding as a desert oasis in 1706 by its mayor, Capitán Martín Hurtado). Arid lands surround it, but forested mountains are visible just east of the city. There are snow-capped peaks to the north and dry volcanoes to the west. Beyond the low volcanoes, further west yet, the snowy peaks of the extinct stratovolcano, Mount Taylor, are visible winter or summer, at eleven thousand three hundred five-foot-elevation, the twelfth highest mountain in New Mexico. Mount Taylor was originally named by the Navajo as *Tsoodzif* (Turquoise Mountain) and was a sacred mountain to many Pueblos and tribes, but it was renamed in 1849 for then president Zachary Taylor after the Mexican War ended.

The Spaniards followed the Rio Grande northward from what is now Mexico and established the city of Albuquerque near the river they called the Río Bravo ("Fierce River") with its green sash of riverine cottonwood forest extending from southern Colorado and continuing five hundred miles southward to near present-day El Paso, Texas. It meanders through a sparse, gray-brown xeric landscape in New Mexico. Like Cairo on the Nile or Babylon on the Euphrates, the desert river of New Mexico meant life for both the Spaniards and the Indians. With the river, crops were possible, life was tolerable and water would be available throughout the year. The Rio Grande made the desert city possible in the past and still does today, though its flow has been greatly modified by dams, irrigation canals and climate change. In fact, in August of 2022 the Rio Grande went dry at Albuquerque for the first time in forty years.

Everyone in Old Town generally knew or was related to, directly or by marriage, everyone else, not only because they shared a neighborhood and history, but because they saw each other at church for mass, weddings and funerals, or worked and celebrated together at fiestas. I, at least as a child, was ignorant of the larger city around me. With few exceptions, Anglos (Whites) lived outside the floodplain of the Rio Grande in the "Heights" and Hispanics lived in the "Valley." Land in the Heights for homes became very expensive in the 1950s with the post-World War II boom. I learned in the 1930s and 1940s, land in the apparently worthless scrublands of the Heights that today support much of modern Albuquerque could be purchased for as little as fifty cents an acre. I asked my dad why he did not buy some land when it was only fifty cents an acre. "I didn't have fifty cents," he replied. It was true. I learned when he was working as an adobe laborer, the pay was fifty cents per day.

A Verdant Park

An exception to the Whites living upslope and the Chicanos living down in the Valley was the neighborhood of the Albuquerque Country Club, which was only four blocks from my adobe home. The glorious houses in the lush green island seemed like palaces to me, when compared to the adobe houses with which I was familiar. In fact, I had a goal as a child of living in a metal trailer someday and getting out of adobe houses. It is a good example of why seven-year-olds should not make major decisions for a family.

To my eye the country club homes looked like the houses one saw in Hollywood in movie magazines, which my Aunt Jessie, who had lived in Hollywood and met movie stars, read regularly. I, of course, who read everything, loved the Hollywood gossip magazines and read all of them. I always assumed the Country Club people were the rich people of Albuquerque and therefore could afford the grand mansions. I did not know Hispanics were forbidden from living in the Country Club area or being there after the sun went down due to sundown laws, even if they could afford it, which few could in any case.

A Barrio

Old Town met the classic definition of a barrio—a Spanish-speaking neighborhood in a southwestern city. Like New Mexico itself, it had different political allegiances over time, which contributed to the various identity crises of the people living there. My maternal great great grandmother, Maria del Carmen Mestas "Carmel" Sanchez, was born in Spain in 1814. My great grandmother, Jesusa "Jesusita" Garcia, was born in Mexico in 1831. My maternal grandmother, Juana Rebecca Gutierrez, was born in the United States in 1874. As mentioned earlier, each woman was born in the same geographical location; only the governments were different.

New Mexico belonged to Spain during the Spanish Colonial Period (1692–1821), then shifted its allegiance to Mexico during the Mexican Period (1822–1846). Then followed the Territorial Period (1846–1912), when New Mexico Territory (including present day Arizona and parts of other states) came under the control of the United States after the Mexican War. New Mexico became the forty-seventh state of the union in January of 1912 (after separating from Arizona Territory), which then became the forty-eighth state.

In many ways, the people reflected these changes in their daily existence. My grandmother, Juana Rebecca Gutierrez Devine, always referred to the dollar as a *peso*, a quarter as two "*reales*" (*dos reales*) and a fifty-cent piece as *cuatro reales* (four reales). The *real* became the unit of currency of Spain in 1497, after the *Reconquista*. Mexico developed its own currency in 1821 after independence from Spain and Mexican *reales* were used throughout the new nation of Mexico, which included New Mexico.

My grandmother could have been familiar with either the Spanish *real* through her grandparents or the Mexican *real* through her parents. Either way, when she needed fifty cents for me to go to the store to buy a bag of Bull Durham tobacco and cigarette papers, she would tell me to go get *cuatro reales*. I would go and get two United States quarters. As her health deteriorated and her eyesight grew dim, I had to roll the cigarettes for her. I also had to read the daily newspaper to her, in English, with emphasis on the obituaries and social gatherings, though she seldom left the house.

The Old Town area in the late 1940s (excluding shop owners) was almost entirely Hispanic although a few Anglos lived there too and at least one Chinese man who had married a local Chicana. Rose, his wife, was always referred to thereafter as the woman who married the China Man (two words). Nothing like that had ever happened before in Old Town in the memories and lore of the old timers, which extended back through periods of living under both Mexican and Spanish rule.

Lazy Mexicans

In Old Town, people always worked, whether young or old, often into their eighties. For all the lazy Mexican talk, I never met or heard of anyone of any age, barring illness or injury, who did not work all the time. A popular cultural item of the day was the Sleeping Mexican. It was a statue, drawing or other representation of a Mexican man leaning against a cactus, wearing a huge sombrero and sleeping. It epitomized the lazy Mexican message of White society toward Chicanos in the United States and was common in those days.

In Mexico, it was not seen as demeaning, however. Drawings and artwork related to the lazy Mexican appeared in the late 1800s, mainly using Indians at first, but then with lazy Mexicans supplanting the lazy Indians (sort of like the scalping practices). Even Diego Rivera, the great Mexican artist, produced some sleeping-Mexican art. To many Mexicans/mestizos in the mid–1900s, however, the caricatured Mexican was the equivalent of the wooden Indian that sat outside many shops when I was a child—same demeaning message. The wooden Indian became famous throughout the world in 1953 when Hank Williams recorded the country hit, *Kaw Liga*: "Kaw Liga was a wooden Indian, Standin' by the door." There was a life size wooden Indian sitting outside a shop in Old Town that I never looked at in the same way after the Hank Williams song became a hit. Poor old Kaw Liga, he never had a chance.

Spanglish

In mid–1945 (the year I was born), almost everyone in Old Town spoke Spanglish (a mix of English and Spanish that is almost a separate language or patois). Curiously, no one in my family ever spoke Spanish to me, though they did speak either Spanish or Spanglish to each other. I was constantly asking, "What did she say?" They would always tell me what they had said. This led to my understanding Spanish but not being able to speak it well. It was very common among Chicanos in the western United States. Richie Valens, the California rockstar who died at only seventeen years of age in a plane crash with Buddy Holly, never learned to speak Spanish either, though one of his hit songs was *La Bamba*, a song with *mas o menos* Spanish phraseology.

Linda Ronstadt, too, the Queen of Rock and Roll and one of my favorite singers—something I share with Barack Obama—also spoke no Spanish, other than a few isolated phrases. When she decided to make two outstanding Mexican albums to honor her father and her Chicano heritage, *Canciones de Mi Padre* and *Mas Canciones*, she had several of her relatives help her with the pronunciation of the words. With her voice, of course, she could sing anything and sing it well. Linda is only one year younger than I, so we listened to much the same music when we were growing up, though she was in Tucson and I was in Albuquerque. In her book, *Simple Dreams* (Ronstadt, 2014), she talks about growing up Chicana and musical in Tucson and adjoining Mexico.

Her family was more musical than mine, but I had a radio. I could listen to KABQ ("*la voz Hispana de nuevo méjico*") with DJ "Pal Al" Tafoya. Sometimes I could even pick up XELO out of Juarez almost three hundred miles from my home, a giant of a station at one hundred fifty thousand watts that outshone the puny U.S. stations, even powerful ones, such as Albuquerque's KOB or Oklahoma City's KOMA with their fifty-thousand-watt transmitters. XELO reached much of the Southwest from Texas to California.

Linda Ronstadt's singing did not fool my dad, who said, "That girl obviously does not speak Spanish, but she has a wonderful voice." He had no idea Linda was the reigning Queen of Rock and Roll and a Chicana to boot (something I myself did not know when she began her singing career), though she was a "lapsed" Chicana when it came to language ability, like most of us it seems.

10

CHILD OF NO ONE

"One of the most egregious behaviors a parent or other caregiver can do to a child is to abandon them, allowing them to suffer alone." (CPTSD Foundation, Complex PTSD)

I was born in 1945, a month before President Franklin Roosevelt died, two months before Victory in Europe Day, four months before the first nuclear test at the Trinity Site near Alamogordo, New Mexico (two hundred miles south of Albuquerque) and five months before the atomic bombs ended World War II. It was a big year by any measure, maybe one of the biggest in the history of our world.

Divorce

My non-religious father had abandoned my Catholic mother in 1942, if not before, and had eventually sued her for divorce, with her countersuing him. She won for cause, with the cause being abandonment. This was unheard of in the Hispanic community. Not the abandonment (men left all the time and frequently returned home), but Catholics were not permitted to divorce. Women just did not sue for divorce. They suffered quietly and prayed for things to get better.

As I was growing up, my folks had some friends who lived together as man and wife, but the "wife" was a married woman who could not divorce the husband who had abandoned her decades earlier. Thus, they "lived in sin" for their entire lives, careful never to say they were married or participate in the sacraments of the Church at mass, though they were both very religious. We always acted like they were a married couple, as I suppose most people did, since what difference did it make? But that's the way the Church's rules were in those days and may still be today. (Steinfels, 1995; Rauch, 1997)

My parents' divorce was granted on my dad's thirtieth birthday, December 28, 1944. His second son was about to be born and he returned to Los Alamos to continue working on the atomic bomb. When the divorce decree was granted, my mother was five months pregnant with me. (The pregnancy suggests they were not totally estranged from one another as the divorce proceeded.) I only weighed five pounds when I was born, so there likely was not much of a baby bump.

My presence would only mean an increase in child support for my dad. My parents had been married in 1936 in a civil ceremony, but I am sure as far as my Catholic family and certainly my maternal grandmother, Rebecca, were concerned, the civil ceremony had zero validity. So, when my mother was pregnant with her first child, my older brother, she must have been under intense family pressure to have a real wedding. She and my dad thus had a second marriage ceremony in 1938 in San Felipe de Neri Church, the same church in which we held her funeral fifty-seven years later. I guess this marriage counted, especially among family members, but it did not turn out to be any more successful than the civil ceremony of 1936.

Living with Relatives

The first four years of my life were spent at my grandmother's and Aunt Nina's house, which was across the street from where my mother lived. I have few memories of this time because I was so young, but I remember my aunts, Florence (Nina) and Carmen, Uncle Billy, Jeanette (Billy and Carmen's daughter) and Grandma. They were the main people in my life who took care of me, and all of us spent our days in my grandmother's small adobe house of four rooms and my uncle's adjoining one-room grocery store. Everyone except Grandma was working, so I assume she bore the lion's share of taking care of me during the day.

I do not know how much time my mother spent with me, but she only appears sporadically in my memory. My mother was a single mother of two and had to work each day. I do not remember ever having spent a night at her house across the street from Grandma's. I was probably raised on baby formula so she could work. Since her immediate family members lived right across the street and were available and willing to care for her children, my older brother and me (and our dog, Lassie), she took advantage of family geography to leave us with them all day and maybe at night, too, in my case. Children can be a bother, more so even than puppies, so I find it remarkable that my aunt and Grandma would agree to take me in as a little boy. Nina was unmarried and childless and my grandmother, a widow in her seventies, had not had a young child around the house since the roaring twenties.

My brother was in grade school at San Felipe School (one block from our house) and was gone each weekday, so it was just me and the dog at Grandma's house. My mother was home on weekends, though I do not really remember. She worked in an office as a secretary in downtown Albuquerque and must have taken the bus to work each day or walked (she never learned to drive). My father had not been around since long before I was born, so not only did I not miss him, I am not sure I had ever met him. I do not know whether my brother missed him or not. I am pretty sure my mother did not miss my father, given the circumstances.

Then the World Changed

So, my world was very small during my first four years of life. Aunts, uncles and cousins would come to visit my grandmother so I got to interact with many relatives in our extended family. Their visits almost always occurred on Sunday afternoons after Mass and Sunday lunch. Mainly, I would play in the backyard, spend my days in the grocery store, or play with visiting cousins, though most were older than I. Nina also worked downtown and Grandma, a septuagenarian, did not have a lot of patience with a very active child. I spent many hours playing with Lassie and I considered her my dog. Neighborhood friends would come over to play with me, but I was reluctant to let them leave and created scenes when they did, which probably bothered them. It was typical behavior of an abandoned child.

Everything changed forever in 1949. Incredibly, my parents remarried each other on the 14th of April, 1949, civilly, because in the eyes of the Church they were already married and had been married since 1938. My parents always claimed 1936 as their wedding date, which was the date of the first civil ceremony. They never mentioned the divorce or remarriage, or the church wedding right before Anthony was born, an emergency wedding, if you will, to have the Church officially recognize their union by the time he was born.

Indeed, when I was twelve and living with my parents I decided to root around through closets and boxes. I discovered my parents' third marriage certificate (the second being the re-wedding in the Catholic Church just before Anthony was born). I asked my mother what was up with a civil marriage certificate from 1949 and she said it was nothing. She then proceeded to destroy it and all related papers pertaining to their various marriages and divorce. So much for preserving documents. Not in my family. It is ironic I went into museum work, where we preserve everything forever.

Fig. 29. Top: Grandma Rebecca Devine, my mother Rebecca Mares, brother Ernest Anthony Mares; lower: Joseph Anthony "Butch" Esquibel, Michael Mares about 1948.

I was four when they abandoned me. At some point, the atomic bomb project ended and my dad finished his work on the railroad and joined the Army. He was going to be posted to Carlisle, Pennsylvania for a year. Now they were faced with a dilemma, or at least my mother was. They had two kids, one only four years old and needing a great deal of attention, the other eleven and more independent. They also had a dog, but I doubt Lassie was much of a consideration. My dad had no feelings for dogs one way or the other, having grown up on a ranch where the dogs took care of themselves and did the work of protecting or herding sheep or cattle. Dogs were never pets to him.

Fig. 30. Rebecca and Michael Mares in 1949 just before she moved to Carlisle, Pennsylvania.

My mother could have stopped working and taken care of me (my brother would be in school in Pennsylvania), but this she was not willing to do. If she did stay home to care for me, she would be back where she was originally, being dependent on her unpredictable husband for support. Moreover, she had a small child, so from her point of view things were unspooling as they had the last time she had been abandoned, only worse since she now had two children.

My dad did not know me at all, so taking off without me was no big deal. He had abandoned the family before and, indeed, that was the very reason the court had found in favor of my mother in her divorce petition. I did not have a say in what was to me a momentous decision, but what she decided was to give me away to my grandmother and aunt—the people who had been taking care of me most days over the last four years—and move to Carlisle, Pennsylvania for a year, where my dad would learn drafting and other skills and be assigned to military intelligence.

An Abandoned Child Never Forgets

My dad had to have been in Albuquerque on April 14, 1949, as indicated on their marriage certificate. My fourth birthday had been on March 11, just a month earlier. My father had enlisted in the Army and was headed for Chicago where he would meet my mother and Anthony. I mis-remembered my mother's goodbye, not too surprising since I was only four years old and did not understand what was going on. I thought the three of them (mother, father, brother) left together from Nina's house after telling me they would see me in a year and that a year was not very long. Seventy years later, after almost everyone involved in my early childhood was dead and my older brother was dying, I told him I remembered their leaving in a green car and I always assumed it was my dad's car. I had had the image of that car engraved in my memory since I was four years old, three quarters of a century earlier.

Anthony said Uncle Billy had given them a ride to the bus depot and the green car was his. My dad was in Chicago waiting for them. Since I did not know my dad, I can understand my not getting the specifics of the leaving perfectly. In addition, I am sure I was not totally aware of what was happening but I had many questions. Where are you and my brother going? Why are you leaving? Why are you leaving me? The green car backed out of the driveway and into the permanent tracks of my memory and they were gone.

Anthony told me they rode all night on the Greyhound bus to Chicago. He said when they got there, the "newlyweds" had the biggest fight he had ever seen and he had seen a lot of fighting. It was a rough start to the new/old marriage. He said I was lucky to have been left behind; all they did was fight. "You were better off with Nina," he said. I asked him how he felt when they moved away from Albuquerque to Carlisle. He said he really missed his dog, Lassie. No surprise there. I did not miss him either, since I hardly knew him in those days, but Lassie would be my dog for the rest of her life. My not missing them surely applied to my dad, as well, and probably, and maybe especially, to my mother. My family defined dysfunctional. I was not a Mares anymore.

Write to Me

They must have left shortly after my fourth birthday in March after their April wedding, because in July 1949, just three months later, I received an envelope with a booklet of postcards that unfolded and showed me what Carlisle looked like. I doubt it meant anything at all to a four-year-old-boy who had never been anywhere. It was addressed to Michael A. Mares at Grandma's house. The whole message was: "Hello Precious. Here is a folder for you so you can see what Carlisle looks like. We live very close to the college shown here. I have put an arrow where Daddy works. Be a good boy and we sure miss you. Write to me. Love Mommy and Anthony."

I doubt the set of colorful cards meant anything to me at all—still doesn't seventy-five years later. The only reason I have it is that it was in Nina's papers when she died. Poor Nina, she was stuck with the abandoned little boy and I doubt the card made her feel better either. And while I could read a bit at four, I could not write, so I was not going to be sending any missives to Pennsylvania. By the way, where and what is Pennsylvania? Did it make my mother feel better to send this card to me and ask me to write to her? Maybe. She was out of touch with children and how they thought—and what they felt.

The U.S. Census

As I was writing this book, the 1950 U.S Census was published (U.S. Census New Mexico) after the mandated seventy-year delay. I went to check the results for Old Town and Grandma's house, expecting to find myself there. There were Nina and Grandma. Billy and Carmen were there too. Jeanette too. Where am I? Nothing. I am as absent as Lassie. What was up with that? Was I hidden in the closet when the census person came by, like they used to hide me in the closet so I would not get kidnapped by the roaming bands of gypsies that visited Old Town periodically? Where was I?

Weeks later, as if reading my mind, a note arrived from Ancestry informing me a search of the 1950 census throughout the country had found me. Where was I? Not in Old Town according to the U.S. census. I was found living in Carlisle. Although I lived in Pittsburgh for eight years in the seventies when I was a professor at the University of Pittsburgh, have traveled much of the world and visited six continents, all fifty states and sixty countries, to this day I have never set foot in Carlisle. But the U.S. census has me there in 1950.

What did my folks say to the census taker? Oh, he went over to his grandmother's house to visit (in Old Town, Albuquerque, New Mexico), but he lives here. He just stepped out. He went down to the corner for gum. This really makes me doubt the accuracy of the United States census. I guess my mother did not want to admit she had abandoned her child and I was living two thousand miles away without her. She was very good at not admitting things and constructing her world and the family's world to fit her needs and lifestyle.

Child Abandonment

There are many kinds of abandonment confronting children. One or both parents can die and while that is difficult for a child to understand, death is a part of life, as every Catholic learns early in life. The parents did not choose to die. Divorce can lead to a parent leaving, although some divorced parents maintain close connections with their children. Also, especially in Chicano homes, it is usually the man who leaves, not the mother. A mother abandoning her child is extremely uncommon.

The effects of abandonment are significant in young children and in the adults they grow up to be. The CPTSD Foundation (cptsdfoundation.org) conducts research on children and adolescents who have been abandoned and attempts to alleviate Complex Post-Traumatic Stress Disorder, which characterizes abandoned children, often throughout their adult lives.

II

Chicano Childhood

Juana Rebecca Gutierrez Devine

My grandmother was born in Old Town on January 30, 1874 to Juan de Jesus Gutierrez and Maria de Jesus Simona Garcia Gutierrez. She had two brothers, Macedonio Amado Gutierrez (1857–1916), Antonio Gutierrez (1865–?) and a sister, Maria Feliciana Geronima del Refugio Gutierrez Martin (1852–?). In 1892 at the age of eighteen she married James Devine (1864–1926) of Irish ancestry. Grandma was a flinty woman who had little patience with children, other than me and my cousin, Butch (Joseph Anthony Esquibel Shenuski). She was born two years before General Custer was killed at the Little Bighorn and as a child had been hidden from Indian raiding parties.

I would refuse to take in a four-year-old boy to rear as my own now, given my age and other issues. It is a big enough challenge raising my American Eskimo dog, Lobo, who's five years old. I am too old with too little time remaining to even think about raising a child. Yet Grandma and Nina agreed to take in a little boy and his dog. They were both heroes for agreeing to do it. We use the word "hero" too readily these days, but two women (a widow with no income and an old maid with very little money) were committing a significant part of their lives to take care of a rather active and probably unhappy little boy with issues, as they say, especially issues related to abandonment.

I am not sure why they agreed to take me in. Maybe they thought I would be dumped at the orphanage if they did not step up. Of course, my Aunt Nina would shoulder most of the burden for my missing mother, who was her younger sister and my other aunt and uncle helped too, especially Uncle Billy, who was a lieutenant in the Albuquerque Fire Department, which meant he was responsible for running one of the firehouses. I spent a lot of time in the firehouse. He was the male figure in my life for years.

Fig. 31. Nina, Grandma Devine, Rebecca Mares, Ernie Mares, Chris Mares about 1956.

Throwing Rocks

My friends and I would vex Grandma periodically and she would take after us with rocks, or spray water from a water hose if one were handy. At seventy-plus, she was never able to hit us with the rocks, although it was not for lack of trying. She had a very good arm (better than mine is today, after a fall in the high Andes of Argentina damaged my rotator cuff), but cataracts left her with failing eyesight. Her aim was poor and we were adept at racing just outside her range where we would stop and taunt her about her poor throwing ability. In the book, *The Milagro Beanfield War*, written by my friend, the late John Nichols of

Taos, there's an old woman in the town of Milagro who throws rocks at passersby. The old lady depicted in the film version of the book could have been my grandmother. Maybe throwing rocks is a mestizo old-lady thing.

After she began her long decline in health with a series of strokes, I became the person who spent most time with her, since Nina was at work. Nina did not retire until she was eighty and then only because she fell and lost the ability to walk. I read the newspaper to Grandma each day, concentrating on the obituaries. I also learned to roll cigarettes for her using Bull Durham tobacco and rolling paper. She was finicky about her cigarettes and if they were not rolled properly, the whole process had to be done again. I never became a smoker, but even today, more than seven decades later, I could still roll a packed cigarette that would meet her strict specifications.

I was nine and in the fourth grade when Grandma was diagnosed with diabetes after falling and breaking her collarbone. After her diabetes was discovered, Nina and I were the people who had to check her blood sugar using urine, chemicals and test strips. Had she not broken a bone, they would never have taken her to the hospital and discovered her disease. That was her first visit to a hospital in her life. I was in the fourth grade at the time and though she recovered from the broken collarbone, she never really recovered her vitality. The diabetes affected her in many ways. She died when I was a senior in high school.

A Long Life and the Gift of Death

Grandma had been born during the presidency of Ulysses S. Grant and died just a month before John F. Kennedy was assassinated. She had been having small strokes over her last few years and was very unhappy and undoubtedly depressed, although no one used the word in those days. She could not really walk or see very well, much less throw rocks anymore, but her mind was good. I would play the piano for her and knew her favorite songs. I played for her the day she died. Shortly after

I finished playing, she had a stroke and knew it was all over as she fell. Her last words, in Spanish, were *"Estoy muriendo y estoy feliz."* (I'm dying and I'm happy.) And she did and she was. She was eighty-nine. After we carried her into bed, I raced off in my car to get the priest from San Felipe Church, as Catholic families do, but by the time he got his stuff for the dying together and I drove him from the rectory back to her house, only four blocks away, she was dead. I was sure she was dead before I left the house to get the priest in any case, so I was not surprised to find she was gone. He anointed the body anyway. Our family physician stopped by and pronounced her. The family matriarch was gone.

Jumping Tarantulas

When Grandma was a child in the 1870s, she traveled by covered wagon to visit relatives in the Manzano Mountains just east of Albuquerque, a journey of eighteen miles that in those days began long before dawn and ended well after dark. (Today, the trip takes fifteen minutes on Interstate 40, a highway whose bridges and roadways I helped build as a laborer.) She often recounted how the family had once encountered a tarantula on the trip and she distinctly remembered the spider jumping over the wagon and bounding away. Of course, as a desert biologist I know tarantulas cannot jump. In fact, if you were to drop a tarantula from any height at all it would likely burst its abdomen and die. It has a brittle exoskeleton. But in those days, when such a trip was an infrequent and possibly dangerous adventure, it is easy to see how a young girl could conjure up a myth around a chance encounter with an unusual desert invertebrate she had never before seen. Of such singular observations are myths made. Each time I run across one of these large, hairy spiders after a desert rain, I am reminded of the little girl from Old Town who, nearly a hundred fifty years ago, made an exciting journey in a wagon to the mountains near Albuquerque and saw the remarkable jumping tarantula of the New Mexico desert.

Grandma was religious, but she was too ill to go to mass anymore. She prayed the rosary now and then, but it was not an overt religiosity.

After making long trips across the desert in a covered wagon from Albuquerque to Phoenix and back, there was one thing that made her fall back on her faith—thunderstorms. She was scared of lightning, which would indeed be frightening crossing the desert in a horse-drawn wagon, where the horses might bolt even if the lightning did not strike the wagon and kill the occupants directly. As soon as we heard thunder, she would take out the holy candles kept for just such an eventuality. She might say a rosary during the storm. Being in a desert, such storms were few and far between but could be violent. Her profound reaction caused me to be nervous of thunderstorms too. Alas, I ended up living in Oklahoma, where some of the most violent thunderstorms on the planet are common and where all movies about tornadoes are filmed. I don't use holy candles, however, but follow the weather radar on television, like all other Oklahomans. I became a private pilot and thus have a deep interest and understanding of the weather.

Grandma loved professional wrestling. In those days of black and white television and three channels, none of us knew wrestling was phony. We were definitely rubes. Her favorite wrestler was a Chicano named Juan Garcia, a super handsome and well-built good guy who always got battered around until, when all appeared lost, righteousness eventually won out over darkness. Each match was a morality play. Grandma would be watching and giving Juan audible advice in Spanish on what to do or what to watch out for: *¡Cuidado Juan! ¡Pégale! ¡Allí viene!* Perhaps she liked him because she had a granduncle named Juan Garcia on her mother's side.

Whatever her motives, wrestling, Liberace and Lawrence Welk were her favorite shows. Liberace was, of course, a flamboyant gay man, but none of us knew what gay was in those days and Grandma loved his sweet personality and outstanding talent for playing the piano. I think she liked the Welk orchestra because her late husband had been a band leader and while he was alive the house was filled with music, trips with his orchestra, dances and so on. When he died, all that stopped—no more husband, no more music and no more dances. Everything stopped for her and never restarted.

The other show we always watched was Father (later Monsignor and then Bishop) Fulton J. Sheen's "Life is Worth Living." Sheen was a brilliant Jesuit religious philosopher who spoke in clear terms about morality and the challenge of living a good life. We all listened raptly to his logical arguments. Sheen has made progress toward being canonized a saint in the Catholic Church. So Grandma's and Nina's (and my) remarkably diverse television viewing consisted of a popular orchestra, a Chicano pro wrestler, a gay pianist—whose outlandish outfits would influence Elvis two decades later—and a saint.

A Mestizo Lawman

My own television watching consisted of everything Disney, "The Mickey Mouse Club" (especially the blooming Annette Funicello), "The Cisco Kid," "The Lone Ranger," "Dragnet" and everything Roy Rogers and Gene Autrey. One time, Disney produced a movie about a remarkable New Mexican Chicano lawman, Elfego Baca, who had danced with my grandmother when she was a young woman. He was a lawman extraordinaire. The television series was called The Nine Lives of Elfego Baca," which later became the movie "Elfego Baca: Six Gun Law." Elfego was also known as The Man Who Couldn't be Killed. He was an outlandish character who became a defense attorney and once purportedly told a client who called him in Albuquerque from El Paso and said he had been arrested for murder, "Say nothing. I'm on my way with two eye witnesses."

Fig. 32. Elfego Baca as a young man. Center for Southwest Research, University Libraries, University of New Mexico

After the Disney show, Elfego Baca became a legend throughout the world, though he had always been a legend among Chicanos. Even my dad was afraid of Elfego Baca. He said once he and some Albuquerque High School friends (all at least mildly inebriated), decided to roll a couple of water heaters down Central Avenue, Albuquerque's main street, from the Heights to the Valley, letting gravity do the work. This was just teenage hooliganism, but who should stumble onto the shenanigans and come after them but Elfego Baca himself.

The boys abandoned the tanks and took off on foot. All were athletes, young and fleet of foot. Baca was in his sixties. He identified himself and told them to stop, but of course who would stop under those circumstances? So, the race began. Youth won out over old age, as it usually does in such a situation. The abandoned water heaters rolled to the curb and Baca had to let the students go. My dad was really afraid Baca would catch them later. "That guy was tough," he would say. Baca's legend preceded him.

For all the good Disney did in boosting the legend of Elfego Baca, when it came time to cast someone in the roll, it was the fine New York Italian actor, Robert Loggia, who played Elfego, and not a Mexican actor. Hollywood seldom cast Mexican or Chicano actors as Mexicans or Chicanos. For example, Telly Savalas, from New York Greek ancestry, played Pancho Villa, as did Wallace Beery, Missouri born. In the film, "Viva Zapata," Marlon Brando played Emiliano Zapata, the revolutionary Mexican leader who rode with Pancho Villa, although Emiliano's brother, Eufemio, was played by Anthony Quinn, a mestizo wetback whose father really had been a soldier in Pancho Villa's army and little baby Quinn and his mother followed the troops around.

It was interesting to watch the show with someone who knew Elfego Baca personally. Baca was nine years older than Grandma. Grandma liked him and thought the movie was pretty accurate, given what she had heard rumored over the decades. He was the first Chicano ever to take on a small army of Gringos and win. He arrested a drunken cowboy and put the cowboy in jail. Shortly thereafter, a judge released the cowboy from custody, but the man's friends were not about to let a lone Mexican lawman arrest one of them, so they attacked Baca. Baca returned fire and killed one cowboy and wounded another. Baca took refuge in a tiny one-room adobe jail. The cowboys attacked again, firing their guns and Baca killed another one.

From forty to eighty heavily armed cowboys then gathered together as a mob and attacked the one-room jail, firing more than four thousand bullets into the small space. (Bryan, 1993) The assault went on for thirty-three straight hours. Baca was never hit by a bullet but kept returning fire. Eventually he was persuaded to surrender. He was then brought up on charges of murdering two cowboys and injuring others. The door of the jail was admitted into evidence. It had four hundred bullet holes in it and everyone knew the jail itself was torn to pieces by the thousands of bullets fired at Baca by the cowboys. After the door evidence was introduced into court, the jury acquitted Baca of all charges.

Lost Children

I have become the genealogist for the family and recently discovered burial records for an Albuquerque cemetery (Santa Barbara Cemetery) that no longer exists. As far as everyone in my family was aware, Grandma Devine had six children, beginning with my Aunt Nora in 1900, followed by Florence (Nina 1902), Billy (1904), Vincent (1910), Rebecca (my mother, 1916) and the youngest sister, Jessie (1920). Except for my mother, all lived into their nineties. Grandma was forty-six years old when she had her last child.

This is the family I thought I knew so well, but things are not always what they seem. In my family, and maybe this was typical of the people of Old Town generally; things were *never* what they seemed. People kept secrets. What happened in the family was nobody's business, including other members of the immediate family. It was almost like security in the CIA. If you were not directly affected, you did not know and had no need to know. So things would take place that people did not know about, although sometimes certain actions or situations would come out in gossip or arguments. If you were a child, you never had a need to know.

I obtained the burial records from the lost Santa Barbara cemetery that had been subsumed into a larger newer cemetery in the early 1900s (Mt. Calvary Cemetery), with most of the burial locations being lost. The records included the names of the dead and their immediate relatives. I was stunned to learn my grandparents had two children who died shortly after being born: Adelina Devine, their first child, who died at age fourteen months in 1898 (one of Nina's names was Adelina) and Joseph Devine, who lived for only twenty minutes and died in 1909. In over seventy-five years of close interactions with my extended family never had I heard any of the six brothers and sisters or my grandmother mention a dead sibling, let alone two dead siblings. I am convinced her children did not know about them. Perhaps it was too painful for her to talk about the deaths.

No doubt losing two children colored my grandmother's view of life. Losing an adult son some years ago certainly colored my view of life. When I was very young and digging through drawers and boxes looking for anything interesting in Grandma's house, I was fascinated by a sepia tintype of a dead baby kept in a box of old photos. My guess is the dead baby was my uncle, Joseph Devine. I asked Nina who it was and she said she did not know. She said it had always been around the house and must have been some relative. She had no reason to imagine it was her older brother. A half century later, she tossed the tintype and many other historic family photos into the garbage when she was getting ready to head to a nursing home, a bit of dementia already becoming evident. I wanted those photos, but they were lost forever. The tintype was the most fascinating picture of my childhood, during a period when poorer families had few family pictures of any kind, much less tintypes.

Maria Adelina Florencia Devine (Nina)

In a number of Hispanic families, it was not unusual for one of the children to dedicate their life to taking care of their aging parents, especially if they themselves did not marry. There were no old folks' homes in those days. People got old, stayed with their married children or had an unmarried or widowed daughter take care of them or lived alone and eventually died. My grandmother did not want to stay in any of her children's homes (and with her difficult personality I doubt she would have been welcomed in any case), so she pressured Nina to stay with her as an old maid who would become the person Grandma would be able to count on in her infirm years, which were fast approaching by the time I was born. This, of course, demanded a great sacrifice by her daughter, who would spend *her* final years alone. Men were seldom selected for this lifelong commitment. No thought was given as to what Nina herself would do when age or infirmity defined her life. Of Grandma's six children, all were married or widowed and remarried, except for Nina. Grandma did not want Nina seeing men, which often led to heated arguments between them.

My mother, Jessie and Nora had all married Chicano men, with varying degrees of unhappiness. My mother was in and out of divorce and remarriage with the same person, so her life was too complex for Grandma to hope for any elder care from her. Besides, by abandoning me she showed everyone that she was a pretty poor bet for becoming a caregiver, even for her own mother. Jessie's husband had drunk himself to death by the age of thirty, leaving her pregnant and with a six-year-old boy, Butch. Jessie, with an infant and a young boy on her hands, wanted to remarry and quickly, while she was still young.

Grandma, who had married an Irishman, for some reason did not want her daughters marrying Gringos and would raise hell about any suitor who was not Chicano. And by raising hell, I mean there were screaming arguments where dishes, including knives, would be thrown at one another. I tried to stop these arguments by screaming and cursing loudly at them, but my attempts to use curse words, which I really did not know then, were pathetic. I would break down crying in frustration, but sometimes my efforts led to the argument's ending. Those were stressful times for everyone involved. To a little boy, women fighting is much worse than men fighting.

Fortunately, those kinds of outbursts were rare, but they put pressure on everyone involved. Ironically, after Jessie's Chicano husband had drunk himself to death, she brought home a remarkably kind, hardworking and gentle Gringo Air Force man whom she eventually married. Tom Shenuski, a machinist and Chief of the Fabrication Branch of the Technical Service Division of the Air Force Weapons Laboratory at Kirtland Air Force Base, was a truly fine person, a good provider and was great with her children whom he agreed to adopt. Together, they had a girl. After a few years, Grandma came around to realizing what a catch Tom was and there was peace in the family.

When Tom died in a tragic fall many years later, Jessie (or Morena as we called her) asked my historian brother Anthony to write Tom's obituary but, like my mother's rewriting family history, she placed many restrictions on the obituary's author. She did not want any mention of Joe Esquibel, her first husband and the father of two of her children (he was never mentioned to his children by their mother) or any hint she had been married before. The obituary should only mention Tom and all of her children were to be described as his children. Anthony could not mention the duration of their marriage or questions would be asked. A timeline had to be constructed to make the legend fit the facts. He refused to write the obituary.

Fred Astaire, John Wayne, Elvis

Nina's job as a salesclerk in various businesses gave her a Zelig-like ability to meet famous people but often not recognize them. One of the stores where she was employed was just down the street from the Fred Harvey House at the Santa Fe Railroad Station in downtown Albuquerque. The Santa Fe Super Chief, known as the Train of the Stars, came through Albuquerque every few days on its run from Chicago to Los Angeles and back. Flying was sketchy in the early days, so movie stars and other famous people took the Super Chief when they had to cross the country safely to get to Los Angeles or Chicago, a forty-hour train trip.

One day in 1933, a tall (by Nina's five foot zero standards) thin man came into Nina's store and wanted to purchase a number of items. She helped him shop and then got ready to ring him up:

> "Do you know who I am?" he asked.
> "No, I don't", Nina said.
> "You've never seen me before?"
> "No, sir, I'm sorry, but I haven't."
> "Do you go to movies?" he asked.
> "Oh, I love movies," replied Nina.
> "Did you ever see 'Flying Down to Rio' with Fred Astaire?"
> "I did and I love Fred Astaire," she said.

"Well, I'm Fred Astaire," he said proudly.

"No, you're not," said Nina.

Fred was taken aback. I am surprised he did not do a soft shoe move for her.

"But I am. I really am."

She looked at him more closely; then the penny dropped.

"Oh my goodness, you really *are* Mr. Astaire!"

That was Nina. Some decades later she was working in a small curio shop in Old Town that specialized in Indian jewelry, weavings, Kachina dolls and southwestern trinkets. One morning John Wayne walked in. Nina recognized him all right. He was making a movie in New Mexico. It turns out he collected Kachina dolls and was looking to purchase a few, since Old Town was famous for its Kachina dolls. She showed him what Kachinas they had and he bought three. Years later I saw those Kachina effigies at the National Cowboy and Western Heritage Museum in Oklahoma City, where he had donated them.

Nina and her friend, who worked in the curio shop, were in their late sixties or early seventies. They were both five feet tall, and John Wayne, with his boots and Stetson hat, which is what he was wearing, was almost seven feet tall. She sold him a few other items and he said, "Say, I have to be here tomorrow too, and there's no place I can go that people don't bother me. Would you girls mind if I came into your store early tomorrow and just sat around for a few hours?" "That would be fine, Mr. Wayne," replied Nina nonchalantly.

So, next morning, John Wayne arrives with coffee and donuts for everybody. He spent a few hours there hiding out and then left. When Nina told the story, she said, "John Wayne is such a nice man." I asked her how he was dressed. "Like John Wayne," she said. "Big hat. A red shirt. Boots. Just like you see him in the movies."

Mia Farrow came through the shop one day. She may have bought some jewelry, but the thing that impressed Nina was how small she was and how perfect her features were. Somebody must have told Nina who she was because I doubt Nina had ever heard of Mia Farrow. Nina had not gone to a movie at a theater since 1950 and there were no movies on TV in those days.

The topper for meeting people came the day young Elvis Presley walked into her shop. He started talking to Nina and asked her about her family. "I don't have any children," Nina said. "I've dedicated my life to taking care of my mother, who is very old now." That impressed Elvis and he told her, "There is nothing more important than a mother and taking care of your mother is a wonderful thing you are doing." Then Elvis left the building. She was never really impressed by celebrity, but enjoyed meeting famous people, if only for the stories she could tell, as she noted when she got home: "Elvis is such a nice boy."

Nina beamed with pride over her nephews' educational accomplishments and our advanced degrees. My mother was not a hands-on mother to say the least and Nina had helped raise all of her children, especially me. When I got my Master of Science degree in biology from Fort Hays State University in Hays, Kansas, Nina, who did not drive, got on a train and rode it overnight to Kinsley, Kansas, where I drove down from Hays to pick her up. She wanted to see the ceremony where I was awarded my degree. Cynical me was going to skip the ceremony, as I did my Bachelor's and PhD commencement ceremonies, but Nina was not having any of it. So I marched and she swelled with pride. She was my surrogate mother, so I was happy for her to be able to make the long train trip to Kansas to see me receive my degree. It meant a lot to me and to her. She and my wife were the only family members present.

A Boyfriend

Nina had to have been lonely taking care of her frequently difficult and ill mother and a hyperactive little boy who had issues with abandonment.

To top it off, she was the person called upon to take care of my mother's other children whenever my mother was at work. Nina was active in the church and various women's social organizations but must have longed for social interactions with a man. I do not know how many men she might have known (likely not many), but there was one man to whom she was clearly attracted. This caused some enormous fights with Grandma, who sniffed out the relationship almost instantly. How she did this, I do not know, because she never left the house.

Victor, Nina's suitor, came with several unhelpful attributes. He was a Jew, which was perhaps a bit better than being a Gringo, but not a helpful situation for deeply Catholic women. He said he was an FBI agent. He carried a gun he let me fire when we were parked on the West Mesa above Albuquerque. It was a .44 Magnum (think "Dirty Harry") and kicked like a mule in the hands of a ten-year-old boy when I fired it in the desert. It almost knocked me over with a deafening ear-ringing blast. Today we have the Internet to range across time and space as if life were a mobius strip with no beginning or end, permitting us to snoop in on everyone's life, past and present—where someone was born, where they married, when they died, where they are buried, and so on. I learned Victor was a car salesman, not an FBI agent, which also made him a liar.

I was the chaperone on the parking (sparking?) trips they occasionally took to the mesas west of Albuquerque and like a good witness, I have to say I never observed untoward behavior, though I am uncertain if I would have recognized such behavior if I had witnessed it. Moreover, I would never have said a word against Nina. I was not a rat that would turn on the one person in the world who was most responsible for my care. She loved me unconditionally and I knew it. Victor had a much bigger downside than being a Jew, however. Somehow Grandma, with her feral instincts regarding men on heightened alert, found out Victor was married. *Ay yay yay*. The sins were stacking up on many levels for an unmarried, very religious but likely desperate Catholic woman.

Grandma's accusing him of being married led to a horrific screaming match where items were thrown at each other. Whether or not Nina knew he was married (which he was), Grandma knew or assumed it was true and would loudly describe the kind of women who dated married men. She had known some in her time and they were invariably tramps. How could her daughter do this to her? How could she do it to her family? It led to difficult times for Nina and the chaperone (me). The breakup of Victor and Nina was probably inevitable, wife or no wife. I seem to recall their breaking up amicably, but I know after their last trip to the mesa, I never saw Victor again. Poor Nina. As far as I know, that was her last attempt to get involved with a man, married or otherwise. She made a life of giving unconditional love to the flotsam and jetsam of my mother's children.

When Grandpa Devine died in 1926, the children old enough to work got jobs as salesclerks or mechanics in the Santa Fe Shops. Uncle Vincent (Chepe), Billy's younger brother, was also a gifted athlete. He worked as a boxer for a while and was a very good baseball player, before going to work as a laborer. He spent his life as a laborer, dying in his nineties. Aunt Nina went to work in various shops in downtown Albuquerque and later at Old Town Plaza.

For the rest of her life (she died at ninety-six), she had a great love for education, since poverty had denied her the chance to go to school, along with almost every other member of my family, male or female, Mares, Martinez, Devine or Gutierrez. I was the first PhD in the family and my older brother was the second PhD. My younger brother, Chris, was the first MA in the family (in music therapy and psychology). He is also the true master of the piano, the gifted musician, mainly jazz piano, but he can play any type of music and play it well.

My mother had purchased a Steinway upright for Chris and he worked most of his life as a professional musician. The noted country western singer, Charlie Pride, heard him play in a small Albuquerque bar and came up and told him that he was the best piano player he had ever seen.

He told him he needed to get out of Albuquerque and take his talent to a place it would be appreciated. Chris decided to move to Miami where he might find an opportunity as a professional musician, but the gods are not pleased with Chicanos who leave the Southwest. He arrived one day before Hurricane Andrew devastated much of Miami, including the area where he had decided to live. He ended up living in a damaged apartment and out on the street for more than a month until he could return to Albuquerque. He has spent the rest of his life as a musician in Albuquerque and has now retired there. It is hard to pull Chicanos out of New Mexico in any case. They might move to California, but going east is an anathema.

William Leslie Devine (Uncle Billy)

When Grandpa died, it was not a good time for the family to collapse financially. Uncle Billy, an outstanding baseball pitcher, had just been offered a professional baseball contract before his dad died but had to turn it down since the salary was too low. Billy had been a star pitcher for the Albuquerque Grays (later the Albuquerque Broncos, which became the Albuquerque Dukes), the city's first professional baseball team in 1931. Together, he and his brother Vincent, also a pitcher, were responsible for much of the Dukes' success. Billy had been a high school star athlete at Saint Mary's High School, playing football and basketball. He even boxed professionally for a while. He ended up working for the railroad as a freight car repairman for seventeen years, before joining the Albuquerque Fire Department.

The House of David

On April 9, 1928, the House of David Jewish baseball team showed up to play an exhibition game against the local team, the Albuquerque Broncos. This was a big deal for a small western town. How big a deal? The Mayor of Albuquerque caught the first ball, which was pitched by the state's governor. The House of David was characterized by the players having very long hair and beards, some hairdos growing past their belt. The players were ascetics with extremely strict moral codes. Many famous major league baseball players had played with the team, including Hall of Fame legends Satchel Paige, Grover Cleveland Alexander and Babe Ruth. The major leaguers would put on a fake beard and play as teammates of the religious team. The House of David thought of signing Babe Ruth to a contract but found he was too hedonistic to be around the players for any length of time. He would corrupt them.

Fig. 33. Albuquerque Dukes professional baseball team, 1932; Billy Devine third from right standing.

Despite their hirsute appearance, the visiting team had outstanding players and enjoyed demolishing local teams across the United States and Mexico, much as the traveling Harlem Globetrotters would do decades later in basketball. When they rolled into Albuquerque they were considered the finest House of David team ever. Pitching for the Broncos in the newly formed New Mexico league, was Billy Devine. Family lore had Uncle Billy beating the visitors, but I found the newspaper story about the fifteen to five blowout in favor of the visitors under the headline "Devine might have had better luck if his support hadn't wavered: good early showing." The second baseman for the House of David said Billy had "...a good fastball and a nice curve, but he did not mix up his pitches enough and lacked a change of pace. If he learns to do that, he will be hard to hit." Billy was twenty years old.

Fig. 34. House of David Jewish baseball team. Baseball Hall of Fame Library.

12

Hard Times in Old Town

Being Poor

Old Town was an economically depressed community, but I never noticed we didn't have much money. My grandmother used to send me out to the vacant weed-filled lots to pick edible weeds for dinner, which may have been a clue to a lack of extra cash. The plant I remember picking is the verdolaga, also called wild purslane or Mexican parsley. It has thick leaves and grows close to the ground and, with its red stems, was easy to identify. Grandma would wash it, then fix it like a spinach stew with a chopped hard-boiled egg, some pinto beans and onions. It was delicious and essentially free. Beans were about eight cents per pound, an egg was about a nickel and onions were about seven cents a pound. The verdolagas were free.

Turns out wild purslane was a depression-era food for many people and that may be how my family came to know of it. I still make a very similar dish, but I use spinach in place of the purslane. Money is no object nowadays with my stew, but my grandmother's stew was better than mine and it cost only pennies. White bread was a dime a loaf, but we hardly ever ate white, store-bought bread. Grandma hated it and called it *pan aguado* (watery bread).

They would get old bread from my uncle's store and lay it out in the open air to use it in cooking. We almost always ate either white tortillas or sopaipillas with our meals. We would have corn tortillas if we were making enchiladas. There were no corn chips in those days, although one could get potato chips and Fritos. I longed for white bread like so many of the kids at school ate for their lunch, but I had to stick with the fresh tortillas and sopaipillas. Today, sopaipillas are considered a delicacy with meals and store-bought white bread? What can I say? It's *aguado*.

Maternal Grandfather James Devine

James Devine was a clerk during part of his working hours but a noted bandleader during evenings and weekends, even playing music accompaniment for the silent films shown in the movie houses of the day. When my grandparents married in 1892, my grandfather was in the Army. They moved to Arizona because Grandpa was the director of the Phoenix Indian School Band. Under Grandpa James Devine's tutelage, the band became one of the finest bands in the Southwest, a renowned marching band that traveled to many states, from California to Albuquerque, Kansas City and Nebraska. The surprising orchestra and marching band was composed entirely of young Indians boys. There is a certain irony to the fact Grandpa was a musician training Indians to play instruments and march, whereas his dad, John Devine, had been a dragoon sergeant in the U.S. Cavalry engaged in fighting Indians across the West.

Phoenix Indian School Band

As Handel and Humphreys noted (2005: 150), "By 1900, the Phoenix Indian School served more than 700 male and female students, and the band under the direction of James Devine, had become an elite group on the campus." Students had to have good grades and agree to the rigorous practice schedule. "The band had become the most popular activity on campus and the school's greatest public relations asset. The popularity of the band is further evidenced by the fact that seemingly every major event in Phoenix gave the Indian School Band top billing."

(Handel and Humphreys, 2005: 151) The band was called on to perform before every high official from Washington, DC who visited Phoenix and band members had to be "... in uniform, pronto, to play." (Handel and Humphreys 2005: 151) The band played mainly classical pieces, eschewing trashy modern music such as ragtime. Grandpa instituted Sunday afternoon band concerts that became highlights for the school and even for the City of Phoenix.

Fig. 35. Phoenix Indian School Band, James Devine in center, 1890.

The band toured on trains and presented concerts wherever they could schedule a stop along the railroad. Grandma went with them in most cases. I have to wonder now if she lost any children in Phoenix. There are no records of lost children, but there were not any records in Albuquerque either until I got lucky finding the list of burials for the lost cemetery. However, she got married at eighteen in 1892 and it seems unreasonable to think that she did not start having children in Albuquerque until 1898. She continued having children for almost thirty years, so I would not be surprised to learn she lost one or more children in Phoenix, Arizona or Gallup, New Mexico, where they lived for a while as well. When they returned to Albuquerque, she proceeded to have babies regularly.

A bandleader was often called "professor" in those days, so when stories would appear in newspapers, Grandpa would sometimes be referred to as Professor Devine. At other times he was referred to as Master Sergeant Devine and his Indian band. Later he was the Sergeant Director of the Regimental Band of Albuquerque. My grandmother told me grandfather once combined his Indian School band with the band of John Philip Sousa at a festival in Kansas City. Sousa, founder of the U.S. Marine Corps Marching Band, author of the greatest marches in this country's history and arguably the most famous musician of the 19th century, was the equivalent of a rock star in those days. It was considered a great honor for any band to have played with his band. I am certain the young boys of the Phoenix Indian School Band never forgot their trip to Kansas City. Grandma told me Sousa let my grandfather direct Sousa's own band, a hat tip to the leader of the famous Phoenix Indian School Band. Unfortunately, I have been unable to verify her memories with hard data.

Instant Poverty

I never knew my maternal grandfather as he died nineteen years before I was born. When he died of several strokes over a short period my grandmother and most of her children were left destitute. He had been the sole breadwinner and suddenly he was gone at sixty-three, well before he intended to be, I am sure. The family was left with nothing (no income, no property, and few savings). He had played and taught every instrument in the band and owned a large collection of band instruments, with his favorite one being a violin. My grandmother was forced to sell all his instruments and everything else he owned that had any value just to get by for a short period.

His many instruments turned out to be his only monetary legacy to the family. It did not amount to much. Grandma kept his baton as the only artifact that recalled her talented husband and the father of her children. The baton is made of ebony, silver and ivory. I have it to this day and will donate it to the Albuquerque Museum at some point. His Albuquerque band used to play on the bandstand in Old Town Plaza, where I once danced dressed as a Mexican boy of course (what else?) in the mid–1950s for the Old Town Fiesta.

James' brother, Robert Devine, also a musician, gave my grandmother the small adobe house where I grew up, so she and her children would not end up on the street—a generous brother-in-law indeed, but one who had shared grief with his brother and sister-in-law. Like my grandparents, an examination of the lost graveyard records showed he too had lost two children. A son, Berto, had died at six years of age in 1901, and a second son, Jacobo, died in 1911 at age fifteen. The families were close and lived together in a compound of small adobe houses. There were no social programs to support people in those days, no social security, no retirement programs, nothing. There was only family, and if the family was poor, you were out of luck. If you did not work, you did not eat. If you starved, so be it.

What about the Church, you ask? I doubt the Church would have been of much use to them, even though my family had helped build Old Town's San Felipe de Neri Church. I never found individual Catholic churches to be very charitable, despite the gospels and the encouraging words of Jesus Christ. *Au contraire*. Churches were very good at asking for money, but they fell far short in spending money on the poor.

San Felipe School, the local Old Town Catholic school, had a two-dollar per month tuition fee when I attended there in 1950. Whatever the tuition was in 1926, my newly widowed grandmother could not pay it, especially with four children in school. So, my mother dropped out of school for two years and then set about making those unpleasant impoverished years disappear from her life. When her father died, my mother was ten years old and had to drop out of grade school and look for food in garbage cans, foraging with her little sister, Jessie, who was six. The family did not have enough money to buy food. My mother was a proud woman and her pride must have become more important to her when she had to search for food in trashcans. She never mentioned this to me, of course (no one talked about anything in our family), but her sister, Jessie, told me about it after my mother had died and Jessie was on the road to death herself. Family secrets again.

Reinventing Your Story

When my mother died in 1995 at the age of seventy-eight, we learned she was two years older than she had always claimed. Even my dad did not know her age after fifty-nine years of marriage. All of her legal documents were incorrect, as she had made certain not to include those two years of desperate poverty on any written record. She had erased them from her life even if it meant reaching retirement age and receiving social security benefits later in life than would have been the case otherwise.

Things are what you make them and she was not going to be two years older than her high school classmates or friends or have to tell them why. Just before she died, she asked me not to put her birthdate on her tombstone. We all knew she had been born in 1918, but if she wanted it that way, I would get around her request in some way. In her obituary notice I wrote that she was born during the last year of World War I. I thought that way the birth year was not listed, as she had requested, but anyone who knew history would know when she was born. How clever I was.

As part of the paperwork of death, I had to gather many of her documents from various agencies, social security, unions, insurance companies, churches and so forth. She handled all of the books and records of the house and had destroyed all such documents at home, including marriage licenses and divorce papers. The two missing years in her life were not found until I went to San Felipe Church to get her baptismal certificate.

The certificate listed her date of birth. (Various official documents had her birth year listed as 1916, 1917, 1918 and even 1920.)

I learned she had been born in 1916, not 1918. I took the baptismal certificate to my dad to show him. "Well, I'll be goddamned. She was only nineteen months younger than me." Married almost sixty years and he knew nothing. That pretty well describes my family. He had no need to know. I made certain on her tombstone her birth year is listed as 1916, which was the actual year she was born.

My mother loved "Gone with the Wind," Margaret Michell's opus and academy-award winning film. She had read the book (she was a dedicated reader, mainly of novels but also many non-fiction writers like Helen Keller, Bishop Sheen, Tom Dooley or Eleanor Roosevelt), but she also loved the movie version of the book. I would guess like all women she was attracted to Clark Gable. But I think she would also have recognized parts of her own life in Scarlett O'Hara's comments as the City of Atlanta, her plantation Tara, and everything in her world lay destroyed and burning all around her.

For all practical purposes, that is the position my mother found herself in as a ten-year-old girl. She was forced to drop out of school, leave her friends, look for food in garbage cans and would be unable to graduate from San Felipe School with her classmates. She was too young to go to work. If her mother had had a job instead of counting on her husband when death took him so suddenly, perhaps the children would not have had their lives so terribly disrupted. She reconstructed her world to fit her desperate situation. I am reminded of the last lines in the film "Gone with the Wind" as a starving Scarlett O'Hara falls upon a carrot buried in the mud she has discovered in the garden and devours it. Afterward, she stands up and gestures toward heaven. "As God is my witness, I'll never be hungry again." That could have been my mother's mantra.

13

A Green Island in a Brown Sea

Albuquerque was founded as a locality for trading goods between the Spanish colonists and neighboring pueblo Indians. The city has annual rainfall of less than ten inches (and even less today with the increasing aridity of global climate change), which is the classic definition of a desert. The seasonal flooding of the Rio Grande provided the forested and seasonally-flooded areas of Old Town with rich soils in which to grow crops, including a wide variety of fruits and vegetables. Of course, the major crops of the Southwestern Native cultures were beans, corn and squash (called the "three sisters" of vegetables) and originally imported into North America from Mesoamerica. Alas, in recent years it has gotten too dry to grow pinto beans in New Mexico as large commercial crops. The pinto bean along with *chile* are New Mexico's state vegetables, but most pinto beans are now grown in North Dakota. *¡Por Dios!*

The deep greens of the Rio Grande Valley in the 1940s and 1950s made a striking contrast to the pale gray/brown surroundings of the arid *bajadas*. The Albuquerque Country Club had beautiful buildings with red tile roofs and a glorious golf course set within the Rio Grande floodplain, but few of my neighbors had grass in their yard—just the hard-as-stone pale *caliche* dirt. We played baseball, football and basketball on that hard substrate, which seemed mainly to support angry ants and crops of goat-head stickers (thorns that punctured flesh, footballs and bicycle tires with equal facility).

The Country Club

There were few parks in the poorer parts of town, so the country club seemed like the Elysian Fields to me, a green and glorious park with giant cottonwoods providing shade to the darkest of green grass and with the Rio Grande flowing gently by just to the west. Even on hot summer days it was cool on that grassy golf course. The club was surrounded by a chain link fence and one had to pass security to enter.

Country club homes were beautiful and looked for all the world like the homes one saw in photographs of Beverly Hills. It truly was another world from the adobe huts of Old Town. These very homes, with their white walls and red tile roofs, were later highlighted in the television series, "Breaking Bad," where the character, Jesse, lived in the Country Club neighborhood. In 2011, one of my screenplays won the Beverly Hills Film Festival and I was able to walk through Beverly Hills. Other than the palm trees, it did resemble the early Albuquerque County Club.

In contrast to the white stucco homes with red tile roofs, we lived in a small adobe house, a plastered mud hut if you will, only four blocks from the country club, with a flat tarpaper roof. I did not know at the time the country club had sundown laws to keep "Mexicans" like me out of the neighborhood after sunset. Hispanics could not live there, but during the day maids had to be allowed in, workers had to access the country club's golf course, restaurant and bars, landscapers and domestics were needed each day and caddies were allowed into the most sacred place of all, the huge deep green golf course.

Golf and Caddying

I decided to become a golf caddie. Almost all the caddies were Hispanic, as was the caddie master (the guy who either gave you a job carrying golf clubs or said "not today"). I had tried to make money as an eleven-year-old by cutting lawns in the country club with a push mower. It was hard work on a hot day and I was paid two dollars per lawn, including trimming the edges with hand clippers. It worked out to about a dollar an hour. As I got older, I finally decided I could make more money as a caddie. The work looked easier. Alas, I was not a very good caddie. I had bad eyes and found it almost impossible to follow any ball hit a great distance at high speed—and not always in the direction of the hole. It was one of a caddie's main duties in addition to carrying a very heavy bag of clubs for miles.

I needed money to buy baseballs—so my friends and I could play baseball at every opportunity, day or night. We did not play on grass, but on hardpacked dirt with chips of glass, sharp gravel, goat-head stickers, nails, and other things that ate away at the soft horsehide of the baseball. Our baseballs did not last as long as they would have had we played on grass, so we had to adjust and were always trying to find a way to get new baseballs. Those that had lost their hide could only be repaired with electrical tape for so long before we were down to the small cork ball at the core. The going rate for a caddie was three dollars for nine holes. If a person played eighteen holes, the pay was six dollars. It was a job that took all day, which meant a caddie earned about a dollar an hour—again.

All of the golfers I remember were Anglos. Generally, I was treated well if I could see where the ball went, but that was always difficult for me. Much later in life, I learned my eyes were not only severely myopic, but out of alignment as well, leading to double vision, and it was progressive. I sort of remember when it got more pronounced because I suddenly could not hit a baseball anymore and even had trouble catching flyballs.

I got tossed out of the Country Club for laughing at a man playing golf who happened to be the fellow for whom I was caddying. He had hit the ball into a deep sand trap and had to then hit the ball onto the green to finish the hole. He swung mightily and peered toward the green, but he missed the ball completely several times—sand scattering to all sides and his anger building. Finally, he connected. His club carried the ball up the overhang of the sand trap over his head and deposited it in the sand right behind him. His hand covering his eyes, he peered across the green as Lewis and Clark must have gazed at the endless ranges of the Bitterroot Mountains from Lemhi Pass in Idaho. Where was that ball?

I could no longer contain myself and fell on the grass laughing, rolling around as tears poured from my eyes. He never saw the ball sitting right behind him but I, the kid who could almost never find the ball, had seen exactly what had happened. It was one of those times where forbidden laughter leads to uncontrollable laughter. He got very angry, threw his club into the rough and fired me saying, "Goddamn Mexicans." It was the first job from which I was fired. I survived to caddy another day. Over time, I learned it was much more fun to caddy for women. They didn't hit the ball very far and I could generally follow the ball. They never cursed at their caddy and sometimes they even tipped us. I never saw a woman throw her club after a bad shot.

The Country Club remained a white-bread island in a blue-corn-tortilla sea until civil rights legislation was passed in 1964 that changed the sundown laws, but I was in college by then and no longer working at the Country Club. Curiously, today I could afford to live in the Country Club area and, indeed, my wife and I looked at a number of Country Club homes in the late 1990s when we were going to buy a house in Albuquerque. We ended up buying a home in Old Town only a couple of hundred yards from my grandmother's house where I grew up. Our condo was just across the street from my grade school and a few blocks from the fancy homes of the Country Club.

The year we bought that home in Old Town, on the Fourth of July we sat on the porch of our new condo sipping wine and watching the fireworks and the tethered hot air balloon display (a "glow") from the golf course at the Country Club where the giant balloons that have helped make Albuquerque famous were set up on the fairways I knew so well. The Anglos of the Country Club were working hard for my patriotic enjoyment.

Rich and Poor

Captain Maximiliano Luna was an upper crust Chicano Republican politician who grew up in a wealthy and influential family in Los Lunas, just south of Albuquerque. (Melzer, 2017) The family home was known as the Luna Mansion and is described at length by Melzer, along with photos. In many ways the house reminds me of the Martinez ranch house where my paternal grandmother grew up—a huge multi story ranch house on the prairie west of Wagon Mound New Mexico.

In contrasting rich and poor Hispanics in New Mexico, with the Lunas being exemplars of wealth, Melzer (2017) reports on a letter written by an unnamed curious Anglo railroad engineer who visited one of the poorer Chicano families to see how his Hispanic neighbors and employees spent the day. The description of the economically poor Hispanic home was that of a whitewashed small adobe house. The photo the author selected to illustrate the railroad man's description of the sad adobe house could have been a photo of my maternal grandmother's house, the house where I grew up. So, my paternal Martinez ancestors came from money, but the Devine and Gutierrez ancestors were by no means wealthy.

There were some differences from the humble home described by the railroad man and the house where I grew up. By the time I was born, the dirt floors of my grandmother's house had been replaced by wooden plank floors that bent under the weight of everyone, even a child. The house had electricity early on too, at least from my point of reference as a child, but it was clear we may not have had electricity for that long a period. My grandmother used to ask me to blow out the lights, since she was used to having hurricane lamps or candles in candle holders on tables and walls. I would blow on the electric light bulb just to irritate her. Once, when we actually had a hurricane oil lamp lit because the electricity had gone out, she asked me to blow out the light. I grabbed the glass hurricane lamp cover with my hand to remove it before blowing out the wick. No wonder she told me to blow out the light. I burned my hand rather badly.

The observant engineer as quoted in the Maximiliano Luna book also noted something peculiar in his description of Chicano behavior: "They do a great deal of sweeping about the house, inside and out." The comment brought back a flood of memories of watching my grandmother sweeping the inside of our house and then sweeping the front and back yards, which were hard-packed dirt. She did this every day, except for the exceedingly rare days when it rained. After sweeping outside, she would wet down the dirt using a large pan of water from the backyard handpump. I asked her why she swept the yard and she said it was to keep down the dust, so she would not have to sweep the inside of the house later, after the dusty New Mexico winds and visitors with dirty shoes had filled the house with dirt and dust.

We always laughed at her seemingly unyielding, yet hopeless, battle with dust and dirt, which we knew Grandma could never win. It reminded me of the story we heard in grade school religion class about the child who in the year 400 CE was sitting on a beach using a seashell to dig a hole. Saint Augustine, walking along the beach and, thinking deep Augustinian thoughts, saw the child and realized the little boy was trying to empty the ocean into a hole he had dug with the seashell. As luck would have it, Augustine was working on a book that described the Holy Trinity and he was having a great deal of trouble understanding the concept himself. He told the child how hopeless it was for him to try to empty the entire ocean into the large hole he had dug. You will never be able to do it, he said. The precocious, smart-mouthed little beach urchin looked Augustine in the eye and said he had a lot better chance of emptying the ocean into the hole he had dug than Augustine had of ever understanding the mystery of the Holy Trinity.

At least when I was a child, Grandma's house did not have an outdoor *horno* (oven) for baking, like the house the engineer described, though there must have been one long before I was born. We did, however, have a woodburning stove with burners over the coals and an oven. We also had an upright, insulated, non-electric icebox that could keep a small number of items cool as long as the large block of ice added each day or two had not melted away. We had a sink that drained out into the yard through the kitchen wall. The icebox drained into a pan below the icebox.

When I was five years old, we got linoleum for the floors. Linoleum is made from linseed oil, gums, pine resins and ground cork dust formed into sheets. It was a big deal in the 1950s, this hard, colorful floor covering. We used it in the kitchen, bedrooms and living room to cover the boards. It must have been expensive, because we had to clean our feet very well before entering the house so as not to dirty what appeared to me to be indestructible linoleum.

Indians used to come to my aunt's and uncle's little one-room grocery store, which was the fifth room of my grandmother's house. My aunt gave credit, which turned out not to be a good idea when the store closed with hundreds of people still owing thousands of dollars and never paying their bills. My uncle and aunt were angry at the deadbeats, some of whom were family members who did not have the money to pay their food bills or just never got around to paying. It led to family friction. The people who owed the money felt guilty and would seldom come around to visit and those who had provided credit were cheated. Perhaps because of this, I do not believe in personal loans. If I have the money, I will give it to a friend or family member who needs it and not expect repayment. That way there are no hard feelings.

Billy's store closed because a Piggly Wiggly supermarket had opened a quarter-mile away and many of its customers were the very same people who owed money to their family's store for food eaten long ago. There was damn sure no credit at Piggly Wiggly. My aunt's and uncle's little store had no chance of competing with the variety and prices of a huge supermarket. It was true for mom-and-pop grocery stores throughout the country—anywhere a modern supermarket opened nearby.

Siempre Los Mexicanos

My dad had a saying, "*Siempre los Mexicanos*" (literally, "always the Mexicans"), used colloquially to refer to Chicanos either never getting a break or always failing to make the right or profitable choice. If someone got scammed over a foolish get-rich-quick scheme and lost their money, what could one say? *Siempre los Mexicanos*. It was how one might describe Jackie Gleason's character, The Poor Soul, who could never catch a break.

The Indians who would come to our small grocery store, like many Hispanic customers, had no money. They did have woven blankets, pottery, jewelry and other items they would offer to trade for food. My aunt did not want to barter since bartering brought in no cash, which she needed in order to replenish the shelves, but she did not want to withhold food from the hungry Indians either, so we would end up with beautiful pots, jewelry and weavings. The problem was, no one in the family liked these items, nor did most people in Old Town in those days. They would never have bought such goods. To us they were practically worthless.

Grandma and Nina, in order to keep the New Mexico dirt off of our "beautiful" linoleum floor, used to put rare Indian weavings on the step outside the house for cleaning our feet to avoid dirtying the linoleum. Large pots were used as wastebaskets. *Siempre los Mexicanos*! My Uncle Christie knew Maria Martinez, the famous potter from San Ildefonso, when she was a young woman. (I do not know if she is related to my family). He bought one of her pots during World War II and it set him back eight dollars or thereabouts. Today of course that pot might be worth tens of thousands of dollars at least, maybe more. Indian art had no market demand and little value in those days and certainly not among the mestizos.

14

CHICANOS IN THE VALLEY, ANGLOS IN THE HEIGHTS

That was the unwritten rule for Albuquerque in the mid–1940s and 1950s. For a child growing up in Old Town, the inhabitants of the Heights were as remote to me as people from exotic places. Old Town was probably unusual by Anglo standards. Friends, acquaintances, and family included a cross section of people whose incomes were low, whose Catholic faith was strong (going back in some families for at least fifteen hundred years) and who had large, extended families. Most were not educated beyond the primary or high school levels.

In 1956 many of the boys in San Felipe School came to idolize Elvis Presley, his persona and his music. He was new and rock and roll would never be the same. I grew my hair like Elvis, sang his songs in my little band and generally tried to become a clone of him. When the movie "Love Me Tender" came to town, it was playing at the Highland Theater in the Heights. I told my friends I wanted to ride the bus to the theater to see the film. "Are you crazy? There are stomps there. They'll beat the shit out of you, a little Mexican. You'd better not go without a knife, man."

I really wanted to see the movie, which was making headlines everywhere. I got a hunting knife and strapped it to my leg, then took a bus to the Highland Theater. It turns out that the Anglo girl who would marry me forever lived only a few blocks from the theater, but of course I did not know that since I would not meet her for another five years. I was as jumpy as a long-tail cat in a room full of rocking chairs as I rode the city bus up the *bajada* to the dangerous Heights, my first time there. I got to see the movie and, if there were any stomps around, I did not see them. After the movie I got on the bus and rode it downhill all the way to Old Town. Whew. Safely back in Chicanoland. In my mind I had cheated death to see Elvis.

Get an Education

My mother and dad graduated from high school, but I doubt Grandma Devine had more than a sixth-grade education, if that, although she was taught by a putative legitimate saint, Sister Blandina Segale, Servant of God. At age seven, Grandma first attended Our Lady of Angels School under Sister Blandina Segale when it opened in 1881. The school offered elementary education and grammar, with music and art available in the convent next door. The school's name was changed to San Felipe de Neri in the early 1880s. Subjects offered included writing, arithmetic, spelling, English, Spanish, geography and U.S. history. I don't think the curriculum had changed much in the seventy years that had passed from the time Grandma enrolled in the first class to when I enrolled there, though we did not have language instruction, other than English. Nina, who was highly intelligent, never made it to high school. She had to go to work.

Nina always insisted each of us had to be highly educated. We had to work hard in school and learn something. She told us everything depended on our education. We had to make something of ourselves. She hoped we would go to college, though no one in the family ever had. She helped me and my brothers pursue our education as far as possible, taking care of us when there were no parents available, even giving us some loose change or a few bucks now and then to help with expenses for books, cars and whatever. She was as poor as the proverbial church mouse, but always saved some small amount of money for her nieces and nephews. Had we not accepted it, she would have been devastated.

My older brother and I were the first in our extended family to ever receive PhD degrees and my younger brother, Chris, received his Master's. Nina was so proud of us. When senility eventually came calling during her final years when she was in her nineties and in a nursing home, she awarded herself a PhD in clinical psychology. "I needed to study and get my degree to be able to deal with some of these patients. They are pitiful, Michael."

With the exception of a pharmacist who was a Chicano and an extraordinary individual in many ways, the only people I met who had graduated from college were doctors and were invariably Anglos. As a child, I never met a lawyer, dentist, professor or artist who was not an Anglo. The people of Old Town were laborers, railroad workers, barbers, road workers, painters (of the house variety), firemen, owners of diners and delivery men. In the 1900 census, the most common occupation for men in Old Town was day laborer.

Forty-five years later, when I came along, being a laborer was still a common occupation for men in the area. My neighborhood was definitely not Mr. Rogers' neighborhood. Years later, when I was a professor at the University of Pittsburgh, where the actual Mr. Rogers was also on the faculty, my children would watch his television program, set in a more gentle neighborhood than Old Town and more reflective of the Anglo neighborhoods where my boys were reared.

Barbers and Perverts

My neighborhood had more than its share of alcoholics, some of whom, when they were in their cups, would gather to serenade my grandmother at night. She would throw buckets of water on them to drive them away, treating them like stray cats screeching on a fence. I mentioned to her the singers probably liked her but she wasn't having any of it. "I don't want to be serenaded by drunkards," she replied. The men who came over most frequently were survivors of the Bataan Death March and I wonder today if they were suffering from PTSD that led them to the bottle. We did not know anything about war-related mental injuries in those days.

I was also told all house painters were alcoholics due to the chemicals in the paint. I do not know if that was ever true, but the singing drunks were indeed house painters. Research published in Business Insider (Lubin and Giang, 2011) showed house painters were ranked in the top four of jobs with deaths from alcoholism (with bartenders being number one, for understandable reasons). I remember watching the body of one old alcoholic who had died of cirrhosis being carried from his miserable, bedbug-infested apartment, his yellow cast and distended abdomen providing an indelible memory.

There was at least one pervert in my immediate neighborhood, I'll call him "Nick the Barber" (who lived next door to, I'll call him, "Pablo the Plumber"). People were often identified by their jobs. Nick was an old man who had even flashed my mother when she was a little girl. She swore his pants were on some sort of cord that could be released at will and then pulled back up quickly. The barbershop's remarkable collection of pornographic magazines and filthy photographs would be the introduction to female anatomy for most of the neighborhood boys, as well as the only place we could see such remarkable photos that came from Mexico of women interacting pornographically with animals. What amazing things those people and their dogs and farm animals did to each other. There were no videos back then, but the tiny black-and-white photos seemed to tell a story. Nick was born at the wrong time. Instead of being a degenerate barber, he might have become a rich purveyor of pornography and filth and had his own web channel today. He might even be an influencer.

Each New Year's Eve, Nick would come out of his house at midnight, drunk as a skunk, and fire a high-powered rifle into the dark sky. The report of the five shots at midnight would reverberate throughout the neighborhood and announce the arrival of the New Year. My home office in Santa Fe is situated immediately above the Santa Fe National Cemetery. Each day I hear the three-rifle-shot salute for another veteran as they are buried. The shots often make me think of Nick's holiday rifle shots. He was my barber for years until he cut my neck while he was drunk. When I got back home Nina went to his shop immediately and raised holy hell with him about cutting me and that was my last visit to Nick's barber and porn shop.

There were also a few wife-beaters in the neighborhood, men who generally pummeled their spouses after having drunk too much fortified wine or cheap tequila. It was a cross many poor women bore in silence and the children of the neighborhood never talked about, but we were aware whose father had to be avoided at particular times. I remember one girl who had a house full of friends visiting her for an after-school party when her father, a violent man when inebriated (though charming when sober) arrived roaring drunk. He was a veteran of the U.S. Marines and may have been in combat. He and his long-suffering wife were good friends of my mother and dad. As soon as we saw him walking unsteadily toward the front door, we poured out of every door in the house to race back into the safety of the neighborhood. We felt both guilty and helpless as we watched his daughter watching us run away. (I still feel guilty about this sixty-five years after it happened, with everyone involved, except me, now being dead.) I see her standing alone, a lovely doe-eyed innocent teenager, waiting to deal with the onslaught that would follow. She later became a drug addict and an alcoholic, a mother of five (but lost one infant who was likely murdered by her ne'er do well live-in lover) and spent part of her life in institutions. She died in her forties. Her drunkard dad reformed and became an AA counselor in California and was known for his outgoing, friendly and gracious nature.

A Boxer's Family

A family friend had a son who had been a professional boxer and was punch-drunk. (Today it is called chronic traumatic encephalopathy.) He would shamble along, often not knowing where he was going. His arms usually flopped around, but sometimes he held them in a boxing stance. Seeing Leo, I knew early on boxing was not for me, although to this day boxing attracts poor Blacks and Chicanos who see the ring as a way to escape the ghetto or barrio, beating themselves senseless for the enjoyment of people with money. (Curiously, my older brother, who was a poet, historian and a far-left activist with a very strong social conscience, loved boxing matches.) The boxer's mother, Lola, had had a difficult life. Another woman's husband had stabbed her husband to death as he attempted to make a hurried exit through his paramour's bedroom window. The woman's husband had come home early, finding Lola's husband and his wife doing the dirty and, since everyone carried a knife, the outcome was inevitable. The unfortunate widow was never quite the same after the murder.

Children in Old Town

Life in Old Town was not merely a succession of peculiar individuals and unfortunate incidents. We had great times playing baseball almost continuously during the spring, summer and fall, and playing football and basketball during the fall and winter. My basket for basketball was actually made by my uncle out of a wooden peach basket nailed to a locust tree—shades of Dr. Naismith, himself. In summer we lived on our bicycles and, in some respects, our childhood was probably not too different from that of Anglo children living in east Albuquerque. Nevertheless, my childhood was radically different from that of my own children, who had a much more Anglified upbringing than I. They were raised in upscale neighborhoods and attended schools where they did not experience mental or physical abuse. They never encountered the oddballs who peopled my old neighborhood. Unless we were living at a field station, where I was teaching and doing research, they were never permitted to run unfettered for hours on end without our knowing their whereabouts. Indeed, they were reared like I imagined Anglo children were reared.

Here is an example of a game that we played in my neighborhood that I would not have allowed my children to play. One of our favorite pastimes was climbing onto huge metal empty fuel storage tanks that were left lying on their sides in the lot behind the Hedges gas station behind my grandmother's house. They were the kind of tanks that are buried in the ground to store gasoline and diesel fuel for gas stations. They were about six feet in diameter and twelve feet long. Old Man Hedges, as we always called him, kept coming over to visit with Grandma and kept trying to buy her property so he could expand his gas station and storage lot to serve tractor trailers. She was always nice to him, but made it clear she would never sell. Hedges died before he could ever convince her.

The only people who used the large metal gasoline tanks were us kids. Like loggers in a log rolling contest, four or five of us would get on top, running on the tank to make it move. We rolled the tanks across the vacant lot and against one another in a type of slow, but massive, battle charge. Two great tanks would be crashed into each other at full speed after long runs across the lot and those who remained standing on top of their tank after the collision were the winners. Being kids, we never thought it was a dangerous game, but once a friend fell into the path of the oncoming, unstoppable tank and the edge of the tank rolled slowly over his head. We thought he was surely dead, but when we leaped off to help him he seemed to be in fairly good shape, except for the fact his head was misshapen and compressed. Obviously the soft sand substrate had helped keep him from dying, but he did not know who we were or who he was for some time. We were worried about his obviously laterally compressed head, so I squeezed it back into shape by wrapping my arms around it and applying strong pressure. After this "therapy" he began to come around. He finally recognized us and was able to walk, if a bit unsteadily, but said he had an awful headache and went home. A few days later, he seemed okay. I lost track of him shortly after that incident and have occasionally wondered if he had any lasting effects of what must have been a significant concussion. No, my children would never have been permitted to do that. That was my world, but it would never be theirs.

A favorite pastime of ours was to throw rocks at the rich kids from the roof of their private elementary school just across the vacant lot from my grandmother's house. This ruffian behavior developed because we were not permitted to use the playground of the private school, whose swings, slides, teeter-totters and other equipment sat idle most of the year, especially in summer. There were no classes at the school in summer and it was the only playground in Old Town to which we had access. To use the playground we had to climb across the rooftops of the school or had to scale tall, chain link fences. I suppose in response to a general ban on our being on the school grounds playing with what were clearly indestructible heavy steel yard toys (a ban we invariably ignored, in any case), we assaulted the children regularly. Usually, we pelted a few of them with pebbles before they realized we were there. Eventually, they would call a teacher and the teacher would call the police, but we were off the roof and well away from the school by the time the police arrived, their patrol car rolling slowly through the empty hard-packed dirt lot.

Sometimes just to be ornery we would climb over the roof and sneak into the classrooms at a time we knew teachers and maintenance people were present. I disliked school, so it is difficult to imagine breaking into a school. We enjoyed getting on the nerves of the people in the private school, however, and we dared them to catch us, which they never did. Eventually, we outgrew this annoying behavior as we grew older than the children in the school. Picking on younger kids was no fun.

Bees

There was little wild nature in the neighborhood, so we interacted with animals as we encountered them and as our curiosity led us to explore their habits, often in destructive ways. My cousin and I once found a large beehive in the tall locust tree in the backyard of grandma's house. Bees were swarming around the hive, but we decided to knock it down for reasons I no longer remember. As Steve McQueen said in "The Magnificent Seven" about why the man took his clothes off and jumped into the cactus patch, "He said it seemed like a good idea at the time."

We searched for very long sticks and then smacked at the hive until it came crashing down. It broke into several pieces, helped greatly by our sticks. We may even have killed the queen bee. We certainly tried. The angry bees swarmed at us and we leaped through the screen door into my grandmother's kitchen. Her house had a screened window as well as the screened back door and both opened on the back yard with its beautiful locust trees and dense swarm of angry bees. The bees covered the screens so densely that the house grew dark. My grandmother was furious that we had disturbed the bees and intimated that she was considering putting us back outside to face the angry, buzzing insects. Fortunately, she was no more intimidated by the angry bees than she was by the drunks who would sing in the front yard. She decided to adapt her method for dealing with singing drunkards against the furious bees and began hurling pots of water on them. The bees wanted no more to do with my tough grandmother than did the drunks and dispersed to buzz and make honey another day. My cousin and I spent the rest of the day hiding in the house. No way we were going outside. What if bees had memories?

A Talking Crow

Lola, whose son was the addled boxer, had forgiven her wandering husband immediately after his demise and, with her gentle and religious nature, would surely have forgiven him even if he had survived the stabbing. Shortly after his death, she would talk about how her husband continued to visit her in the guise of a talking crow. She knew the bird was her husband in disguise because it had human buttocks (and they were the buttocks of the only man she had ever loved). Those were simpler times in many ways and people often lived hard lives. One struggled to fit the frequent tragic occurrences of daily life into a framework of understanding that permitted a person to endure. Perhaps if your only son had been beaten senseless and consigned to a confused and shambling existence and your spouse had been stabbed to death while engaged in an adulterous liaison, you would talk to crows too.

The crow visited her for many years and she would often recount their lengthy conversations, which dealt with everyday happenings, rather than with portents of the future or descriptions of life in the hereafter. I asked her if she ever asked the crow what was going on in the world of the dead, but she said he only wanted to talk about what was going on in the neighborhood. I guess he missed it, removed too soon from the Old Town barrio by a cuckolded husband. The crow with her husband's buttocks was her constant companion until the day she died. Some would certainly think her daft, but Lola was a wonderfully gentle person with an unshakably sweet and optimistic personality. She always called me "Sugar" as I was growing up. There are many stories that could be told about her, for the fact that she was visited by a talking crow was not her only unusual characteristic. One significant accomplishment was managing to maintain her driver's license long after she had gone blind.

Driving Blind

Decades before a "blind" Al Pacino drove a Ferrari in "Scent of a Woman," my elderly Aunt Nina, and another ancient friend—both of whom never learned to drive but who were blessed with excellent eyesight into their nineties—would team up with their sightless friend and drive around Albuquerque, the sighted old women giving loud advice to the unseeing driver. As frightening as this sounds, they managed to maneuver about town very well, except when the octogenarian advisors disagreed (e.g., "The light is going to change. Stop." versus "No, go ahead, this is a long light, go on, go on."). Fortunately, such disagreements were rare.

My aunt had excellent vision and hearing. ("I can hear a pin drop" was a phrase she used to the day she died). She felt obligated to accompany Lola when she was driving around Albuquerque. Part of the reason was Lola, a close lifelong friend, had told Nina not to worry about her driving alone even though she could not see. She had discovered the car more or less knew where it needed to go. It had a mind of its own and she was sort of going along for the ride. Perhaps the crow was helping.

Nina would relate how difficult it was for them to negotiate streets that had three lanes, for then the fearless dowagers had to give directions that referred to the movements of traffic on either side of the car, as well as ahead of them. If there were vehicles in those lanes, their rapid-fire, audible instructions and close tolerances became a feat worthy of the Blue Angels, the U.S. Navy precision aerobatics team. Curiously, over the years, they had never had an accident, gotten a ticket or been stopped by a cop.

The Blue Army

While not exactly the Blue Angels, the women were members of the Blue Army, the official name of a small group of deeply religious, extremely old, Catholic women who venerated the Virgin Mary, did good deeds for the church, went to each other's funerals and spent inordinate amounts of time praying—perhaps to Saint Francesca Romana, the patron saint of safe drivers. The small Blue Army of Old Town had perhaps ten teeth apportioned among its nonagenarian troops. These old women had seen it all. Some had been married and had grown children and grandchildren, even great grandchildren; some had never married; some had lost children; and most had lost husbands and lovers. All were deeply devoted to the church. To them, priests and nuns were saintly, even if there may have been some doubts about the true character of individual priests or nuns.

Even a parrot knew nuns were saintly. My mother had a yellow-headed Amazon parrot when she was a little girl. Its name was Lorito, meaning little parrot, and he was well known in the neighborhood. Parrots get attached to a single person and the only person for Lorito was my mother. Everyone else was scared of the parrot, which had an evil streak manifested by his habit of sneaking up on people and trying to bite them on their feet and legs. Nina was bitten when she was a teenager and carried the scar on her foot for the rest of her life. Lorito never bit my mother and the parrot would allow her to play with it any time she wanted.

Unlike most Chicano children, Lorito spoke both English and Spanish and would spend time in the screened-in front porch watching people walk by and chatting with them. Whenever nuns walked by the house, Lorito would say in English, "Good girls. Good, good girls." Lorito could count, too. The parrot would say, "*Uno, dos, tres*," then pause for a bit and repeat the "three": "*tres, tres, tres*." Then he would try it in English, "one, two, three, three, three." Eventually, he stopped counting and began chuckling.

A Religious Superstar

One priest, Father Roberto Sanchez, was made Archbishop, which was even greater glory for his people—the first Chicano Archbishop of the Archdiocese of Santa Fe and, indeed, the first in the entire United States. *Caramba*! He did many good things. He recognized the atrocities inflicted on Indians by the Church and apologized to the Indians for the evil the Church had done. No one had ever done that before, much less a church leader. He selected and named the first ever Native American bishop.

He knew he was a mestizo and wore vestments that reflected his dual Chicano/Native American ancestry. He was a proud mestizo. That was a first, too. He encouraged parish priests to recognize the cultural differences within their flocks and to be sensitive to the needs of their different cultural members. He had studied in Rome, was smart and worked on high-level papal commissions dealing with immigration problems throughout the world. (Hevesi, 2012) He was a star and a Chicano star at that. He was one of our own.

At San Felipe, he spent part of his priestly time with teenage girls in the rectory. My Aunt Nina used to clean the rectory as part of her work for the church and the Blue Army. Like Jesus with the money lenders, she would drive the girls out when she found them in the priest's private quarters, saying "What's wrong with you girls? Don't you know he's a priest?" Of course, the girls were not the entire problem. It was the handsome young priest, in whom we invested such pride because he was a Chicano, who was the real problem.

Catholic bishops are held to very high moral and religious standards.

(Danel, 2019) Their oath of ordination includes the following statements and questions, and responses:

> "Will you refrain in all your ways from evil and, as far as you are able, with the help of the Lord, direct them to every good?"
>
> "I will."
>
> "Will you observe and teach, with the help of God, chastity and sobriety?"
>
> "I will."
>
> "Will you, as far as your human frailty shall allow, always be given up to divine affairs and abstain from worldly matters or sordid gains?"
>
> "I will."
>
> "Will you yourself observe, and likewise teach others to observe humility and patience?"
>
> "I will."

Ah, human frailty. Aren't we all frail? Even bishops?

As Marc Antony said of the dead Julius Caesar: "The evil that men do lives after them; the good is oft interred with their bones." The evil the archbishop had done by turning a blind eye to child sexual abuse running rampant in his New Mexico diocese and, worse, by himself being involved sexually with teenage girls while still a young priest, came roaring back to haunt him years later. A Mike Wallace "60 Minutes" exposé in 1993 revealed the sordid story to the whole world.

As I write these words in Santa Fe in June, 2022, the historic Santa Fe Cathedral, built by Bishop Jean-Baptiste Lamy is being mortgaged to pay settlements for victims of child abuse by priests in the archdiocese. The archdiocese filed for bankruptcy and it was granted at the end of December, 2022. The Church could have saved over one hundred twenty-one million dollars and a lot of embarrassment, not to mention the lives it would not have destroyed, if it had only listened to Nina.

15

Outhouses, Pachucos, Rock and Roll

At Least We Had Electricity

When I first started living with my grandmother and aunt, we did not have running water. We had a hand pump in the backyard of the house where we would pump water from the well for cooking, drinking, washing and other needs. Pump water always seemed to be cold, winter or summer. I loved drinking from the pump. On Saturdays, I was bathed in a round galvanized laundry washtub placed on the kitchen table with water heated on the wood stove. My hair was rinsed with vinegar.

We had a one-hole outhouse in the backyard, a small wooden building that, in addition to being the place to go to the bathroom, also served as one of the great breeding sites of all time for black widow spiders. They were everywhere: behind you, above you, below you and in the dark interior of the toilet. They demanded alertness and caution. The outhouse was freezing in winter and exceedingly ripe and hot in summer.

Life With a Wood Stove

Before the installation of a natural gas line, we had a woodburning kitchen stove. Wood had to be chopped and glowing charcoal formed from the burned wood before it could bake anything, otherwise the smoke would ruin the food. The stove had a large stovepipe that went through the adobe wall and into the backyard. Grandma and Nina took great pride in preparing Thanksgiving and Christmas dinners. They would chop the wood the night before and get it burning and crystalizing into charcoal early in the morning. Then, and only then, would they put the turkey in the oven.

They began working on the turkey and charring the wood at four in the morning, while it was still dark and cold outside, sometimes even snowing lightly. Bread had been drying for days in the arid New Mexico air for use as stuffing. This was the only time they bought commercial white bread. As the stuffing was made and the bird stuffed, they would debate the ingredients of the stuffing. More celery? More sage? It all had to be done early because they wanted to put the food on the table at precisely noon for reasons I never understood. We only ate turkey twice a year. It was not a law and no one else was joining us for lunch, but Grandma and Nina seemed to think it was a holiday requirement. For as long as I lived with them, they hit the noon mark with the holiday meal each time. Quite remarkable when you think about all the work it took to get the stove, turkey and other dishes ready. It became easier after the gas stove arrived.

Now in my dotage, I do a lot of cooking for the holidays and I also want the food to be on the table at noon sharp. It seems to be the thing to do. A requirement? Perhaps it is a psychological requirement to know you can control the preparation and cooking of a complex meal with astounding precision. I still remember Grandma's and Nina's turkeys as the best ones I ever ate.

A Gas Stove at Last

When I was five years old, indoor water and an indoor bathroom were added to the house (with a buried cesspool outside that always seemed to flow over with foul exudate in summer, when it would have to be pumped out). We also had a natural gas line installed for the living room and kitchen. A small electric refrigerator was added to the kitchen. Gone were the wood stove and the ice box. I have no idea where the infusion of money came from to make all those changes happen. I assumed it was Uncle Billy and Nina who covered the costs, but whoever it was, it improved our lives immensely. What marvels. The outhouse was no longer needed and eventually, while still a small boy, I grabbed a hammer and tore it down, watching the black widows run for cover, victims of modernization.

Donkey Deliveries

The sweet *chiles rellenos* and *calabacita* squashes with green *chile* and whole corn kernels, and a hint of meat, were also a memorable part of the holiday meal. And of course, *sopa* (not soup, but Spanish bread pudding) was a superb holiday dessert. A syrup was made for the bread pudding (from burnt sugar), then boiled raisins and other fruits and spices were mixed in. Cheddar cheese was added.

Every two weeks or so a man with a donkey laden with white goat cheeses would come by the house selling moist cheese balls. They were about the size of large softballs and were delicious. We sometimes ate them with a bit of syrup or honey on top, or better yet, *capulín* jelly that was homemade from chokecherries we had picked in the mountains. And of course there were *sopaipillas*—puffy, pillow-like fried bread that seemed an ideal accompaniment to goat cheese or anything else.

The donkey vendor also came by periodically with tamales, which are tough to make, so people loved buying them already made, if the *chile* and pork were well prepared. I doubt goat cheese or tamales are sold off the backs of donkeys anymore, but it was a good way to get the food to outlying homes and was a welcome treat. Few people in my neighborhood ever went to restaurants, so you had to make things yourself. There were few stores in our neighborhood, so vendors who brought cooked food to the house were appreciated. Of course, the ice cream man had delivered frozen treats for years, but who would not prefer a warm tamale delivered on a quiet little donkey to an ice cream cone delivered by a van with ear shattering chimes?

Pachucos

Unlike today, there were few gangs in Albuquerque in the fifties, but there were some *pachucos*—Chicano hoodlums who were good with a knife, had a cross tattooed between their thumb and forefinger, always fought at dances, smoked, drank, went to prison and often ended up dead at a young age. Some of my friends were *pachucos*. One, who got in a fight with me in grade school was, even to my child's mind, especially violent. I remember telling him in sixth grade, after we had had a fight, that he would end up killing someone someday. Years later, he stabbed his older brother to death.

His brother was a big fellow who lived for fighting, especially with Anglos, often seeking out situations where he was outnumbered just to make it more interesting. He loved post high-school football game fisticuffs. He was a very tough guy. I figured he would get killed someday, but I never imagined his own brother would be his murderer. The older brother was much tougher than the younger one, but a knife tends to equalize things. Both of them were friends of mine at one time in Catholic school, although our paths had parted long before the murder took place.

A family who lived behind our house had several children. The father and one of his sons had unusually distinctive deep voices that made them sound like croaking frogs. It was hard to distinguish the father's voice from the son's, even though the boy was only ten. A second son, an epileptic, earned his living selling blocks of ice to tourists on Route 66. We spent a good part of each hot summer's day at his ice house, a large, insulated, wooden box cooler set up on stilts along Central Avenue

(Highway 66). We would gather up and eat the bits of ice that fell on the ground as the large ice blocks were chopped up to be put into the coolers of the tourists driving westward to California, an eight-hundred-mile journey.

In spring and summer, tourists faced a very hot trip through Gallup, Holbrook, Winslow, Flagstaff, Seligman, Kingman, Needles, Barstow and Los Angeles. In summer it was a long hot journey across mountains and deserts. Most people rented motel rooms during the day and crossed the desert at night. That is what we did when we drove to Los Angeles, even in the 1960s. Cars could not deal with the desert heat very well and it was even more difficult for the people in the cars. My dad knew many of the towns along the way because they were railroad stops where he had spent a good deal of time in the 1930s working on the Santa Fe Railroad.

The coolers in the cars were designed to hold snacks and cold drinks much like modern ice coolers, except they were made of metal. There were a couple of other contraptions I do not think are made anymore but that every traveler had in those days. The automobile air conditioner had not yet been invented, so when families were traveling by car, they looked like Gary Larson's cartoon of the dog family on vacation. Windows were open, the deafening roar of the road noise and wind filled the car and people roasted on the inside of the really hot car, hoping the blowing hot wind would cool them down a bit through evaporation.

Eventually, an evaporative cooler was developed for cars that held ice or cold water with chipped ice in the body of the cooler that was then attached to the window. As the car moved forward, a fan in the cooler spun as it caught the wind and pushed cool air into the hot car. It was an evaporative cooler that did not cool the car very much, but every little bit helped. Each car also had a large canvas bag filled with water that hung in front of the hood's grille where the rush of air would evaporate the water on the outside of the canvas bag and cool it. It could be used for a cool drink of water or to cool the engine when it inevitably overheated climbing the mountains, hills and *bajadas* between Albuquerque and Los Angeles (or Albuquerque and Santa Fe, where La Bajada Hill had water barrels strategically placed to be used when the vehicles overheated).

Rock and Roll Arrives

The iceman's parents ran a small café just a couple of doors down from the ice house and only a half block from my grandmother's house. Mainly they served Mexican food, burgers and ice cream. The café also had a jukebox which, when rock and roll was becoming popular, played the earliest rock and roll songs I can remember. It's where I really heard rock and roll for the first time emanating from something besides a tinny radio. I loved that jukebox. It was five songs for a quarter and I always had a quarter saved up to play the latest songs. This was in the mid-1950s, so rock and roll was just getting started.

Their café was the place where I heard my first rock and roll song ever in 1954, "Earth Angel," sung by The Penguins, but written by my aunt's neighbor in Hollywood, Jesse Belvin, who used to watch over me and my cousin while my aunts and grandmother went off to tour Hollywood. Mainly we played marbles together. Jesse did not sing "Earth Angel," but his singing career was developing with another song he wrote, "Goodnight My Love." Jesse was considered the new Nat King Cole and had a super smooth voice.

Unfortunately, Jesse died in a car wreck at the age of twenty-seven, along with his wife and driver in Hope, Arkansas (hometown of Bill Clinton and Ross Perot). It was 1960, just as his career was taking flight. He had been part of the first-ever concert tour of black rock and roll stars to perform before an integrated audience in Arkansas. The rock stars included Sam Cooke, Jackie Wilson and Marv Johnson. White supremacists in the audience had hurled racial epithets and insults at all of the performers. After the concert, as Jesse's car was traveling on the highway, it suddenly veered into oncoming traffic resulting in the accident. Given the ugly atmosphere, the police thought Jesse's car had been tampered with to cause the wreck, but they were unable to prove it. Whatever the cause, the only rock star I would ever know was dead.

Another early rock song was "Why Do Fools Fall in Love" in 1956, by Frankie Lymon and the Teenagers. I loved Doo Wop and could listen to it all day. Music by The Diamonds, The Spaniels, The Drifters, The Del Vikings, The Platters, The Crests, The Cadillacs, The Chantels, The Clovers and other early rock groups was heard on the radio and eventually on records. Chuck Berry, Fats Domino and Little Richard loomed large in early rock and roll, as did Elvis of course, and all of us neighborhood boys loved them too. I would buy 45-rpm records for a nickel from the used record store where very worn jukebox records went to die. The most used records, i.e., the most popular ones, had their grooves worn down to almost nothing, but the music did not sound too bad when played on a cheap record player.

Chicanos reflect many cultures and they do so in their tastes in music as well. In the late 1940s and early 1950s, many popular singers I listened to were Bing Crosby, Frank Sinatra, Perry Como, Doris Day, Louis Armstrong, Glen Miller, Tommy Dorsey and even Al Jolson, my dad's favorite, who had been the most popular crooner during the Great Depression of the 1930s with a host of uplifting and positive songs. Of course, since I was in New Mexico, western music was also popular, with songs by Hank Williams, Bob Wills, Tex Ritter, the Sons of the Pioneers, Gene Autry, Roy Rogers, Marty Robbins and Johnny Cash. Generally, we listened to radio, or on records or television (after we got a TV in the 1950s). In 1947, I was taken to a live performance by Tex Ritter at the Kimo Theater in downtown Albuquerque. Ritter even had his horse on the stage, but I was only two years old and remember nothing of the show.

Mariachi Music

Most people in my neighborhood also listened to Mexican music, especially mariachi music. The top performers I recall included the so called "Los Tres Gallos" (the three roosters), the greatest mariachi singers of all time: Javier Solis, Pedro Infante and Jorge Negrete. All were singers and actors in Mexican films, which we also watched. They all died young. Solis, who had a remarkably smooth voice, died of complications from gallbladder surgery at only thirty-four. Infante was a pilot and owned a B-24 Liberator bomber he would fly regularly, logging three thousand hours as pilot in command. One of his engines failed on takeoff from the Yucatan Peninsula and he lost control. He was thirty-nine. Negrete died at forty-two in Los Angeles from cirrhosis and hepatitis. He had trained as an opera singer and with his remarkable voice would record operas in New York City under a pseudonym so as not to ruin his reputation as the king of the mariachi singers. He had also attended medical school and been a combat officer in the Mexican Army. The deaths of these almost mythical performers brought sadness to the people of Old Town. They were beloved as actors and singers and their music was part of our lives. I still listen to them today.

Other mariachi singers were Lola Beltrán, Lucha Villa, Miguel Aceves Mejia, Vicente Fernandez, Luis Aguilar and José Alfredo Jimenez (who wrote a thousand of the most famous mariachi songs ever recorded though he could neither read music nor play an instrument). Albuquerque had Spanish radio stations and they often played mariachi music. Mariachi music was mestizo music and Chicanos were definitely mestizos, so it was our music.

Pastor Versus Jukebox

As much as we loved hanging out at that little neighborhood café, the owner got in trouble with the pastor of San Felipe Church for having that damned "tool of the devil" jukebox in the café, moreover one that played rock and roll music and attracted children (e.g., me) to gather there. The café was put off limits to Catholic children, which really hurt their sales since everyone in the neighborhood was a member of the church. I do not know whether or not the priest announced the ban on the restaurant in church, but I would bet he did (and neighborhood rumor said he had), thus shaming and punishing the woman economically at the same time. That jukebox was one of the few highlights of my pinche neighborhood and the goddamn priest took it away.

I, of course, paid no attention to the pastor's edict. My friend's parents owned the café and I was sure, even at a very young age, that a ban on the café was baloney. Still, eventually they had to close the café due to the ban. My friend's mother's maiden name was Mares, but I did not learn that until I started researching this book seventy years later. We may have been related. Other than my being dumped by my parents and some negative nun-or priest-student interactions at school or at church, the café imbroglio was one of the first injustices involving the church of which I was cognizant.

The third and eldest son in their family was shot in the head while cooking hot dogs in his backyard near the Rio Grande, dropping dead on the spot in front of his family. No one ever determined whether it was a stray bullet from some hunter in the *bosque* cottonwood forest along the river or a murder. One minute he was there and the next he was gone. It was thought to most likely be an accidental shooting.

16

LEARNING TO READ AND CALCULATE

My aunt Carmen and Uncle Billy had a one room grocery store in a plastered cinder-block room attached to my grandmother's house that could be accessed by me through a large window between the bedroom and the store. As a child, I hung out in the store every day. Grandma was old and most people were at work every day, so there was not a lot for me to do to keep busy. The grocery store was where Carmen and her daughter, my cousin Jeanette, who was seventeen years older than I, taught me to read and do sums when I was four. I learned from reading soup-can labels and other products in the store. It was not hard to do.

Fig. 36. William (Billy) Devine and Carmen Nicolaci Devine.

Since I was sitting around the store all the time anyway, they also decided to teach me math using the prices of goods, making change and operating the old hand-cranked cash register. I also found this easy to do, but ended up figuring the change in my head, which was much faster than using the cash register. I still do them in my head seventy years later and today when I tell the cash register operator the amount of change due me after a purchase, they always look at me strangely.

Once I could do the cashier duties, they had me label the goods with a price punch marker with an ink pad. Every time you punched a price on a can or box, the ink pad put more fresh ink on the number pad. It was fun. I think they were just thinking up ways to keep me busy all day so I might talk less. Soon I was able to run the cash register, too, and they required me to use the register to give change, since it produced a small paper tape receipt for the customer. I took great pride in being faster than the cash register, paper tape or no paper tape. I sort of became a little freak for customers to watch, since I ran their purchases and handled the large cash register. I had just turned five.

Firemen and Cops

Uncle Billy had a number of friends in the police departments of Albuquerque and the New Mexico State Police. He had known them for years. They faced off in firemen versus policemen baseball charity games each year at Tingley Field. He always took me to the games. Sometimes he and the police worked together at wrecks, fires or on other first responder calls. For them it was like making friends in combat. Billy told me about one terrible motorcycle accident where he was responsible for finding all the body parts. The last thing he found? The tongue. I guess these were gruesome stories, but they did not upset me.

I hoped to be a fireman. How could I not? I hung out in the firehouse with Uncle Billy. When the calls came in, I was left behind in the fire station and told not to touch anything, while they sped away with sirens and red lights blazing. It was too cool. Right, don't touch anything. I explored every inch of the fire station and slid down the pole from the upstairs dorm. How I longed to climb on the truck with Torr, the dalmatian, and race to the fire. When the alarm bell rang, Torr was the first one on the truck, standing on top and ready to go, while the firemen were still sliding down poles and putting on their fire gear. In those days, the firemen stood on the tailboard of the firetruck on the outside hanging on for dear life as it roared away from the station, red lights flashing and siren wailing. It looked like so much fun and adventure to me.

Uncle Billy rode in the cab because he was the lieutenant and had to develop the strategy, they would use to put the fire out or deal with whatever emergency they encountered. Today all firemen ride in cabs. He was part of the team that fought Albuquerque's largest conflagration, the great Sears fire in May, 1953, where nine fire trucks and seventy firefighters battled the blaze for twelve hours overnight. Seven firemen were injured.

It was the city's first four-alarm fire, which meant almost every fire station and fireman in the city was called to fight the multistory fire and to keep it from spreading to the rest of downtown Albuquerque and destroying the entire town. They even called in help from the Santa Fe Shops fire brigade and the Kirkland Air Force Base fire department. The blaze was set by a fourteen-year-old girl wearing two actual, loaded six-guns and hiding in the store after hours, waiting for the store to close so she could "burn it down." If the papers of the day ever followed up on the story of this weird pyromaniacal girl, I could not find evidence of it. A fourteen-year-old pyromaniac armed and dangerous with real pistols and trying to burn down a city would definitely go viral today.

Hinkel's Department Store went up in flames in downtown Albuquerque in February, 1954, in another huge fire. This time Billy was not as lucky as before, as he and another fireman were overcome by smoke and ended up in the hospital. A third fireman fell into the basement of the building where the store's records were kept. Other firemen brought hoses and sprayed them down and pulled all three to safety, saving their lives. Remarkably, other than some bruises and a few minor burns, they were unhurt. As he told me afterward, any fire can be dangerous. It does not have to be a four-alarm monster, referring to the previous year's Sears fire. In newspaper clippings of this fire, the station's dalmatian was photographed in the smoke. The caption gave his full name: Jolly Torr. Who knew? I never heard anyone call him Jolly Torr.

I heard lots of stories about the work of being a fireman. I learned how a young man had been swimming in a water tower and drowned. Billy the fireman and Red Dow, badge No. 1 in the New Mexico State Police (a person who a little Chicano boy considered a friend), had to climb the tall tower and then take turns diving to the base of the tower's tank to retrieve the body. Billy said it took quite a few tries diving over and over into the pitch blackness of the water tank. They could not really see the body since they were inside a huge metal tank and had to hold their breath and feel around, but eventually they found it and brought it out. When the police would come around, I always liked being near them. They befriended me, the little boy without a mother or a father, but with an uncle who was a friend of theirs. Red gave me a real policeman's whistle. Another policeman gave me a badge. Uncle Billy gave me a fireman's hat. I was ready to go to work.

Bringing Order from Chaos

We lived very near the intersection of Highway 66 (Central Avenue, perhaps two hundred feet behind our house) and New York Avenue (today it's called Lomas Boulevard), which was maybe fifteen feet from our front door. Just west of us (in fact only a block away, right by my grade school), New York Avenue and Central Avenue merged and continued westward as Highway 66, the only highway to southern California. It was a two-lane highway then. In later years it would become I-40, still the major road to Los Angeles, but today a four or more-lane ribbon of concrete heading toward the setting sun and, eventually, the California beaches. What the merging of the streets meant for me was the traffic on both streets was extremely heavy and slow, sometimes bumper to bumper. Anybody traveling from the East Coast to the West Coast by car drove by our house and the crowds increased during summer vacation season.

One day, I decided a police presence was required to bring some order to the traffic, which seemed especially dense and noisy that day. I put on my fireman's hat, policeman's badge, grabbed my whistle and my six-guns and waded out into the afternoon traffic. I was four years old and fearless. I started blowing my whistle and stopped the traffic on Lomas in both directions. Of course, no one past the first couple of cars could see me since I was so small, but my whistle kept them from moving. It was a real police whistle after all and I had practiced a lot to blow it like a traffic cop. The line of traffic backed up for several blocks, with me trying to impose some order on the drivers.

The horn honking became deafening. It got the attention of Uncle Billy in his grocery store who came out to see what was going on. *Ay yay yay*! The four-year-old had stopped all westbound and eastbound traffic. Uncle Billy waded through the cars and I could almost see the smoke coming out of his nostrils. Boy, was he angry. I had never seen this side of his personality before. He picked me up by my hair and arm. He took me to the curb and chewed me out royally. I could see people in the cars laughing at me. He also took away my badge, guns, hat and whistle. It took some time, but I got them back after he had cooled off. I never did that again, though. What a humiliation for a police officer.

Police Friends

Since I felt I was friends with several police officers who would come through the neighborhood most days, I never felt threatened by them. They were like my uncle—heroes who helped people in desperate situations and went after bad guys. I spent a lot of time playing in the large vacant lot behind my grandmother's house. There were all kinds of things to do among the waist-high weeds or on the flat *caliche* dirt. There were fallen down adobe walls, giant empty oil storage tanks at least fifteen feet tall, large underground storage gasoline tanks that lay on their side, abandoned metal sheds, parts of the undercarriages of tractor trailers and other wonders. Whiptail lizards abounded.

One day when I was five, I saw a dog coming towards me. I liked dogs, but this dog was snarling, unsteady on his feet and foaming at the mouth. Before he could get near me, I ran to get Uncle Billy. He took one look at the dog and called one of his policeman friends, who came on a motorcycle to where we were. He was there in minutes. The dog had rabies. The policeman made sure we were standing behind him, then took out his gun and shot the dog. BANG! One shot and it was over. The officer explained the dog was a deadly threat to every person and every dog in the neighborhood and had to be killed. The policeman thanked me for finding the dog and telling Uncle Billy so the policeman could deal with it. We waited with the dead dog until the animal control people came and took it away. I was proud I had done my duty to help save my Old Town neighborhood and all of its dogs from rabies—especially my dog Lassie.

Skipping a Grade

Kindergarten and first grade were not only boring, but way too easy for me. I already knew how to read a bit and do basic math. The nun's decided that I would skip first grade and go to second grade. This was great news since my cousin Butch was in second grade and now he and I would be together. Unfortunately, something went very wrong with my tonsillectomy at age five, and I had to stay at home in bed for more than a month. I assume I got an infection, but I am uncertain and, of course, no one ever told me. Nina was there every night when I was ill and did her best to take care of me.

I must have been sick enough that my memory was affected since I remember very little of my recuperation, though I remember the surgery and kicking the doctor when they tried to put the ether mask on my face to knock me unconscious for the operation. Eventually the doctors and nurses overpowered me and when I woke up I was in a lot of pain that continued for over a month. The nuns said I had missed so much school I had fallen behind what the second graders were doing and could no longer skip a grade. I thought that was malarky then and I still do, though my life would have unspooled differently had I jumped to the second grade.

17

SAN FELIPE DE NERI SCHOOL

Sister Blandina

The roots of San Felipe School (originally called Our Lady of the Angels) reached back through the history of New Mexico and the West. Jesuits invited nuns from the eastern United States to come to Albuquerque to open a Catholic school in Old Town. Sister Blandina Segale was among the first to answer the call. In recognition of her pioneering work in the founding of a Jesuit-based Catholic school in early New Mexico and perhaps also in recognition of a life well lived, she recently achieved the first step toward canonization, having been beatified. She is now being considered for sainthood. If successful, she would be one of the very few Americans to reach that exalted plateau in Catholic lore.

Eventually, she will become one of eight Americans to be canonized, joining, among others, fellow Italian nun, Mother Cabrini and another nun, Sister Elizabeth Ann Seton, who was born Gay Betty Bayley and was a high-society Episcopalian. (Her maternal grandfather was a deacon in the Church of England and Gay Betty had social interactions with George Washington.) Seton was canonized by Pope Paul VI. She had been married, had five children and was then widowed. She never neglected her children despite her punishing schedule as an educator. Maybe that fact alone is enough to make her a saint. She did not give them away. She established the first Catholic girls' school in the United States.

Blandina, who taught my grandmother was, according to Grandma, a very mean woman, or more colorfully as Grandma put it, "mean as a snake." My grandmother, a tough woman herself, did not use such terms lightly, which tells me Sister Blandina, whether saintly or not, was probably similar in behavior to many of the nuns who succeeded her at the school. One cannot learn these things by reading her autobiography, which tells about the times she shone and made herself out to be a hero of the west. When I took Bob McKee's screenwriting course, he cautioned us to always remember biography is fiction and autobiography is fantasy.

Blandina had been brought to Albuquerque by Bishop Jean Baptiste Lamy, who himself arrived in New Mexico along with the United States government in order to bring the light of French Catholicism and Anglo rule to the benighted Mexicans of the Southwest. Some early New Mexico history is germane to my story, for my grade school, through its founder Sister Blandina, only came about because of larger forces on the march in the territory.

Blandina's heart was often with the mestizos. She reported on a visit with an Anglo lady who wanted Blandina to approve a deed for a ranch. Blandina had complete respect from the citizenry and her signature as a witness would make the deed legal. She asked if there was anyone living on the ranch. "Only kangaroos," said the wealthy woman. Her sons had told her those living on the ranch were like kangaroos or coyotes. They needed to be shot so the boys could take over the ranch. Blandina quickly figured out what was going on between the ignorant mother and her two criminal sons. She asked her over to the window of the convent which opened on Old Town Plaza where people were passing by. Some prominent mestizo citizens walked past. Do you know these people, she asked? Oh yes, they are wonderful people. Blandina pointed out these were the people her criminal sons called kangaroos and coyotes. "You may tell them for me that there is a Vigilant Committee which would be highly pleased to meet them. The committee always carries a rope for just such emergencies as your sons are trying to create." (Segale, 1948: 193)

New Mexico Under Spain, Mexico and the U.S.

Mexico had obtained its independence from Spain in 1821 and its early period was characterized by many weak and short-term governments unable to control its vast territory. In 1836, Texas declared its independence from Mexico and, after several short, but bloody battles, including the Battle of the Alamo in San Antonio, General Santa Anna was defeated decisively by Sam Houston in the Battle of San Jacinto, which finalized independence for Texas. After going to war with Texas, Mexico then had to fight a war with the United States (termed the Mexican War in this country and the United States Intervention in Mexico). Of course, Mexico also lost that war. As the saying goes, "Poor Mexico, so far from God and so close to the United States." Differences between the two countries were "settled" with the Treaty of Guadalupe Hidalgo in 1848. The treaty ceded to the United States the territories of New Mexico, Utah, Nevada, Arizona, California and parts of Colorado and Wyoming.

Spanish-speaking New Mexico had owed allegiance to Spain for almost two--and-a-half centuries, more than any other territory turned over to the United States by the treaty. After its brief participation in the Mexican Republic (only twenty-five years), it now became a territory of an English-speaking country that had won control over it through a war many people thought was illegal, including the Great Emancipator himself, Abraham Lincoln. The war had at its base the tenets of Manifest Destiny. Turbulent times were ahead and the history of New Mexico and its people would be forever changed.

Fig. 37. Bishop Lamy statue in front of Santa Fe Cathedral. Wikimedia Commons, photograph by Camera Fiend.

A Vain Frenchman

Bishop Lamy was imbued with a feeling of superiority over the long-isolated clergy of New Mexico and the brown-skinned mestizos of the territory—or maybe it was just that he was French. As the brilliant

Fray Angélico Chavez, New Mexico's premier religious historian (and another mestizo from Wagon Mound) noted in *My Penitente Land* (Chavez: 258), "Lamy was chosen on the Philistine assumption that French priests, for speaking a language derived from Latin, were ideally suited for a people who spoke a Latin-derived language of their own." Perhaps because the mestizos of New Mexico were Spanish, Mexican or Indian (perhaps simply because they were not French), Lamy attempted to reorganize the way the Catholic Church did business in New Mexico. His way of showing the people the path to the truth and the way of Christ was to run roughshod over their native religion (a mix of Catholicism and Indian beliefs) and to subdue their priests. Most people accepted Lamy, though they might be discontented with him, but not Padre Antonio Jose Martinez, the curate of Taos, who felt himself every bit the equal of Lamy—intellectually, spiritually, and politically. Martinez was more educated, more experienced, more charismatic and more intelligent than Lamy, and perhaps Lamy knew it. The arrogant Frenchman did not cow Martinez, as Fray Chavez also wrote in *My Penitente Land* (1921: 259):

> The few native priests were a part of their pastoral life and landscape, proud and easygoing like desert partriarchs [sic]. Besides, they had been educated in Durango when the spirit of Mexican independence was at its highest and, while some resented the American occupation as Mexican patriots, all balked at having an American prelate so close to home. The resentment grew stronger when they felt themselves regarded and treated as dust by the new broom. Chief among them was the famed Padre Martínez of Taos who, unlike his brethren who either left the ministry or exiled themselves to Mexico, stuck to his post and continued the good fight for his people against all abuses, whether civil or ecclesiastical.

The Only Printing Press in a Vast Territory

Shortly after General Kearny entered New Mexico to claim it for the United States, he sent a special invitation and an armed escort to Padre Martinez and other notables from Taos to come to Santa Fe as "a gesture of honor and highest esteem." (Chavez: 79) After Padre Martinez returned to Taos, Kearny wrote to him attempting to purchase his printing press or to have the Padre rent it to him, since it was the only printing press in the territory. The Padre, not being interested in money, responded by lending it to him at no charge and, so, the first American document ever printed in the new territory, *Kearny's Code of Military Laws*, was printed on the press of my distant uncle. The press was then returned to Padre Martinez at Taos so he could continue publishing his newspaper, textbooks, religious tracts and law books.

The Making of a Hero

Lamy has been made famous, as well as sanctified for all intents and purposes, in Willa Cather's novel, *Death Comes for the Archbishop*. In the novel (and too many people forget Cather was a novelist of fiction, not a historian), Cather gratuitously vilified, if not demonized, my fourth great uncle, Padre Martinez. (Cather, 1927: 141, 148) Her description in the novel juxtaposes the evil native clergy with the holy and refined Frenchman in a way that left little doubt as to Cather's sympathies. Fray Chavez (1921: 258), in discussing the Cather novel, wrote: "In *Death Comes for the Archbishop*, Willa Cather...makes a lecherous ogre of... Padre Martinez...while also demeaning his people...."

In fact, the immensely popular and historically inaccurate Cather book notwithstanding, Martinez was a brilliant man who was excommunicated by Lamy on possibly false charges of, among other things, living with a woman as if she were his wife and having children by her. No one knows the true facts of the case and the clash of the personalities and egos involved were immense. What is known is Padre Martinez, who owed allegiance to Mexican bishops and Spain and then Rome, was not compatible with the haughty Frenchman with the Gallic airs who found nothing in New Mexico he liked and who was closely allied with the Americans and the French (and through Paris to Rome).

The cultural clashes of Europe were thus transposed to the isolated mountain villages and valleys of northern New Mexico and sprinkled with the westward expansion of Manifest Destiny. French, Anglo, and Mexican interests were interlaced with the political machinations of Rome, which also wanted to get along with the Americans in this vast new country ripe for great numbers of conversions (almost as important in the Church's eyes as gold itself). History has not yet been able to winnow out the truth of the Martinez-Lamy situation, but the accomplishments of the New Mexican priest were many and Lamy's claims to godliness are open to question. As often happens, however, politics, power and political connections trample the truth and those who write history, or even "historical" novels, become its heroes—the truth be damned.

Today, Lamy is a larger-than-life pillar of Catholicism, while Martinez is a conflicted villain—a gifted, politically active priest who brought the first printing press to New Mexico and who taught Indians to read and write. He was the intellectual and spiritual leader in northern New Mexico who provided native New Mexicans with pride in their Spanish, Mexican and Indian ancestries. He was intensely devoted to education and books. Even Cather had to admit, "The Padre's study table was... piled so high with books that they almost hid the crucifix hanging behind it. Books were heaped on chairs and tables all over the house...." (Cather, 1927: 144)

Lamy, for his many good works, could not accept the New Mexican priests as equals. He clearly felt the French and Americans (but especially the French) were superior in all ways to the swarthy native clergy. According to the historical account of the Martinez-Lamy clash by Ray John de Aragon, Lamy wrote, "Our Mexican population has quite a sad future. Very few of them will be able to follow modern progress. They cannot be compared to the Americans in the way of intellectual liveliness, ordinary skills, and industry; they will thus be scorned and considered an inferior race."

This is how the Frenchman who founded my grade school through Sister Blandina spoke of the Spaniards who had "discovered" the New World, exploring and colonizing a vast landscape larger than all of Europe and many times larger than France. For good or for ill, those Spaniards were giants of world history. And Lamy? He could not even finish building his cathedral, which stands unfinished to this day. I make this critical comment as someone who built a major museum building—a cathedral to science and evolution if you will—completed in 2000. I too ran out of money as we neared the end of the construction project, but unlike Lamy, who gave up and left the cathedral unfinished, I raised the needed funds and completed the building. (Mares, M. A., 2001)

An Educational and Religious Leader

In the political infighting of the day, Martinez, from the recently conquered New Mexico Territory, was no match for the Lamy-Anglo alliance, which had strong influence in Rome. Martinez was an indefatigable educator who insisted girls, as well as boys, be educated—Indians as well as Hispanics. These were very radical ideas at the time. This in spite of the fact that the good Padre's father, my fifth great grandfather, Antonio Severino Martinez, who was once mayor of Taos, kept Indian slaves. The slaves were Indians who had been captured on raids he led to reduce the danger of attacks from Indians in the Taos area and to recapture white slaves who had been taken by the Indians on their raids into Taos. It was a regular give and take, raid and counterraid, losing captives and retrieving them.

Antonio Severino Martinez's *hacienda* stands to this day as an example of classic historical *hacienda* architecture. (Weber, 1996) During the early days of the *hacienda*, however, Martinez abandoned the *hacienda* each year after the harvest and, in order to obtain manufactured items (axes, saws, ploughs, tools, etc.) from Mexico, would journey south. He took the entire family, for it was far too dangerous to leave people behind where they could be raided by Indians and either be killed or enslaved. Everyone would travel to Chihuahua, Mexico, a journey of more than a month. They would reach Chihuahua around Christmas and in March would head back to Taos for the planting of the crops. Antonio Severino's son, José Antonio (Padre Martinez), would also make the trip when he was a youth, long before he became a priest.

Padre Martinez used his significant intellectual and spiritual powers to convince parents in the small villages of northern New Mexico to send their daughters to school with their sons. Martinez's school produced many of the important early legislators of New Mexico. At least sixteen priests, lawyers and judges were trained at his school and with his books, as well as the first New Mexico delegate to the United States Congress. Martinez's ideas regarding education and his activism were considered subversive by some and he was accused of being a ringleader in an abortive Christmas Eve 1846 attempt to kill Kearny's soldiers and their New Mexican collaborators. Padre Martinez was cleared of any complicity in the plot, but the next month, Charles Bent, the first civil governor of New Mexico and a remarkably arrogant and ignorant man, several of his associates and some prominent Taos citizens (including the sheriff and the judge) were scalped alive and then, mercifully, killed by a mob of Pueblo Indians in Taos.

Bent loathed Padre Martinez with singular venom and the governor's semiliterate rantings about the priest were mainly sarcastic diatribes steeped in jealousy. As he had noted in a letter about the "greate literary Martinez,":

> His greate name deserves to be written in letters of gold in all high places that this gaping and ignorant multitude might fall down and worship it, that he has and done condiscnd to remain amongst and instrkut such a people.

Bent's rambling, hate-filled missives stand in marked contrast to the careful and literate writings of the educated clergyman. In perusing the writings of the two after more than a century has passed, it seems clear Bent, despite his military academy graduation, remained an Anglo yokel.

He was unable to accept an Hispanic whose intellect and education far exceeded his own, and moreover, one who was not shy in speaking out publicly against Bent. There was a great deal of grumbling against Martinez at the time Bent was scalped and subsequently murdered, especially given the animus between the two men, but witnesses came forth to say Martinez had saved at least one of the victims of the attack and tried to stop the mob from killing many of the other victims. He berated the rebels, who hoped in vain he would join with them in the uprising. However, he would not support them and they did not dare assault the intellectual and moral leader of Taos.

Eventually, as many as two thousand rebels were involved in the uprising and an Army of four hundred eighty troops under Colonel Sterling Price (soon promoted to General Sterling Price) was sent from Santa Fe to quell the rebellion. Various battles were fought, including the decisive Battle of Taos Pueblo. After the battle, Padre Martinez administered the last sacraments and buried the dead, assisting where he could. Although the padre again attempted to stop the rioting mob, asking them numerous times to surrender and assisting Colonel Price throughout the confrontations, Martinez's many enemies used the unstoppable weapon of malicious gossip (the social media and fake news of that day) to insist he had been the ringleader of the rebellion, bearing false witness throughout the territory and across the centuries. As has been said, "A lie can travel halfway around the world before the truth can get its boots on." Certainly, Padre Martinez was subjected to gossip lies, malicious lies, best-seller lies and religious lies during and after his lifetime. He was too old to emerge victorious from his difficulties with the bishop or the calumny heaped upon him. Death always wins.

Martinez fought Lamy's edicts throughout the territory, particularly those that required parishioners to pay tithes for the services of the Church. He convinced many that Lamy was not good for the Church in New Mexico. That led Lamy to call upon the power of God, as interpreted by Lamy himself, of course, to excommunicate Padre Martinez, damning him to the eternal fires of hell. Martinez scoffed at Lamy's actions, never accepted his excommunication and continued working with his flock, preaching and saying the Mass, fighting against Lamy to his last breath. In July of 1867 as he lay dying, Padre Martinez dictated his last statement, saying in regard to the Catholic Church, "I have professed its holy truth, and my conscience is quiet and tranquil. God knows that this is true." (De Aragon, 108) When he died, many, if not most, of my Martinez and Mares relatives left the Church.

At his death, the New Mexico Legislature proclaimed him "the Honor of his Country." (De Aragon: 109) The late Fray Angelico Chavez said of Padre Martinez in *My Penitente Land*, "...his headstrong character caused him to be gravely maligned, even by a few of his own—and finally by the Cather novel—when he should long ago have had a heroic monument as Hispanic New Mexico's greatest son." (Chavez: 259) Chavez had a suspicion Padre Martinez really did live with a woman as a wife and had children with her. He could not prove it, however, and neither could Lamy.

In 2006, a larger-than-life statue of Padre Martinez was installed in Taos Plaza, a fitting monument to a giant in New Mexico history. It stands only a few miles from the Martinez *hacienda* where he grew up. Alas, ignorance is rife in America as we seem to be desperate to become the world depicted in the film, "Idiocracy." Red paint was poured on the statue's foot in 2017 in the belief Padre Martinez, defender of Native Americans and Chicanos, was somehow involved with De Vargas, a man who died almost a century before Martinez was born. Fools. Ignorance, anger and a paint can—what a combination.

New Mexico history was not taught in the Catholic schools I attended and I doubt my distant relative would have received fair treatment had it been. The nuns were, after all, spiritually descended from the Lamy-Blandina alliance. In grade school and middle school there was no biology or science taught. We learned the three "Rs" plus a fourth—Religion. We learned to read and write well, to understand the rules of grammar, to understand basic math well and to express ourselves effectively. Religion was mainly rote learning through repetition of hard and fast rules of the catechism and dire threats of eternal damnation. We learned even (or, perhaps, especially) saints suffered, everyone died and if you ate meat on Fridays or missed Mass on Sundays you would spend eternity in Hell. What a tough religion.

Fig. 39. Ten-foot-tall bronze statue of Padre Martinez in the central plaza of Taos, New Mexico. Wikimedia Commons, Carole Henson.

18

Altar Boy

My family, especially the women, was strongly religious. Most women on my mother's side of the family had come from long lines of Catholic ancestors going back for centuries, many through Ireland. On my mother's side, members of the Gutierrez family had even helped build San Felipe de Neri Church in Old Town. Women on the Martinez side of the family were also religious but they left the Church over the unfair treatment of Padre Martinez by Bishop Lamy. Because of Lamy's injustice, my paternal grandmother became a staunch Methodist, as did the rest of the Martinez clan. If the Church could do that to a great man, then they wanted nothing more to do with the Church.

Becoming an Altar Boy

I became an altar boy at San Felipe Church, as did my older brother a few years before I joined. Anthony was seven years older than I. Several of my friends also signed up. We never knew anything about sexual abuse in those days and I doubt anything was going on with the altar boys when I was there. I know it happened to some altar boys at San Felipe long after I was gone from the Church, actually and metaphorically, but nothing untoward ever happened to us. I have not been to mass in more than a half century.

I do not remember exactly why I became an altar boy but it seemed sort of cool at the time. The new altar boys had to learn the basics of serving mass and other church functions, how to help the priest get his own vestments on, the proper responses to prayers in Latin, how to put on our own robes, how to check the altar to make sure everything was ready for mass, provide a backup in case the host was somehow dropped and how to help the service move along at funerals and weddings.

We checked the wine levels in the bottles behind the altar and lit the candles that would glow during mass, then put them out after mass. There was quite a bit for us to learn and do. I learned years later my older brother and his friends used to drink the church wine regularly. Not me. I tasted it once and found it sickeningly sweet. Those were my teetotaler days in any case. Of course, I was ten. The downside of being an altar boy was having to serve the six a.m. mass, which in winter meant getting up in the dark and walking the four blocks to the church in the cold. They always hung this duty on the younger kids, probably because we were fired up to be altar boys and happy to be there in the freezing winter or at rosy dawn in summer, walking to church all alone from our homes. One had to arrive early enough to help get things ready, so I was usually there by five-thirty after Nina woke me at five.

The priest's vestments reflected what happens in the Church calendar: for example, purple for Lent, green for regular days, violet for funerals, white for Christmas and Easter. Altar boys at San Felipe de Neri Church always wore black surpluses and white chasubles. I do not know who cleaned them after we used them but the chasubles were always impeccably white and nicely starched. Mass was in Latin in those days, so our responses to the priest were always in Latin. Our prayer books were bilingual (Latin-English), so we more or less understood what was said in mass and what our responses had to be. It unspooled unchanged from day to day in any case, so practice made perfect for us altar boys.

Fig. 40. San Felipe de Neri Church, Old Town, Albuquerque. Wikimedia, Camera Fiend.

There were some benefits to being an altar boy. For one thing, you were part of the show and spectacle of mass. There were no girls allowed in those days, just boys. (In fact, maybe girls are still not allowed to be, what? Altar girls?) At San Felipe, there was a percussion bell that the altar boy sounded as the host was raised during mass. We used a small percussion mallet with soft velvet tips. This is my body. Ding, ding, ding. It was an important part of mass, indicating the transmutation of Christ's body, a basic Catholic belief. Again, when the host was raised in veneration, the chimes would sound.

I loved playing those hollow tones during mass, like playing a really small xylophone that marked the progress of the mass. These were rung even at low mass. Serving high mass was a big deal because there was music from the organ and choir and there seemed to be more going on. Christmas and Easter were the biggest deals and there were more priests, altar boys and worshippers in attendance for those ceremonies. Weekday masses took place before school, so if I were serving one of those masses, I was looking at a long day. Another fun thing altar boys did if they were serving the six in the morning mass was ringing the large bell in the bell tower of the church. It was something I really loved to do, when the thick rope would pull me off the ground with each peal. I also knew I was waking up the whole neighborhood for a mile around. "Hey, it's six, time to get up and get to mass." I was a veritable Chicano Quasimodo. Early the other morning, I was having my coffee and sitting on my patio listening to the bell of Lamy's Santa Fe Cathedral ringing at six. I wonder if there are still kids who are excited to pull the rope, or could it be a recording now?

You Never Know What Might Happen at a Funeral

Serving weddings and funerals was a part of the altar boy's duties too. I loved serving funerals because they were always on a weekday and got me out of school for an hour or two. My first limousine ride was in a hearse, sitting in front of the coffin. Usually, we rode with the priest in one of the black (or, rarely, white) limousines. While a funeral got one out of school, the raw grief at most funerals was troubling. I saw a mother try to throw herself on the coffin of her child as the coffin began its descent. When I first started serving funerals, the coffins were sometimes lowered by hand-cranking. In later years, an electric motor did the job. Some people would faint (this also happened to the groom at one wedding.). A downside of funerals (well, there are many downsides to a funeral, starting with the dead body), but a major one for altar boys who wanted to buy baseballs, was no one ever tipped the altar boys at a funeral. Eventually, everyone got planted in the ground, the service was over, everyone felt bad and it was time to go back home or to school. No tip. *Adios*.

My mother told me of a most unusual rosary that took place at San Felipe Church. One of the parishioners was extremely ill and scared to death of dying. He had somehow gotten involved with a fundamentalist preacher who told him if you believed in the risen Christ with enough fervor you could not and would not die. It was the answer he was desperate to hear considering the unbearable terror caused by his impending death. He and the preacher met several times and the preacher told him not to worry about his fatal disease; he would not and could not die. Period. His family was concerned he had gotten involved with some sort of religious crackpot and strayed from the Catholic fold, where death was accepted as an inevitable part of life.

He died, of course, and was laid out before the altar in a coffin for the recital of the rosary to help speed his soul into a glorious afterlife. The family was praying and grieving. The corpse was on display (unlike most funerals, where the coffin was closed). As they were praying, they heard a loud voice from the back of the church: "Get up! Get up. You cannot die." At first people could not figure out what was going on. It sounded like a madman had wandered into the church, but it was the fundamentalist preacher, three sheets to the wind, weaving down the aisle toward the coffin.

People were transfixed. No one moved. What was happening? Was this a nightmare? As he approached the coffin, he began to yell again. "You are not dead. You cannot die. You must believe in Jesus' name that you are not dead." (The preacher obviously did not understand death, much less embalming.) There is always a pause in the action when something truly unexpected is happening and we do not know how to respond. During the pause, the inebriated preacher grabbed the corpse by his lapels and started yelling even louder, "Get up! Get up. You are not dead."

Now the family and the priest finally began to respond, as well as the shocked morticians. The preacher had the corpse half-way out of the coffin yelling into the dead face covered in embalmers' heavy makeup. Then the family got to him and tried to pull him away, but he had a death grip on the body and refused to release the corpse, who was really paying no attention to the drama surrounding him. He truly was the corpse at his own funeral.

As the family pulled the preacher away, the coffin tipped over, opened up, and the corpse came tumbling out. The corpse did not have pants on since the "viewing" was of his upper body only. Women screamed. Someone fainted. The men of the family started beating the shit out of the preacher. The funeral guys hustled to wrangle the corpse back into its coffin. The police were called. Eventually a shaken priest continued with the rosary. The family was traumatized, but it had been the most memorable and exciting rosary ever.

The most impressive funeral I ever served was when the pastor of San Felipe Church died (not the one who stole my money, unfortunately, which I will discuss next). The pastor's body was laid out in the coffin and they had positioned his gold-bejeweled chalice in his hands. The mortician had done a good job, too; he really looked like he was asleep, which is unusual for most corpses. People always say someone looks like they are sleeping, but it's hardly ever true. I have seen a lot of corpses, but few look like they are asleep. They look dead. Very dead. In fact, if you saw someone sleeping and looking like the average corpse, you would dial 911 ASAP.

I had served mass for the dead pastor, so I knew him. (In fact, he's pictured in my first communion photograph.) He was always nice to me. He looked great. At his funeral, I was assigned the brass incense censer, which would put out dense puffs of smoke as I moved it about. The incense crystals were spread over live coals in the thurible. I would hand it to the priest to use in part of his blessing of the corpse and the congregation but then he would give it back to me while he sprinkled holy water all around. I could not resist moving the thurible around to make more smoke, plus I liked hearing the little metallic clicking sounds it made.

The memorable part of the funeral, however, was not the dead priest or having fun with the incense censer. As we walked out from the sacristy to start the funeral, the church was filled with anywhere from fifty to sixty monks in their habits with their cowls up. They were everywhere.

My jaw gaped and I was taken aback by their presence. What were these monks doing here? They filled the altars, the side aisles, the pulpit, the choir loft. I had never seen such a thing. I had seen a few monks now and then, but generally San Felipe de Neri Church either had diocesan priests or Jesuit priests. Perhaps the monks were Franciscan, since the church of San Felipe was founded by Franciscan priests and was originally named St. Francis Xavier. The Duke of Alburquerque required the name be changed to honor King Philip of Spain (El Rey Felipe) and eventually the church became San Felipe de Neri in 1776, just as our nation was being born.

San Felipe de Neri Church was built under Spanish Colonial Rule in 1793 (after the original adobe building, built by a Spanish Franciscan priest, had collapsed). San Felipe de Neri is not a large church but can hold several hundred worshippers. All pews were filled for the funeral. The school's students were required to be there for the pastor's funeral and were brought there with each class. I, of course, had a front row seat. The monks stood during the entire service.

Shortly after we got the funeral underway, the monks started singing Gregorian chants *a cappella*. I had never heard such music in that church or anywhere else for that matter. It was haunting, remarkable, ethereal and pulled one's imagination to other times in monasteries in deserts across the globe. Men's voices reciting the prayers of the mass in song: it felt ancient, almost biblical. They made our pitiful little church choir even more pitiful by comparison. I thought, if these guys could sing at all of our services, we would have massive attendance at mass. They were amazing. I still listen to Gregorian chant as part of the music I prefer. I do not remember accompanying the priest's body to the cemetery. Perhaps the body was shipped somewhere else for burial. Too bad he was unaware of his terrific sendoff. He would have loved it.

Weddings Were Another Story

The downside of weddings was that they were always on Saturday, one of the two non-school days during the week. They were usually in the morning. People were usually happy. There was often music. In later years I was the church organist, so I supplied the music. Even better, unless the groom or best man or father of the bride was especially stingy, the altar boys would get a tip—as little as five dollars or as much as twenty (i.e. five baseballs) in other cases. Serving a wedding, the altar boys were definitely front and center. We got to see, up close and personal, the feelings and emotions of the wedding party and the closest relatives.

Generally, everyone is on their best behavior for the nuptials and they have not yet started drinking. I watched one extremely nervous young groom already gasping for air at the start of the service. Looking back with the maturity of years, I am sure he was having a panic attack and, who knows, might even have suffered from asthma. What was clear to me was he was not going to make it through the wedding ceremony, which included the preamble, the vows and the mass. Sure enough, a few minutes into the wedding, his eyes rolled back in his head and down he went. He was carted off to the sacristy, where they worked on him like a prize fighter who had taken a sucker punch, slapping and moistening his face, giving him water. Within twenty minutes, he was shakily brought back in to face the music. The mass and ceremony went on and he seemed to man up. The mass proceeded without further incident. It was a rough start to their marriage, but the worst seemed to be over.

19

MUSIC AND THE CHURCH

A Cardboard Piano

When I was five years old, someone, probably Nina, decided I should learn how to play the piano, maybe because her dad was a musician and she hoped just maybe I got a drop or two of his musical talent. I did not want to play the piano, or any other instrument for that matter, except perhaps the guitar, like my hero Roy Rogers. Playing the guitar was off the table, however. What I really wanted to play was outside with my friends. Also, and this seemed like a deal breaker to me, we were poor and we did not own a piano. How can I play a piano without a piano? But Nina signed me up anyway. Piano it would be, with me complaining all the way. Being a kid, I dutifully went to my first piano lesson from an Anglo woman, Wanda, who lived in the neighborhood.

She was very nice and had two pianos in her home, which was only a couple of blocks away from my grandma's house. She and her younger sister had never married. One had orangish hair (my teacher); the other had very white hair. Their mother, who was silver haired, lived with them and seemed ancient to me, even compared to Grandma. All were remarkably pale, almost translucent and definitely not Chicanos. As a family of three old women of very short stature (under five feet), they had a large, lovely *pueblo* style house. Uncle Billy used to call them

Arsenic and Old Lace, referencing the 1943 Frank Capra film about two old women who turned out to be serial killers. My teacher had a few other students, but after a couple of years it was clear I was her best pupil, so she began having me play for the public.

I got to hear a real piano for the first time at her home. I had never played a piano, or even seen one played for that matter other than on television. Nina, ever the clever one, got a long piece of heavy blank cardboard and measured, cut, drew and reproduced a full-sized, 88-key cardboard keyboard she taped to the kitchen table. She had me practice my music for an hour each day. It must have taken her a lot of work, for the keys were the proper size and were black and white. That was my piano for the first year of weekly piano lessons. It worked. I made very few mistakes and I was able to then play the real piano at my piano teacher's house and actually hear the notes, which was fun. Each week, I showed progress.

Somehow, Nina worked hard over the next year to scrape together enough money to buy a real full-sized upright piano for me. Ironically, for someone who never married, she was a seamstress in her spare hours, specializing in wedding hats and other wedding apparel mainly made from tulle and wire, or she tailored people's clothes. If there was any extra money around the house it came from Nina's sewing. She was a good seamstress. She taught me to sew and I specialized in monogrammed towels, pot holders and monogrammed pillow cases on the electric sewing machine. She worked each day, then sewed at night or on weekends. The piano was a used Chickering piano and cost her twenty-five dollars (over three hundred in today's money).

That was the piano I played the day Grandma died, by which time, thirteen years later, I actually knew how to play the piano pretty well. I do not know what happened to that old piano, but I think Nina just had someone haul it away when she got too old to take care of the hundred-year-old house and had fallen ill herself. Today that same piano, reconstructed and refinished, might sell for thousands. *¡Siempre los Mexicanos.*

Performing in Public

I played only classical music. I did not play "by ear" at the start, but always read music off the sheet music or music books I got from my piano teacher or from Nina. My sight reading was excellent, so I could pick up any piano piece that was within my skillset as a pianist and play it in short order. I gave a number of recitals, generally at my teacher's house, for very small audiences.

Gradually, I performed for larger crowds around Albuquerque, always playing complex classical pieces, such as "Finlandia," by Jean Sibelius, which is a *tour de force* for the pianist. In 1960, I was part of a statewide youth concert in Las Cruces, New Mexico at New Mexico State University. I dressed up in a sport coat (I have no idea where I got it, but my mother probably borrowed it) and played the long and complex piece, the "Spinning Song" by Mendelssohn, which went pretty well. I was the final performer in a group of twenty-seven young people, closing out two days of music classes and performances.

I was totally frightened when I had to perform in public as a solo performer, never having done such a thing before, sitting at a magnificent Steinway concert grand piano in a large auditorium in front of hundreds of people. The Steinway was the first grand piano I ever played and a long way from my silent cardboard keyboard. We had to memorize the pieces. I made a small mistake, but covered it pretty well. I learned performing solo piano pieces was not for me. It was a strain on my equanimity and some of the kids who played the piano at that concert were more serious students of piano and quite more talented pianists than I. If I wanted to be best at something, it was not going to be performing as a classical pianist, not without much more dedication of time and effort to studying and practicing than I was willing to invest (and even then, I might lack the talent). I was pretty good, but pretty good was nowhere near good enough for a concert pianist. However, being able to play the piano well opened a number of doors for me.

If you can play a piano, you can play an organ (and even find your way around a xylophone or accordion). It turned out the principal of San Felipe School, Sister Anne Lorraine, needed someone to play the organ in school musical performances. I was always getting into trouble as a school kid, but I was happy to play her small folding electric organ, which made pretty good organ sounds. "Sure," I said. "I can do it." How hard could it be? She was a good person and we got along well. She could have expelled me many times from junior high school, but she always supported me, no matter how much trouble I was in or what crazy things I had done. She was definitely one of the good nuns.

She told me I was very smart, but somehow she felt I wanted to fail and kept getting into trouble. It was true. For example, I was a patrol boy wearing the beautiful red coat and white Sam Browne belt and badge (almost like the Canadian Mounties and Sergeant Preston of the Yukon). I loved it. We were crossing guards at all roads, including Route 66, and also had to put up the flag and take it down each day, so we learned flag etiquette and how to properly fold a flag. Unfortunately, we had to keep ourselves and our uniform jacket and belt impeccably neat and clean, which meant if we got into a fight or played football or baseball, or had red *chile* for lunch, we were likely to get demerits for being sloppy. *Chile* really stood out on that white belt. So many demerits and you were tossed off the force, which is what happened to me. It was fun while it lasted though. It was a break from the normal humdrum of school.

Baseball Interlude

I was a fanatic Dodger baseball fan in 1955 when the Dodgers played in the world series against the mighty New York Yankees. Uncle Billy was a Yankees fan, but I loved Dem Bums. I don't know why I picked the Dodgers to support, but I had read about Duke Snider, Pee Wee Reese, Gil Hodges, and African Americans such as Jackie Robinson and Roy Campanella on the team, so I always rooted for them.

The Dodgers were never a World Series threat—until 1955. I knew that most people thought the Yankees (think Mickey Mantle, Yogi Berra,

Whitey Ford) would walk away with the series, as they always did, but hope springs eternal for Dodgers fans. Games were played without lights in those days, as baseball should be played, so on weekdays all of the games would take place when I was in school. The problem was, how could I follow the team's radio broadcasts if I was in school? God bless the crystal radio.

Crystal radios were remarkable devices that could pick up radio signals using only the power of the radio signal itself. No batteries. No amplifier. No speaker. No electric plugs. It was like magic. Just a simple receiver and an ear bud to hear the broadcast. They were small and silent. It is as if they had been invented to allow boys to hear the World Series during school hours while being supervised by suspicious nuns. Which is exactly what I did. I do not remember anymore where I got a crystal radio, but I assume that either Nina or Uncle Billy was involved. The thing was, I had to keep the nuns from finding out, or it was goodbye radio, or knife, or water gun, or whatever contraband I might have smuggled into school. Most nuns, even the decrepit ones, were sharper eyed than eagles. I knew if the teacher saw the radio, she would take it away, so hiding it was extremely important. In more ways than one, those of us boys who were a bit loose with the rules were like the prisoners in the movie "The Great Escape" always taking risks, but sometimes they paid off.

We had old desks with an inner book storage area under the desk's top. I set up the radio inside the desk before class started, while the teacher was occupied elsewhere, and ran the earbud wire through the ink bottle hole. If the teachers were good at seeing us boys all the time, we had also become very skilled at keeping track of where their attention was focused, so we would know when to fire the bobby pins, toss the erasers and so on. It was sort of like the predator-prey interactions I studied as a professional ecologist, like the kangaroo rat and the owl. Perhaps that is why I became an evolutionary ecologist in my professional life, and a desert biologist at that. I had been the prey species in grade school. I was able to hide the radio's tiny ear bud while taking time to answer questions, or read, or whatever was required. As class proceeded, I would drop a pencil or otherwise lean toward the desk, anything to get the earbud into my ear. Being on heightened alert in this manner, I was able to keep up with the games. The difficult part was not being able to tell my friends what was happening on the baseball diamond. The radio was never discovered. Having to hide the radio from the ever-watchful nun made the games even more exciting than they already were.

When not in school, I would listen to the games on the real radio at home. Amazingly, my Dodgers won the series, even though the poor Dodgers had never won before and the great Yankees never lost. This had seemed to be an immutable law of the universe. Maybe that is why I rooted for the Dodgers. Chicanos love the underdog. Wonder why? To this day, I still say the best game I ever "saw" was the seventh game of the World Series as called by Vin Scully on the radio in 1955. It was time for Dodger baseball. I had never been to Brooklyn, never seen a major league game, and here I was in Old Town in Albuquerque listening to the Dodgers beat the Yankees in faraway Yankee Stadium. The invincible Yankees, who had not lost a World Series since before I was born, were beaten by my Bums. I lorded it over Uncle Billy who had to listen to his Yankees go down in almost inconceivable and ignominious defeat. It was a great win for a ten-year-old. Too bad I didn't bet a baseball on the series.

The Dodgers left Brooklyn shortly after their series win for their new home in Los Angeles. I did not know at the time that the construction of the new Dodgers Stadium would uproot and displace a whole tightly knit community of Los Angeles Chicanos. I am sure they were much like Old Town inhabitants, but the city did not really care if they were left homeless, nor did the corporations involved. (Nusbaum, 2020) They never do. I never really forgave the Dodgers for leaving Brooklyn, except for one day when the whole Dodger team stopped in Albuquerque and played an exhibition game at Tingley Field, home of the Dodger's farm team, the Albuquerque Dukes. It was the very stadium where we would hang out in the parking lot late on summer nights during games to collect home run or long foul baseballs to use in our own baseball games. Uncle Billy was a star pitcher for the Dukes in the 1920s, long before I was born, and when he coached in the policeman-fireman games, which were held there too, I was usually in the stands. The Dukes eventually became a Dodgers farm team. Tommy Lasorda, legendary manager of the Dodgers, was the manager of the Dukes in 1972.

It was my Dodgers once more, but this time in the flesh. The faces I knew so well from sports magazines and baseball bubblegum cards were in my neighborhood. They played against the University of New Mexico Lobos, our local college baseball team. On that afternoon all was forgiven and the fact they were moving to Los Angeles did not matter. I would frequently watch the Albuquerque Dukes play in that stadium.

The arrival of the Dodgers was my wildest fantasy coming to life for a twelve-year-old boy stuck in flyover country far away from major league baseball. The World Champion Dodgers were going to play in our local ballpark. Thus, for one glorious afternoon in spring, 1957, I watched Sandy Koufax and Don Drysdale pitch against each other. Koufax pitched for the Lobos and Drysdale pitched for the Dodgers. I guess the professional players did not want to destroy a young college pitcher's fragile confidence by beating their pitches to death. The Dodgers pitched a no hitter against the college team. No surprise there, what with one of the greatest pitchers in baseball history pitching against them. After the Dodgers left Albuquerque for Los Angeles, I switched my allegiance to, who else, the Yankees. Change had never been very good for me and I have never liked change in anything, so when the Dodgers left, I sided with the people of Flatbush. How could you not be loyal to your town, your stadium, your neighborhood and your fans? Chicanos are loyal to a fault: to their friends, family, barrio, state and country, whether or not that loyalty is reciprocated.

Music in School and Church

Apparently, there were not many people who played the organ or even the piano in San Felipe parish so it did not take too long for the pastor of San Felipe Church to approach me about playing the organ in church. He knew I had been playing the principal's small organ in school.

"Can you play a full-sized organ?" he asked.

I thought, How hard could it be?

"Sure," I said, but I had never even seen one.

"We can pay you," he said.

"Great," I said. "How much?"

"Well, if you play at mass and other things with our choir, I could pay you two dollars per week."

That was like mowing a lawn each week with a push mower, but we were not talking about hard work here. Fifty-two weeks in a year. That's over a hundred dollars. What couldn't I do with that? Ka-ching, ka-ching. "Okay," I said. We shook hands on the deal and I was now the organist for San Felipe School and for San Felipe de Neri Church. I was twelve years old.

I met the choir when I went to choir practice for the first time. It consisted of three old ladies, all of whom knew my mother and Nina. The choir loft was up a winding dusty stairway like a ship's ladder, and the loft overlooked the church. It was in the rear of the church and faced the altar. It had a very low rail. There was no OSHA and no building codes during the period when the choir loft was built more than a century earlier, and apparently no required updates.

The loft was home to an ancient upright pump organ, which must have been all the rage in the 1800s. They must have pulled it up with ropes after delivering it in a wagon. I fiddled around with it and figured out how to play it, while pumping with my feet. It had many stops that had to be adjusted to give the proper tone and it also had a peculiarly pump organ sound, much like a giant accordion, sort of wheezy notes like an old squeezebox.

We practiced once a week in the evening for a couple of hours. Before we knew it, it was Sunday high mass where the organ and choir would put on a show for the folks down below with a performance of religious music. I had known most of the songs from serving high mass as an altar boy, so it was not a very steep learning curve, and the written music was no challenge. It seemed to be written by or for an inexperienced organist. Church music is basically simple; think "Silent Night." I could read music easily in any case. Studying and playing classical music will do that for you. Music is a language and learning to read music was like learning to read and write Spanish or any other language, with the difference being the letters of the language translated to notes on the instruments or in the song lyrics.

We practiced regularly and finally got to where we were working well together, but always within the limits of our talent and ability. The old ladies loved singing, even though they were not always on pitch. Perhaps they had been better in their younger days back when Al Jolson was popular in the 1930s. Still, there were moments when we sounded pretty good. Shortly after I became the organist, the church got a new electric organ, probably a Hammond. Now I could make some real sound come out of it without pumping madly like the Wicked Witch riding her bicycle in "The Wizard of Oz." The old pump organ was relegated to a dusty corner of the choir loft, a reminder of the past, unless the Hammond malfunctioned or the electricity went out.

The transition to the new organ took place in 1957. Like most young boys, I had become interested in rock music, thanks to Elvis and the Doo Wop rockers, and had worked out a number of piano pieces of

Elvis, Fats Domino, and Ricky Nelson hits, as well as the song Tequila. So, after Elvis came on the scene, along with Frankie Lymon and the Teenagers, various Doo Wop groups and others, all my nonchurch music was rock and roll. I still played classical music for my piano teacher or an occasional recital, but my heart was in rock and roll. I was part of a small rock band with some classmates in 1958. The first time we had a "paid" gig, they paid us in tamales and enchiladas. The second time we played was at a dance and a fight broke out, chairs were tossed, cops were called (always the police). We were not paid at all for that performance. Fights were typical at dances in our part of town. The main thing you needed to know was to keep playing, no matter what.

I Quit

I played for a year with the church choir. Like Scrooge McDuck, I was counting my money and planning on getting paid after a year of practice and performances, thinking not only of baseballs but presents I could buy for Nina and Grandma. Remember the old saw, don't count your chickens? One day I was called out of class in the middle of the day to meet with the pastor. Ruh roh. Pastors were all powerful. They reported directly to the bishop, a Wizard-of-Oz-like character whose cathedral was in Santa Fe and who was seldom seen, except at major church functions. Even the school principal had to bend to the wishes of the pastor who ran the whole parish. What could such a powerful person want with me? I felt like Dorothy in the presence of the great and powerful Oz. A wild thought entered my mind, maybe he was going to pay me.

We met in the principal's office, a place of authority for him. And who was I? I was an eighth grader with some musical ability and a smart mouth and maybe a Chicano "cheep" on my shoulder, as my wife says, but not much else. Father Joseph Malloy. Old, heavyset and very bald with a sparse fringe of white hair on the temples and ears. He was a very white Irishman wearing a very black and not very clean cassock. I will never forget him. It was clear shortly after our meeting began that *Siempre los Mexicanos* was about to come true again.

He buttered me up, telling me how much he enjoyed my playing the organ with the choir and how it made masses more spiritual, how talented I was. Blah, blah, blah. This was not looking good. "There is one problem," he said, "we just don't have the money to pay you." I was at a loss for words, which was unusual for me.

"You owe me one hundred dollars," was all I could muster.

"We don't have that kind of money," he said.

"I think the best thing for you to do is to donate your money to the church. That will help the church and be a good way to honor God."

He said all this with a straight face. I was a young kid, but not an idiot. "You're just trying to steal one hundred dollars from an eighth grader. Stealing from a kid. You owe me one hundred dollars and I expect to be paid, or you can find another organist."

I then quit the choir. Word got out fast. The choir ladies went to see my mother. I doubt my dad gave a shit one way or the other, so they did not bother talking to him. My mother browbeat me into continuing to play, tossing every guilt trip there was my way. Due to her pressure, I continued playing without pay, since the pay business was a sham in any case. The church was conning me. What a weakling I was to return.

I Quit Again

Another year passed (and, if only theoretically, I lost another hundred dollars) but I continued working hard with the choir. Christmas was fast approaching and we were practicing for high mass, which is a big deal—lots of people, music and drama. It is the second biggest feast day of the year, after Easter. We were trying some new pieces I had worked out on the piano at home. Unfortunately, the old women of the choir were really in their cups with Christmas cheer, having started celebrating earlier in the day. They usually smelled like rum or brandy and, in my innocence, I had mentioned to my mother that the perfume they used smelled like rum. My teetotalling mother said they were probably having a "little drink" to get ready for choir practice.

This time they did not emanate a pale hint of rum, like maybe rum flavoring for a Christmas cake. Oh no, they smelled like a barroom filled with drunken sailors; they were pickled in it. Could they carry a tune? No. They found it a challenge to carry a tune even when they were sober, but there was no chance in hell they could sing if they had been celebrating with some Christmas libations before mass—and the Christmas high mass at that.

The practice continued. The low railing in the choir loft was maybe two to two and half feet high, if that. No problem if one were sober. But drunk? I imagined their teetering over the railing as they searched helplessly clawing for the correct notes, screeching all the while and falling to the pews twelve feet below. Death on Christmas.

I told them they were drunk and had to stay away from the railing. They could sing from behind the organ, rather than from the rail, where they usually stood. They took umbrage and insisted they were not drunk. What a thing for a kid to say to an adult, they said. I did not drink at all in those days (maybe because I was still fourteen?) so I could easily smell the booze. I was not going to be responsible for the deaths that would surely follow. So, I quit. That's two.

The choir members called my mother, again. Still no sense telling my dad, who was not even Catholic and not a believer in any case. I walked home on that cold afternoon and my mother was waiting. She asked accusingly how I could quit on Christmas before midnight mass? I explained that the three drunk old ladies were going to topple to their deaths over the railing. Did she want that? No, of course not.

"I'll go back with you and talk to them." So, that's how we worked it out. She told the choir ladies (all friends of hers from their younger days) that they had to position themselves behind the organ or there would be no midnight mass with the choir. It turned out okay. The organ was good and loud; the singing was not good and not loud and, best of all, no one died. That was success in my book. No one was any the wiser, since the choir was often off tune. I never played with the choir again.

20

FAMILY GATHERINGS, PLAYING IN THE BARRIO

Picnics

A highlight of family social life as a child was the occasional Sunday picnic, perhaps twice each summer, which involved a large group of twenty or so relatives traveling either to the east side of the Sandia or Manzano mountains east of Albuquerque with their pine/juniper and ponderosa pine forests, or to the more mesic Jemez Mountains, at least two hours (in those days) northwest of the city, with their richer and denser forests of piñon pine, ponderosa pine, blue spruce, Douglas-fir and aspens. There were many rivers and streams with birds, fish and other creatures along the water (especially in the relatively water-rich Jemez Mountains).

In the mountains, exploration took on a new dimension. Once, while trying to grab a fish, I fell into the Jemez River and almost drowned. My cousin, Butch, who was a year older than I, grabbed a large branch and held it out to me so I could grab it as I tumbled downstream. I was five at the time. The water was frigid, fed by snowmelt from the high mountains and I think Uncle Billy was both furious and relieved. How could he explain my drowning to my absent parents? He bundled me naked into a blanket and threw me into the back of the pickup truck for the long, cold trip back to Albuquerque. Butch and I rode all the way back in the bed of the pickup truck, although he had his clothes on and I only had a blanket. I was embarrassed and returned in shame.

On picnics to the Manzano Mountains, we passed a cave where, in the late 1800s, a relative had stood his ground to a charging black bear, killing it, while a frightened friend who was backing him up sprinted away in fear. The story was told in such a way that it was clear the good guy stood there, shot straight and killed the bear, while the craven coward crept away when danger appeared, leaving his friend to the mercy of the bear. The cave is still there, but few who race past it on south State Highway 14 know the story of the coward and the bear, a small moment captured in the lore of early New Mexico and used to teach a lesson in courage, loyalty, and friendship to children. You do not abandon your friends, no matter the danger.

Nature

Sometimes on those picnics deer or other animals would appear. If my grandmother had little to say about animals, my mother had no qualms in her dealings with them. Birds were good, especially parrots and mockingbirds. Big mammals that could not hurt you (e.g., deer) were to be left alone, not hunted and definitely not eaten. Big mammals that could hurt you (e.g., bears) were to be avoided by staying out of their territory. Snakes? As far as my mother was concerned, the only reason God put snakes on earth was for them to be killed. Any snake, anywhere, anytime. Invertebrates such as spiders, scorpions, roaches and, especially, the dreaded centipedes, filled the same niche in God's plan as snakes.

Mostly her dealings with wild animals were based on fear and ignorance. Ironically, I ended up being an international biologist for my life's work, studying mammals and other animals in rain forests, deserts, grasslands, mountains and thorn scrub across the globe, from Albuquerque to Africa, Pennsylvania to Patagonia, Idaho to India.

Once my extremely myopic mother had just finished a bath and was drying off when she felt a spot that would not get dry. Putting on her glasses, she discovered a large desert centipede sitting on her shoulder, its size magnified by her nearsightedness and by its proximity to her eyes. The panic that followed could only be described as blind, as she was unable to scream or even to open the bathroom door to escape. The centipede never stung her, but she was as jumpy as a toad on a dancefloor after that every time she took a bath.

Many years later, the terror of her impending death was less pronounced than the horror of the centipede in the bathroom. She had asked me when she was diagnosed with diffuse interstitial fibrosis, a fatal lung disease of unknown cause, how I thought she would die. She said she was afraid to choke to death trying to get air. I told her she would most likely enter a coma before she died and would be unaware of anything going on, including dying. She thought that did not sound so bad and, for a moment, was less afraid of death. Unfortunately, she went to see her lung doctor and told him what I had said. He responded by saying, well, you could strangle to death. He had the MD, not the PhD of her son, but he was way off base on how to deal with old women petrified of dying. When her time came to die, she was in a deep coma, just as I had predicted, and she slipped away from life without having the awareness to be afraid. As so often happens, anticipation of death is much worse than the actual dying.

Rattlers and Rats

My mother died without ever understanding why I study mammals and other vertebrates, knowing only that after such a long education, my research should have been limited to finding a cure for cancer. Animals were best left alone.

There was another time my mother was frightened into a paralyzing fear and I may have had something to do with it. When I was in high school, I got interested in rattlesnakes and collected them around Albuquerque in nearby mountains, hills and deserts. I wanted to preserve a rattler and had caught an especially large, six-foot-long diamondback rattlesnake near Los Lunas, just south of Albuquerque. It was an enormous and frightening animal with a large triangular head, beautiful coloring, long fangs, a thick body, bright contrasting black and white bands on the tail and a long, beautiful rattle on the tip of the tail. Now I faced a dilemma. Collecting a large rattler is one thing, but killing it is another. How does one kill a large rattlesnake before preserving it? There was no Internet in those days and no one to talk to about such things.

I had read about people freezing to death and learned how it was a relatively peaceful way to die. After one got over the feeling of being very cold, a person just slipped away. In fact, Rainbow Valley on Mount Everest is filled with people who died in just that manner. It is called Rainbow Valley because of all the brightly colored climbing outfits on the many frozen corpses forever lying on the snow.

How about freezing the snake? It would gradually go to sleep thinking (if it thought at all) it was experiencing an especially cold winter as it hunkered down in its den. So, I put the animal in a clear gallon jar and placed it on the top shelf in the dark freezer in the garage. We hardly ever used the freezer in any case. Neither my dad nor my mother liked food after it had been frozen. About the only stuff we froze was orange juice, ice cream, *chile*, beans and *posole* (and that was mainly at Christmas), so this little-used freezer seemed to offer the ideal way to kill the rattlesnake.

The plan would have worked fine, except about twenty minutes later, while the snake was still warm and pondering its situation, my mother made one of her very rare visits to the freezer to get something for dinner. She had a visceral fear of any snake and, as far as I know, had never even seen a rattlesnake. A friendly garter snake at a picnic was alarming to her. Question: Had any snake ever done us any good? Answer: No. (Just ask Adam and Eve.)

So, there she is in the dark garage and she opens the freezer with its bright light inside. Rising up in front of her only a few inches away from her face, at eye level and rattling away in the clear gallon jar was a giant diamondback rattlesnake. She must have thought it was a nightmare come true and it was happening in her own peaceful freezer in her nice tranquil garage. How could this be? What was happening? Her first instinct was to call for my dad, but he was not around and she had no voice anyway. Then it dawned on her, still with no voice to even scream: Michael. It had to be Michael.

She finally screamed my name. I was in the living room reading and I heard her scream from the garage. Uh oh, I thought, she must have found the rattlesnake in the freezer. What is she doing in the freezer? I went racing out to the garage. There she was, transfixed by the snake, unable to even close the freezer door. The snake had risen up to the level of the closed lid and was rattling away to beat the band and threatening everyone with a deadly poisonous strike should they try to touch it. I closed the freezer door.

"What are you doing out here?" I asked, perhaps trying to divert blame? She was not easily diverted, however.

"There's a giant rattlesnake in the freezer. What's it doing there?" These sentences were almost screamed at me.

"I collected it and I was trying to freeze it to death so I could work with the specimen. In a few hours it would have all been over."

She was not really understanding at that moment and did not want to see how the rattlesnake could not have hurt her unless she dropped the jar or something. We have a saying in Spanish, "*No hay pero que valga*," which sort of means there are no excuses that will excuse this thing that was done. Mine was definitely a *pero que valga* moment. I finally calmed her down enough for her to go back inside the house and tell me what she wanted out of the freezer. I promised to get the snake out of the freezer after it died and promised to never put a snake of any kind in her freezer again.

Sometime later, however, I had a five-foot-long bull snake that was a sort of a pet. I had collected it on a field trip to an arid grassland in eastern New Mexico and it was both beautiful and friendly. Bull snakes are large and can hiss and bite, but every once in a while, one of them will be especially tame with people and will not bite at all. My snake was one of the tame ones. You could place it around your neck and handle it easily. I decided to hide the bull snake at home where no one would find it. I knew if my mother saw it, I would have to get rid of it after some dramatic scene, since she did not distinguish one snake from another. After the freezer incident, I thought any snake would look like a rattlesnake to her.

My dad knew his snakes pretty well, being a cowboy raised on a ranch, but I doubted even he wanted a big bull snake loose in the house. I had a good cloth bag I kept it in when I was away from the house and would take it out to play with when I was home. Bull snakes are beautiful snakes, sort of a golden-brown and black checkered. They are rather heavy bodied and are pretty fast, too.

One night when I was away from home, my mother and dad were watching TV. The house was rather dark except for the flickering lights of the television. Suddenly this very big-bodied and very long snake came out of my room and slithered in front of the television set. My mother thought she must be seeing things, but shook my dad awake so he could see it too. Seeing them and the TV images move, the bull snake rose up like a cobra and hissed loudly, sounding like a rattlesnake and vibrating its tail.

My mother thought it was another rattlesnake, of course (but I had learned my lesson about vipers), but my dad, old shepherd that he was, said it was a bull snake. He went to get a broom or something to pin the snake, but it was faster than he was and took off through the house. My dad chased it, but it got away. When I got home there was hell to pay about hiding snakes in the house. Again. The sad thing is the snake was never seen again. I only hope it worked its way into the backyard and then reached some of the nearby farmland to feed on rodents.

The only other animals-in-our-house story concerns some very large albino white rats I had decided to raise. Again, I did not tell anyone. What good could come of that? I had them hidden very well in the garage. When I got home, I would watch them or play with them in the evenings. As luck would have it, they got out of their cage when I was not home. Where do large white rats with pink eyes and pink tails go when they escape from a cage in the garage? To my mother's clothes washer, apparently.

Once again, my mother came into the garage, this time to do the laundry. She opened the washer and tossed in some clothes. Suddenly a big white rat climbed to the top of her laundry and was looking at her with large pink eyes. "Eek." is not the sound a woman makes when surprised by a large rat The next word out of her mouth was...Michael! My dad came into the garage, found the abandoned cage and then the new nest in the insulation in the garage wall. *Ay yay yay.*

Over the years I have learned wild animals almost always escape from their cages, usually to the consternation of people sharing a house with you. In fact, it happens frequently with people who have such wild and often dangerous pets as African lions, leopards, crocodiles, pythons, or poisonous snakes. Animals are good at working their way out of situations not to their liking. Even zoos have a hard time keeping their animals contained. It is best not to keep wild animals at home where if things can go wrong, they will go wrong.

Hollywood

Growing up in New Mexico in the late 40s and 50s, I was aware there were Chicanos and Anglos (or gringos, as we called them), but I never saw an African American until I was four years old, and that was on the Santa Fe Super Chief going to Hollywood, California. The conductors were mostly Black. Numerous members of my maternal grandfather's family had migrated to California in the early 1900s. We would visit various aunts and uncles after the long train trip to Los Angeles, sitting in our seats all night long. I was so young when I went to California the first couple of times the visits are just a dim memory, though I do remember having lunch at the Brown Derby Restaurant. Who could forget having lunch in a hat? My uncle Joe (Butch's dad), who died of alcohol poisoning at thirty, worked in a cleaners and was a tailor to several Hollywood stars (including Fred Astaire and Bing Crosby). He would drive us around Hollywood pointing out actors walking along Hollywood Boulevard. I mostly remember his chartreuse convertible, my first time in a roofless car. Hollywood seemed very exciting to me. Over the years, we lost track of the Devines of California.

Joe's name is of interest in that his actual baptismal name was José Inés Esquibel. Inés is not a common name for a man. Joe was born in 1920 and three years before he was born, General José Inés Salazar, one of Pancho Villa's officers in the Mexican Revolution, had died. He had once been incarcerated in New Mexico and was defended by none other than Elfego Baca. Almost certainly, Joe was named in honor of the colorful Mexican general who fought for liberty for the people of Mexico from the dictator, Porfirio Díaz, the *de facto* lifetime president of Mexico.

My maternal grandmother was the matriarch of the Devine family and she, my aunt Florence (Nina) and I, made at least two trips to California. I was convinced I was a cowboy and wore two cap guns in a fancy holster and a cowboy hat, like Roy Rogers. I would regale train passengers with stories of my ranch and cattle. As Nina said, "We didn't have enough money to buy a goat and you were constantly talking about your cattle, your horses and the ranch."

Constantly talking. Sounds like me all right. I truly was all hat and no cattle, as the saying goes.

21

SISTER BLANDINA AND SAN FELIPE SCHOOL

Everything Was Green

After my parents left me, I attended kindergarten at San Felipe School, which was in the basement of the old Bernalillo County Courthouse that had been converted to a parochial school. I did not like kindergarten at all. I was bored. Little industrial-green tables and little green chairs, everything Lilliputian and green, as if we were illiterate Irish dwarves. Even the lettercards were green. I already knew how to read, so playing with lettercards was a very unexciting way to spend the interminable days. Even worse was the time we had to spend with clay. What are you going to do with a rather dry ball of gray or green clay? You could stick lettercards into it and make boat propellers or even plane propellers. You could roll many tiny balls of the rather dry clay, broken off from the larger ball and throw them at your friends or use an ice cream stick to get some speed on them when you shot them. Clearly, I was not a budding sculptor.

I could not wait for the time to pass. We had recess, lunch and naptime. I walked to my grandmother's house for lunch. Those were the highlights of my day. I do not know what I would do without naptime today, when I am seventy-nine and a poor sleeper, but at five years old, who naps? I knew when I got out of school at the end of the day my faithful collie Lassie would be waiting for me at the schoolyard gate, just as she had waited for me at lunchtime, and we would walk the block back to my grandmother's house. She never failed to be there. She was one of the few constants in my life as a little boy.

No Mares Here

Since my folks had abandoned me, I saw no reason to keep their name, thus in first grade I changed my name to Devine. The teacher would call on me, "Mr. Mares," and I would stare straight ahead as if I were deaf. "Michael Mares." Nothing. She would walk up to me and say, in my face, "Mr. Mares, I'm talking to you." "My name is Michael Devine," I told her. She argued with me for a while but then went back to her desk. She would not call me Michael Devine and I would not answer any questions put to Michael Mares, who did not exist as far as I was concerned. So, they called for my Aunt Nina. Poor Nina, who had never married or had children, now had to deal with all of the problems of her sister's troubled five-year-old, 24/7/365.

I do not remember if Uncle Billy came to school with his older sister, Nina, or not, but he probably did. After meeting with the teacher, Nina came back home and said I could not just change my name because I wanted to. "Why not?" I asked. "There's no one named Mares around here." She said my parents would be coming back soon and everything would be all right then, so just keep using the last name Mares. I kept using Mares, but things did not turn out all right. Nina was seldom wrong and I believed everything she told me, but that time she was way off the mark.

Psyops For the Boys

I am not sure exactly what students in the 2020s are supposed to learn in elementary school, but grade school mainly taught me to survive in a challenging and often hostile environment. The nuns we encountered included some of the meanest people I have ever met. They utilized terror and physical abuse to control the children, especially the boys. They were bullies and used physical punishment, threats of eternal damnation, death threats and other psyops techniques to break the will of the boys. Always the boys. Most nuns favored girl students, unlike what one hears in current politically-correct studies showing males are favored in school. Not in our school. I never saw a girl tortured or beaten.

In third grade, a Chicana nun from Arizona, Sister Mary Nolasco Sanchez, who resembled a five-foot tall, stocky ape, would position boys who had caused some minor problem in class (usually talking, laughing or throwing something) about six inches from the blackboard and then proceed to hit them hard in the back of the head with her hand moving upward and forward. Bang! Thump! Bang. Thump. Bang. Thump. It happened fast with a definite rhythm. This resulted in their head snapping forward, hitting the board and bouncing back again, when the process would be repeated.

The nun was able to get a fairly consistent rhythm going between the board, her hand, and the oscillating head of the third-grade boy, almost sounding like Joe Louis working out on a punching bag. Usually, the boys were hardly able to stand after a period of pummeling. I have no doubt the repeated insults to the head led to minor concussions. After about five of her vicious hits, the boys would have trouble walking and making it back to their desk. All the rest of us could do was watch helplessly and be glad this time it was not our turn at the board. One student who was interviewed for an article published long after this cruel nun had died said that Sister Nolasco "...never got old, remaining youthful looking and vibrant." Must have been her regular punching bag exercise regimen. She worked out every day.

The sister was good at meting out punishment and had developed her talent for head-banging over many years, no doubt. She had been one of the first teachers to arrive at San Felipe school, even assisting the legendary Sister Blandina Segale, the supposed saint-to-be. Sister Nolasco was sixty-three years old when our paths crossed, unfortunately for me. When I researched her on the web, I found the following comment: "Noted for her guidance, concern, and love for the students, she was a legend in the parish." Oh, she was a legend all right. Could my memory be wrong? She sounds like an absolutely wonderful person, a veritable caring angel. Alas, my memory is not wrong and whoever wrote this claptrap obviously never had her as a teacher, or was a girl at the school or was one of those writers who never speak ill of the departed, whether or not they even knew the person. She punished boys for almost anything, probably causing brain damage.

If your penmanship was not perfect (and mine was awful), you spent hours after class cleaning blackboards, writing as perfectly as you could on the lined blackboards and killing an hour or two each day working after school just for the sake of being punished. I cleaned thousands of erasers in my day and can only imagine what the chalk dust did for the allergy problems I have suffered from throughout my life. I cannot remember how many blackboards I filled throughout all the school's classrooms writing "I will not talk in class" over and over and over. My hand and arm got tired, but it did not affect my talking. It only made me angry for missing my baseball games.

A Frontier Nun

When Bishop Lamy arrived in Santa Fe in 1851 and started his battles with my distant uncle, Padre Martinez, he decided the diocese was in desperate need of teachers. Although Padre Martinez himself was the director and teacher in a grade school for children in Taos, boys and girls, Lamy wanted a larger commitment to education across the territory than a single school in a single mountain town could provide, much less one paid for and overseen by a mestizo priest with a fiery personality. Lamy knew the Bishop of Cincinnati, John Baptist Purcell, an Irishman who had studied in Paris. Purcell oversaw a convent of nuns available to serve in the new territories. They were called the Sisters of Charity.

I might have suggested a different name for the group, for charity is far too charitable.

When the newbie nuns heard there was a need for their services in New Mexico in the West, Sister Blandina and her fellow sisters answered the call. Blandina was a gutsy Italian who was able to deal with anyone, from bandits to renegade Indians, from Billy the Kid and his gang to difficult Indian Chiefs. In Trinidad, Colorado, she talked Billy the Kid out of scalping the local physicians who had refused to care for his wounded bandit henchman whom she had cared for herself. As Billy himself said to the bandits after Sister Blandina asked him for the favor of not scalping the local physicians, "She is game." Sister Blandina had kept the killer alive for many months before he finally succumbed to his wounds and perhaps found Christ due to her efforts. Blandina felt fear, of course, but her core belief in the righteousness of God led her to deal with everyone without prejudice and with acceptance.

Fig. 41. Sister Blandina Segale sketch.

Oh Pancho

The highlight of my grade school years occurred for me in the fourth grade on Thursday, January 28, 1954. For us, the day began as just another school day in our usual humdrum existence. However, we were suddenly asked to stand and walk outside as a class to see something special. What on earth could it be? As we walked into the hallway, we saw all the classes coming out of their classrooms. Was this a fire drill? There was none of the fire drill urgency, however. No bells were ringing. No one was telling us to keep calm. We were led outside to the hard-packed dirt schoolyard in front of the tall imposing school building. And then things suddenly became dreamlike.

One of the favorite television shows of all the boys at San Felipe School was the Cisco Kid. Not so much for the performance of the Romanian, Duncan Reynaldo. playing a Chicano (natch) but for his lovable companion, Pancho, played by Leo Carrillo, a real-life bonafide Chicano. Given his role—he was in part playing the buffoon ("Let's went, Cisco" or "I hear footprints")—but he was always wise, the hero's stand-up partner and quick with his gun or his fists. Carrillo was proud of his Hispanic heritage and traced his family in California back through medieval Spain, just as I have traced my family back a thousand years. (Carrillo, 1961) He was trained as an artist and worked as a cartoonist for a while for the *San Francisco Examiner*. But then acting called and he worked his way steadily up the acting ladder through Broadway, the silent films, the talkies and eventually television and the Cisco Kid. He took on the role of Pancho when he was seventy. Amazing, considering all the riding, fighting and stunts he had to do during the show. So, why this disquisition on Leo Carrillo?

Fig. 42. Leo Carrillo as Pancho from the "Cisco Kid" television series and his horse Conquistador. Wikipedia.

Because, as we stood in the schoolyard on that cool, sunny January morning under the brilliant blue sky, who should we see walking up to us? Oh Pancho. It was Leo Carrillo himself, in the flesh, wearing his cowboy outfit, packing a six-gun and in full color. (I had never seen him in color.) Our day was made; our year was made. Pancho made a little speech to us about studying hard and doing well in school and, as he prepared to say adios, he pulled out his pistol and fired it into the air, with the loudest BANG any of us had ever heard and a good deal of smoke. Oh Pancho, you are forever in our memories.

Carrillo was in Albuquerque to meet with schools that had participated in the March of Dimes as part of his effort to fight the dreaded disease of polio that was sweeping through schools, including ours. He visited some of the larger upscale gringo schools in the Heights, was in a parade with his horse, Conquistador, on Central Avenue in the Heights and then little San Felipe School was added to his itinerary because we were one of the poorer schools that he insisted he visit. He wanted to visit a Hispanic school with poor Brown kids. He did not want his visit limited to Gringo schools having only White kids. Thank you, Pancho. Gracias. I wish I could have ridden away with you on Conquistador to California and away from San Felipe School and Old Town. Forever.

Fig. 43. Bernalillo County Courthouse later converted to San Felipe de Neri School. 1900 historic photograph.

22

A "Murder" by Nuns

We'll Have to Kill Him

Our teachers wore black habits with stiff, white hoods draped with a black veil and a large stiff, white collar. The women were shapeless in their flowing robes and for many years as young boys we debated whether or not they were anatomically complete. We were never able to prove they were or were not, however, and like the sophists, debated at great length and in complete and baffled ignorance, about whether nuns had breasts. Some suggested they had them surgically removed so they could never leave the nunnery. It sounded logical. Why else stay with an organization that seemed to make you so malicious toward children and never have children of your own?

Nuns had ways of breaking little boys. I saw two nuns hold a mock trial followed by a mock execution of a poor first-grade boy who had been talking too much. Talking was not tolerated and it is one of the main reasons I got into trouble regularly. I was then and continue to be today, even at seventy-nine, a talker. As I tell my wife, "You'll know I'm dead when I stop talking." Our school had been the county courthouse for decades before being turned over to the church and converted to a school building. The top floors must have been cells at one time, for they still had bars on the windows (why else would you need bars on windows on the third floor, fifty feet above the ground?) There was nothing friendly about the building. It rose ninety feet or more into the New Mexico sky and was an imposing stone structure.

In our classroom, there was a massive walk-in safe with a heavy, black, steel door. This must have been where county records had been kept in territorial days. Inside, the safe was as silent and as black as the tomb. The door was black painted steel with delicate gold trim and so heavy it was difficult to open and close. The safe was in my homeroom and was used to store class supplies. Its combination lock had been removed, leaving a small hole in the door, probably for safety reasons. One could not get locked inside the safe, supposedly, but little kids did not know that.

The two nuns had set up a dramatic staged prosecution of the little boy and brought the child (who was already crying) into an office adjoining our classroom. I had a clear view of what transpired and could see and hear them berating him for his behavior and telling him his talking could no longer be tolerated. They went through the motions of a trial and informed him since he refused to stop talking in class (and they had given him many, many chances before), he would have to be killed by being placed in the gas chamber.

The child practically fainted with fear, the snot running out of his nose, but the nuns dragged him into the dark safe, telling him in a loud voice it was the execution chamber. They then slammed the heavy steel door, enclosing him in the black, airless room. Like Poe's *Telltale Heart*, I could hear the muffled screams of the little boy and hear his fruitless banging on the heavy steel door.

Then one nun told the other, again in a loud voice so that the child could hear, "Go get the gas." The other nun promptly went to her office and returned with a bicycle pump. It was inserted into the small hole where the lock had been and, with a yell to "turn on the gas," the nun began pumping madly with the small air pump. In the black, silent interior the child must have heard the hissing begin, for his muffled screams increased.

The nun stopped pumping and let his cries die away. Then they opened the door and said that this time they had decided not to kill him, out of mercy (why not charity?). They said if he ever misbehaved again, he really would be given the gas. Clearly this was a well-rehearsed act of perversion and cruelty. Why do I think they would not have done this with an Anglo kid? They would not have done it in front of Leo Carrillo, either, but they felt free to do these kinds of things in front of and to helpless children. Know this, Sisters, I will remember. ¡*Nunca mas!*

The incident with the safe was the worst act of cruelty (of many) I witnessed in my ten years at the school. To this day I feel guilty for watching them torture that little boy and not trying to help the child. I was ten years old. Surely I could have done something. I could have cracked the nuns over the head with a baseball bat or something. I felt I was an honorary cop and fireman. But I did nothing. I sat there and watched this horrible tragedy run its course. This is one of the reasons I do not tolerate injustice quietly, even as a seventy-nine-year-old man. If you do not stand up for what is right, you will carry that very heavy burden forever. Or as Edmund Burke noted in the 18th century, "All that is necessary for the triumph of evil is that good men do nothing."

I think we all started out as nice little boys and I have a photograph to prove it, where all of us boys and girls are dressed in impeccable white at our first communion looking like pure little angels and standing in front of the nun's convent. How did we go from those beautiful children on that innocent Sunday morning in May to being such troubled and difficult school children, almost in the blink of an eye? One could blame the parents, of course, as many would do in these modern times, but I will put my money on the abusive nuns and the bullying priests, with maybe some blame thrown in for the parents too.

Fig. 44. San Felipe de Neri School, first communion class outside Sister Blandina Convent, 1952.

Low Expectations

In these racially sensitive times, I wonder if we could have been experiencing the soft bigotry of low expectations, as George W. Bush described it. Almost all the children at San Felipe School were Chicanos which, after all, is why Leo Carrillo came to see us. His visit was the only benefit of being in an impoverished Chicano school as far as I could tell. None of us was likely to amount to much in the world, as the nuns surely knew. What did it matter if you were bashing a future ditch digger's head into the blackboard? It was not as if the boy's wealthy parents would descend upon you in protest, waving lawsuits, or as if you were damaging the brain of a future neurosurgeon. These kids were not going to write books, after all, they might not even read books; these were Chicanos, the people that Bishop Lamy had described as "not as intellectually lively as Americans," and it was Lamy who brought the Sisters of Charity to New Mexico and founded San Felipe de Neri School.

I have a small frame of comparison regarding the influence of low expectations. My Anglo wife attended Holy Ghost School in Albuquerque. Her school was situated in the Heights, not in the Valley. This meant all her classmates were Anglos. If a Hispanic happened to be present, it was because their dad was in the Air Force, since the Catholic children of military families attended Holy Ghost School, which was near the military bases. My wife recalls only a single Hispanic child during grade school or middle school. By contrast, I only recall a small handful of Gringos at San Felipe. The nuns who ran her school were Sisters of the Immaculate Heart of Mary, not the psychopathic Sisters of Charity of Cincinnati. She tells me she never saw or experienced anything like what I describe for San Felipe School. No beatings, no bullying, no torture, no mock executions and no schoolmates doing the kinds of things that I did. She loved school. White versus Brown? Or could it just be me?

Pigeons or Squabs?

In the sixth grade, while cleaning blackboards throughout the building, I discovered a couple of seemingly secret doors on the third floor of the old courthouse that would permit one to enter the bell tower, which of course was now an inaccessible part of the school building and off limits to everyone. A key was required, but I discovered where the keys were kept. It was a key no one would ever miss since no one ever went up there. I had to clean blackboards all afternoon after filling them with promises to stop talking or to write better, thus I had access to all offices and other spaces in the school. I rooted around and found a key closet holding many keys. It was just a process of elimination to find the key to the secret door. I saw that one particular key was never moved.

The key opened a small door just past a larger door leading to a very narrow, dusty and steep wooden stairway with steps much higher than normal. There was no handrail and if one slipped, it would be a long fall to the wooden floor below, although the foot-thick layer of bird guano might help cushion your fall. The place was ripe with the smell of pigeons and guano built up over a half century or more. Dead mummified adult and baby pigeons were everywhere. Oh, the *odeur*.

The stairway led to a very large room where a large bell sat on the guano covered floor, but it had been silent for a half century or more. The belfry was filled with pigeons, perhaps a hundred of them, making a loud and constant cooing sound. The pigeons had been living and crapping here for decades. What a great thing to discover at school. And no one would know anything about it since we could lock the door behind us. No one else had a key. What an adventure.

A group of four boys and I decided to capture the pigeons and I offered to set up a pigeon coop, about which I knew nothing, so that we could keep the birds. We got hand nets and pillowcases and gradually began to chase the pigeons around the belfry. It was hard and dangerous work. Sometimes we were working on windowsills twenty feet above the floor and seventy feet or more to the schoolyard below. Of course the pigeons were cooing and flapping and trying to get out of the belfry, though we had closed off most of their potential exits. It was wings noisily flapping, dust clouds of pigeon poop, nets swinging at the birds, leaping down on them if they crashed into the floor in their panic and generally having a great time as eighth grade boys, alone in what seemed to be a dangerous space designed just for us.

Since I was taking many pigeons to Grandma's house (only a block away), it was getting tougher and tougher to take care of them in cardboard boxes. Pigeons are eating and pooping machines. Then Uncle Billy came through again and made a pigeon coop with chicken wire and places for them to roost. I took care of at least twenty-four pigeons for months, until they got too expensive and troublesome to care for. Man, could they eat.

What to do? I could either let them go (after working so hard to get them and keep them?) or kill them and eat them. No one in the house wanted to eat pigeons, so I decided to ask the nuns if they would like squabs to cook for the sisters. I called them squabs, which are immature pigeons and sometimes considered a delicacy, because I had already seen that calling them pigeons did not get peoples' taste buds salivating. "Squabs? Oh, that would be wonderful." Nuns and priests will eat anything if it's free.

I figured I was racking up points with the nuns and perhaps would catch a break when the next bit of trouble came around that I was sure I would get into, despite my wanting to "be a good boy." I also guessed, correctly, the nuns would not be able to distinguish an adult pigeon from a young pigeon. So, I slaughtered the poor pigeons, cleaned off their feathers, took out their guts, washed them and gave them to the good Sisters of Charity. Turns out they loved the feast and I got a lot of "attaboys" from the sisters for my donation of slaughtered pigeons.

Back to Eighth Grade

I liked the eighth grade and the nun who taught us, Sister Mary Louise. There was always some new thing sweeping through the school among the boys: knives, clothespin guns, popsicle sticks. Knives are self-explanatory. We always had a pocket knife to play with outside class or use as a tool to make something, like the clothespin gun, for example. We used the popsicle sticks to shoot the small, round, green, hard fruits of the cottonwood trees that were abundant in the Rio Grande floodplain where we lived and would shoot them with popsicle sticks. We called the fruits *tatonies*, but there is no such word as far as I can find, not in English or Spanish.

Water Guns

The latest craze to sweep through San Felipe School in 1958 among the boys was water guns. Shooting water was not only fun, but an ideal toy for the hot weather in Albuquerque. It did not hurt anyone and after shooting someone, or getting shot yourself. It dried off quickly in the dry desert air. It was even refreshing. The guns were tiny and could to be hidden in our underpants where the nuns never looked. The teacher would walk out of the room for something and long streams of water would be shot around the room. If someone were acting as a lookout and sounded the alarm, the water guns would quickly disappear into our undershorts.

One day, as luck would have it, the principal, Sister Anne Lorraine, caught us in the act when several of us were firing our water guns. She appeared suddenly in the doorway, as nuns seemed to be trained to do, and somehow we had not set a guard in the hallway to give a warning. She had us dead to rights.

"Give me the water gun, Mr. Mares." "I'll put it away, but I won't give it to you. They cost too much money and I do not want to lose it." She started walking toward me ominously. "Give me the water gun." Closer and closer she came, holding out her hand as if I were actually going to give her the gun. Imagine that. To paraphrase Charlton Heston who would say many years later when he was addled and appeared in a pro-gun commercial: "You can have my water gun when you take it out of my cold wet hands."

"Sister, I can't do that. I'll put it away." "No, let me have it." "I can't just let you have it. Don't make me do this. If you keep coming, I'll have to shoot." And that's how people rope themselves into doing really stupid things, especially teenage boys. On she came, implacable as a battleship, as I pointed the water gun at her face.

"Don't force me to shoot," I begged. She was only a few feet away. She stopped for a second, wondering how this was going to go down, then decided to make a lunge for the gun. I was faster. I emptied the water gun into her face and wimple.

Now was I ever in trouble. I had just shot the principal in the face with a water gun. Moreover, she was someone I liked and respected, except when she tried to take my water gun away in front of the class. She took the gun away from me and told me to accompany her to the office. I spent so much time in the office it was almost like another homeroom, but this time I had done something beyond the pale and I knew it.

She told me to go home, while she thought about what to do with me. She was really angry. Since everything had unspooled in front of the entire class, it was embarrassing for both of us, though mainly for her, I am sure. Although the thought crossed my stupid thirteen-year-old mind to ask for my water gun back before I went home, I decided not to do that. I went home and of course said nothing to my parents. How can you tell your mother you just shot the principal you really liked in the face with a water gun? No way she would understand that. This was far worse than the rattlesnake in the freezer incident.

A Second, Third and Fourth Chance

Next day I reported to the office rather than to my home room. The principal said she was not going to let me expel myself from school. She said I could make something out of my life if I tried. You are smart and you have talent, but you need to start behaving properly. You need to stop getting into trouble. She ordered me to get the big washtub from the storeroom (the kind of laundry tub that I used to be bathed in as a little boy) and put it in the main hallway.

"Here's your water gun. Start filling that tub. Go to your classes, but every spare minute, including lunch time and every time the bell rings to change classes, I want you filling that tub in the hallway with your water gun. Before class, after class and for an hour after all classes are over for the day, keep filling the tub. You will come in early in the morning and keep filling the tub. You will do this for three days and when the time is up, you will bring me the water gun."

My punishment was a mix of public-shaming and physical punishment for my tired, aching hands. Even at that age, I was not so dense as to not recognize the great favor she had done me. I could have been history at San Felipe and out of school with just a word from her. So I emptied the little water gun into the giant tub for the next three days. Word had gotten out about what I had done, since it had occurred in front of the whole class. I wisely refrained from shooting my classmates as they passed by in the hall making snide comments. It was sort of like being in the stockade during colonial times, but with very tired hands and a little water gun. At the end of the three days, I returned the water gun to her and said I was very sorry it happened. She told me to go back to class and never mentioned it again and neither did I. I never got the water gun back, either.

In researching this book, I learned Sister Anne Lorraine's real name was Mary Catherine Kelsey. Why do nuns change their names? She was born in Denver and died at the ripe old age of 94 in 2012, 54 years after the water gun incident. She had been born one year after my mother, 1917, and entered the nunnery in 1937. She received a Master's degree in education from Creighton University, a private Jesuit university in Omaha, Nebraska, in 1955 (not long before I met her). She went on to receive a second master's degree in guidance counseling from the University of Northern Colorado in 1969, nine years after I last saw her. I would guess she was an outstanding guidance counselor.

I never heard anything about Sister Ann Lorraine later, but I know she would have remembered me, though not for the best of reasons. Still, I would bet dollars to doughnuts no one else during her long life as a nun and principal ever shot her in the face with a water gun. Maybe she even told the story at nun gabfests: "Sisters, I can top that story..." Sister, you were definitely one of the good ones. Oh, and by the way, you were right; I made it, thanks to you.

The *Kraken*

In some ways things had not gotten much better by ninth grade. We had been hassling with a cranky and very old nun as the school year was winding down. We were approaching our release from so many years of incarceration at San Felipe School through our upcoming graduation. One day the old nun did not show up in class. Was she ill? Did she die? We never found out. Nuns keep their own counsel. However, there was an Anglo student teacher who arrived to take her place, a petite blond. The student teacher was very nice and very cute, at least to us ninth grade boys. (She was not a nun.) She did not look much older than we were. But we had been out of control and had even driven away (or killed?) the elderly nun who fought with us each day. We were on a roll.

What I never could figure out is why they brought in this very nice, innocent, newly-minted teacher to try to control what was likely the most challenging ninth grade class in the long history of the school extending back to territorial days. We had been honed by years of psychological and physical abuse and other bad behavior on the part of the nuns. We had responded in kind.

Talk about a trial by fire for the inexperienced teacher. She absolutely did not know how to handle us. We talked, we threw things (erasers, chalk, spitballs, *tatonies*), we got out of our desks and walked around the room, we went to the bathroom when we felt like it, we laughed and in general we were complete jerks. She kept trying to get our attention, but we would not listen to her. She had no chance of controlling the class. It went on for at least an hour or two, then she broke down and started crying and ran from the room. We had never seen such a thing from a teacher and that made us quiet down and feel bad for her.

When the principal came in a short time later, she gave us a well-deserved tongue lashing. Were we trying to destroy a young teacher? The teacher was so upset she had been forced to go home. She lived only a block or so away from school, just off the plaza. The boys were ordered to walk to her house as a group and apologize and beg her to forgive us. We felt suitably chagrined. We all went together and found her at home and really did apologize to her. We felt terrible. We were sincere. And she was so nice, too. She was still crying. Poor thing. I do not know if she forgave us. She said that she forgave us, but I am not sure I believed her. If the tables had been turned, I doubt I would have forgiven such an unruly class of ninth grade morons. We knew we had gone way too far. What was wrong with us?

In "One Flew Over the Cuckoo's Nest" in the mental hospital where Jack Nicholson and other men were being treated for psychological problems, the staff hoped to exert strict control over the patients who had been taking more and more liberties with the regulations of the hospital. Like San Felipe, everything was about control in the mental institution and, like the ninth-grade boys at San Felipe School, things were out of control. In the film, the mental hospital administrators brought in a sadistic sociopathic nurse, Nurse Ratched, who some have likened to the Antichrist. She exerted ironclad control over the men and was merciless in putting them in their place, demeaning them, and even putting their lives at risk. In essence, she emasculated them in front of each other.

After we broke the pretty teacher down and possibly made her consider giving up the teaching profession altogether, the bat signal glowed over the evening New Mexico skies calling forth the most frightening nun we had ever seen, or even imagined, to deal with our wild class. The school brought in Sister Ratched. The *kraken* was now in charge. She was mean to her rotten core and was our worst nightmare come to life. She made it crystal clear that our days of cutting up and upsetting teachers were over. We belonged to her now. She was built like a professional wrestler and carried a large, heavy wooden rubber stamp (the kind used to stamp the inside covers of textbooks). She did not need the reflective glasses of the walking boss in "Cool Hand Luke" to be the perfect villain. Her wooden block would do just fine, thank you. She would use it to underscore her willingness, or even eagerness, to hit boys over the head with it (always the head). She tapped her fingers against it as she walked around the room, tic, tic, tic. She gave the impression that her major goal in life was to crack the head of some smartass ninth grade Chicano asshole at San Felipe School, which included most of us boys.

Something was different and "off" about her. We thought she was nuts and well she may have been. For one thing, she was always in motion and hardly ever at the front of the room (all the better to sneak up on miscreants). Generally, teachers stayed at the front of the class, where they might teach, for example. The front of the classroom was where they could watch us and, more importantly for us, we could watch them. Not this one. She loved standing at the back and we were not allowed to turn around to see her. Eyes forward. The better to surprise you when you misbehave, my dear.

We had encountered a new predatory hunting behavior we had not been trained to avoid. We were like the little marsupials in Australia that had no chance of survival against the new and terrible predator, the house cat, that had been released on the continent, leading to their eventual and unavoidable extinction. We tried to get a handle on her strategy beyond fear or the air of insanity she projected, but she was hard to fathom. I had a friend named Tommy who was talking and passing notes one day and did not see the looming figure of this massive nun coming our way from behind. Tommy was just across the aisle and one desk ahead of me. I tried to warn him *soto voce*, "Tommy. Tommy," but I could not get his attention. Plus, I knew the predator would get me too if I made my warning too obvious.

One second Tommy was laughing and, suddenly, WHAM! She struck a lightning-fast blow none of us saw coming. She hit him hard on the head with the edge of the wooden block and split his head open. He fell to the floor barely conscious. Blood flowed everywhere. His parents were called and he was taken to a doctor for stitches. Chaos reigned. The big nun probably received a medal from the other nuns when they were in the privacy of their convent sharing a glass of wine, since she had finally quieted down the incorrigible ninth grade boys with fear, violence and blood. She had deadly force and was not afraid to use it. The boys had it coming. (Look what they had done to the poor young teacher.) This time, however, the crazed woman had picked on a child who was old enough to tell people what had happened to him without worrying about a feigned date with the imaginary gas chamber like the poor little first grader years earlier.

Like us, Sister Ratched was obviously out of control too, even the control of the other nuns. Like a pederast priest, she had to be removed. She never appeared in our classroom again. I assume she was sent to a mountain retreat to relax in the beauty of the sunny Jemez Mountains, along with many pedophile priests from New Mexico who stayed at the Servants of the Paraclete. They were all child abusers after all; they should get along just fine. She had clearly earned her spurs in the convent and had earned a paid vacation free of restless and smartass boys. She had met and harshly dealt with the ninth-grade boys of San Felipe School. It was a victory for control. Control at all costs. Yay, Sister.

There were some good nuns in our school, but frequently the women we had to deal with (ironically called the Sisters of Charity) were wicked. As I have traveled the world, I have met incompetent bureaucrats, anti-*yanqui* paranoids, people envious of me or filled with hatred for the United States, angry policemen, scared soldiers, intelligence agents who felt the need to interrogate me and people who were just plain mean. (For example, there were people who cheered wildly when they heard my field crew had burned alive when their VW bus burst into flames. The crew escaped the flaming vehicle and were okay, but the early report was they were literally toast.) But the most difficult foes I ever encountered were amateurs compared to some of the nuns of San Felipe de Neri School who made our childhoods miserable, but who taught us to endure, whatever the cost.

From these women, I learned to keep my wits about me when the situation appeared to be deteriorating, no matter how frightened I might be. The more threatening the circumstances, the calmer I would force myself to be. Sometimes the difference between getting hit over the head with a board or slipping out of danger had to do with keeping one's cool in the line of fire or defusing a situation with humor. It was very good training for fieldwork; I have been able to meet difficult situations with great equanimity.

23

HIGHWAY LABORER

Working for College

I think my family did not want me to have the impediment of a Spanish-speaking background, as it might condemn me to a life digging ditches for a living, so they did not speak Spanish to me. If one peruses the neighborhoods of Old Town in the U.S. census of 1900, 1910, 1920 and later, most of the men's occupations were "day laborer." Despite their not wanting me to spend my life as a common laborer, I did dig ditches as a pick-and-shovel worker each summer over five years during high school and college in order to pay for my education (a dollar ninety an hour for forty to sixty hours a week). It was extremely hard, hot work under New Mexico's blazing sun, especially when highway paving was involved, with the asphalt being spread at three hundred degrees Fahrenheit and the laborers (me) walking on it to make sure it spread evenly and to fill in and smooth out any discontinuities. I had good metal-toed boots, but they would get so hot I had to get off the asphalt periodically to keep my feet from burning up. To this day, when I am traveling by car and pick up the smell of asphalt along a highway under construction I am transported instantly to the heat and hard work of a highway laborer in the blistering New Mexico summer. It is engraved somewhere in my brain, like the aroma of roasting green *chile*.

During my high school and early college years, the Interstate Highway System was being built (thank you, President Eisenhower) and laborers were needed. Most laborers used the work to earn money for their families, but some, including my cousin, Butch, my older brother, Anthony, and I used the developing highway system to pay our way through college. I thought I was well paid as a union laborer (always a union man as a member of the Hod Carriers and Laborers Local #16) until one extremely hot and long day. We had begun work at five in the morning and quit for the day twelve hours later building the runways at the Albuquerque Sunport. Curiously, my uncle Christie Mares had worked as a laborer and helped build the first runways at the Albuquerque Airport during the Great Depression. Later in my life, when I became a pilot, I would take off and land on the very runways I had built.

After work, I stopped in at the local supermarket to get a cold soda pop. While checking out, I asked the sacker, who spent the entire day in air-conditioned luxury and carried nothing heavier than a bag of groceries, what his salary was. He said two dollars and ninety cents an hour. A dollar an hour more than I was earning. Aagghh! For carrying little paper bags of groceries? Good lord, was I in the wrong business.

Work Habits

Most of the laborers were Hispanics or Indians, and several of them were drug addicts with the tracks of their injections on their forearms. They worked hard, though, as we all did. It was difficult, often dangerous, dirty work, but such menial laboring jobs were readily available to poor people willing to work. (Zuehlke, 2009) All you needed was muscle and stamina. I dug ditches to go to college at the University of New Mexico. What did I know about other schools, college rankings, prep courses, and so forth? Nothing. To me college was college. I did not know anyone who had gone to college in any case, except an Anglo doctor who had married my cousin, and my older brother who had gone to Notre Dame for a year, then transferred to the University of New Mexico when he found Notre Dame's Catholicism oppressive. I was very impressed by the laborers who worked with me under the brutally hot summer sun and also in the freezing winter. They were never going to do anything but be laborers. Since I was working to go to college and hoped never to dig another ditch, I sometimes felt like an imposter.

That hard work clearly helped my cousin, my brother and me develop work habits that included being unafraid of hard physical labor, long days and jobs that had to be done whether we liked them or not. We carried the lessons learned as laborers throughout our lives. My brother became a PhD professor and a highly respected teacher, historian and poet. My cousin (who had grown up in a bedbug-infested apartment near my grandmother's house after his alcoholic father had died very young) became a multimillionaire executive of IBM and AOL and was probably a CIA or DIA agent, making him the richest family member since Epimenio Martinez, the owner of much of northern New Mexico. I used my experience with hard physical labor to work diligently in university classes and became a PhD field biologist and a professor working in the field under very difficult conditions throughout much of the world. (Mares, M.A., 2002) I became a museum builder and museum director and used my experience as a laborer in building and road construction to oversee the development of a major museum for the State of Oklahoma. (Mares, M.A., 2000–2001)

Once we were doing a difficult pick and shovel job and had been given short-handled shovels. Digging hour after hour with such short shovels was really tough on a person's lower back, even a young person like me. I thought this might be a chance for me to do a favor for my older coworkers and help the company. I went to see the Anglo foreman with the best of intentions and told him my big idea. I suggested he get long-handled shovels so the laborers did not hurt their backs while being stooped over all day. They would be happier and get more work done, I offered. He asked me to get in the back of his pickup and drove me off the worksite and told me I was fired. The man was neither a visionary nor a natural leader, but he was decisive. I was sixteen.

My laborer's job paid for tuition, books, gas and other expenses like field trips to the surrounding desert. I think tuition at that time was about one hundred dollars a semester. Books may have been the main expense, because at the University of New Mexico I was a pre-med student with lots of expensive science books to buy. I also had to buy many other books, since I was in the Honors Program and we read a book each week in each of our classes. A voracious reader since childhood, I loved it. I read *War and Peace* over a weekend in forty-eight straight hours.

Dangerous Jobs

Laboring on large construction projects could be dangerous. I had some close calls. Once while working on the first Big-I interchange of Interstate 40 and Interstate 25 in Albuquerque (the present "Big-I" is the second iteration since I worked on the first one sixty years ago), I was assisting with the concrete pour for the lanes of the highway bridge. The steelworkers had already put in the iron rebar and steel forms for the highway. The concrete masons were getting the concrete (called mud) spread throughout the forms. I was using a powerful vibrator I would immerse in the newly poured concrete and it would almost liquify the concrete to spread it into all the corners and cracks. There were no safety barriers along the edges of the highway since we had not built them yet. The edge was perhaps thirty feet above I-25.

The silent concrete bucket hanging from a crane and weighing more than a ton snuck up behind me and pushed me over the edge of the roadway. Not knowing what else to do, I grabbed the edge of the bucket as it swung out over the roadway far below. I hung on for dear life. Nothing could stop the enormously heavy bucket as it took me for an exciting if very slow ride over I-25. Luckily, I was young and strong then, and weighed a lot less than I do now, so I hung on to it until it slowly swung back over the bridge we were building. When it got back over the work site on the bridge, I let go of it and went on helping with the pour.

Jackhammer

We were working at the cement factory in Tijeras Canyon, just east of Albuquerque. My brother had worked there years earlier when they were building the factory. Its purpose was to eat the mountain next to it, literally, then convert all that rock and gravel to cement to feed the insatiable demands of the Interstate Highway System. It had massive rock crushers inside tall metal structures that the stones and gravel were put into to be crushed for cement to be used to make concrete. We were told the crushers were sinking into the earth and we had to break the massive concrete pads surrounding the crushers so that they could be reinforced to reverse the sinking. It was a problem similar to that of the Leaning Tower of Pisa in Italy. I had never run a jackhammer before, but when the foreman asked if I could run one, I said sure. (How hard could it be?)

Turns out it is *very* hard to handle a jackhammer properly, especially in the old days when there were no protective devices for the operator and no padded handles or other safety features. Within an hour of starting to break up the concrete, I knew immediately this was a really tough job and agreeing to do it had been a major mistake on my part. My coworker (who knew how to run a jackhammer) and I were busily drilling away at the thick concrete, but it hardly yielded to our jackhammers. I could tell my piano-playing fingers were about to be damaged, but what could I do?

Jackhammers in those days ran on very high-power compressed air with a gasoline compressor supplying the air. The work was violent with deafening noise, choking dust that was generated by the vibrating chisel and nerve-destroying vibrations that were surely damaging my hands, arms, neck and shoulders. Add to all that, the summer heat and the dense concrete we were trying to break and it did not take me too long to discover that this was the worst laboring job I had ever had. I was rapidly learning once and forever just how hard it could be.

As I am having this sudden realization while trying to break up the apparently indestructible concrete, the connector between my compressed air hose and the compressor broke. Now the housing for the compressed air hose, which was a heavy metal buckle, broke loose. Suddenly the compressed air line looked like a cobra rising up to strike someone. It would swing by us with enormous speed. With the weight of the metal coupling and power of the compressed air, it could easily have crushed a skull. I had steel-toed reinforced work boots and was wearing a hard hat, but the heavy metal housing of the hose swung at me with enormous speed and hit me across my instep, flipping me completely in the air and down on the concrete slab and knocking off my hard hat. It rose again and headed toward me for a second shot, but this time it seemed to be aiming for my head, since I was lying injured on the ground.

I was trying to crawl out of range but my foot was very painful and I thought I had surely broken it. Just as the hose reached its maximum height before striking again (it almost seemed to be a sentient creature), my fellow laborer dove on the hose and the coupling and wrestled it to the ground. It dragged him here and there, while he battled it, refusing to let go. I was able to crawl to the compressor and turn it off. Whew. My foot was swelling up quickly, so I told the foreman that I had to go to the hospital to have my foot X-rayed. I had to remove my boot before driving to the emergency room, since it was swelling up so fast, I would have trouble removing it if I waited.

A heavy equipment operator had died the day before I was injured while he was working on the rock pile and his caterpillar had turned over, crushing him, so they let me leave work. Too many injuries were happening. The hospital staff X-rayed me and said the foot was not broken, but it was badly bruised. I went home. While I was there, my fingers began swelling up to the size of small bananas, so much so that I could not dial the rotary phones of the day because they would not fit into the holes in the dial. There was a lot of pain in my hands, even more than in my foot. The man who saved me was a hero but I do not even remember his name, although I think his last name was Garcia. Maybe we were related. He was a quick thinker and stubborn enough not to let go of the angry hose, no matter how it tried to whip him about.

24

Ranch Life During the Great Depression

Education

My uncle, Christie Mares, was my dad's younger brother. An older brother, Solomón, had died of diphtheria in 1920, when he was seven years old. Christie, like my dad, was highly intelligent, but with no formal education beyond high school until after he joined the Marines. They shared the same tight-fisted grandfather/granduncle who was rich as Croesus but would not loan them the fifty dollars required to go to college. As a child on the ranch, Christie had distinguished himself by deciding to climb on the new barn roof using poles with spikes on the end. He was imagining climbing mountain glaciers and to keep from falling off the roof he used the spiked poles to provide purchase on the slippery metal of the shiny new roof. He climbed all over that roof. He was six years old and imagining himself a great adventurer. When his dad and grandfather/granduncle saw the roof there was some question as to whether Christie would live to see another day. They had to re-roof part of the barn at great expense during the Great Depression when almost no one had any money. The owner of the barn was one of the great misers in our family. It was some years before Christie and my dad could laugh about the incident—perhaps eighty years. I could feel the power of the horrible deed as the story was told to me eight decades after it happened.

The Mares boys grew up on a huge ranch (fifty-five thousand acres) near Wagon Mound, New Mexico, but the ranch did not belong to their father or grandfather, rather it belonged to their extremely wealthy and tough grandfather/granduncle, Epimenio Martinez, who owned much of northern New Mexico. My paternal great grandfather, Don Pedro Martinez, had twenty-one children, fourteen by his first wife, Adelina Paltenghe, and seven by his second wife, Simonita Lucero. Being left with so many children while trying to run a ranch must have made him desperate to find some way to deal with three-year-old Alice Martinez (my grandmother to be), so he gave her to his wealthy and very tough miserly brother who had no children. His brother promised to adopt little Alice and took her in as an only child.

Fig. 46. Epimenio Martinez (third from left) and his family; top row right is my grandfather Eduardo Mares. Photograph late 1890s.

A Large Ranch House

My paternal grandmother, Alice Martinez Mares, thus grew up in a wealthy part of the Martinez family. The family eventually lost their ranch, like so many New Mexican Hispanics and, when she was in her eighties, I took her to visit the ranch she had not seen in more than a half century. It was owned by some Texans (natch) and we did not know if they would let us into the house. My garrulous dad, however, talked to the big, tall rancher and explained this was the house where his mother grew up, married and had children more than seventy-five years earlier. The rancher graciously let us walk through his ranch.

Fig. 47. Grandmother Alice Martinez Mares on her wedding day in 1910 wearing an ermine-trimmed gown.

It was a remarkable walk back in time. My grandmother showed us the bed where she had given birth to several of her children. The furniture had been made by a great grandfather. I especially remembered a knickknack shelf made of wooden spools of different sizes and styes that had been sanded, fitted, varnished, and glued together making a unique piece of furniture that bespoke of art. Most of the furniture in the house had been made by various ancestors.

I would guess there were few furniture stores in those days, particularly on a ranch where the nearest town was Wagon Mound, hours away by wagon and with a population less than eight hundred seventy-five. (New Mexico 1910 census, 1913) "This is where your Aunt Eppie was born. This is the bed where your uncle Solomón died when he was seven years old." She was clearly reliving those days of joy and heartbreak. Then we entered the third floor—a ballroom. She recalled dances, her coming-out party (*quinceañera*), her wedding. We had literally walked back in time more than seventy years and her memories, some from the 1800s, came flooding back.

Grandma Alice had started out with money and had even been sent to St. Louis to a girl's music academy to study piano, something most people could never hope to do in those days, and certainly not the downtrodden mestizos. Alas, she married my grandfather, her step-uncle, who never climbed above the economic level of "broke."

Grandma's husband, Eduardo Mares, had attended Haskell Indian School in Kansas. He was a short (maybe five foot two) feisty alcoholic. My dad always said his father could sit on a curb and swing his feet. He was the brother of her stepmother/step-aunt, the mean woman who reared her, making her step-aunt her sister-in-law too. Caramba. No wonder my dad would periodically break out in song to the tune of "I'm My Own Grandpa." My grandfather had worked as a jockey for a while in addition to raising sheep. Eventually he found the job with the Santa Fe Railroad shipping coal on coal cars. He worked for the railroad until his retirement.

He was unable to pay the debts he had with various banks and lenders. Grandma's father/uncle was the owner of the only bank in Wagon Mound and wrote a note to Grandpa saying he was a man without character since he would not do the honorable thing and pay his many debts. Grandpa paid many bills a bit at a time, one dollar here, five dollars there, but then borrowed again. "Prove me wrong," Epimenio scolded, "and pay me what you owe me, then I will reconsider my opinion of you." In today's money, he did not owe his wife's uncle/father much money, but the old man was a noted miser and to him, even a nickel was a big deal. Grandpa was his more or less son-in-law and his brother-in-law too (mountain people), but what with his drinking problem and inability to hold a job until he joined the Santa Fe Railroad, he was unable to pay back most of the loans he had taken from his very rich relative.

We left the ranch knowing none of us would ever return and realizing how abrupt the change from living as the daughter of a wealthy ranch owner to being just another poor Chicana had been. It seemed as if they had been tossed out too quickly to take their things with them. As my dad said, "*Siempre los Mexicanos*. They had it all and they lost it."

Fig. 48. Marine Christie Mares with his father, Eduardo around 1940.

My grandmother, a teetotaler, suffragette and highly religious person, eventually divorced him. Why did she marry him in the first place? She was so anti drinking and opposed to whoring that there are stories of her taking an axe to bars and whorehouses along with her fundamentalist politically-active sisters. I have not been able to confirm the stories, but was told by several people, including one of her sons, and have no reason to doubt them. She died two months shy of age one hundred three.

A Self-Made Man

Grandma called her uncle father and her father uncle. She said her father/uncle's second wife (her step-aunt/stepmother) was a witch and the meanest person she met in over a hundred years of living. Giving Alice away to her uncle led to family confusion as to who was who, and who was related to whom, that continues to this day. As my mother said, "Those mountain people...." Grandma's stingy father/uncle made Ebenezer Scrooge look like a philanthropist. I recall the movie "The Professionals" again, where Ralph Bellamy tells Lee Marvin, "You bastard." Marvin, nonplussed, replies, "Yes sir. In my case an accident of birth. But you sir, you're a self-made man." That was my grandmother's father/uncle: a self-made man.

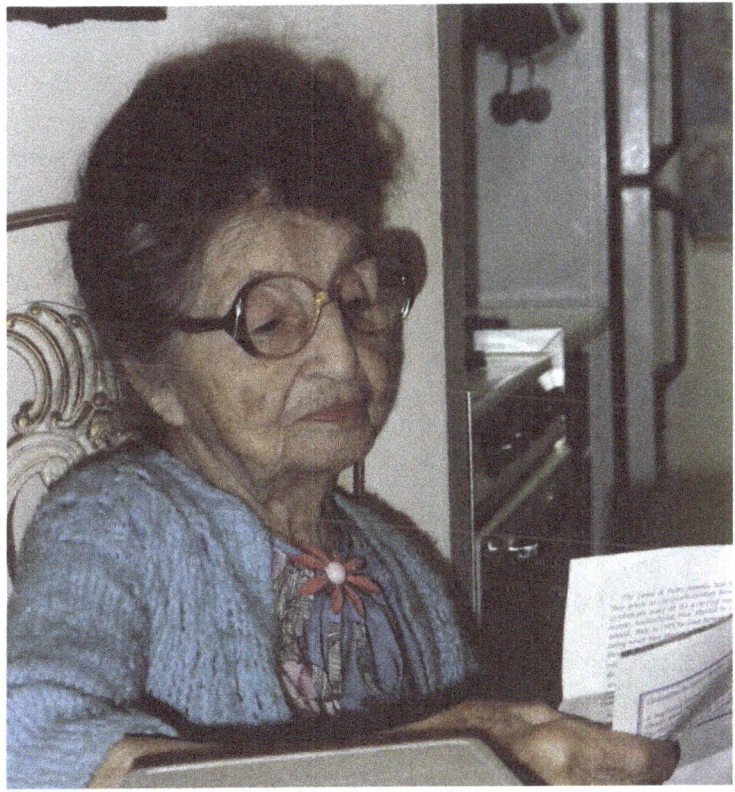

Fig. 49. Grandma Alice Martinez Mares nearing one hundred years old.

After he died, my grandmother was left out of sharing in her father/uncle's enormous estate. She sued for a part of the inheritance but the court found her uncle had in fact never adopted her. He had promised his brother he would do so and for many years the whole family, perhaps even Grandma, thought he *had* adopted her. In his will, he left her a small house in Wagon Mound that had little value, but he left her none of the enormous ranchlands and other property of his estate.

I would guess the reason for essentially cutting her out of his will (she was in effect his only child) is that he didn't like her husband, Eduardo, who, truth be told, had many issues. Maybe Epimenio thought my alcoholic grandfather would end up with part of his fortune and the enormous ranch properties and drink it all away. Why should he inherit the ranch when he never got around to repaying loans from Epimenio worth a total over the years of perhaps a hundred dollars (three thousand in today's money)? This was an enormous sum to the miser.

Grandma cared about Epimenio, however, and called him father from the time she was three years old and was given to him by her biological father (my great grandfather, Don Pedro Martinez). Among the many jobs Grandfather Eduardo held was working for the undertaker that buried Epimenio in the largest funeral held in northern New Mexico for many years. His bronze coffin cost five thousand dollars (more than ninety thousand in today's money). Grandpa told Grandma there was some funny business afoot with the mortuary that had buried her father. Never one to be afraid of the courts, or anything else, Grandma monitored his gravesite day after day and noticed the dirt had been moved around several days after the funeral.

She went to court and filed for an exhumation order for her uncle's body. The court agreed with her and they dug up the coffin. They found Epimenio's very expensive bronze coffin, perhaps the only one in the state, had been exchanged for a very cheap pine box. The crooked mortuary wished to sell the expensive coffin again and again and again. Grandma had her uncle/father placed in his original container and reburied. He had no children of his own, but his never-adopted only child, who was basically left out of his will, saved his fancy coffin for his rotting corpse.

Mares and Martinez

Grandma was a strong and disciplined woman. When she was sixteen, she felt she was putting on a bit of extra weight and vowed she would get up from the table a bit hungry at every meal thereafter. She then proceeded to do just that for the next eighty-six years. As a teenager in the very early 1900s, she climbed Cabezón Peak by herself. Cabezón Peak is one of the more dramatic volcanic necks in New Mexico, along with its more famous cousin, Shiprock, of Tony Hillerman fame.

Many dramatic volcanic remains, if not most, are sacred to Native Americans. Cabezón Peak is not a technically difficult climb, but neither is it easy to do, especially for a sixteen-year-old girl. It is considered a Class 3 climb, which means ropes may be required, but it can be completed without technical climbing gear. Grandma, of course, had no climbing gear, just a lot of spunk. Every time I drive through northern New Mexico and see the protuberance on the horizon—and it is visible from most of the northern parts of the state—I think of the teenage girl from Wagon Mound clambering to the top of that volcanic rock one hundred twenty-five years ago.

We did not visit my Grandma Alice very often. We traveled to Santa Fe on a Sunday (in fact she was referred to as Grandma from Santa Fe) perhaps three or four times a year. Santa Fe was home to dozens of relatives and extended family members of my dad. I know he liked going up there to see his two sisters, their husbands and his mother. However, I always got the impression my mother did not like Grandma Alice. No one ever told me why, of course, but I gathered that Grandma had moved in with them at one time and two women in the same house is a recipe for disaster. Grandma would frequently travel on the bus to see relatives from northern New Mexico to Arizona, and for some reason this bothered my mother, who never went anywhere without my dad. "I always remember her with a suitcase in her hand, going off to see some relative." Perhaps Grandma thought my mother, a Catholic, was a poor choice for a life partner for my dad and, as things turned out, she was correct, but not because of religion.

I barely knew Grandpa Eduardo, but I remember him. He used to wrestle with me and tickle me until I would fall on the floor, laughing till I cried in frustration. I did not like it. He bullied me—one of the few people around who was shorter and weaker than he was. He died of cirrhosis at the age of sixty-eight, when I was four years old. His deathbed conversion to Catholicism notwithstanding, he is buried in Fairview Cemetery in Santa Fe, the only non-Catholic cemetery in the largely Catholic city during the early to mid-20th century, although technically he died a Catholic. I remember his funeral, which was my first of oh so many funerals. As a four-year-old child, I recalled the funeral taking place in Albuquerque at Mt. Calvary Cemetery, which was basically the Catholic part of my family's burial grounds. However, he is buried in Santa Fe and my four-year-old's memory had been faulty.

Separated For Eternity

Grandpa Eduardo Mares, being a Mares and not a Martinez, and facing death, decided to cover his bases and, like John Wayne, convert to Catholicism on his deathbed. Grandma Alice, a staunch Methodist, was incensed over his deathbed conversion. They had been divorced for many years in any case, but she never forgave him for that conversion—at least not for the next half century. Grandpa is buried near the southern edge of Fairview Cemetery in Santa Fe, where deceased prisoners from the state pen got their final lodgings. Time heals some wounds, however. Before Grandma died, she decided she wanted to be buried next to the only husband she had ever had in one hundred three years of living, but the historic old cemetery made that impossible. So they lie, buried at opposite ends of the cemetery, a Mares and a Martinez separated for all eternity because of a divorce more than a half century earlier.

25

New Bishop in Town

A Bishop and a Priest

Padre Martinez, the leading religious figure in northern New Mexico, had married and had a child while still a very young man. His wife died in childbirth and his only child, a daughter, died some years later. He knew passions, loss and love. He had little confidence in Bishop Lamy. What on earth did that French youngster Lamy know about anything other than his seminary studies in France? Book learning at best, and mainly religious tracts at that. Both he and his lifelong friend, Father Machebeuf, had only recently been ordained. To Martinez, they were kids, and especially arrogant youngsters at that, not because they were French, but because they were, indeed, arrogant.

When Jean-Baptiste Lamy became a bishop, Padre Martinez at first told him that his allegiance was to the bishop at Durango, Mexico, not some quasi-French American Jesuit young person who was determined to control everything in the vast territory of New Mexico. Eventually, Martinez tried to be obedient to Lamy and to follow his orders in the early days, as the priesthood required, but Lamy, who wanted money to build churches and schools, decided to make tithing mandatory by Church law. Martinez had done away with tithing in his parishes, believing it hurt poor people. Follow the money.

Fig. 50. Archbishop Jean-Baptiste Lamy. Creative Commons. Wikipedia, public domain.

Lamy wrote a letter to Padre Martinez saying New Mexicans lacked the intellectual liveliness of the Americans and had primitive morals. Martinez must have loved that letter. Lamy was White and French and very closely allied with the WASP Americans. The mestizo priests were a bother to Lamy, especially Padre Martinez, the intellectual giant of northern New Mexico, who was likely much smarter than Lamy, much older and much more experienced in the ways of the world and of New Mexico. He was also more powerful in his dealings with people and was the *de facto* religious and education leader of northern New Mexico. Lamy had to find some way to control him and the other mestizo priests who refused to treat Lamy as a newly arrived French deity.

Money, Money, Money, Money

Lamy's henchman, Father Machebeuf, later Monsignor (and eventually Bishop of Denver), actually released personal information gathered from the sacred privacy of the confessional to threaten parishioners to pay their tithes. Fooling around on your wife with the maid? Pay me or I will tell everyone in a sermon. Breaking the seal of the confessional is the greatest sin a priest can commit, far more serious than molesting little boys or deflowering teenage girls, for example, yet Lamy's dearest friend-for-life was so accused.

A group of parishioners from noble (but Hispanic) families approached Lamy with this thorny problem, saying they had respect for Machebeuf because he was a priest, but they did not respect him as a person. He cared only about bleeding tithes out of the poor and even threatened them by releasing in public sermons the sins they confessed in the sanctity of the confessional. Lamy was furious with the parishioners, but was not angry with his dearest bosom buddy, Machebeuf. He asked for juridical proof because this was such a heinous crime for a priest, the worst charge that could be made of a man who was a Catholic priest. He then threatened those making these accusations of malicious calumny with severe punishment. In effect, he was blaming the victims, a classic move to protect *mon frère* Machebeuf.

Padre Martinez felt tithing was not acceptable to the poor people of New Mexico. Indeed, Martinez used his personal fortune to build schools in Taos. He did not feel churches should make money off worshipers. If people wanted to donate to the church to help out with a project, that was one thing, but to extort the money out of the flock through the force of law was, in Martinez's mind, the equivalent of a crime against the faithful. And to use the secrets learned in the confessional? My God, that was truly beyond the pale. What were they teaching these priests in France for God's sake and just how close were Lamy and Machebeuf? (Anders, 1999)

Lamy was not a giant and Martinez knew it and told him so. He was a young inexperienced bishop who was in way over his head in a very complex land of which he knew nothing, including the language and culture of the people in his ministry. Eventually, Lamy excommunicated Martinez. Many, if not most, people in the Martinez family became Methodists, or followed other Protestant branches of religion, as a result of Lamy's actions. Lamy and his foolish pride had undone my family's faith that had lasted for millennia.

Martinez was the man who brought the printing press to New Mexico; who published the first book in the territory; who taught boys *and* girls, Indians *and* Whites, to read and write in the first Catholic school in New Mexico; who unselfishly served the people's need for religion; who fought for land rights for the Hispanic residents of New Mexico who were going to lose their land-grant properties; who was himself a delegate to the Territorial Legislature, as well as an official observer as the First Territorial Constitution of New Mexico was adopted. The influential Martinez family in New Mexico—whose members had been Catholic for at least a thousand years and had a saint and a pope in their ancestry—left the Church.

Lamy, by his self-centered drive to control religion in the state and his efforts to control the mestizo priests and their followers, had managed to force these deeply religious Catholics to abandon their faith. They were people whose religion could be traced all the way back to the Middle Ages, including the battles where Santiago himself, the patron saint of Spain, had appeared as a miraculous knight on a white horse to lend the Spanish soldiers a hand (as he supposedly did at the Battle of Acoma in 1599). The ancestors of the people of northern New Mexico had fought alongside Santiago for God's sake. And now they were leaving the Church in droves.

Willa Cather

Heroes need foes and in the Cather 1927 novel, *Death Comes for the Archbishop*, Lamy (or Bishop Latour as she delicately referred to him), is described as practically a saint, but with a major enemy in the form of the looming and evil Padre Martinez, who had "yellow eyes and yellow teeth." Yellow eyes and yellow teeth do not run in my family, even to this day. Interestingly, Cather changed Bishop Lamy's and his oh so dearest sidekick Machebeuf's names in the novel, but Martinez was named directly, the better to destroy his and his family's reputation.

Grandma Alice always said, with great irritation, when referring to Cather, "*¡Esa mujer! ¡Esa mujer!*"(That woman! That woman!) Cather had referred to Grandma's uncle, the padre, as:

> ... the powerful old native priest [who] was rather terrifying...with his big head, violent Spanish face, and shoulders like a buffalo... an old scapegrace, if there ever was one; he's got children and grandchildren in almost every settlement around here.

Cather's evident racism had destroyed the reputation of a giant of a man of religion and letters in New Mexico, one of the state's great intellectuals, a religious icon, and Alice's granduncle to boot. Martinez, not Sister Blandina, was the first and most important educator in the huge territory of New Mexico, which stretched from California to Oklahoma and Utah to Mexico. His students (politicians and priests) would eventually serve their territory, the Church and the nation at many levels, including as members of the United States Congress. (Cather: 76)

When the young, nugatory Lamy arrived in New Mexico, Martinez was an old man of fifty-seven and in his waning days. Still mentally alert, but no longer the remarkably strong priest and horseman who would ride regularly to Durango, Mexico, more than fifteen hundred miles away across deserts and through hostile territory, often alone, to see his bishop or to study. Martinez had been a strong and vital priest, legal scholar and educator, but in age, Lamy definitely had the edge: a mere youth of thirty-six. He would beat the old man merely by outliving him and the other elderly Spanish priests, too, for that matter. Time was on his side.

26

Wagon Mound

The 1930s

The Great Depression was a tough time for all poor people in New Mexico and even for some wealthy families. New Mexico at the turn of the century was still close to Mexico and Mexican politics and very aware of the challenges faced by the forces of revolution in the "mother country," where the people were trying to unseat a cruel dictator and establish a democratic nation. The United States was never the mother country for New Mexico until the territory filled up with Anglos. When the intellectual President of Mexico, Francisco Madero, was murdered in a *coup d'etat*, along with his two brothers, Ernesto and Gustavo, in 1913, Mexico was plunged back into civil war. My dad, born in 1914 in Wagon Mound, New Mexico was named Ernesto Gustavo Mares in honor of the murdered brothers Madero. Such were the connections between New Mexico and Mexico a half century after the United States had taken over New Mexico Territory.

Ernesto Gustavo (Ernie) was a wrestling champion in high school at Raton High. He was only five foot six, but was especially tough and was an extraordinarily gifted athlete. He played football and was also a champion swimmer, having learned to swim in Black Lake. The lake itself, at eight thousand six hundred feet in elevation, has very cold water year round and was located on one of the Mares ranches. You may be familiar with the lake as it was used for the final scenes of the television series, "Lonesome Dove," where it masqueraded as Montana. The cabin the cowboys built in that beautiful forest was on the shores of Black Lake. The forest and lake were part of the Mares Ranch. The owner of the ranch at the time of filming "Lonesome Dove" was my cousin, Carmen Mares Cook, who may have actually been the first Mares to visit (and work in) the White House. During World War II, Carmen was a translator in the East Wing of the White House for President Franklin Roosevelt.

Sinbad

Ernie's best friend and teammate on the football team was Everett Allen Malcomb, an Anglo who came from money and was an outstanding athlete. Malcomb joined the Navy in World War II and attended the U.S. Naval Academy from 1937–1941, where he was a standout football player and picked up the moniker, Sinbad. Malcomb was stationed on the *USS Arizona* in Pearl Harbor in 1941. My middle name, Allen, was in honor of my dad's friend who everyone thought had died at Pearl Harbor when the Japanese sank his ship. I had a chance to visit the Pearl Harbor monument in the late 1990s and was able to examine the wall of honor placed above the sunken battleship *Arizona* with a complete list of the crew members killed in the attack. Malcomb was not listed.

When I got back to New Mexico, I told my dad Malcomb was not listed on the *Arizona* monument. He replied that things were really mixed up when the war began, so he didn't know officially if Malcomb was alive or dead. He knew he was on the *Arizona* and they never heard from him again. Turns out Malcomb was on shore leave on December 6, 1941 and was returning to the *Arizona* just as the Japanese fighters began their attack. He went on to have a very distinguished Navy career, being present at the beginning of the war at Pearl Harbor and at the end of the war, when he led a detachment of Marines ashore in Tokyo Bay to secure the Yokosuka Naval Base. My dad and Malcomb never contacted one another across the years. They died only a month apart in 2005.

Ernie was very smart, as his Army IQ test showed. Of course, IQ is one thing, but what you do with it is another. He wanted to go to college and learn scientific and medical illustration, and other medical subjects. He was a naturally talented artist. He approached his extremely wealthy grandfather/granduncle, who was largely uneducated but was nonetheless a self-made Republican titan of New Mexico capitalism, president of the bank and one of the richest men in the state. My dad asked if he could borrow fifty dollars to go to college in Colorado. His uncle said, "You can have what I had when I started out in life," and he gave him one dollar. He did not hold with book learning in any case and thought it was a waste of time.

My dad was also an expert horseman and cowboy and this same grandfather/granduncle, who had a fifty-five-thousand-acre ranch, among other properties he owned, told my dad that if he could ride his horse around the periphery of the ranch in one day, he would give him the ranch. Of course, it was impossible to do that across mountains and canyons for hundreds of miles. Obviously my grand uncle had a streak of mean in him as well as a streak of the skinflint.

During the early part of The Great Depression, Ernie worked as a fur trapper. He always said he ate a lot of squirrels and rabbits during the early thirties, and he also collected coyotes, deer and other animals for their pelts and meat (in the case of deer). He noted the family was so poor during the 1930s they hardly noticed the Depression had occurred. They had to read about it in the papers. He had been a newspaper boy in May of 1927 and remembered selling papers and shouting, "Lindbergh lands in Paris." He said he had two questions: Who was Lindbergh and where was Paris? The Great Depression similarly came to them in newspaper stories about bread lines and unemployment.

The ranch where he was born was about fifteen miles east of Wagon Mound, New Mexico. Wagon Mound is not much of a town today. It is still the home of the Wagon Mound Bean Festival, though the beans are long gone from northern New Mexico due to climate change. But in

1918, it was a major stop for travelers crossing the western Great Plains on the way to Santa Fe, Albuquerque and Denver. The town reached its maximum population size in 1950 with around one thousand inhabitants. In 1920, there were eight hundred seventy-five people living there. Today there are fewer than three hundred residents. (U.S. Census) I still have a few relatives living there, but most are in the *campo santo*, which is brimming with Mares and Martinez graves. Indeed, the population of Wagon Mound's graveyard is greater than the population of the town. When my Uncle Christie applied for a job at the CIA and was asked where he was born, he referred to Wagon Mound as "the middle of nowhere."

Fig. 51. Wagon Mound New Mexico in 2008. Creative Commons, Wikipedia, public domain.

The first time my dad was taken to town as a four-year-old he peed his pants because he couldn't find an outdoor toilet. He had never seen indoor plumbing. For someone living on a ranch in the middle of nowhere, Wagon Mound must have appeared to be a metropolis, with a few buildings reaching the dizzying height of three stories. My dad did not speak English when he first went to school, only Spanish. However, in order to prepare for school, he had memorized Lincoln's Gettysburg

Address in English. It was all the English he knew, but he was a bit of a sensation in his grade school. He was paraded around through all the grades to show that someone who didn't speak English could learn and recite from memory Lincoln's great address: "Four score and seven years ago...." He remembered the address eighty years later. He learned English quickly and grew up without a Spanish accent.

Working on the Railroad

After high school, he got a job on the railroad as a fireman, which meant his job was to keep the steam engine's boiler going by shoveling coal into the insatiable creature. This was hard manual labor and it built up his arms and torso, as well as his legs. I am sure being an athlete helped him carry out the hard work he had to do. He basically lived on the train (in the caboose) and was on call day or night to keep the boiler functioning at a rate that would meet the conditions of the track and landscape.

He always talked about Raton Pass in New Mexico as being the highest point on the Santa Fe Railroad line at seven thousand eight hundred thirty-four feet and noted how hard the boiler had to work to get over the pass. He was the person who had to do the hard work of feeding the boiler during its passage. If other problems arose, the train's fireman fixed them too, including working on the massive wheel assemblies with giant wrenches. Very hard work.

In later life, my dad, who became a master machinist, could make or fix about anything. He could work with wood, plastics or metals. He made a telescope and a magnifying glass which included pouring, making and sanding the glass. In 1936 he decided to go to Spain to fight with the Nationalists against the Republicans, but married my mother instead that same year, eliminating any dreams of a romantic war in Spain and tying him down to New Mexico in perpetuity. From 1937–1941, he studied to be a machinist at the Santa Fe Shops in Albuquerque, both in formal classes and as an apprentice. Just before the war, he received a diploma as a machinist. He would be a proud member of the machinists' union for the rest of his life. He was hired to work on the atomic bomb at Los Alamos. Machinists were in such short supply, even Chicanos were welcome.

Fig. 52. Ernesto Gustavo Mares working as a draftsman in the U.S. Army, 1950.

Working as a model and instrument maker for Sandia Laboratories, his major work was making wind tunnel scale models of rockets and planes. There were no computers in those days, so the models had to be exact scale replicas to be placed in the wind tunnels for studies of stability, flyability and so forth. The work was classified, so we only learned about it after he retired. He made telescopes to track rockets, the rockets themselves and even the early rocket planes. He was most proud of his work on the FB-111 Aardvark, one of the most advanced supersonic low-level variable-geometry wing fighter/bombers of its time and one capable of flying at more than sixteen hundred mph.

My dad as a young man was also a hard drinker. Who knows what kind of issues he carried from his alcoholic dad, his tightfisted grandfather/granduncle or his hard scrabble upbringing? The family's significant Native American heritage may also have influenced the heavy use of alcohol. (Ehlers and Gizer, 2013) In the early days of their marriage, Ernie made things miserable for my mother who, like his mother, was also a teetotaler. All the women in my family from the parental and grandparental generations at least, maternal and paternal sides, were teetotalers, but not the men, for the most part.

The pattern of alcohol use makes me wonder if an alcoholism gene is sex linked on the Y chromosome. Recent research has shown some influence in alcohol dependency behavior being linked to the Y chromosome in European men. (Zuo *et al.*, 2014) My older brother, Anthony, remembered as a child having to accompany my mother from bar to bar in Albuquerque searching for my dad. Eventually, they would find him and big arguments (and maybe more) would ensue as they took him home. Curiously, my Irish grandfather did not drink. I don't know whether his dad, John Devine from Northern Ireland, master sergeant in the dragoons and soldier in the Indian wars, drank or not. I never heard stories of either of them drinking, putting the lie to the old joke: An Irishman walks out of a bar.

When my older brother was six years old, my parents divorced. With my dad traveling on the railroad all over the central and western United States, drinking and very likely chasing women, divorce was probably inevitable. He clearly did not want to be married and did not want a family. There were rumors of a half-brother of ours in Kansas but I was never able to find an actual link to a Kansan, who would be dead now anyway. Although my parents divorced, my mother, as a Catholic, could not be a divorced woman and do things like date or remarry. To do those things would be a scandal of the first magnitude for the family, greater even than the divorce itself, and so it was out of the question for her. She was still married to her forever husband in the eyes of the Catholic Church (where till death do us part was an iron clad rule not a romantic suggestion).

My mother went to work as an office worker, something she had trained for in high school. She had been the fastest typist in her class at one hundred twenty words per minute on an old Royal typewriter. She worked either as a secretary or as an office manager and bookkeeper for the next half century, always an active member of the Office Workers Union. After the very rocky start to their marriage, she would never again be caught without a job or having to depend on a man. She had been dirt poor after her father had died, so she was determined to make her own way through life with her own income and nothing would stand in the way.

The Atomic Bomb

After my dad abandoned the family, he went to San Francisco to spend time with his sister, my Aunt Alice, and they both considered going to work on the Panama Canal. Bilingual people were especially needed to work on the Canal's operations. Ernie had been exempt from the draft due to his working for the railroad, including helping with troop trains and war equipment trains, things that were vital to the effort to prepare for the coming war. These were considered reserved occupations. Neither of them ever went to Panama, but my dad ended up at Los Alamos where the A-bomb was being developed and Alice eventually worked for the U.S. Government in helping rebuild Germany after the war under the Marshall Plan.

As someone affiliated with research and development at Los Alamos on the Manhattan Project, my father was again exempt from military service. He had a Santa Fe address where his mother lived, but he actually lived in Los Alamos. I think all or most of the Los Alamos bomb project people had Santa Fe addresses. He never said what he did exactly but I gather he made the bomb parts and other metal equipment that was needed for testing the science of nuclear fission and for the final bomb design. No scientist could make a bomb, other than in theory. It took machinists and engineers to actually develop and produce the parts for the bomb.

He knew all the Nobel Prize winning scientists—the friendliest, Enrico Fermi, the least friendly, J. Robert Oppenheimer. Fermi was a warm Italian, always willing to hug someone, tell jokes, and join in sports. My dad was invited to go to the Trinity Test Site near Alamogordo to see the first atomic bomb detonated on July 16, 1945. He turned down the invitation. I asked why, considering it was such an historic event, and he said there were a lot of conflicting views on what the bomb would do—fears about its power and radiation or even if it could be controlled at all. Some believed it would ignite the Earth's atmosphere. (Yuen, 2020) He decided it was safer to stay in Santa Fe.

27

Tracks Across New Mexico

My dad was tested in the Army and found to have a genius IQ of one hundred fifty-five (only five points below Einstein). He once applied for a job and the man doing the hiring told him he was clearly the most qualified person, but "you're the wrong color." That's how it was in those days. My dad started out working as a shepherd on his family's ranch, worked for a while as an adobe maker (one of the dirtiest, hardest jobs there is), was a lifeguard for several years (saving perhaps twenty-five people from drowning). I asked him how many people he saved and he said he never kept track, but he figured about twenty-five would have drowned without him. He worked as a hunter and trapper during the Depression and worked at other unskilled jobs.

Languages and History

I took Spanish in college, but only became fluent when I taught university classes in Argentina. When I returned to the United States and my dad heard me speak Spanish he would say, "You talk like a foreigner." It was true. I did. Moreover, although I can understand New Mexican Spanglish perfectly, I cannot speak it. It requires a rapid mix of English and Spanish I could never master.

Some New Mexicans spoke Mexican Spanish, others took pride in speaking Spanish from Spain, (not true Castilian, but a Spanish more allied with Spain than with Mexico). Such a language mix is not surprising. Old Town had been around for more than two hundred fifty years when I was growing up and the language trails of the conquistadors across the Southwest were visible in much of what had originally been Spain, then New Spain, then New Mexico as part of Mexico, then New Mexico as a part of the United States.

My paternal grandmother Alice would say, "We didn't come to the United States, the United States came to us." She should know. She had once sat on the knee of her great-grandmother (Maria Dominga de la Nieves Lujan, who was born in 1797), when George Washington was president. My grandmother Alice was born in 1891, when Benjamin Harrison was president. She died at one hundred two during the Clinton Administration. Her sister died at one hundred three. So, Grandma and my great great grandmother had been alive for the terms of the first forty-two presidents of the United States.

They were long-lived ranch people. Her sister broke her leg when she was one hundred. The doctor worked with her to get her to the point where she could walk again. She had a successful recovery, but she refused to use a cane. He pleaded with her to please use the cane. "You don't want to fall again," he'd warn. "Why won't you use the cane?" "Because it makes me look old," she replied. The doctor said she was the oldest person he knew.

Grandma Alice's great-great-uncle was the Taos curate, Padre Martinez (mentioned earlier) whose personal printing press printed out the articles of incorporation of New Mexico into the United States for General Kearny after the Treaty of Guadalupe Hidalgo was signed. He also printed the first book published in New Mexico, *Cuarderno de Ortografía*, a spelling book. He was a firebrand and a highly educated intellectual at a time when New Mexico had few people with such training, education, or inclinations, especially mestizos. Depending on which historical account is consulted, the Padre had the first or second printing press in New Mexico Territory that he purchased in 1834. He was also the first or second person in New Mexico to publish a newspaper, *El Crepúsculo de la Libertad* (Dawn of Liberty), in Taos. (McMurtrie, 1929; Wagner, 1937) To this day, more than a century later, the Taos newspaper publishes a Spanish section called *El Crepúsculo* in honor of that original newspaper of Padre Martinez.

Fig. 53. Michael Mares and his fourth grand uncle, Padre Martinez, in Taos Plaza. Photograph Lynn Mares.

The Padre knew the mestizos had been defrauded by the United States and knew mestizos and the Spanish had victimized the Indians, who had also been exploited by the United States. He tried to right these wrongs as best he could, through charity and education. For him, education was the most important tool for both the Indians and the mestizos, the key to a better life. He did not want semi-illiterate people among his flock, such as his arch enemy, Charles Bent, who became governor of New Mexico, or his occasional antagonist, the illiterate diminutive bumpkin, Kit Carson.

The Old Paths

New Mexico's highways followed the trails of various conquistadors, including those of Coronado and Oñate. There were only so many ways to get across deserts, mountains and rivers, so the early explorers developed the first paths; they were, literally, the pathfinders. So many things in New Mexico today reflect Spanish and Mexican history, as well as that of the United States after the Mexican War. Is it any wonder the people themselves often debate their heritage? More recent immigrants (from the 1900s) were largely of Mexican origin, whereas the original families that extended back in time for hundreds of years were Spanish (emphasizing their links to the "pure" Spaniard of the Conquista in the 1600s and 1700s). In actuality, they were, unknowingly, complex mixes of world civilizations across both time and space, as we would learn with the advent of 21st century genetics, as my earlier list of genetic origins makes clear (and as presaged by the Spanish *casta* system, Davis-Undiano, 2017).

Just the simple word for "grass" conjured up one's roots. If one used *zacate* (as I did), the word was of Nahuatl origin going back to the place and the time of the Aztecs (also my ancestors, not to mention my 13th great grandfather, Hernando Martin-Serrano I, the blacksmith for Hernán Cortés). If one used *pasto*, it was the word for grass in Spain (again, ancestors of mine and of many New Mexicans). Such differences and many others led to a hierarchy among New Mexico's Hispanic natives.

Those who claimed to be Spanish believed that they were less Indian than the "Mexicans." Time-honored families claimed the older Spanish origin and believed they were somehow superior to the disadvantaged Mexican newcomers, often termed wetbacks (a term now considered a pejorative) for wading across the Rio Grande to enter the United States, though in truth almost everyone who colonized New Mexico across the Rio Grande from Old Mexico had to wade, swim or ride their horses and wagons across the river. There were no bridges or boats in the early days. I have waded the river myself several times from the United States to Mexico and back again doing field research collecting fish, so I guess I, too, am a *bona fide* wetback several times over.

Crossing the Border

On a field trip of several month's duration in the 1980s studying mammals across the Southwest, I decided to take a small field class to Mexico for a day so they could experience a foreign country. We walked across the Mexican border at Nogales. After spending part of the day in Mexico, it was time to return to the United States, where I had left my camper truck parked, and continue our fieldwork. One of my doctoral students was from Argentina. "Getting back is no problem," I told him. "Just show them your passport and visa and the agents will let you return to the United States." "I left my passport back in Tucson," he said. "What?" I replied. Now we had a problem. This could really mess up our field trip and schedule. "I'll find a way to get you in; come with me."

I had the other students cross back to the States on foot and wait for us at the truck, while he and I went in search of a cab driver. I found a cab and explained to the driver that I had to sneak my student back into the United States because he had forgotten his G%dd$@$&d passport. "We have to smuggle him in," I said. "No problem," he said. "I do it all the time." Before we drove to the border, I had my student practice his pronunciation. I had been to Mexico dozens of times over the years entering from near Brownsville all the way to Tijuana and most crossings in between. There were several crossings with no border patrol or official border points and I crossed there too, entering both on foot and in vehicles, so I worked to get him ready to sneak back into the U.S.

"They're going to ask you, where were you born? You'll say, "I was born in Pittsburgh." He was living in Pittsburgh at the time, so I thought if the agent asked what part of Pittsburgh he lived in, he could say Squirrel Hill, which would be true. We practiced over and over. I was born in Pittsburgh. I was born in Pittsburgh. I was born in Pittsburgh. It wasn't perfect, but it wasn't bad either. Okay. Here we go.

Years later I saw Cheech Marín in one of his films teaching undocumented Mexicans how to handle the border patrol when trying to enter the country without papers. Over and over, he had them say, "I was born in Cheecago. I was born in Cheecago."

We drove to the international border where the cars were stopped and officers were going from window to window. We were in a Mexican cab and I was on the driver's side.

> "Where were you born?" "Albuquerque, New Mexico."
>
> "How about you," he said to my student. "Where were you born?" "I was born in Pittsburgh."
>
> "Why are you in a taxi?" (This was asked of me, thank God.)
>
> "We left our truck in Nogales so as to not bring it down and park it in Mexico. I thought it would be safer there."
>
> "Good idea," he said. "Go ahead."

And we were in. I justified my actions because my student was a legal immigrant who had gotten himself into an awkward situation *vis a vis* his passport, the U.S. border and other things. We were fortunate this happened more than forty years ago. With today's immigrant problems we might have ended up on Martha's Vineyard. Had it blown up in our faces, we would have both been in hot water. As it happened, we drove into the U.S. in a Mexican cab. We didn't drive through the river, so we were not wetbacks.

The derogatory term "wetback" would be used in 1955 by President Dwight D. Eisenhower, who oversaw the largest deportation ever of 1.3 million Mexicans from the United States to the hot desert town of Mexicali, Mexico, just south of Calexico, California. The deportation program was officially called Operation Wetback.

> July is scorching in Mexicali [with] temperatures up to the 120s. In 1955, thousands of disoriented people roamed the city's streets as the sun bore down on them. They had just been dumped there by American immigration officials—snatched from their lives and jobs in the United States and thrown into a city where they didn't know anyone. (Border Police, *Sarasota Journal*, 1954)

U.S. citizens (Blakemore, 2018; Border Police in Drive on Wetbacks, 1954) were gathered up for deportation too. They just had to be Brown and off they went, nabbed by the "Wetback Raiders," as they were called. In the 1930s, when there was an earlier wave of deportations to Mexico of "Mexicans", sixty percent of those deported were actually U.S. citizens. People were pulled out of hospitals and clinics regardless of how ill or crippled they were and tossed into deportation trucks. U.S. citizen? It did not matter. Round 'em up like cattle. They're Brown. They do not belong here.

Clearly, the United States has frequently had problems with Brown immigrants crossing our southern border and has been only mildly sensitive to the citizenship status of those it deports. Like my dad when interviewing for that job, they were the wrong color, so off they went. Donald Trump, in his incomparable ignorance, was enamored of Operation Wetback (Canizales and Vallejo, 2021), where the Mexicans "never came back." Most did, of course, especially when they were needed as farm laborers. I have always joked that when the *Mayflower* landed at Plymouth Rock in 1620 my ancestors who had arrived more than a century earlier had a taco stand on the beach to feed the poor starving Pilgrims.

It's What Dictators Do

Deporting people *en masse* rarely occurs in a democracy. It is more likely to be the stuff of dictators (think Hitler or Stalin). In fact, as I write these words in the 2020s, the pathetic and weak despotic dictator wannabees (the governors of Texas and Florida) have kidnapped Latin American immigrants who are legally seeking refuge in the United States and shipped them out of Texas (without informing them where they were being sent) to largely Democratic cities and towns in the northeastern United States. This was a new low in U.S. history, especially for tin-pot governors salivating to be the next president or vice president of the United States. About three centuries ago, the Frenchman and friend of Voltaire, the Marquis Luc de Clapiers, without ever meeting the two pathetic governors who would live so far in the future, described them thusly: "The greatest evil which fortune can inflict on men is to endow them with small talents and great ambition."

In fact, the governor of Texas, Greg Abbot, a man suffering from uncontrollable ambition to be president of the United States someday at any cost, sent Mexican immigrants from Texas to Washington, DC in winter, though they lacked shoes, jackets and other clothes to protect them from cold weather. He did not tell anyone they were coming and he did not tell the immigrants where they were going. They were Mexicans, so it was okay to treat them as less than human. He had them unloaded in the snow in front of the Vice President's residence. How does one explain such viciousness of a hack politician who is willfully cruel and unable to control his political ambitions?

Both the Governor of Texas and the Governor of Florida acted like sociopaths and took great pride and joy in the "lost" immigrants and how the towns to which they had been sent, which had not been given a heads up, responded to a sudden immigrant crisis. It is a very cynical way for anyone to behave, no matter how badly they wish to be the big dog. Most people had never seen anything like this behavior before, but I had.

I worked for many years in the deserts, forests and mountains of Argentina as a field biologist studying mammals. (Mares, M.A., 2002) For a while, I was a university professor at the National University in San Miguel de Tucumán, in a verdant and small province in the far Northwest (where my two sons were born on different field trips). Once, when the government had been overthrown in a military coup and the dictator president *de jour* was busy executing people, he decided to pay a visit to Tucumán city, the "Garden of the Republic" and the birthplace of Argentine liberty, for a national celebration. Being situated in the subtropics, the warm weather of Tucumán, like southern California, attracted many homeless people to the densely populated and economically depressed province. Some of the homeless lived outside the city limits well out of sight of tourists and visitors, but not all of them—and therein lay the problem.

As the time of the proposed visit approached, the military governor of the province and city leaders realized their town was looking less attractive than it should look for the glorious visit of the new dictator/president. Everything seemed rundown and dirty. Paint was needed. White paint. Everyone in the city who lived near the miles-long presidential motorcade route was ordered to paint everything below two meters high with white paint—buildings, walls, fences, trees, park benches, garbage cans, telephone poles, light poles—everything.

That was not good enough, however. They also wanted rows of stately palm trees from the airport to the government building in the central plaza, like you see in Beverly Hills or Rio de Janeiro. Workers raced to cut palm trees from throughout the province of Tucumán and from neighboring subtropical provinces as well, and ship them like telephone poles on flatbed trucks where, like telephone poles, they were stuck into holes dug along the motorcade route. No roots. No water. No nothing. Just palm poles with palm leaves waving on top. They looked beautiful.

Oh, and one more thing. There were too many blind, crippled and mentally unstable people on the streets begging for coins and food (*los locos*). "Get rid of them." "How?" "Just get them out of town." Tucumán Province abuts several provinces that have small populations and are very hot deserts. They are extremely impoverished and sparsely populated. The army decided to collect the homeless and drive them into the cactus desert of a neighboring province. Military trucks came rolling along and gathered the halt, lame and blind of the capital city. They were then left abandoned and wandering amidst the cacti of a neighboring province, where they could no longer embarrass the good citizens of Tucumán during the visit by the latest glorious dictator of the Republic. They had no food or water. What if they died of the heat or lack of water and food? *¡Que se caguen!* (Let them shit themselves.)

When the president showed up the next day with all the news cameras following him, the city looked great. So clean. Green lawns and everything else white. And the palm trees. So majestic. He left the following day, charmed by the Garden of the Republic (Tucuman is known as *El Jardín de la República*). As his plane headed east to the great metropolis of Buenos Aires, the palm trees began to dry and bend and had to be removed immediately before they fell on someone.

People joked about the paint, saying if a person did not keep moving, they too would be painted white. The homeless? People in the neighboring province found them wandering helplessly amidst the cacti and thorn trees in the blazing hot desert and helped them with food, water and shelter. Eventually, each of them returned to their original street corners in Tucumán and life returned to normal. That's how it was in Argentina during the dictatorships and how dictators respond to things they do not like. How things looked was more important than how things actually were. Politicians and military leaders literally could not handle the truth. Few dictators or wannabe dictators can.

Fig. 54. Sergeant Christie Mares, USMC, South Pacific, 1944.

28

A Mexican Marine

Horse Soldiers

Christie Mares (Cristobal Gilberto Mares) joined the Army as part of the New Mexico National Guard in 1939. The depression was still underway and military service was a way to get paid for doing something you loved doing anyway. Having grown up with horses on his family's ranches, he joined the horse cavalry. The cavalry of that day trained with their horses in many kinds of environments where war might call them. He loved the paintings of Frederic Remington that portrayed the cavalry. He would describe the paintings as if they told a story and would often remark, "I've been in that very situation." The time for using horses in battle had passed, but the Army, or at least the New Mexico National Guard, was not yet aware of that fact. So, they trained on horseback, like the cavalry of old. In 1940 he left the national guard and joined the Marines.

Christie related how when he was a sergeant in the Marines in early 1942 his unit was in the Chocolate Mountains in the Mojave Desert, the hottest and driest desert in North America, during an especially brutally hot day. All deserts are tough habitats in which to survive, something I know intimately as a desert biologist, but the Mojave is among the most challenging. It is the desert where part of the adventure film, "The Professionals," was made. As Robert Ryan's character, Hans Ehrengard, notes in the film:

"Broiling by day. Freezing at night. Alkali dust choking every hole in your body. How in the name of God does anybody live here long enough to get used to it?" Lee Marvin's character, Henry "Rico" Fardan, responds, "Men tempered like steel. Tough breed. Men who learn how to endure." Lee Marvin was a tough decorated ex-Marine who had been wounded during the Battle of Saipan and knew what it took to be a member of that rugged breed of men.

Christie's squad of cavalrymen and their horses were trying to find a bit of shade in the barren mountains, while mapping the area and performing other military field preparedness duties. They carried water for themselves and their horses, for none was available anywhere nearby. Suddenly, in the far distance, he spotted a dust cloud. Some sort of vehicle was working its way through that arid empty landscape and apparently heading toward the squad, since there was no one else around. As the vehicle got closer, he saw it was a military jeep.

Christie was in charge of the cavalry patrol, so he went down to meet the jeep and see what was up. As the jeep reached their camp, who should alight but General George S. Patton. Patton was six feet two inches tall and my uncle was five five. Patton must have seemed like a giant to Christie. The general had been assigned to the Desert Training Center (also known as the California-Arizona Maneuver Area or CAMA) for training his armored tank force in desert tactics.

"Sergeant," Patton said, "I have to take your water. My men might die in their tanks in this heat and we don't have enough water." Patton was training for the North Africa campaign and the Mojave Desert served as a surrogate for the African desert, as they prepared to begin the hunt for Field Marshal Erwin Rommel, the "Desert Fox," and his Panzer divisions.

I asked Christie what he said to Patton. "What do you *think* I said? I said, 'Yes sir, General.'" I asked how he knew he was a general, did he have an insignia on the jeep or something? "I knew it was General Patton and that's all I needed to know," he said. "You couldn't mistake General Patton for anyone else." Before Patton left, he said, "Sergeant, I promise you I will get water to you and your men, and your horses, by nightfall." And then the old horse cavalry officer was gone.

Christie and his squad hunkered down as best they could in whatever shade they could find in the broiling desert heat. As hot as it was, they were glad they were not encased in steel tanks in the full sun. That evening, as night fell, trucks arrived with water for Christie's cavalrymen and the horses.

I asked Christie if he ever regretted his decision to join the Marines and leave the cavalry, seeing as how he got into the thick of the fighting in the Pacific. "No," he said, "every one of the guys I served with in the New Mexico one hundred eleventh Cavalry (later the 200th Coast Artillery) became part of the Bataan Death March. Those guys really had it rough."

Rough indeed: nine hundred New Mexican soldiers were starved, tortured, bayonetted, beheaded or beaten to death on the Death March, along with almost seventeen thousand other soldiers. Only two of Christie's men in the New Mexico Cavalry survived the Death March. Many of the New Mexico contingent were from Old Town and all of us in the neighborhood knew one or more survivors of the Death March.

When my older brother was Curator of History at the Albuquerque Museum in Old Town in 1979, the museum hosted an exhibit of Japanese art. No one came to the exhibit except people from other parts of Albuquerque outside the surrounding Old Town neighborhood. The director asked him why the people of Old Town weren't coming to see the exhibit? My brother told him very few people in Old Town did not have a grandfather, father, son, uncle or brother who had not been on the Bataan Death March. Many had been tortured and many had died. Survivors of the Death March still lived in the Old Town neighborhood near the museum. People in Old Town hated the Japanese with a passion and though the Death March took place more than three decades earlier, 1942 to them had happened only yesterday. In fact, as a kid, everyone I knew referred to dirty flies (for obvious reasons), dirty Republicans (for Herbert Hoover and the Great Depression) and dirty Japs (for the Bataan Death March).

U.S. Marine

After Christie was in the Marines in 1942, he was sent to the South Pacific. He traveled first to New Zealand, where he was put in charge of the photogrammetry training section for the Navy in the Pacific. He then had duty stations in Espiritu Santo, Malakula, and Efate islands in the Pacific Nation of Vanuatu; all of the Hawaiian Islands; American Samoa; New Caledonia; Eniwetok Atoll; Guadalcanal; Tarawa and, finally, Saipan.

While training on Pacific islands, he contracted malaria, which kept him out of action for a while. He had recurrences of malaria for years thereafter. His job on the ship was working to calculate range, accuracy and targets for the big guns that shelled the coastal areas where Marine landings were going to take place; this involved his photogrammetry skills and the use of aerial photos. He was part of the Fire Control System on the ship.

Marines were not only the Navy's infantry, but they carried out shipboard duties as well, hence Christie's being assigned as a fire control officer. The job involved map reading and complex mathematics to calculate the trajectories of the large shells. Part of his training to meet the needs of the Marine Corps was to take two years of college math in California. Because of the work of these men, the shells fired by the big guns were remarkably accurate and both terrorized and slaughtered the Japanese soldiers on the various islands where the Marines would land and attack. I don't know all the battles he was in, but he was at Guadalcanal, Tarawa, and Saipan.

Saipan

The ships began bombarding Saipan on June 13, 1944, with battleships, destroyers and other vessels involved, delivering more than two thousand four hundred sixteen-inch shells before the Marines went ashore. (Hallas, 2019) Four of the older battleships involved in the shelling had survived Pearl Harbor and were present for the Battle of Saipan, which would affect the outcome of the war. On Saipan, thirty-one thousand Japanese awaited the assault from seventy-one thousand Americans of the 2nd and 4th Marine Divisions and the 27th Infantry Division of the U.S. Army. Overall, the United States forces totaled five hundred thirty-five ships and one hundred twenty-one thousand troops in an operation that was the second largest combat sea and land operation of the war—second only to D-Day in France, which had taken place a week earlier. The U.S. Marines on Saipan were the first U.S. soldiers to set foot on Japanese soil since the attack on Pearl Harbor.

Christie, who was a sergeant, said at Saipan his company was held in reserve in case things went wrong on the beach landing on D Day. The United States military needed to take Saipan because by controlling Saipan they would also control the Island of Tinian immediately to the south. Tinian had an airfield long enough to support the new Boeing B-29 super fortresses designed to reach Japan and drop the atomic bomb. Taking Saipan would mean the end of the war was in sight. It was worth any cost to move the nation closer to ending the bloody and costly conflict.

The bombs were being developed in New Mexico, not far from Christie's home in Santa Fe. His brother, Ernie, was part of the group that was making the atomic bomb. Wars put everyone into jobs and places they never would have considered possible absent a world war.

Two Chicano brothers from Wagon Mound, were each engaged in the world war in very different situations and a world apart, one a U.S. Marine infantryman on Saipan and one a machinist working with the Manhattan Project at Los Alamos.

The land Battle of Saipan in the Mariana Islands began with the first wave on Green Beach and ran into stiff opposition from the entrenched Japanese, with more than two thousand Marine casualties on the first day. For perspective, nineteen hundred fifty U.S. troops and CIA agents were killed over the entire twenty-year span of America's war in Afghanistan. Christie said he spent almost all that long first night of the assault on the ship carrying amputated limbs from wounded Marines to toss into the sea, knowing he would be part of the early morning assault group.

Banzai

Next morning (D Day plus one), more Marines hit the beach to support their comrades. The Marines encountered withering fire, suicidal banzai charges by the screaming Japanese and hand-to-hand combat. Christie had an artillery round hit right next to him that blew him twelve feet in the air. He said his vision went red and it looked as if the whole world was red. After he fell back to earth, he was amazed to find he was unhurt and his eyes were fine, so he resumed fighting.

In late afternoon, as the fighting continued, another mortar round hit him, this time almost severing his left leg at the ankle. His best friend who was fighting next to him told him to take off all equipment, including his rifle. His friend then picked him up, threw him over his shoulder and ran under fire to the medics who were a half-mile away.

His buddy managed to carry Christie to the rear and saved his life. Christie was given emergency medical treatment and eventually sent to New Zealand for treatment and rehabilitation. There he learned his entire platoon had been wiped out in a banzai charge. The Japanese fought until July 9 with the loss of twenty-nine thousand Japanese troops and thousands of civilians. Losing this crucial battle led to the suicide of General Yoshitsugu Saitō and the resignation of Japan's Prime Minister Tōjō. After the Battle of Saipan, the seas were now open all the way to the Japanese home islands. The end of the war was much closer than it had been before the Battle of Saipan took place and was won by the U.S. Marines and the U.S. Army.

Christie spent an extended period of time being rehabilitated in New Zealand and recovering from his wounds. These were called million-dollar wounds—a ticket out of combat and a return home. Such wounds had to be bad enough that the soldier could not recover enough to be sent back into combat. Christie had won a Purple Heart for being wounded. His buddy was awarded a Bronze Star for saving Christie's life.

Love With Complications

Christie's buddy met a woman while in New Zealand. She was a professor of psychology and looked, according to my uncle who ought to know, like the twin sister of Greer Garson, the famous actress—which is to say she was beyond beautiful. As frequently occurs in wartime, the beautiful psychologist and Christie's war hero buddy fell deeply in love. Such situations were especially common in World War II, where soldiers were in the military for the duration of the apparently endless war.

"Dear John" letters were famously sent by wives or fiancés in the States who had found new lovers during the years-long separations of war and wrote to inform their serviceman husband/lover about it. The reverse happened too, where fighting men fell in love with someone from a foreign country and had to write "Dear Jane" letters to their wife or girlfriend to let them know things had changed. As the English said about the main problems with the World War II GIs, "They are overpaid, over sexed and over here." Christie was single, but his buddy was married—definitely a complicating factor in the whole scenario that was about to play out.

His buddy asked Christie to marry the psychologist in his place since, as the wife of a serviceman, she would receive automatic U.S. citizenship. Obviously his friend couldn't marry her, God knows, because he was already married. He said if he could get her back to the States as a U.S. citizen, Christie could divorce her there and she would then be free to be with her lover in one form or another. So, with the three principles in agreement (Christie, his buddy and the psychologist), Christie married her.

Christie had never met his bride-to-be before their wedding day; he had only heard about her from his buddy. Suddenly he was marrying this drop-dead gorgeous woman. He said he kissed her chastely after the wedding ceremony. His buddy, the best man, then stepped forward and kissed her passionately, which drew some serious stares from the preacher and the guests.

Even before the invention of social media, those types of situations had a way of getting out, no matter how hard someone worked to keep them quiet. In this case, it was the bride who was about to be divorced by Christie, as they had all planned, who let it slip out (telephone, telegraph, and tell a woman, as they used to say when I was a child). She called her father in New Zealand and told him about the whole plot. The father was apoplectic. He wanted Christie arrested and returned to New Zealand to be jailed for something, anything, surely there was something with which to charge him. What? Marrying a girl under false pretenses? She had agreed to the plot. She had an advanced college degree. Getting divorced on his return to the States? Nope. Marrying his buddy's lover? Hardly. Well, something, surely. Her father went to the New Zealand courts.

Congressional Assistance

One member of our family, Antonio Fernandez, who was born and lived for years in the town of Raton, New Mexico was a U.S. Congressman from New Mexico. He was married to our cousin, Cleo, who was a talented artist. Representative Fernandez specialized in issues affecting the military and was a major supporter of the G.I. Bill, passed in June, 1944—the very month when the Battle of Saipan was fought—so he carried a lot of weight in Washington with the Roosevelt administration. Not only was Christie a close relative of the congressman who had grown up in the same small town, but he was also a wounded and decorated Chicano war hero as well. Christie's unusual marital problem was practically invented for his cousin's congressional acumen, legal experience and influence. Congressman Fernandez opened up official channels with the people" down under" and dealt directly with the government of New Zealand. He even involved the Chief Justice of New Zealand. In the end, Christie's still unconsummated marriage to the psychologist was annulled by the court, leaving Chris free of entanglements and leaving his "ex-wife" free to marry her lover.

Yet Another Woman

A marriage can be annulled months or even years after a wedding, depending on circumstances, so the woman's U.S. citizenship was not affected. There was only one problem that reared its ugly head as things got even more complicated. His friend had been promoted to captain after he got back from the war and was now moving in more elevated social circles than those of the simple enlisted man he had been before. He met a beautiful teacher who lived in Washington, DC and fell madly in love with her. Now Christie's buddy was torn between two lovers and his wife. ¡Por Dios!

"What should I do?" he asked Christie. "Marry the girl from New Zealand; she's beautiful, she's smart and she was willing to take part in our crazy scheme in the first place. You owe her." But the buddy chose the teacher. His dad was absolutely disgusted with his son and the whole mess of his son's personal life. He told him to call the New

Zealand woman and tell her what he had decided. However, he did not believe his son (his promotion to captain and medals of valor in battle notwithstanding) had the courage to call his soon-to-be ex-lover and tell her the truth. His dad insisted he listen in on the phone call between his son and the woman he was dumping to make sure he would tell her the whole unvarnished truth. His son made the call, telling her it was all over. His buddy then divorced his first wife and married the teacher. After all the personal turmoil, they stayed married for the next 50 years, until his death did they part.

There is one more twist to this story. More than five decades later, as he lay on his deathbed, Christie's friend decided to track down his original New Zealand lover. He learned she had married a very rich man in Canada. He wrote her a letter with deepest apologies, emptying his soul and saying he had been an unfair and uncaring jerk and he now finally recognized how badly he had hurt her. He was sorry and filled with remorse for everything bad that had happened a half century before, but now he was dying and he wanted her to understand how terrible he felt about the past. He begged her for forgiveness. She never opened the letter, but instead sent the unopened envelope to his wife. It arrived just after Christie's friend had died but his widow opened the letter and got the whole story. He had never told his wife any of the specifics. Only he and Christie and the New Zealand woman, herself, had known the whole story of what had happened.

A Celebratory Drink

When Christie returned to the States, he had a pronounced limp and needed to use a cane to walk. The doctors and therapists had managed to save his leg but the limp remained for a long time. The family was so proud of their warrior who had come home safe, albeit wounded. One night he and my dad went out to a bar for drinks to celebrate his return. My dad in those days was, of course, a hard drinker and not opposed to getting into a fistfight in a bar. Christie, who had a very gentle nature, was recovering from being wounded on Saipan and the emotional scars of the other battles he had been in, as well as his annulment problem.

Christie had gotten a load of "nice" in the family genes, but my dad had gotten a bucket of "mean" in his genetic complement. Christie had been a fighting master sergeant in the Marines, but he wasn't really a tough fighter without his rifle and bayonet. My dad was.

Christie was in his uniform greens with the Marine hat and his medals. They were sitting in an Albuquerque bar enjoying themselves. They were two New Mexican mestizos, one who had helped take the Japanese island of Saipan, thereby influencing the end of the war, and the other who was helping build the atomic bomb that would end the war. Then a great big gringo (a "stomp"), obviously looking for trouble, walked up and noticed the two short Mexicans, one of whom was in the uniform of a United States Marine and holding a cane. He didn't notice, apparently, my dad's arms were developed like Popeye's after years of working on the railroad. The gringo came up to their table and said in a very loud voice for the whole bar to hear, "Well, well, well. I never thought I'd see the day they let Mexicans into the Corps. A Mexican Marine."

He had no sooner gotten the words out of his mouth than my dad hit him with an uppercut on the jaw. His jaw shattered, some of his teeth flew away and the big guy went down as if he had been poleaxed. The whole bar broke into a donnybrook with gringos and Mexicans fighting each other. Christie got up using his cane and my dad got him safely through the fighting crowd and outside the bar. Meanwhile the fighting continued after they left and they could hear things breaking as they walked away. Though it could be argued my dad started it all with the jaw-breaking sucker punch, neither of them had been hurt and they made a clean getaway. No one had laid a finger on the Mexican Marine. As Christie told me, "Ernie was as tough as nails and that guy was down for the count."

War is Tough

Saipan was some of the worst fighting of World War II in the Pacific Theater. It was a battle that had the Navajo Code Talkers stationed with the troops. I asked Christie if he knew any of them, because many were also from New Mexico. "Yes, I knew them. I tried not to get too close to them, though. If we were overrun by the Japs, it was my job to kill the code talker so that the Japs could not take him prisoner and crack the codes that were used in combat by the Marines."

> "Would you have done that?" I asked him.
>
> "Of course," he responded. "If they ever got that code, we could lose the war in the Pacific and many Marines would die. It was my duty."
>
> "That's pretty tough," I said.
>
> "War *is* tough," he responded.

The Japanese never cracked the Code Talkers' code. They recorded the calls but could not figure out what kind of strange language or code it was.

I asked Christie if he had ever seen any war movies, and, if so, did they bring back the feelings he had in combat. "I never saw a war movie until I went with my grandson to see "Saving Private Ryan." The beach landing was very well done, except no one was really dying and everything else was phony. You knew you wouldn't die and everyone around you in the theater was going to get through the movie battle. In combat, you and everyone around you are likely to be killed and you know it. There is no way a movie can make you feel what war is really like."

CIA

After first having been in the Army and then the Marines in World War II, Christie joined the nascent CIA after the war as a photogrammetry specialist. In 1962, it meant he was part of the team that examined aerial photos obtained from the overflights of Cuba by U-2 spy planes; it was called Operation Brass Knob. He also worked with aerial photos from other countries to determine what was going on in different parts of the world, especially things pertaining to the Soviet Union or other Cold War rivals. He traveled the world as a part of his job, but always had to have clearance to travel to a foreign country and contacts to protect him when he was on the road, because his security levels were so high. He was too important to be captured by the enemy.

A Very Fine Wine

Once on assignment in Portugal, Christie was in a bar (he loved his drinks) and asked the bartender to give him a glass of the best wine in Portugal. It was expensive and after he was served the wine, he sipped it for a long time. He said it was wonderful. He then asked for another glass. The bartender said no. "Why not?" Christie asked. The bartender said it was because almost no one in Portugal could afford to drink the country's finest wine; they only dreamed of someday having such a wonderful glass of Portugal's best. Then a rich North American comes into the bar and wants to have two drinks? No, he could not in good conscience serve him another. Since he agreed with the bartender, Christie was so moved that tears fell from his eyes. He hugged the bartender. Christie was always far and away the most sensitive of the Mares men.

The Bay of Pigs

As the Cuban situation post Bay of Pigs developed, Christie was approached by CIA operatives to go to Cuba as a spy. He spoke perfect Spanish (in fact, like my dad, Spanish was his first language). They said they would have to surgically alter his face with scars so he would be harder to recognize as a North American. They would get him into Cuba and he would start to do the dangerous work spying on Cubans and Russians in Castro's Cuba. It was a perilous assignment, to say the least. I asked if he would have accepted such an assignment. My country needed me, so I said yes. However, they decided I was more valuable to them with my photographic work, so the idea was dropped. He would never say this but I'll say it for him: Whew!

Cuban Missile Crisis

When the Cuban missile crisis occurred in October, 1962, Christie was one of the few analysts who examined Lockheed U-2 CIA reconnaissance aircraft photos of Cuba. It was Christie's job to determine whether or not the Soviet missiles were offensive weapons or defensive missiles and the conclusion by his small group of specialists that the missiles were, indeed, offensive weapons, initiated the whole Cuban missile crisis. His group met with President John F. Kennedy in the Oval Office to explain to the President how they had distinguished the offensive missiles from defensive weapons. He was selected to be in the group that would travel with the President in the event of a nuclear holocaust so their expertise would be available to him. He would work with the photos made at great risk to the pilots who flew unarmed missions over Cuba. On October 17, 1962, the anti-aircraft missiles that had been stationed on Cuba by the Soviet military, downed a U-2 spy plane while photographing Soviet weapons and killed its pilot, Rudolph Anderson Jr. The attack came close to igniting the fuse to World War III.

My girlfriend (now wife), Lynn Brusin, was a student at St. Mary's High School, which is where we met. In 1962, we were both juniors and assumed we would always be together and in fact have been together over the intervening sixty-plus years. The night we waited for the U.S. Cuban Naval blockade of Russian ships to either succeed or fail was like a countdown to doom. I had convinced her Albuquerque was a primary target for the Soviets because of its air force and army bases—and the fact that nuclear bombs were stored at both Sandia Base and Manzano Base under the Manzano Mountains. It was an open secret in those days that the Manzano Mountains were filled with H-bombs. Students in Albuquerque never had "duck-and-cover" drills, perhaps because everyone knew we were sitting on top of the country's hydrogen bomb storage site.

I said there would not be much to live for if the Russians rained their ICBMs down on our heads, so why not get together in the local park and watch them come flying in? We could say goodbye to each other and to the world. Like a good high school girlfriend, she understood my logic and said okay. We needed twenty minutes lead time if the missiles flew, so I watched the news constantly and listened to the radio as the world counted down to the end of days. Then the ships in the Russian convoy stopped. Then they turned around and left. "We're eyeball to eyeball and I think the other fellow just blinked," remarked Secretary of State Dean Rusk. Life went on and the doomsday clock was moved back just a bit.

It is as close as the United States has ever come to nuclear war and it was set in motion in part by my uncle and his team of analysts. After the ships turned around, Christie had to verify the dismantling of the Cuban missiles and see them reloaded on Russian ships. Of course, he never talked about any of this until twenty years after he retired and the work was declassified. He was also then able to receive his CIA medals and numerous official recognitions and awards for his work.

I was reading a history book once and Christie was in the room. I found the page describing the Cuban missile crisis complete with aerial photos. "You want to tell me how you could tell that these were offensive and not defensive weapons? I can barely tell they're missiles." He looked at the photos and laughed. "Those aren't the photos I used," he said. "Those are the photos we released to the press. You can't see a damn thing in those photos, but the ones I used were remarkably clear. People died getting the photos we used. They are still classified."

Get an Education

Thirty years later, when he retired from the CIA, Christie enrolled at George Washington University and received a Bachelor of Fine Arts degree. When he was in the Marines in California he was ordered to enroll in college for some needed training. He got two years of training. His majors? Math and art. He had wanted to go to college since he was a teenager and, after leaving the CIA, he finally had the opportunity to do it full time in his sixties and was awarded a college degree in art with honors. He always had been an excellent artist, but after getting a degree in the subject, his work became even more interesting and mature and he won several art contests in the Washington, DC area. He painted and also made pottery, *a la* his mestizo/Indian relatives in New Mexico. His work was highly respected in artistic competitions and he had a unique style in painting and potting.

As an old man, long retired as a CIA analyst, Christie would read any book cover to cover, including an entire encyclopedia and then would want to discuss many topics from the book. To the day he died, at the age of ninety-three, his mind never slowed or faltered. He had a remarkable memory, like my dad. As far as I am aware, he did not read fiction, only things that improved his mind. He was always trying to make up for the education he had lost as a young man. He lamented that loss all his life, as did my father. I edited the large volume, *Encyclopedia of Deserts* (Mares, M.A., 1999) and Christie read the whole seven-hundred-page book. Afterwards, he wanted to discuss the deserts of the world with me and seemed to remember all the chapters.

Fig. 55. Christie Mares in the Marine Corps, 1942.

My Uncle Christie was a patriot. Long after he was no longer a Marine, when he was in his seventies and retired from the CIA, he told me he was walking in front of a Marine Corps recruiting office and the Marine's Hymn was playing over a loudspeaker. He said it was all he could do not to go in and sign up again, a half century after he had been in the Corps. He finally figured they did not want an old man in his seventies for the modern Marines. That's how deeply the pride of being a World War II Marine gets drilled into you.

Was he seeking to recapture his youth? Perhaps he wished to once again be part of something enormous and global, where you knew you were fighting for something good and millions of your brothers and sisters were also engaged in the same enormous and historic undertaking. I doubt he wanted to be involved in repelling a Japanese banzai charge again, which he found the most fearsome thing he had ever experienced. ("I shit my pants twice that day!") I think he was simply longing to be a part of a group of Americans fighting for a just cause.

Fig. 56. Christie Mares, helping develop photogrammetry for the Navy and the CIA.

The Pied Piper of Saipan

There were a number of Chicano Marines on Saipan. One became known as the Pied Piper of Saipan. Guy Gabaldon, a Chicano from Los Angeles, whose parents had been born in New Mexico, was raised in part by Japanese neighbors in Los Angeles, when he left his parents' home as a troubled youth of twelve and moved in with the Japanese family next door and essentially became their son. He became fluent in Japanese and, since his new Japanese family were immigrants, he learned the Japanese language used in the home islands. He joined the Marines at seventeen.

In combat on Saipan, the naturally independent Chicano Marine went across enemy lines and started talking to the Japanese in their own language as they hid in caves and holes. He convinced them to give themselves up, rather than die in battle or commit suicide. Remarkably, he was able to gain their trust, even with the battle raging around them. His commanding officer did not approve of his working alone behind enemy lines and chewed him out, reminding him he was a member of a group (for the most part Chicanos are not in favor of being members of a group), but Gabaldon kept going out alone anyway. Night after night, he brought back more and more Japanese soldiers and civilians whom he had convinced to surrender. His commander finally accepted this Chicano was not very controllable and let him continue. Besides, he could not argue with success.

By the time his work was done on Saipan, Gabaldon had brought in fifteen hundred Japanese, soldiers and civilians (ten percent of all the prisoners captured by all the other Marines and soldiers on Saipan). It was the capture of the most prisoners taken by a single U.S. soldier in the history of warfare. He was compared to Sergeant Alvin York, who had captured one hundred fifty Germans and won the Medal of Honor. Gabaldon, too, was recommended for the Congressional Medal of Honor (CMH), but instead he was given a Silver Star Medal. Gabaldon was also badly wounded on Saipan and won a Purple Heart Medal, but being ignored for the CMH was an obvious slight to his heroism. His heroic exploits were likely ignored because he was a Chicano.

"Hell to Eternity" (1960), starring the handsome, six foot one tall, blue-eyed Jeffrey Hunter as the five foot four-inch, swarthy true-life hero, Guy Gabaldon, told the story of Gabaldon's heroics. (The movie also starred David Janssen, Vic Damone and George "Mr. Sulu" Takei.) The year the movie was released, the U.S. Government and the U.S. Navy upgraded Gabaldon's award to the Navy Cross, the highest Navy medal there is, except for the Congressional Medal of Honor. Gabaldon noted he probably could have been awarded the Medal of Honor and his not receiving that award may have had something to do with his being a Chicano, but he was proud of his service, proud of the Navy and proud of his Navy Cross. Guy Gabaldon died before the Medal of Honor could be awarded to him. His case is still being reviewed.

In an interview, Gabaldon (2000) recalled how, after he was released from the hospital and had returned to Los Angeles from Saipan, he would go out drinking with his Chicano buddies, who were all combat veterans. He noted how they would be attacked by what he called big "Okies," who wanted to beat them up for being Mexicans. They did not realize we had been killing people and fighting for months in combat, he said, so we took care of them when they tried to beat us up.

Marcario Garcia

That was certainly the case with another Mexican/Chicano soldier, Marcario García, who received the Congressional Medal of Honor from President Harry Truman at the end of World War II. President Truman, a war hero himself, told García he would rather have the Medal of Honor than be President of the United States (which recalled General George Patton's comments on the medal (Yardley, 1998): "I'd give my immortal soul for that medal." Marcario's family had crossed into Texas to pick cotton and young Marcario was a cotton field laborer throughout most of his youth, unable to go beyond grade school. He was born in Coahuila, Mexico, but grew up in south Texas from the time he was a small child. Today he would be called a wetback, an illegal, or an undocumented immigrant.

When he was twenty-two years old, he joined the Army and was soon headed to Europe. He took part in the D Day landings as a member of the Army's 4th Infantry Division, the lead division on the D Day beaches of France and was badly wounded. After recovering from his wounds for four months, he was sent to Germany with the infantry. In November, 1944, acting as squad leader, he single-handedly engaged two enemy machine-gun nests that had pinned down his entire company. He was badly wounded approaching the German machine guns but ignored his wounds and destroyed the first position with grenades. He then approached the second gun emplacement alone and destroyed it too, receiving more wounds in the process. He stayed with his unit until the battle was won and only then accepted medical attention. As the Medal of Honor citation said, he had total disregard for his personal safety. Garcia later said he was scared during the whole battle but knew what he had to do.

After recovering from his wounds, he returned to Texas and tried to get a cup of coffee at the Oasis Café in Richmond, Texas, which did not serve Mexicans. He was in full uniform wearing the Medal of Honor and his many other medals, but that did not matter. A fight erupted and Garcia was badly beaten by the restaurant owners who assaulted him with a baseball bat. Marcario was saved by the quick action of a bunch of Gringo sailors who jumped to his defense. The owner even pressed charges against García for entering the restaurant and fighting, and García was the only person in the restaurant who was arrested. (Olivas, 2008)

The incident recalls the epic fight with the restaurant owner in the movie "Giant," where Mexicans were not allowed to eat, even if they were the mix-blood grandson of the rich, white-as-snow millionaire Texas oilman played by Rock Hudson. Indeed, the Marcario García case is presumed to be what influenced the book's author, Edna Ferber, to include the redneck restaurant fight scene between Bick Benedict and the café owner in the book and the film. (Olivas, 2008)

No Mexicans or Dogs

In the movie, "Giant," the sign that the roadhouse owner tosses on Bick Benedict after beating him up so he was prostrate on the floor, notes that the restaurant reserves the right to deny service to anyone. That was not the actual sign involved in the Macario beating, however. At the time the Texas fight took place, the Texas Restaurant Association had signs printed for display in all Texas restaurants that read, in English and Spanish: "No Mexicans or dogs." When the story hit the national news media, all charges were dropped. Some years later, García received his high school diploma and became a U.S. citizen, eventually going to work for the Veteran's Administration. He was a noted activist for civil rights and died in a road accident on Christmas Eve in 1972 at the age of fifty-two. Streets, schools, and a veteran's center are named in his honor in the Houston area. Marcario won the Medal of Honor and other recognitions, including: Combat Infantryman Badge; Legion of Merit with one Oak leaf cluster; Bronze Star; Purple Heart; American, European, African, Middle Eastern, World War II medals; Campaign Medal; Campaign Medal with two Service stars; Victory Medal; and the Mérito Militar (from Mexico).

Another Chicano killed in battle by a Japanese sniper on the island of Luzon whose remains were treated poorly in Texas was Private Felix Longoria, who was also from Sugar Land, Texas, and had died in the Philippines in 1949. (Carroll, 2003) This incident was also depicted in the movie, *Giant*. The hero's family wanted him buried in Three Rivers Cemetery near his hometown. The cemetery had a Mexicans Only section separated from the Anglo section by barbed wire (works for cows and Mexicans, apparently). Cemetery officials said the chapel could not be used by Mexican Americans, including the war hero, Longoria. As the funeral home man said, it did not matter that he was a heroic veteran killed in action, "You know how the Latin people get drunk and lay around all the time. The last time we let them use the chapel, they got all drunk and we just can't control them—so the White people object to it, and we just can't let them use it."

This became a minor *cause célèbre* and finally reached the desk of Senator Lyndon B. Johnson of Texas who received permission from President Harry S. Truman to bury Longoria in Arlington National Cemetery, which is where his remains are interred. Senator Lyndon Johnson, who used to teach English to impoverished Mexican kids in elementary school, and his wife Lady Bird, were in attendance at the funeral. (Patterson, 2023)

Gabaldon's and García's and the other Chicano post-war stories are so similar to that of my Uncle Christie in the Albuquerque bar, it suggests a pattern of ethnic hatred that was faced by returning Chicano soldiers during and after World War II, heroes or not, wounded or not, medals or not, dead or not.

29

"Time just gets away from us."

(Mattie Ross. "True Grit")

I have presented a non-traditional history of Spanish-Mexican-Chicano-Mestizo cultures from my point of view with my own experiences throughout. The story stretches from the Iberian Peninsula during the Medieval Period of the Middle Ages into the New World, including New Mexico and parts of the American Southwest, after contact was made between the European invaders and the Native peoples. My ancestors were a part of this history all the way back to Medieval times, at least to the end of the first millennium, and centuries before Spain was even a country. They were a part of the exploration of the New World, the era of the conquistadors, the conquering of Native peoples in Mexico and in the American Southwest, the Indian Wars, the Mexican War, the Civil War, and other wars.

My genome is composed of parts of the DNA of all those peoples and more, as are the genomes of almost all mestizos in present-day Mexico and the United States. We are an amalgam of cultures. My ancestors were the conquerors and the conquered. They fought in many wars and killed their enemies. Some may have eaten their enemies. Some were eaten by their enemies. There was no shortage of cruelty over this long span of time, and for humans, war and cruelty are the defining characteristic of our species, though we frequently struggle to be morally superior to our bloody nature and are loath to admit our inherent barbarity.

The story of humanity is a history steeped in warfare and slaughter on a massive scale, where there were no good guys, only warring factions, some of whom won and some of whom lost. Data demonstrate gene exchange across cultures and nations with the ultimate survival of those genes found today in the surviving mestizos and Indians that tell the deep history of our people across time and space. The historical record tells the story of cascading deaths from introduced diseases, unimaginable cruelty by all peoples toward their enemies and the illegal taking of enormous tracts of territory in parts of what would become the United States.

As *The New York Times* noted in 2003, over the last three thousand four hundred years, peace has reigned on the planet for only two hundred sixty-eight years, or only eight percent of recorded history over a time span of more than three millennia. (Hedges, 2003) During that period, perhaps a billion people have died in wars, maybe many more. Even as I write these words, there are twenty-eight armed conflicts underway worldwide. As a letter between two Parthian monarchs, Mithridates and Arsaces (as recorded by the Roman historian Sallust, 66 BCE) noted:

> In fact, the Romans have one inveterate motive for making war upon all nations, peoples, and kings: namely a deep-seated desire for dominion and for riches ... Do you not know that the Romans ... have possessed nothing since the beginning of their existence except what they have stolen—their home, their wives, their lands, their empire? ... no laws, human or divine, prevent them from seizing and destroying allies and friends, those near them and those afar off, weak or powerful, and from considering every government that does not serve them, especially monarchies, as their enemies ... it is by this audacity, by deceit, and by joining war to war that they have grown great. Following their usual custom, they will destroy everything, or perish in the attempt.

We cannot rewrite history, though we can reinterpret it with new data. Part of this history in the 1800s was driven by the interests of the United States and Texas in promoting slavery across the nation, supported by the almost crazed doctrine of Manifest Destiny for Protestant White America, wherein God ordained America's hegemony from sea to shining sea. (De Gree, N.D.) Some people, perhaps most, still believe this doctrine, which they have sometimes conflated with the phrase American Exceptionalism, another national myth having little substance.

The enormous and fascinating lands of Mexico and New Mexico under Spain and later under Mexico were eventually arrogated by the United States government in an illegal war that had the goal of taking Mexico's territory by force and making the newly acquired lands a part of the existing territory of the United States, thus extending the United States all the way to the Pacific Ocean. Ideally, at least for the slave holders, this would have had the additional advantage of extending slavery into the new territories, slavery being an abhorrent practice Mexico had made illegal in 1829. This helped lead directly to the war of Texas Independence and the Battle of the Alamo. Texas lore has made the Alamo a heroic story of the fight for freedom, but in fact the truth describes a much darker story of a fight for the freedom to own slaves. That part of the Alamo myth seems to have been well covered up and slipped away over the centuries. The Civil War intervened in any plans to extend slavery to the new territories and states and eventually the United States, as Mexico had done more than three decades earlier, prohibited slavery.

Siempre Los Mexicanos

The Treaty of Guadalupe Hidalgo was signed guaranteeing the rights of Chicanos to keep the lands that had been gifted them by the King of Spain in gratitude for their conquering, colonizing and holding an enormous new territory for Spain, a territory on the far side of the world that was much larger than Spain itself. The U.S. State Department and the Mexican government were careful to protect the rights of the Mexicans and Chicanos in the peace treaty that was signed to end the Mexican War, since these people were about to become proud new citizens of the United States. They had been living in the newly recognized American territory as Spanish or Mexican settlers for hundreds of years, long before the nascent USA was colonized by Europeans. Now suddenly they were in a territory that belonged to another country. Unfortunately, in ratifying the Treaty of Guadalupe Hidalgo, the U.S. Senate changed many of the fundamental agreements on how the new citizens of the U.S. should be treated and their lands protected (Adams, 2006), and things were not changed to benefit the citizens to be. On the contrary.

Local Anglo governments went about busily finding ways to steal the land-grant ranches and move the Chicanos into poverty. Part of their strategy was destroying all legal documents in New Mexico that described land holdings. Wills were also destroyed so heirs would have a difficult time maintaining their family's property. In Texas they simply forced Chicanos off their ranches at gunpoint. Leave or die.

The State Department officials who had painstakingly negotiated the protocol [between the two nations] found...the rights of people they were trying to protect left in the desert...The difference...was more than one of 'opinion.' Mexican and American statesmen had agreed on words that were designed to protect and crafted for clarity…. American politicians had altered the reality in order to renege on the protections and obscure their purpose. (Adams, 2006: 149)

In California, the Gold Rush complicated land ownership, but by the 1900s, "Mexicans had been largely dispossessed of their property.... Lynchings and murder of both Mexicans and Indians were so common that they often went unreported.... The dominant (Anglo) society, profoundly racist, found it entirely reasonable to relegate Mexicans to a colonial status within the United States." (Estrada *et al.*, 1981: 109) Chicanos fought for their property rights, and in a few cases were successful, but overall, the new citizens went from being the old ruling families to brute-work laborers in two or three generations.

Sometimes Brown-skinned Mexican Americans were lynched. (Hall, 2020; Table 6) Between 1848–1928 at least five hundred ninety-seven Mexican Americans were hanged (Carrigan and Webb, 2003), with violence being especially targeted at Mexican workers or landowners. ("Anglo mobs were motivated by racism and greed for Mexican-American land.") (Bishop and Shu, 2016) There were other excuses, too, including "... the Catholic religion; conflict with Mexico; anti-Americanism in Mexico; and suspicions that Mexican Americans were not patriotic." (Martinez, 2018) In California and Arizona, vigilantes were active, killing hundreds of men, especially Mexicans. (Rosales, 1996)

State	Number
Texas	282
California	188
Arizona	59
New Mexico	49

Table 6. The top four states for lynching Mexican Americans (1880–1930)

If someone like my distant uncle Padre Martinez dared step forward to alert the populace of New Mexico about these underhanded land moves, the Church hierarchy in New Mexico excommunicated him and an Anglo writer from Nebraska destroyed his reputation across the ages with her fictional account of a giant of intellectual accomplishments in frontier New Mexico. Even after the newly acquired lands became part of the U.S., there were still continuing troubles in dealing with the Brown people of the Southwest and California. (Rosales, 1996) The first person hanged in the new Territory of California was a Mexican woman who had been assaulted and raped by a drunken Anglo. Her husband killed the Anglo and was exiled, but the wife who "allowed" herself to be raped was hanged. (Estrada *et al.*, 1981: 110)

Forty years before fourteen-year-old Emmitt Till was lynched in Mississippi, a fourteen-year-old Chicano, Antonio Gomez, was lynched by a mob after being forcibly taken from the custody of law enforcement officers in Thorndale, Texas, about fifty miles northeast of Austin. Gomez had been hassled by a group of adult white males for whittling and letting the wood chips fall on the ground. One man grabbed Gomez, cursed him and took away his piece of wood. Gomez responded reflexively, stabbing him and killing him. In 2023 a national monument was established to honor Emmett Till and his mother with President Joe Biden personally dedicating the monument. There is no monument to mark the lynching of Antonio Gomez.

The year before Antonio Gomez was beaten and hung, a Mexican ranch hand named Antonio Rodriguez was captured and put in a jail cell because some people believed he had murdered a woman. A mob pulled him out of jail, tied him to a post, then burned him alive. After this, they lynched the burnt remains. In response, mobs of Mexicans on both sides of the border attacked businesses and assaulted White people. Just as the investigation of the hanging was beginning, the Mexican Revolution broke out and Mexico was thrown into turmoil for ten years.

When the Japanese invaded the United States in the Aleutian Islands in 1942, it was the young Chicano soldier, Joe Pantillion Martinez, of Taos, New Mexico, who died stopping a major assault and winning a posthumous Medal of Honor for his actions. Before the U. S. was invaded by Japan, however, it was invaded by the Mexican bandit/soldier/revolutionary Francisco "Pancho" Villa in the little town of Columbus, New Mexico on March 9, 1916. Villa invaded the U.S. because he wanted the U.S. to invade Mexico in response to his attack and not support the dictator Carranza. However, Villa's raid killed eighteen Americans (eight soldiers and ten civilians) and almost immediately, Villa, who led the raid, was pitted against part of a U.S. 13th Cavalry Regiment stationed in Columbus. Villa's forces fell back to Mexico and President Woodrow Wilson responded by sending the

"Punitive Expedition, U.S. Army" led by General of the Armies John J. "Blackjack" Pershing to capture Villa. Pershing led sixty-six hundred cavalry and infantry into Mexico chasing after Villa. Soon this army expanded to ten thousand men.

My uncle from Albuquerque, Elfego Garcia, was a soldier in Pershing's army and was a part of the Expedition. He fought in the battles that ensued in Mexico. At one point, Mexican regular troops, not Villa's army, attacked Pershing's men. Eventually the Mexican government threatened to drive the intruding American Army out of Mexico. By January, 1917 the Expedition force returned to the U.S. and peace negotiations with the Mexican government followed. Pancho Villa was never found by Pershing's men. He was assassinated by Mexicans in 1923. He was forty-five years old.

The Mexican Revolution and Pancho Villa's raid in the United States led to increasing dislike of Mexican Americans. In early 1915, a plan of rebellion had been drafted in San Diego, Texas (the Plan de San Diego). The Plan was to seize all the former territory of Mexico from Texas and the U.S., including as far west as California and kill all non-Hispanic males over sixteen years of age throughout the southwestern United States. It involved a hoped-for uprising of Hispanic Texans, Mexican Americans and Indians, former adversaries who were expected to act in concert.

No one knows who put forth this deranged plan or whether Mexican Americans or Mexican revolutionaries were involved. (Weber, 1978) However, it understandably upset the inhabitants of the U.S. Southwest and dozens of raids against American and Mexican American citizens subsequently took place. Texas Rangers and the U.S. Army were deployed to the Texas border to control the raiders. Investigations of the Texas Rangers later showed between 1914–1919, as many as five thousand ethnic Mexicans were murdered.

During those turbulent times there were ongoing skirmishes and battles along the Mexican-U.S. border. The Brite Ranch in Presidio County, Texas was raided by Mexican raiders who may have been with Pancho Villa or another faction of the Mexican army or may have just been banditos. No one was certain. They killed three Texans, then were chased back to Mexico by the U.S. 8th Cavalry, which killed some of them. Texas Rangers and Army troops then decided, based on no evidence, that the raiders were from the small Hispanic town of Porvenir (which means future). Soldiers and rangers broke into homes in Porvenir in an early morning raid and dragged fifteen Hispanic men and boys (one was only sixteen years old) into the desert and shot them repeatedly, so many times that it was difficult to identify the bodies. The rangers and soldiers then burned the entire town to the ground.

Hispanics fled from the town and across the river to Mexico. Porvenir became a ghost town. The future it could no longer look forward to was ended by the acts of racist criminals in the guise of Texas Rangers and U.S. soldiers. Porvenir no longer had a future. Elected officials and the Texas Rangers tried to justify the attack. This story came to light only because the sole survivor of the Porvenir Massacre, who was a twelve-year-old boy during the raid, witnessed the attack but said nothing until he was ninety-five years old. Then the truth came out.

Periodically over the last century, and as recently as a few years ago, the U.S. Government would sweep up mestizo U.S. citizens illegally and deposit them in Mexico, along with Chicano and Mexican legal and undocumented immigrants. What other ethnic or politico-ethnic group of American citizens could the government do this to with impunity? What other group would tolerate it? None.

Black and Brown

African Americans would gather together into large groups of people to protest such high-handed and illegal treatment. Blacks have spokespersons on television 24/7, as well as many news anchors among the major networks and newspapers. If something bad happens to a black person because of police actions (a lamentably common occurrence), protests are mounted within minutes from coast to coast. The airwaves are instantly filled with a cadre of informed and respected Black people, such as Reverend Al Sharpton, or a coast-to-coast gaggle of experienced attorneys, including many Harvard or Yale law school graduates, to speak up for the Black people who were killed or injured. All major newspapers carry the stories. Such stories are soon all over the web and social media.

Such responses are good for Black people; they keep their stories and their plight in front of the public so action can be taken and bad behavior can be changed. I am very proud of their ability to come together and keep the stories of injustice on the front pages and television screens of the nation, informing the populace. Moreover, Black people vote as a group and they vote for Democrats. They are a force in every election and have often provided the impetus for a president's winning an election. Without Black voters, Presidents Obama and Biden would not have won the nation's highest office. As Michael Dawson (1995) suggested, Blacks have a sense of "linked fates," where they vote as a group despite being in different economic or social classes and perhaps not agreeing with each other on many things. "My fate is closely linked with the fate of all Blacks, so I will vote with them to support my issues and their issues. We will rise together."

Not So for Chicanos.

The Romans had a battle formation called the *testudo*, which means the tortoise. In this formation, the warriors form a closed box with their overlapping shields. When properly executed, the *testudo* is impenetrable to arrows and spears. It could seem invincible to enemy soldiers involved in battle. The Spanish used the *testudo* too, but it was not uncommon for one or more soldiers to lower their shields so they could fight individually. This led to the failure of the entire *testudo* and the loss of soldiers to arrows and other weapons. The Romans felt the Spanish were the most likely group to allow their independent natures to cause them to weaken the *testudo*.

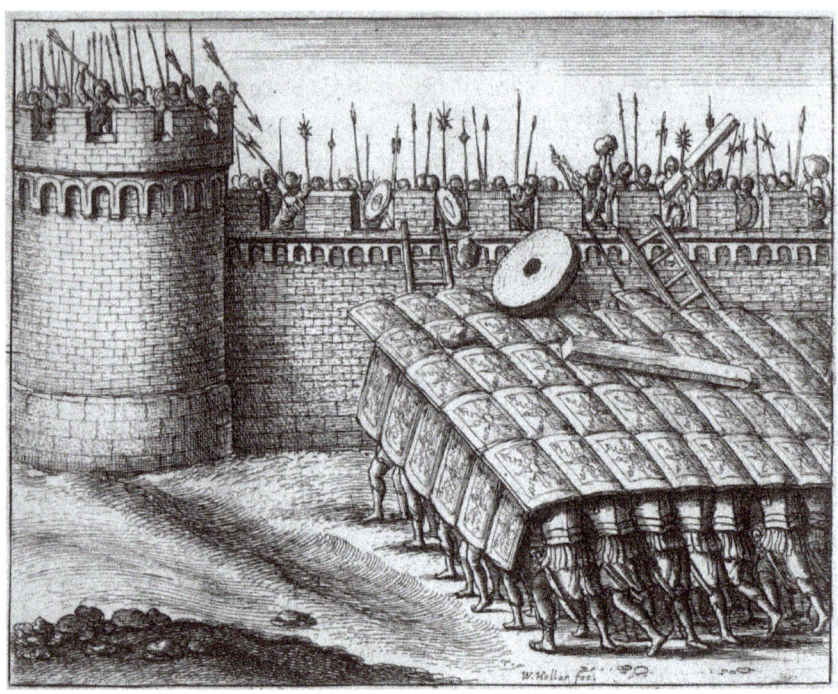

Fig. 57. The Testudo Roman war formation in a castle assault. University of Toronto Wenceslaus Hollar Digital Collection.

Most Chicanos (and as usual I exclude non-Chicano Hispanics) are less social and do not like to be in groups. They are extremely independent and closed off from social groups, except for their extended family and close friends. We are not joiners or members of clubs. We seldom attend activist churches, if we attend church at all. There are few activist Catholic Chicano churches in any case, unlike Black churches. If a Chicano is shot down by police officers in a questionable police action (a common occurrence), the public seldom hears about it. It is never national news and is often hardly even local news. No one takes to TV microphones across the nation for dead Chicanos, keeping the story front and center until corrective action is taken. No Chicano lawyers or social workers appear on national television (or even local television) to sound alarms and demand justice. Nope. Does not happen. In reading about the many Chicanos who won our nation's highest award for valor, the Medal of Honor, it becomes clear they almost always acted alone (Appendix), saving their men and heroically killing their enemies, but not asking their men to risk or lose their lives. It is the way we are.

Moreover, Chicanos do not form a powerful voting block like African Americans. They thus dilute their political power and may even fall victim to being hoodwinked by grifters like Donald Trump, who signed Treasury checks he did not need to sign so people might think he was sending them his money. I laughed at Trump's thinking that people were that stupid. How dumb does he think we are? Well, my stars and garters, many Chicanos thought Trump had sent them his personal money, so they voted for him.

Cruelty With Impunity

What other groups of legal immigrants in their ragged summer clothes—often without shoes and desperately seeking refuge from dangers in their own country—could be kidnapped by tin-pot governors, not told where they were being sent on their first plane flight ever and then be deposited in the snows of cities in the northern U.S.? The sociopathic governors of Texas and Florida and their goon lackeys took great pleasure in the desperate plight of the immigrants and the distress of the townspeople of the places they had been dumped and that had never been notified to prepare to receive immigrants in need.

I am hard-pressed to suggest any other group of people to whom this could have been done without a howl of protest from most Americans. Politicians perhaps? I wish. Blacks? Never. Cubans? Not hardly. They would run the Florida Republicans out of their cushy state jobs. Puerto Ricans? Not with Justice Sotomayor and Lin-Manuel Miranda around. Would not happen.

We must ask why the United States government feels entitled to mistreat its Chicano citizens in this manner, citizens moreover who have contributed and continue to contribute enormously to the quality of life for everyone in our nation. Scores of bonafide Chicano war heroes (Medal of Honor winners) defended our nation during its many wars but were often not recognized for their heroism or were denied medals. They were too Brown I think, like my dad being the wrong color when being told he was the best person for a job but they just could not hire him. He was later able to work on the atomic bomb with J. Robert Oppenheimer, as well as help make some of the most modern rockets, fighter jets and telescopes known at the time (1950s and 1960s), but he never forgot losing that job because he was "too Brown."

Chicanos and Life in the U.S.

Chicano actors, performers, educators, chefs, politicians, artists, intellectuals, social activists, sports champions, authors, reporters, television anchors or business titans have made America a much better and culturally richer place than it would have been had they not been a part of our society. (Appendix) Chicanos have been recognized by major awards ranging from the Medal of Honor to the Presidential Medal of Freedom to the CIA Medal of Merit, from Academy Award Oscars to Emmys to Golden Globes to Grammys to the Nobel Prize. Many Chicanos have been honored on the Hollywood Walk of Fame. Chicanos have been in America longer than the ruling White power structure and, in fact, longer than America has been a nation. Why then do Chicanos remain in the shadows of society?

The first astronaut to play a musical instrument while floating in space was a Chicana, Ellen Ochoa. The fourteenth Director of the National Science Foundation was a Chicana, France Córdoba. Chances are you never heard of either one. (Appendix) The man who discovered and solved the ozone problem that was going to destroy much of life on earth was a Mexican/Chicano, Mario José Molina Henríquez. Chicanos have served as cabinet officers for presidents of both parties, ambassadors, and as elected representatives and senators as well, of both parties. Zorba the Greek was the great Chicano actor Anthony Quinn. Speedy Gonzalez is modeled on the illiterate Chicano comedic actor Pedro Gonzalez-Gonzalez. The uplifting story of a high school math teacher, the Bolivian Jaime Escalante, was played by Chicano actor Edward James Olmos. Wonder Woman was a Chicana. The movie, "McFarland, USA," was about a group of hard-working fruit-picking Chicano students who became some of the finest cross-country runners in the nation. José M. Hernandez was a Mexican American who worked remarkably hard because he wanted to go into space—a fruit picker from Michoacan, Mexico, who was born in a camp for migrant pickers in the United States. Eventually his diligence and dedication paid off and he became a NASA astronaut. He traveled on the Space Shuttle *Discovery* as a mission specialist spending eleven days on the International Space Station. His life was celebrated in the film, "A Million Miles Away."

We have enjoyed the music of Chicanos such as Joan Baez, Vicki Carr, Freddy Fender, Los Lobos, Trini Lopez, Linda Ronstadt, Santana, and Richie Valens. Mariachi music is Chicano music. We have all laughed along with George Lopez ("America's Chicano") or been uplifted by the movie "Flamin' Hot," about Richard Montañez and the Frito Lay company, or "Spanglish," a moving film about a young wetback Chicana high school girl applying to an Ivy League school. Our Chicano heritage is all around us.

Yet as new immigrants have continued to arrive legally seeking refuge in our country, their families have been rent asunder, their children forcibly removed from their parents to disappear forevermore and the people themselves subjected to living conditions in forced captivity that would not be acceptable for farm animals. This was especially notable during President Trump's xenophobic administration with its fixation on building a wall to keep the "breeders" and "rapists" out, regardless of whether they were here legally or not.

Too Brown I Fear

Why does the United States government continue to demonstrate the will to carry out such barbarities on Chicano immigrants, yet manage never to be held accountable? The answer is because they are mistreating Brown-skinned Chicanos who do not form a voting block of their peers, that's why, and who cares about Brown-skinned people anyway? It's called colorism. (Noe-Bustamante *et al.*, 2021; Canizales and Vallejo, 2021) The darker your skin, the harder it is to get ahead in America, which is consistent with the racist underpinnings of our society. (Noe-Bustamante *et al.*, 2021)

In a remarkable paper written in 1931 by the eminent Professor Emory S. Bogardus from the University of Southern California, the attitudes of the Mexican immigrant were discussed. Bogardus noted some of the earliest arriving Mexicans are called conquistadores and are wealthy, educated, and sometimes (sic!) sophisticated. (Bogardus, 1931: 292) I guess that would be me.

But following the educated class and a couple of other groups of Mexicans in the U.S., there is the laboring class. Of course, that was me too when I was a pick-and-shovel laborer. He apparently does not believe in mobility between classes. "In general, these Mexican laborers are unskilled, and socially of low-grade. They are low-cultured members of the main Mexican peoples, that is, of the mestizo classes. They are sometimes called peons, because they have been oppressed laborers." (Bogardus, 1931: 295)

"The employer cannot get native Americans to do the necessary unskilled labor, cannot get European labor, cannot get Japanese or Chinese and does not find Negro labor, Porto Rican labor or Filipino labor as satisfactory." (Bogardus, 1931: 296) (¡Por Dios! Good help is so hard to find these days and they are even darker skinned than we are.) "The employers' attitudes are favorable to the Mexican because of the latter's docility." (Bogardus, 1931: 296) Here he conflates manners and respect with docility. The Medal of Honors winners might have some comments on docility. Finally, Bogardus races toward his racist conclusion: "The employer as a class does not favor the training or education of the Mexican laborer." In the first place he says "...such training would raise the Mexican out of the class of labor where he is needed."

> Second, such education makes the Mexican dissatisfied, restless, desirous of more wages, subject to unionization, and hence 'undesirable.' It is also contended that the Mexican is not capable of being trained, his intelligence is of a low order, and that to spend much money on him is an economic waste. (Bogardus, 1931: 297)

Ah, Professor Bogardus, there goes any pride I might have felt in being awarded my PhD in zoology from a first-rate university. He sounds very much like Bishop Lamy in the 1800s. There are other pearls of wisdom about Mexicans:

> He is hacienda-minded...[having] lived on large estates, which he has never thought of owning or whose owner he has never had a chance to envy.... What he has found lying around on the hacienda he has picked up, examined it if it perchance aroused his curiosity, used it if he felt so inclined, and laid down again—pretty much as an American child would do about his own home. (Bogardus, 1931: 300)

This sounds like a naturalist reporting on the behavior of a monkey.

I actually had one of my well-to-do Anglo neighbors in Santa Fe, who did not know I was a Chicano, confide to me that "…these Mexican people feel that what is yours is theirs and they feel free to take it." She told me to be careful when they were around. I'll have to keep an eye on my granddaughter.

> Since 'right' and 'wrong' do not have the meaning for the

uneducated Mexican that they have for Americans [ouch.], the Mexican immigrant figures more largely in American crime statistics than would otherwise be the case...Stabbing frays are characteristic of personal violence.

It has also been claimed, although proof is hard to obtain, that charity even scientifically administered encourages Mexicans to continue bringing abnormal families into the world.... Climatic conditions, inadequate food, and a dull social routine have combined sometimes to produce a 'lazy Mexican'.... Many Americans possess antipathetic attitudes toward the Mexican immigrant because of current stereotypes. They always think of Mexicans as 'dirty greasers,' as persons 'unclean,' as carriers of dread diseases. They recoil. They object to the presence of Mexican children at the schools where their children attend—for fear that the latter will catch 'some terrible disease.' (Bogardus, 1931: 304)

I wonder if articles like Professor Bogardus's racist screed might have influenced people's attitudes toward Chicanos? His ideas are still current today. These kinds of published beliefs (and many others) have surely made the path of the Chicano more difficult within the United States. Bogardus goes on to say how well Mexican children perform in segregated schools. The U.S. has advanced a long way from its overtly racist past, but there is still a long way to go. Like the *loquitos* who were limited to being a quaint part of life in their small villages long ago, the Internet has permitted racists to crawl out from under their rocks and unite across the world. They are now a force in society The question is, do we have enough time remaining to effect positive cultural changes before our racist/jingoistic psyches decide it is time for the U.S. to kill again on a massive scale in order to preserve the ruling White order? Maybe not.

I noted, Whites live in terror of becoming a minority ethnic group in this country but the shift to Whites being a minority group is already a foregone conclusion. Barring war or some massive calamity, the Whites of America will never be in the largest ruling class again, as ethnicities continue to shift the country toward a multiracial society where Whites are in the minority. Nevertheless, the odious Trumpian xenophobia has captured the minds and hearts of White supremacists and other concerned White people across the country.

Ostensibly the United States would launch a major war (think of the scale of the war against ISIS) and slaughter drug cartel members and any nearby Mexicans or Chicanos who happened to get in the way. (Al Jazeera, 2023) The Mexican nation will not be involved, just as Mexico never declared war on the United States during the Mexican War of the mid–1800s. As Mexican President Lopez Obrador said about this insane talk of war, "…[I]t is an offence to the people of Mexico.…Mexico does not take orders from anyone." He noted if Republicans try to "…use Mexico for their propagandist, electoral and political purposes, we will make a call to not vote for that party." (Al Jazeera, 2023)

Drug cartels are not organized armies, however. They are part of Mexican culture and thus hard to find. Drug laboratories are hidden under tarps in woodlands, cost almost nothing to build, and are exceedingly hard to locate. Destroying such field laboratories does almost no long-term damage. They can be rebuilt elsewhere and be ready to resume operation in hours. (Bhole, 2023) Bombing them can kill some workers but the number of potential drug workers in Mexico, which has a population of one hundred twenty-seven million people, most of them poor, is limitless. The ingredients for the fentanyl used by Mexico to send to the U.S. come from China. Without a ready market of buyers, the drug would disappear.

Fig. 58. Improvised ovens at a clandestine methamphetamine lab in Sinaloa, Mexico. Victoria Dittmar/InSight Crime.

Drug use in the United States encompasses the entire country. There is no red state/blue state division. All states are confronting the enormous drug problem and losing tens of thousands of family members, young people and other loved ones.

Fig. 59. Map of Mexico showing the complexity of the conflicts of the drug cartels throughout the entire nation. Congressional Research Service June, 2022; data provided by James Bosworth, Hxagon LLC.

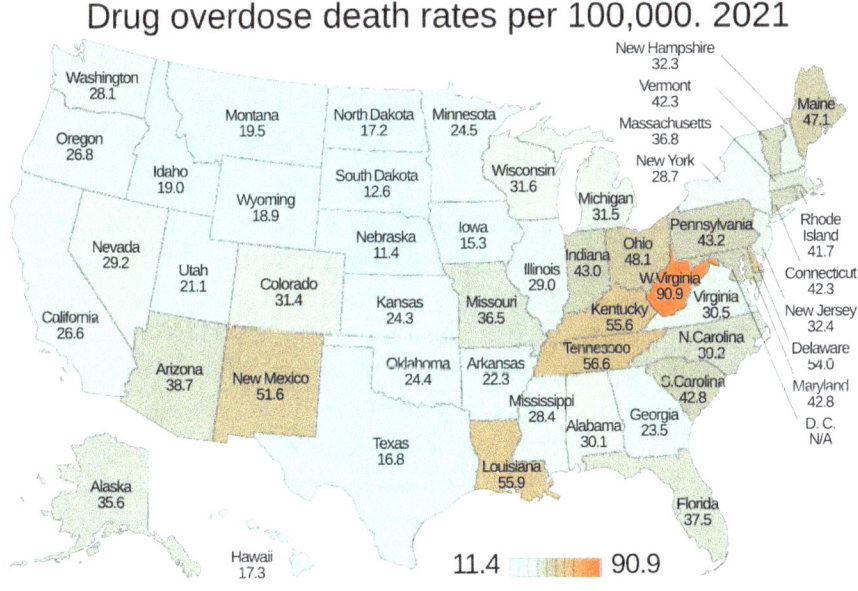

Fig. 60. Drug use in the United States and states most affected by illegal drugs. Data and map from Centers for Disease Control and Prevention.

Perhaps, if we start a war with Mexico we can once again steal additional land by force. Those *Baja* beaches are tempting. As President Dwight Eisenhower presciently noted in his farewell address:

> In the councils of government, we must guard against the acquisition of unwarranted influence, whether sought or unsought, by the military-industrial complex. The potential for the disastrous rise of misplaced power exists and will persist. We must never let the weight of this combination endanger our liberties or democratic processes. (Eisenhower, 1961)

No one listened.

As so frequently happens, Shakespeare said it first when he noted in his play *The Tempest*: "What's past is prologue." This has often been interpreted in a positive manner but, as Andrew MacNeily (2020) noted:

"The alternate, more cynical view, would be that what took place in the past inevitably repeats itself because we don't learn from our experiences and mistakes."

The Mexican War has happened before. At some point, the United States will have to stop killing people throughout the world, otherwise we could go the way of perennially bellicose Rome. Some wars are necessary, but most are not, as Eisenhower noted. The Vietnam War, which was trumped up and phony, damaged the moral fiber of the nation for more than a generation and crippled our military so seriously that the government shifted from drafting soldiers to an all-volunteer military. Politicians and corporations seldom consider the damage done to the spirit and morale of a country from poorly justified wars and conflicts or from general lawbreaking or from nullifying legal punishment for crimes, yet these are serious factors in the happiness and optimism of our citizens.

It seems that Donald Trump might well turn out to be the most corrupt politician to ever serve as president. Yet many people feel he will beat the hand of justice, as he has all his life. (Trump, M., 2020) Like the myth that the United States is not a racist country, the myth of equal justice under law has been smeared across the upside-down star-spangled banner by Supreme Court Justice Samuel Alito. What kind of message does it send to a society if a criminal is given special consideration in court? What does it mean when the top law enforcement officer in the nation, the president, is given immunity from any crimes? It is good to keep repeating the mantra, "Corruption corrupts." I might add a codicil to that statement, to wit: Corruption corrupts and it corrupts us all. When someone slides out from under the rule of law, all citizens are affected and it is the nation that suffers. (Wike *et al.*, 2021)

The United States is at a tipping point. Our country has suffered greatly because of our inherent racism. Blacks are working hard to enter mainstream society, which is dominated by Whites. There was a Black president. There are two Black supreme court justices, and a Black vice president and many other Blacks in high positions in American society.

Puerto Rico was conquered and taken from Spain in large part by the Chicano members of the Rough Riders (aka Teddy's Terrors), where fully a third of the soldiers were U.S. Chicanos. (Westermeier, 1952) It is ironic that Puerto Ricans are now U.S. citizens and the Chicanos in many cases are not. Cubans were able to escape from communist Castro and obtain a special seat at the table of citizenship and political power by becoming fanatical conservative Republicans and voting as a bloc. If their feet touched U.S. soil, they were immediately able to begin the process of becoming U.S. citizens. This is definitely not U.S policy toward the Brown people of Mexico and other mestizo countries.

Who Are We Becoming?

The governor of Texas deployed floating buoys in the Rio Grande that have led to drownings of immigrants who are attempting to reach the center of the river (the actual U.S.-Mexico border). In FY 2022, more than eight hundred immigrants drowned trying to cross the Rio Grande. ("CBS Streaming News" 2023) According to the federal government, the buoys are illegally placed along an international border and are mostly on the Mexican side of the boundary. However, they are effective: drownings are up.

> A state trooper's claims that superiors ordered officers at the border in Eagle Pass to push migrants back into the Rio Grande and deny them water has sparked a state investigation, the Texas Department of Public Safety said Tuesday. The trooper also reported that razor wire deployed by troopers has injured people—including a woman who had a miscarriage while entangled in the wire.

(Garcia, 2023)

The trooper continued in a letter to his sergeant, "I believe we have stepped over a line into the inhumane." (Garcia, 2023) He and other troopers had come upon one hundred twenty immigrants in a very sorry state, "exhausted, hungry, and tired," including small children, babies and nursing mothers. He contacted his shift commander and was told to push the people back into the river so they could swim back to Mexico. With the one-hundred-degree temperatures, one little girl passed out. Others have sustained serious cuts from the razor wire stretched along the river.

The cowardly and apparently sociopathic Texas governor Abbott (Beschloss, 2021) issued a statement saying he never ordered anything like what he was hearing about the mistreatment of immigrants. Right. Like Sergeant Schultz in Hogan's Heroes, "I know nothing! Nothing!" Just like the four-hundred-plus heroic Texas law enforcement officers who charged unafraid into the Uvalde school and stopped the killer before he could kill the Chicano elementary students and their teachers.

Oh wait! It did not go down that way. The armed-to-the-teeth Texas Department of Public Safety and Texas Rangers milled around outside, afraid to go after the lone crazed gunman who had used the governor's buy-your-weapons-fast-and-easy laws and was rewarded by not being bothered by hundreds of pesky police as he slaughtered the school children. Notwithstanding the horror, the governor praised the response of law enforcement saying, "It could have been worse."

A review of databases that track police killings (Police Evidence Report, 2023) shows that while their cases have largely gone untold in the national discussion of police violence, Latinos are killed by police at nearly double the rate of White Americans. And while the national debate on police killings has focused on Black Americans, whose deaths at the hands of law enforcement have been high-profile and outnumber those of other people of color, some activists say the situation for the Latino community has become critical. (Foster-Frau, 2021)

Between 2014 and 2021, more than twenty-six hundred Latinos were killed by police or died in police custody. How many of these did you hear about on local or national news or read about in your local newspapers? The Raza Database Project was founded in 2021 and examined available data on police killings, noting Latinos were underreported in such data by one-quarter to a half. That means the numbers could actually be double or even triple what has been reported. How did the United States, which is basically a caring nation, permit Chicanos to be dropped into rivers to drown or to die in the heat from a lack of drinking water? (LEAD, 2021)

Chicanos are a mixture of people who came to the United States more than five hundred years ago and, if their native American roots are considered, thirty thousand years ago. They also include people who arrived yesterday and today. They form an important part of U.S. society. Chicanos achieve at high levels in any field of endeavor. Reviewing the extraordinary lives listed in the at the end of this book shows many, if not most, began poor, worked at menial jobs and then decided to excel.

Sometimes their success came during the second or third generations in the United States. They often faced racist impediments put in their path to keep them from succeeding. However, the only thing that could keep them from achieving their goals was their own internal drive, intelligence, and *ganas*! They refused to be stopped.

The government needs to expand education programs for immigrants to encourage their becoming active members of society without living separate lives because of language differences. We need to encourage them to pursue education, for that is the true ticket out of the barrio. As Nelson Mandela noted: "Education is the most powerful weapon which you can use to change the world." (Mandela address, Mindset Network July, 2003) College degrees take a lot of work, but the payoff is considerable. Conservatives (especially the uneducated, such as many radio or TV talk-show hosts) speak against education in general and education of minorities in particular. And even liberals like Bill Maher (Cornell Ivy League graduate) feel higher education is a waste of time, a point of view that may be easier to hold when your net worth is north of one hundred forty million dollars. Some actually say publicly they want to burn down the universities, which they believe are education camps run by communists. I do not blame them for not wanting the targets of their manufactured and commercial ire to be educated. It is difficult to deal with an educated person when one is not as highly educated. It is easy to cow the ignorant and uninformed, but hard to dominate the intellectually informed opponent.

Talk radio has influenced much of America with ignorant but highly opinionated political shock jocks spewing poison to a largely uninformed public. Their listeners are hard-working Americans and may not have had the opportunity, the economic means, family support or the intellectual or personal drive to continue their education and become more informed about the world they inhabit. They are ripe for the ignorant messages from hucksters who feed their need for talk, entertainment, paranoia, pugnacity, victimization, validation and worry twenty-four hours a day. As Eli Wallach said in "The Magnificent Seven," "If God didn't want them sheared, He would not have made them sheep." Perhaps, but if they had become educated, they might not *be* sheep.

As a university educator for half a century, I helped hundreds if not thousands of students change their lives for the better, whether they became doctors, lawyers, dentists, professors, veterinarians, nurses, wildlife officers. scientists working for industry or government, and advisors or conservation officials dealing with global challenges. Their education, dedication and hard work made their outstanding lives and accomplishments possible.

Every Chicano child has the potential to lead an outstanding life, just as the abused children of San Felipe School could rise above the cruelty of the nuns and priests and grow to lead fulfilling lives and influence society. Chicanos must learn to fight for their right to be educated, to realize their dreams, and to not let anyone or anything stop them. We are not victims. We are a mix of many of the greatest civilizations in world history. As a group we may be a mix of all the world's great civilizations. As Jaime Escalante said in the movie, "Stand and Deliver":

> There will be no free rides, no excuses. You already have two strikes against you: your name and your complexion. Because of those two strikes, there are some people in this world who will assume that you know less than you do. Math is the great equalizer.

Escalante continued:

> Did you know that neither the Greeks nor the Romans were capable of using the concept of zero? It was your ancestors, the Mayans, who first contemplated the zero. The absence of value. True story. You *burros* have math in your blood.

The system is set up for Chicanos to fail, from grade school through college, but we are smart, are not afraid of hard work and can accomplish great things with our lives. We are better than what the ruling culture expects of us and we always have been. We can learn from our African American brothers and sisters to work together and to share a "linked fate" awareness.

When I was a new PhD student in zoology at The University of Texas at Austin, I was in my biogeography class one morning taught by a famous zoologist, Dr. W. Frank Blair. It was my first class in graduate school at the PhD level and I did not know anyone there. In the middle of his lecture, Dr. Blair stopped the class and announced, "I just received a large grant to study deserts and there is graduate student support in the grant for any student that wants to be part of this research. If you would like to move to Argentina for two years and then work in Arizona at the end of that period, I have salary, travel, and other funds to support you. Just let me know after class."

For me the world had stopped. I looked around—surely every student in the class would leap at this opportunity. What chance did a new Chicano graduate student have to win such a prize? I did not know Blair and he did not know me. I had come from a small college in Kansas and before that from the University of New Mexico. I was well trained in ecology and vertebrate biology and, being a child of the desert, I loved deserts, but the University of Texas was the big time. Its student body was three times larger than the town where my master's institution was located. I had no one to talk to, not even my wife, who would surely have to approve. Yet, I could not let this opportunity slip away.

After class, I introduced myself to Dr. Blair and followed him to his office. When he sat down, I said, "Dr. Blair, I am willing to go to Argentina to work on desert biology. I know reptiles, amphibians, birds, mammals and fish, though truth be told, I am not crazy about fish. I am an ecologist." "I am looking for someone to study mammals." "Then I'm your man," I said, "I love mammals and I worked on the population ecology of grassland mammals in Kansas for my master's thesis. Would you like to see a copy?" "No, that's not necessary. Your job will be to prepare for your comprehensive exams in the fall and to design a research project for Argentina. You'll leave in a year."

That was that. My life had changed forever in a matter of seconds because I was not afraid—or at least would not let fear stop me—of pursuing a major new challenge and grabbing an opportunity when it presented itself. No one else in that graduate class took advantage of the opportunity. As Woody Allen said, eighty percent of success is showing up. I told my wife we were going to Argentina after I got home and she was thrilled too.

Those few seconds when the future knocked and I opened the door ended up changing hundreds if not thousands of lives over my career. My two children were born in Argentina on different field trips. I taught at several universities in the country and influenced hundreds of young people. My own Argentine doctoral students became leaders in their fields of study, as did my North American graduate students who mostly worked in Latin America. I developed friends and colleagues throughout Argentina and, indeed, across the continent. My doctoral research in Argentina changed my life forever.

Fig. 61. Michael Mares conducting field research in the rain forest of Costa Rica.

Only by succeeding can Chicanos change the system that has ruled their lives from day one. That system can be influenced by passionate, educated, informed and committed people who are aware of opportunities to change their lives, who are able to change their attitude about working together with colleagues, Black and Brown. They may be in business, authors, actors, screenwriters, entertainers, politicians, religious people, architects, members of the military, bureaucrats, artists, computer scientists, engineers, medical personnel, reporters, television personalities and a host of other professionals that affect society. Blacks, other Hispanics, Native Americans and Chicanos all need to work together to learn to play the political game to win, though Chicanos are quite different from the Cubans, Puerto Ricans, South Americans and other groups that often fall under the rubric of "Hispanic." It is the only way to win.

All of us must work together to change the system. Together, we can be a force for equality of opportunity and for societal change. Together we already *are* the majority. Together we have remarkable power at the voting booth. We hold power and we must wield it, not let it slip away. That is the operative concept. America is still a land of opportunity, but only if we work together across ethnicities to use the system that is in place and open the doors that have been closed to too many people for far too long. It will not be easy, but success is never easy. If we have the *ganas*, we will succeed. We are an unstoppable force of American society and have been for five hundred years.

30

NOTABLE MEXICAN AMERICANS / CHICANOS

Presidents have often recognized the importance of immigrants to the continued success of America. Lyndon Johnson (1965), for example, while signing the Immigration and Nationality Act of 1965, said:

> This bill says simply that from this day forth those wishing to immigrate to America shall be admitted on the basis of their skills and their close relationship to those already here. This is a simple test, and it is a fair test. Those who can contribute most to this country—to its growth, to its strength, to its spirit—will be the first that are admitted to this land. The fairness of this standard is so self-evident that we may well wonder that it has not always been applied. Yet the fact is that for over four decades the immigration policy of the United States has been twisted and has been distorted by the harsh injustice of the national origins quota system. Under that system the ability of new immigrants to come to America depended upon the country of their birth. Only 3 countries were allowed to supply 70 percent of all the immigrants. Families were kept apart because a husband or a wife or a child had been born in the wrong place....

This system violated the basic principle of American democracy—the principle that values and rewards each man on the basis of his merit as a man. It has been un-American in the highest sense, because it has been untrue to the faith that brought thousands to these shores even before we were a country.

Today, with my signature, this system is abolished. We can now believe that it will never again shadow the gate to the American Nation with the twin barriers of prejudice and privilege. Our beautiful America was built by a nation of strangers. From a hundred different places or more they have poured forth into an empty land, joining and blending in one mighty and irresistible tide. The land flourished because it was fed from so many sources—because it was nourished by so many cultures and traditions and peoples.

President Ronald Reagan (Reagan, 1952, 1989) commented on the importance of the process of assimilating immigrants into U.S. society:

I...have always thought of America as a place in the divine scheme of things that was set aside as a promised land. It was set here and the price of admission was very simple: the means of selection was very simple as to how this land should be populated. Any place in the world and any person from those places; any person with the courage, with the desire to tear up their roots, to strive for freedom, to attempt and dare to live in a strange and foreign place, to travel halfway across the world was welcome here.... A man wrote me and said: "You can go to live in France, but you cannot become a Frenchman. You can go to live in Germany or Turkey or Japan, but you cannot become a German, a Turk, or a Japanese. But anyone, from any corner of the Earth, can come to live in America and become an American...."

Other countries may seek to compete with us; but in one vital area, as a beacon of freedom and opportunity that draws the people of the world, no country on Earth comes close.... This, I believe, is one of the most important sources of America's greatness. We lead the world because, unique among nations, we draw our people—our strength—from every country and every corner of the world. And by doing so we continuously renew and enrich our nation. While other countries cling to the stale past, here in America we breathe life into dreams. We create the future, and the world follows us into tomorrow. Thanks to each wave of new arrivals to this land of opportunity, we're a nation forever young, forever bursting with energy and new ideas, and always on the cutting edge, always leading the world to the next frontier. This quality is vital to our future as a nation. If we ever closed the door to new Americans, our leadership in the world would soon be lost...that's why the Statue of Liberty lifts her lamp to welcome them to the golden door.

Following is a list of Notable Mexican Americans/Chicanos who excelled in heroism, life achievements, or made major contributions to U.S. society. The list is not complete, merely illustrative. Data gathered from numerous pages of military reports, biographical sketches, newspaper and magazine articles and other widely available accounts.

Chicano Medal of Honor Recipients (selected from more than sixty)

Lucian Adams. Port Arthur, Texas. One of fourteen children. He and seven brothers joined military. World War II. Advanced alone against German machine gunners; killed nine, captured two, eliminated three machine gun nests. Used hand grenades and rifle to kill all Germans that were an immediate threat to his men. Called the "Tornado from Texas." Congressional Medal of Honor awarded by Lieutenant General Alexander Patch in Germany on April 22, 1945, in Zeppelin Stadium, Nuremberg. After the medal was awarded, Hitler's giant swastika was blown up by army engineers.

Leonard Louis Alvarado. Bakersfield, California. Vietnam War. Rifleman. In 1969 gave his life fighting to save his platoon and another one they were trying to save. Left his platoon in the firefight and headed toward the enemy disrupting their assault. He was injured by a grenade and killed the soldier who fired it. Badly wounded. Crawled forward through the fire to drag his wounded comrades to safety. He again crawled alone and engaged the enemy, saving his platoon and was killed in the battle. The Congressional Medal of Honor finally awarded posthumously by President Obama in 2014.

Joe Rodriguez Baldonado. Born Colorado, 1930, the son of migrant workers. Corporal Korean War. Held an exposed hilltop position that was attacked by a heavy force. Wiped out wave after wave of enemy soldiers saving his men. November, 1950. Killed by a grenade. Remains were never found. Posthumous Congressional Medal of Honor awarded by President Obama in a special ceremony in 2014 to honor Chicanos, Blacks and Jews denied medals for heroism. Obama noted the reason medals had not been given earlier was due to prejudice. "Some of these soldiers fought and died for a country that didn't always see them as equal."

Raul Perez "Roy" Benavidez. Born 1935 in Cuero, Texas to a Mexican farmer and a Yaqui Indian mother. Very poor. Shined shoes and worked as a fruit picker in several states. Dropped out of school at fifteen. Joined Army at seventeen; 82nd Airborne, then Special Forces. Stepped on land mine in Vietnam and was going to be mustered out because he could no longer walk. Refused to quit. Trained nightly through intense pain to learn to walk again. He was distressed at the lack of support for Vietnam soldiers by the public. Walked after a year of training and returned to Vietnam. He grabbed a helicopter to rush to the aid of twelve Special Forces surrounded by a thousand North Vietnam regulars. His only weapon was a knife. He helped stop the NVA assault and received thirty-seven bullet, bayonet and shrapnel wounds. He was pronounced dead and put in a body bag. His friend asked the doctor to be sure Roy was dead and the doctor said he's dead all right. Benavidez then spit in his face to show he was alive. Benavidez was denied the Medal of Honor at first, but eventually Congress made an exception for him and Ronald Reagan presented the CMH to Benavidez, saying if this battle had been a movie script, no one would believe it. Wrote three autobiographical books.

Pedro Cano. Private first class. Born La Morita, Mexico, 1920. Initial assault on Utah Beach, then combat across France, Germany, Belgium. Company pinned down, Cano crawled under machinegun fire to take out four machinegun nests alone using a bazooka. Next day, alone, he attacked eight enemy machineguns, took out five, then used M1 to kill a German taking his officers prisoner. Distinguished Service Cross mailed to him with no fanfare. The two officers he saved kept recommending him for Medal of Honor. Cano was also denied citizenship. A Texas Senator worked to make Cano a citizen. Cano suffered from post-traumatic stress disorder. Died in a car crash at thirty-two in 1944. The Congressional Medal of Honor was awarded posthumously by President Obama in 2014.

David Barkley Cantu. Born 1899 Laredo, Texas. World War I. Much discrimination against Mexican American soldiers in the First World War. Cantu would not use his last name and even asked his mother not to sign his letters with her last name. Drowned in 1918 on a secret mission to obtain German Intelligence. French Croix de Guerre, Italian Croce Merito de Guerra. Posthumous Congressional Medal of Honor.

Jesus Santiago Duran. Born Juarez, Mexico. Specialist Four. Vietnam. M60 machine gunner 1st Cavalry. His men came under fire from a group of bunkers in 1969. He waded into the fire with an M60 firing from the hip. His bullets were seen coming out of a cloud of dust raised by the enemy fire. He learned two of his men were hit and ran forward firing into foxholes and killing the enemy in four of them. He turned the whole enemy assault around until they were running away. He followed them, killing them as they ran. Congressional Medal of Honor finally awarded posthumously by President Obama to Duran's daughter in 2014—forty-five years after his heroics.

Victor Hugo Espinoza. Born El Paso, Texas. Korean War, Chorwon, Korea, August, 1952. Unit ordered to take a hill but pinned down with withering fire. He single-handedly took out a machine gun nest, found and destroyed an enemy tunnel and then wiped out two bunkers, inspiring his unit to move forward and take the objective. The Posthumous Congressional Medal of Honor was awarded by President Obama in 2014.

Daniel D. Fernandez. Born Albuquerque, 1944, raised in Los Lunas, New Mexico. Vietnam War, 1966. While trying to rescue a wounded comrade the enemy lobbed a grenade into the midst of five rescuers. Fernandez was the only one to see the grenade and threw himself on it saving his four comrades. Posthumous Congressional Medal of Honor was awarded by President Johnson in 1967.

Joe Gandara. Private First Class. Santa Monica, California. World War II. Battle at Amfreville, France. Germans pinned down his men for four hours with constant fire. He decided to take the Germans out and advanced alone voluntarily and destroyed three enemy machinegun nests. Received posthumous Congressional Medal of Honor from President Obama in 2014—seventy years after he died in combat.

Candelario Garcia. Corsicana, Texas, 1944. Mexican descent. Sergeant in Vietnam War. December, 1968. Destroyed two machinegun nests trying to help wounded. Charged a machine gun and jammed two grenades in the gunport. Shot everyone in the foxhole. Cleared out another bunker alone. Received posthumous Congressional Medal of Honor from President Obama in 2014—forty-six years after combat heroics.

Marcario García. Staff Sergeant. First Mexican immigrant to receive the Congressional Medal of Honor. Badly wounded in D-Day landings. Recovered then sent to Germany. Assigned to clear German machinegun nest. He did, but was badly wounded. As they were getting ready to treat his wounds, a second nest opened up on his men and he attacked that nest, killing all the Germans and saving his men. Congressional Medal of Honor awarded by President Truman.

Edwardo Corral Gomez. Born Los Angeles, California. Korean War. Assaulted a tank alone after crossing open ground killing the tank company, then after being wounded led another assault against the enemy until his unit could re-form and enter the fight. He was ordered to retreat but refused and kept the enemy at bay. Although wounded, when his company retreated to set up a new position he kept attacking the enemy until his soldiers were protected.

David M. Gonzales. Born Pacoima, California, 1923. Battle of Luzon, Philippines. Died April, 1945. Company pinned down by heavy fire. Five-hundred-pound bomb hit them, burying five men alive. Gonzales grabbed a shovel and began digging them out. Every enemy soldier fired at him to stop him. He had to stand up to dig more effectively. He dug out a total of three men before being killed by enemy fire, still digging for a fourth man. Posthumous Congressional Medal of Honor.

Silvestre Santana Herrera. Born Carmago, Mexico, 1917. World War II, France. Sergeant. Single-handedly attacked a German machinegun nest, capturing eight enemy. Germans attacked again from a minefield. He decided to counterattack alone. Lost both legs to land mines as he attacked the Germans. Held his position until his men could overrun the enemy. Congressional Medal of Honor and Order of Merit, Mexico, the only person to win both honors from the two countries. Quote: "I am a Mexican American and we have a tradition. We're supposed to be men, not sissies." First Arizonan to win the Congressional Medal of Honor.

Salvador J. Lara. Riverside, California, 1920. Fruit picker. Army, 1942, Anzio Beachhead battle. Badly wounded but kept leading his rifle company. Stopped a large enemy force attacking his men. Shot in leg. Asked to be allowed to wipe out an enemy machinegun nest. He did.

The Germans ran away. Died in Europe in 1945 just after the end of the war. He received the Congressional Medal of Honor from President Obama seventy years after his battlefield heroics and sixty-nine years after his death.

Jose Mendoza Lopez. Master Sergeant. Mexican immigrant, born, 1910 Oaxaca, Mexico. Mother died of tuberculosis when he was eight. Went to work, then became a boxer. Joined Merchant Marines in Australia. Signed up for five years. Was enroute United States when Pearl Harbor was attacked. He was arrested for being Japanese and had to prove he wasn't before being allowed to enter the U.S. Battle of the Bulge. Killed one hundred Germans by himself. Stopped their attack. Could not get a job as an uneducated Mexican so went to work for the Veteran's Administration. Congressional Medal of Honor presented by Major General Van Fleet.

Joe Pantillion Martínez. Born Taos, New Mexico, 1920. Aleutian Islands. Turned around a battle the U.S. was losing by attacking Japanese machine gunners. Shot in head. Posthumous Congressional Medal of Honor. First Coloradoan to receive the Congressional Medal of Honor. First act of heroism on American soil in World War II other than at Pearl Harbor. A naval ship was named in his honor.

Manuel Verdugo Mendoza. Born Miami, Arizona, 1922. World War II. Italy. Single-handedly broke up German counterattack threatening his entire company in 1944. Using a Thompson submachinegun, then a carbine, he wiped out the enemy and stopped their charge. He eventually picked up a machinegun and, firing from the hip, walked into the enemy ranks causing them to run away. He killed thirty enemy and drove over one hundred away. He received the Congressional Medal of Honor from President Obama seventy years after his battle against the Germans.

Michael Castaneda Peña. Born Newgulf, Texas, 1924. Joined Army at sixteen. World War II and Korea. Running low on ammunition, he ordered his unit to retreat while he held off the enemy. Held back the entire enemy force until morning, when he was overrun and killed. Posthumous Congressional Medal of Honor.

Manuel Perez Jr. Born Oklahoma City, 1923. Combat in Philippines, near Luzon. Scout for his 11th Airborne company battling Japanese. Enemy kept trying to overrun his company, but he single-handedly killed eighteen Japanese, holding up their entire advance and saving his men. Congressional Medal of Honor.

Alfred Velazquez Rascon. Born Chihuahua, Mexico, 1945. Grew up in Oxnard California, the son of Mexican immigrants. Joined Army after high school. Combat airborne medic Vietnam. On March 15, 1966, was a medic for an airborne reconnaissance team attacked by a superior enemy force. Rascon rendered aid to the wounded when the enemy attacked with grenades. He shielded the wounded with his body and was grievously wounded himself. After each attack he dragged the wounded soldier to safety and went back for the others, being wounded again each time. Nominated for Medal of Honor but it was "somehow" never acted on, receiving the Silver Star instead. Twenty years later at an airborne reunion his men were astounded to learn he had never received the Medal of Honor. They petitioned the Army, but the Army said no. They went to their congressman and prepared a dossier on Rascon's heroism. It was given to President Bill Clinton who read it and then awarded Rascon the Congressional Medal of Honor in 2000, thirty-four years after his act of heroism.

José Rodela. Corpus Christi, Texas, 1937. Master Sergeant. Airborne. Vietnam War. Action September 1, 1969. Mortar and machinegun barrage. He set up his men in defensive positions and cleared each area of enemy while his men fortified their positions. He suppressed the enemy fire and was wounded in the back and head by a B40 rocket. He then took out the rocket and the enemy using it. Won numerous combat decorations. He received the Congressional Medal of Honor from President Obama forty-five years after his battlefield heroics.

Cleto Rodriguez. Born San Marcos, Texas, 1923. Master Sergeant. Manila Campaign World War II. He and a fellow soldier attacked a heavily defended railroad station. They killed eighty enemy soldiers, wounded many more, capturing the station. His buddy was killed in the operation. A few days later Rodriguez killed six Japanese and destroyed a 20 mm gun, freeing his fellow soldiers to attack. Medal of Honor presented by President Truman in 1945.

Joseph Charles Rodriguez. Born San Bernardino, California, 1928. Korean War. May 21, 1951. Ordered to take high ground held by enemy during a United Nations counteroffensive. Fire from five foxholes stopped the offensive. Rodriguez charged all machineguns hurling grenades as he went. He destroyed them all and the fifteen enemy defenders. His unit then took the hilltop. He received the Congressional Medal of Honor from President Truman in 1952. Retired from the Army as a colonel.

Alejandro Rentería Ruiz. Born Loving, New Mexico, 1923. Combat in Okinawa, Ryukyu Islands. Sergeant Ruiz's squad was pinned down by a grenade and machinegun attack from a pillbox. He grabbed an automatic rifle and charged the pillbox alone, killing twelve of the Japanese soldiers and saving his men. Congressional Medal of Honor presented by President Harry Truman.

Jose Francisco (Frank) Valdez. Private First Class. Born Gobernador, New Mexico, near Dulce, New Mexico, 1925. World War II. Fighting Germans in France took on a tank with automatic rifle, forced it to turn away while his men escaped. Killed three Germans that counterattacked, then had two companies of German shoulders come after him and his men. Stopped them too while his men escaped. Shot in stomach by a bullet that went through him. Despite the pain, he resumed fighting and calling in artillery fire on the Germans. Posthumous Congressional Medal of Honor.

Ysmael Reyes Villegas. Born Riverside, California (Casa Blanca), 1924. Became an orange picker. His military unit invaded the Philippines. Fought the Japanese in the Battle of Luzon. The Staff Sergeant's squad was attacked by a machinegun nest and he wiped it out alone. Won Silver Star medal. Three weeks later, on March 20, 1945, he was ordered to take a hill. Faced heavy machinegun fire. He attacked alone five enemy foxholes, killing all the Germans. He was killed attacking the sixth foxhole. Posthumous Congressional Medal of Honor.

Politicians

Cristóbal J. Alex. Born, El Paso, Texas. Lawyer, Chicano activist, public servant. Founded Latino Victory Project and Latino Victory Fund, both dedicated to increasing the number of Latinos in political positions at all levels, registering voters and increasing civil engagement by Latinos. Advised Hillary Clinton and Joe Biden in their campaigns for president. Andress High School. JD University of Washington Law School. Deputy White House cabinet secretary under President Biden. Head of Tusk Strategies, a political advising organization.

Tony Anaya. Politician, Attorney. Born Moriarty, New Mexico, 1941. BA Georgetown University, American University Law JD. Santa Fe County Attorney, Assistant District Attorney, New Mexico Attorney General. Governor of New Mexico, 1982. Opposed capital punishment. Made New Mexico a State of Sanctuary for Central American refugees. Has worked on Hispanic issues since leaving office. CEO of environmentally friendly companies.

Jerry Apodaca. Insurance businessman, politician. University of New Mexico BS. New Mexico Senate for two terms. Twenty-fourth Governor of New Mexico. First Hispanic governor in U.S. since 1918 (tied with Raúl Castro, Arizona). Reorganized state government. Set up Cabinet system. Limited to one term at that time. President Carter appointed him to head President's Council on Physical Fitness.

Anna Escobedo Cabral. Mexican American from San Bernardino, born, 1959, father a fruit picker. Politician, attorney, banker. University of California Davis BA, Harvard MPA, George Mason Law JD. Chief of Communications Inter-American Development Bank. Forty-second Treasurer of the United States under George Bush. Worked to increase Hispanics in business. Director Center for Latino Initiatives Smithsonian Institution.

Louis Edward Caldera. El Paso, Texas, 1956, family moved to Los Angeles in 1960. Son of Mexican immigrants. BS U.S. Military Academy West Point 1978. Active-duty Army 1978–1983. Graduated Harvard Law and Business School JD/MBA. California State Assembly 1992–1997. Worked for Bill Clinton's Corporation for National and Community Service (1997–1998) then became Clinton's Secretary of the Army. Became the eighteenth President of the University of New Mexico (resigned after two years due to disagreements with Regents). In 2009 as President Obama's Head of the White House Military Office, Caldera approved a low flyover/photo op of Air Force One over Manhattan. The flyover caused panic in New York City after the tragedy of 911 and the brouhaha led to Caldera's resigning after an apology. Caldera is now President of Caldera Associates, a philanthropic organization funding high-achieving low-income students.

Julián Castro. San Antonio, Texas, 1974. Mayor of San Antonio, 2009–2013. U.S. Secretary of Housing and Urban Development under Obama, 2014–2017. Ran for president in 2020.

Raúl Héctor Castro. Politician, Diplomat. Born Sonora, Mexico, 1916. Moved to Douglas, Arizona, attended segregated schools. High school principal told him not to go to college because no one would hire a Mexican. Became a dishwasher to attend college. BS Northern Arizona University, JD University of Arizona Tucson. U.S. Ambassador to El Salvador, 1964–1968 (President Lyndon Johnson). U.S. Ambassador to Bolivia, 1968–1969 (Presidents Johnson and Nixon). 14th Governor of Arizona, 1975–1977, tied with Jerry Apodaca (New Mexico) as first

Hispanic governor since 1918. U.S. Ambassador to Argentina, 1977–1980 (President Carter).

Dionisio "Dennis" Chavez. Born, 1888 Los Chavez, Valencia County (greater Albuquerque), New Mexico Territory. Dropped out of school at thirteen. Family moved to Barelas New Mexico, where his father worked on the Santa Fe Railroad. Studied engineering and surveying. Georgetown Law School JD. Practiced law in Albuquerque, defended organized labor. U.S. House of Representatives, 1932–1934. Ran against Bronson Cutting for U.S. Senate. Lost. Cutting died five days later in plane crash. Chavez appointed to fill the term until next election. Won election in 1936 and served until he died in 1962. Fourth ranking member U.S. Senate when he died. Great Americans postage stamp. Longest serving New Mexico senator. Statue in Statuary Hall, U.S. Capitol.

Linda Lou Chavez. Born, 1947, Old Town, Albuquerque, New Mexico. Author, radio talk show host, highest ranking woman under Ronald Reagan, Director Office of Public Liaison; first Latina ever nominated to U.S. Cabinet for Secretary of Labor by George W. Bush.

Henry Gabriel Cisneros. Politician, businessman. Born San Antonio, Texas; descendent of Spanish settlers in New Mexico. Texas A&M degree, MA Harvard. San Antonio City Council, six years; Mayor, San Antonio, 1981–1989; tenth Secretary Housing and Urban Development (under Clinton); sex scandal and legal difficulties with FBI torpedoed his career. Clinton pardoned him. President and COO Univision.

Catherine Cortez Masto. Born Las Vegas, Nevada. Nevada Attorney General. Elected to U.S. Senate in 2017. Father was attorney and Mexican, mother Italian. Paternal grandfather came from Chihuahua. Voted with Biden ninety-two percent of the time. Supports climate efforts. "F" grade with NRA.

Antonio Manuel Fernandez. 1902–1956. Born Springer, New Mexico. Highlands University and University of New Mexico, JD Cumberland University, Tennessee. Set up practice in Raton, New Mexico 1931 then Santa Fe in 1934. Assistant Attorney General New Mexico. Elected to U.S. House, 1943 until his death. Specialized in military and Indian issues. Married Cleofas Chavez, 1924. As New Mexico legislator, wrote and pushed through the first Rural Electrification Act for New Mexico. Dedicated to New Mexico servicemen, especially combat veterans. Supported GI Bill of Rights.

Ruben Gallego. Born in Chicago, 1979 to Colombian mother and Mexican father. After high school attended Harvard for BA in International Relations. Mother raised children as a single mother. Combat Marine in Iran and Iraq. After the war in 2010 elected to Arizona State House. First bill granted in-state tuition to veterans living in Arizona. Formed a group to recall racist sheriff Joe Arpaio, which failed. Elected to four terms in the U.S. House of Representatives (2016–2024). In 2023 his bill, The Native American Child Protection Act, became law. Ran for U.S. Senate in 2024 and won.

Hector Pérez James Garcia IV. Born Tamaulipas, Mexico, 1914. The University of Texas at Austin, Zoology degree, MD The University of Texas Medical School, Creighton University. Mexican American physician, Civil Rights Activist. Founded American GI Forum (AGIF) to help veterans, especially Hispanics. World War II. Despite being a doctor, assigned as a combat infantry officer in European Theater. Won a bronze star, the European African Middle Eastern Medal with six bronze stars, World War II Victory medal. Practiced medicine in San Antonio, treated all patients whether or not they could pay. Dedicated his life to Hispanic equality; fought discrimination in Texas schools. Presidential Medal of Freedom, 1984; Order of St. Gregory the Great (Pope John Paul II), 1990; Order of Aztec Eagle (posthumous), 1998, highest award by Mexico to foreigner.

Jimmy Gomez. U.S. representative. California Los Angeles district. Born, 1974. Son of immigrants (Mexican fruit picker and a maid). Did not expect to go to college, Target and Subway worker. Then attended UCLA (BA political science), MA public policy Harvard Kennedy School. Labor organizer for health care workers. Elected to California state assembly, 2012 then House of Representatives in 2017. Reelected since then. Very active in international trade. Anti-MAGA efforts: tried to expel Marjorie Taylor Green and Lauren Boebert for heckling Joe Biden in State of Union speech. Assistant whip, Democratic Caucus, Racial Equality Initiative Ways and Means Committee, House Trade Working Group, Subcommittee on National Security Agency and Cyber.

Alberto Gonzales. Born San Antonio, 1955, grew up near Houston. Father with second grade education, migrant worker and construction. Mother sixth grade education, housewife. Family of ten lived in a small two-room house. Air Force in Alaska. Air Force Academy. Rice University. Degree; Harvard Law JD. Attorney in private practice, 1982–1994, one of first Hispanic partners in his firm. Worked for Governor George Bush then became Secretary of State for Texas, then named to Texas Supreme Court. Attorney General for US. Supported Bush's torture program. Supported Patriot Act.

Antonio Gonzalez. Mexican roots in California. Community organizer. Head, Southwest Voter Registration Education Project (SVREP) that registers Hispanic voters. Increased numbers from five million to more than nine million with a voting rate of almost eighty-two percent. His activities have led to an increase in senators, governors and big city mayors.

Enrique Barbosa (Henry) Gonzalez. 1916–2000. San Antonio, Texas. The University of Texas at Austin. Parents fled Mexican Revolution. Law degree San Antonio. Ran a number of times and lost. Lyndon Johnson and Cantinflas campaigned for him when he won a House seat. Was reelected seventeen times. Supporter of civil rights and voting rights. Was with John Kennedy when he was shot. Tried to impeach

Reagan for Iran Contra and George H. W. Bush for Gulf War. National Taco Day celebrated on his birthday.

Michelle Lujan Grisham. Born, 1959 Los Alamos, New Mexico. Lawyer, politician. St. Michael High, University of New Mexico JD. U.S. Representative, Secretary of Health. Chair, Congressional Hispanic Caucus. Twelfth generation Chicana. Twice Governor of New Mexico.

Octaviano Ambrosio Larrazolo. (1859–1930). New Mexico Governor, First Chicano US Senator, fought for Hispanic rights.

Ben Ray Lujan. Santa Fe, New Mexico. Highlands University, University of New Mexico. U.S. Senate, New Mexico. Elected, 2021. U.S. Representative (2011–2020). Assistant Majority Leader, House of Representatives. Strong environmental protection ethic.

Susana Martinez. Politician, attorney. Born El Paso, Texas, 1959. Father professional boxer and Deputy Sheriff El Paso County. BA The University of Texas at El Paso, University of Oklahoma College of Law JD. Governor of New Mexico (two terms).

Joseph Montoya. (1915–1978). Born Peña Blanca, New Mexico. Lieutenant Governor, U.S. House, U.S. Senator from New Mexico (1964–1977). Regis College, Denver, CO. JD Georgetown Law. Youngest New Mexico representative to U.S. Congress. "Little Joe Montoya." Member Watergate Committee. Lost reelection to Senate in 1976. After Nixon resigned Montoya cut his pension. Called himself "a poor boy from Peña Blanca."

Alex Padilla. Los Angeles. Mexican parents. Massachusetts Institute of Technology (mechanical engineering). Software engineer for

Hughes Aircraft. President National Association of Latino Elected and Appointed Officials (NALEO). Fought to lower insulin costs for diabetics. California State Senate, Secretary of State California, U.S. Senator from California, 2021–as of the publication of this book.).

William Blaine Richardson III. Pasadena, California, 1947–2023. Son of a Mexican banker. Tufts University. (BA, MA). Politician, author, diplomat, UN Ambassador, Secretary of Energy, Congressman from New Mexico fourteen years. New Mexico's thirtieth governor. Worked to free political detainees in global hotspots. Nominated three times for Nobel Peace Prize.

Julie Chávez Rodriguez. Born in Delano, California (1978), granddaughter of César Chavez and Helen Fabela Chávez. Political advisor, public service political activity under Obama (U.S. Department of Interior, White House Office of Public Engagement), advisor to Kamala Harris (2017–2019), worked on President Biden's presidential campaign in 2020 and became campaign manager in 2023. Attended Tehachapi High School, University of California Berkeley (BS Latin American Studies). Program director for her grandfather's foundation, the César Chávez Foundation.

Ken Salazar. Alamosa, Colorado. St. Francis Seminary. Colorado College. JD University of Michigan Law School. Lawyer, politician, diplomat. Director Colorado Natural Resources, Attorney General Colorado (first Latino elected to statewide office in Colorado), U.S. Senate, 2005–2009 (worked on immigration reform), Secretary of Interior (Obama), U.S. Ambassador to Mexico, 2021–as of the publication of this book. (Biden). Turned down nomination to Supreme Court.

Antonio Ramón Villaraigosa (Antonio Ramón Villar Jr.). Politician. Born Los Angeles, California, 1953. Abandoned by his mother while a young child and by his father at five years old. Expelled from Catholic school for fighting. East Los Angeles College, University of California at Los Angeles BA(history). Worked for Chicano unity. JD People's College of Law. President ACLU of Los Angeles. Speaker California Assembly, Mayor of Los Angeles (2005–2013)—the first Hispanic mayor in one hundred thirty years. Worked to save the environment and supported poor people, worked on water issues for California. Member Hillary Clinton's and Barack Obama's campaign teams. Tom Bradley Legacy Award, various Honorary Doctorates.

Actors, Musicians, Artists

Jessica Marie Alba. Pomona California, 1981. Mexican and European. Movie and TV actress, businesswoman. *Dark Angel* (Golden Globe nomination). Blockbuster Hollywood films (MTV Movie Award for Sexiest Performance). Star on the Hollywood Walk of Fame. Opened business called The Honest Company selling baby products. One of the few Chicano billionaires. Committed to social activism.

Joan Baez. Folksinger, songwriter, political activist. Father Mexican, mother Scottish-English. Queen of Folk, influenced Bob Dylan, worked with Martin Luther King. Her song *We Shall Overcome* became the Civil Rights anthem of the nation; anti-Vietnam war, survived eleven straight days of bombing of Hanoi by U.S.—the Christmas Bombing. Recorded music in six languages. Rock and Roll Hall of Fame; American Academy of Arts and Sciences; many social justice awards.

Monica Barbaro. Born, 1989 San Francisco, California to Italian father and northern European-Mexican mother. She is one quarter Mexican. New York University's Tisch School BA in Fine Arts, Dance (ballet). Beverly Hills Acting Playhouse. Actress, movies and television. *Top Gun: Maverick*, *The Cathedral*, *A Complete Unknown* as Joan Baez, *Chicago P.D.*, *Chicago Justice*, *Splitting Up Together*.

Patrociño Barela. Taos artist, woodcarver; illiterate; first Chicano to receive national recognition for art. WPA artist as wood carver. Works shown at Museum of Modern Art, San Francisco Golden Gate Exposition, New York World's Fair. Alcoholic, died in workshop fire.

Ana Cabrera. Denver Chicana. News anchor CNN and MSNBC. BA (Journalism) Washington State University. Mark Twain Award for Best Morning Show Broadcast. National Academy of Television Arts and Sciences News Presenter Award.

Florencia Vicenta de Casillas Martinez Cardona (Vikki Carr). Born El Paso, Texas, 1940. Bilingual Spanish/English popular singer over four decades. Won three Grammy Awards (including one for Best Mexican American Performance,1986) and a Lifetime Achievement Award at the Latin Grammys. Established Vikki Carr Scholarship Foundation to pay for college for Hispanic children in California and Texas (1971). More than two hundred eighty students have received scholarships. Ten singles and thirteen albums made the pop charts. Star on the Hollywood Walk of Fame.

Leo Carrillo. Actor, illustrator, conservationist, philanthropist, author. Pancho of the *Cisco Kid* TV series. Proud of his deep Chicano roots in California, extending back to the Middle Ages of Spain. His famous horse was named Conquistador. Star on the Hollywood Walk of Fame.

Lynda Jean Cordova Carter. Wonder Woman. Actor, model, singer, philanthropist, appeared on television, in films and on stage. Voted The Most Beautiful Woman in the World. Named the United Nations' Honorary Ambassador for the Empowerment of Women and Girls, a title later stripped due to Wonder Woman's supposedly objectifying women. Carter has supported many social causes, such as equality for LGBTQ people, alcohol recovery (she is a recovering alcoholic), and has worked to inform people of diseases such as irritable bowel syndrome. Has a star on the Hollywood Walk of Fame and was honored with a Sor Juana Legacy Award for contributions to the arts by women on Mexican descent.

Evelyn Cisneros. Prima Ballerina with San Francisco Ballet Company for twenty-three years; educator, director of the four campuses of the Frederick Quinney Lawson Ballet West Academy in Salt Lake City, Utah. First Chicana Prima Ballerina. Family were migrant workers. Born in California in 1958, grew up in Huntington Beach. Grandparents immigrated to escape Mexican Revolution. Was extremely shy so her mother signed her up for ballet lessons. Discriminated against by some ballet masters who made her powder her skin to look white, but such treatment only made her work harder. Honorary Doctorates from Mills College and the University of California at Monterey Bay.

Moctesuma Esparza. Producer, entertainment executive, community activist. Attended University of California at Los Angeles Theater School. Founded Maya Entertainment. *Milagro Beanfield War, Selena*. Worked to make *Sesame Street* bilingual. Emmy Award, Clio Award, Alma Award (Latin Oscar), Academy Award nomination, Golden Globe Award nomination. Lifetime Achievement Award Mexican American Cultural Education Foundation.

Freddy Fender (Baldemar Garza Huerta). Born in Texas. Tejano country and rock-and-roll singer, actor. High school dropout. Joined Marines. Jailed for drunkenness several times; court-martialed and discharged. The Navy later said it had wrongfully discharged him for drunkenness and he was upgraded to a general discharge. Started to record hit songs but was arrested due to smoking marijuana and imprisoned for three years in Louisiana. Sentence commuted by country western singer governor. Became auto mechanic. Wrote and recorded *Before the Next Teardrop Falls*. Went to Number 1 on the charts. Won various music awards, including two Grammy Awards. Sold five hundred fifty thousand albums. Star on the Hollywood Walk of Fame.

John Gavin (Juan Vincent Apablasa). Actor. Diplomat. President Screen Actors Guild, U.S. Ambassador to Mexico; cultural advisor to the Organization of American States. BA (economics and Latin American affairs) Stanford. Korea, US Navy on *USS Princeton*, air intelligence and translator, rank of Flag Lieutenant. Appeared in many classic films: *Imitation of Life, Spartacus, Psycho, Midnight Lace, Back Street*.

Selena Marie Gomez. Singer, songwriter, actor, entrepreneur. Born, 1992 Grand Prairie, Texas to a father of Mexican descent and a mother of Italian heritage (who gave birth to Selena at age 16). Very poor after her parents' divorce. Spoke Spanish until age seven, two years after parents divorced. Home schooled for high school education. Raised by her Mexican immigrant grandparents. Did small roles acting until *Hannah Montana*, where she played a rock star, followed by Disney's *Wizards of Waverly Place*. Appeared in many TV shows and movies. Began recording songs she had written. Her song *Naturally* received critical and popular acclaim. Her career was growing rapidly in films (e.g., *Spring Breakers*) and music (e.g., *Stars Dance*) and on television. She won eighteen Teen Choice Awards, twelve Kids' Choice Awards and many awards for her philanthropic support of mental health, which she struggled with over the years. Has a net worth approaching a billion dollars.

Pedro Gonzalez-Gonzalez. Illiterate comedic and dramatic actor. Dropped out of school at age seven to work as an actor in Hollywood; his wife would read him the scripts and he would memorize them. Became famous for his comedy and roles in John Wayne movies and many other films. Was the model for Speedy Gonzalez. Star on the Hollywood Walk of Fame.

Michele Dominguez Green. Las Vegas, Nevada, 1962. Irish American father, Mexican/Nicaraguan mother. Actor, singer, author. Emmy Award. *LA Law* TV series star. Several albums of music in Spanish.

Lalo Guerrero. 1916–2005. Father of Chicano Music, National Medal of the Arts (President Clinton). Born in Tucson (family of twenty-one siblings). His music highlighted the Chicano struggle for dignity. Befriended the Ronstadts of Tucson and would serenade little Linda. (Linda sang at his funeral.) Recorded over seven hundred songs, including parodies such as *Pancho Lopez, Pancho Claus, Elvis Perez, Tacos for Two*, and *There's No Tortillas*. Wrote *pachuco* music that was used in a stage musical, *Zoot Suit*. Recorded his final record at eighty-three.

Salma Valgarma Hayek Jimenez. Actress (TV, movies), film producer. Born, 1966 Coatzacoalcos, Veracruz, Mexico. Many movie roles as actress. Founded Ventanarosa movie production company. Produced *Ugly Betty* and won Golden Globe Award for Best Comedy Series and Outstanding Guest Actress in a Comedy Series Daytime Emmy Award, two Primetime Emmy Award nominations, ALMA Award nomination for *Fools Rush In*, nomination for Ariel Award for Best Actress, first Mexican actress nominated for Academy Award for Best Actress for her role in *Frida*, also nominations for best actress for Golden Globe Award, Screen Actors Guild Award and British Academy Award. Works for immigrant and women's rights. Star on the Hollywood Walk of Fame.

Al Hurricane (Alberto Nelson Sanchez). The Godfather of New Mexico Chicano Music (especially ranchera music). Born in Dixon, New Mexico in 1936. His entire family was musical and most performed with him as he traveled around New Mexico. In 1948 the family moved to Old Town. He sang in Old Town restaurants and played for tips at Old Town Plaza, much like Eddie Gallegos, another popular New Mexican singer. His popularity grew and his band performed throughout the western U.S. and northern Mexico with *música norteña* from New Mexico. Appeared with Selena Quintanilla Pérez and his brother in the Al Hurricane Band.

Gabriel Iglesias. Actor, stand-up comedian (one of the top ten paid comedians in the world). Born San Diego, California, 1976. Raised by a single mother; grew up in low-income housing. Cell phone worker in Los Angeles until 1997, switched to comedy and went broke. Stuck to his dream and has had TV specials and has been a voice actor. Had a Netflix show, *Mr. Iglesias*. Always wears Hawaiian shirts (owns five hundred of varying sizes). Weight reached four hundred forty-five pounds and has Type 2 diabetes; working to lose weight and says he lost a hundred pounds. First comedian to sell out Dodger Stadium. Received awards from the City of El Paso, Texas and from Operation H.O.P.E. (provides instruction on financial responsibility and educational programs to low-income people). Net worth exceeds forty million dollars.

Luis Jimenez. Chicano sculptor, 1940–2006. Known for large brightly colored fiberglass sculptures with Mexican themes. His Mustang is a huge sculpture at the Denver Airport. His art was shown at major museums in the Southwest and at the Smithsonian Institution. Art degree from The University of Texas at Austin, with postgraduate work in Mexico City. New Mexico Governor's Award for Excellence in the Arts, Distinguished Alumni Award, University of Texas. Died when parts of an oversized sculpture fell on him severing his femoral artery.

Los Lobos. All Chicano rock band from East Los Angeles. Original name for group was Los Lobos de Este; 1977–as of the publication of this book.. Number one hit Richie Valens' rendition of *La Bamba*. Grammy winner for Best Mexican American Song in 1984. Traveled world as opening act for Bob Dylan and Grateful Dead. Recorded *Papa's Dream* with Lalo Guerrero. Won Grammy for Best Children's Album. Soundtrack for movie *Desperado*, won third Grammy Award. Have had twelve Grammy nominations. In 2001 won El Premio Billboard Award. In 2011 won Latin Grammy Lifetime Achievement Award. Won National Heritage Fellowship, 2021 from National Endowment for the Arts, U.S. Government's Highest Honor. In 2022 won fourth Grammy Award for *Native Sons*, Best Americana Album.

Eva Jacqueline Longoria Bastón. Born, 1975 Corpus Christi, Texas. Actor, producer, model, author, director, soap opera actor, *Desperate*

Housewives. *Searching for Mexico* (CNN food series). Learned Spanish in 2009. Studied kinesiology (BA) and Chicano studies (MA) in college. Golden Globe and Screen Actors Guild Award nominations. Directed the movie *Flamin' Hot*. Founded Eva's Heroes and Eva Longoria Foundation, which support many charities. Star on the Hollywood Walk of Fame.

Constance Marie Lopez. Born East LA, 1961. Actor, dancer. Dancer for David Bowie Tour. George Lopez' wife on his TV show. Played Selena's mother in biopic *Selena*. Constance Marie clothing line. Many TV shows, movies. Soap Opera Digest Award, four ALMA awards, five Imagen Awards.

George Lopez. Born, 1961 Mission Hills, Los Angeles. Comedian, actor, Chicano activist. "America's Chicano." Many awards for his impact on Latino communities (Imagen Vision Award, Latino Spirit Award), star on the Hollywood Walk of Fame. Founded Ann and George Lopez Foundation. Humanitarian of the Year Award by Harvard Foundation. His TV shows have been circulated internationally.

Trinidad "Trini" Lopez III. Mexican American singer, actor, guitarist from the Little Mexico section of Dallas, Texas. High school dropout to support family. His first big hit, *If I Had a Hammer* went gold. Las Vegas Walk of Stars, Palm Springs, California Walk of Stars, International Latin Music Hall of Fame. Appeared in films and on television. One of *The Dirty Dozen*. He sold more than five hundred thousand albums of Trini Lopez at PJ'S. Quote: "My problem was always being a Mexican in America...In Texas, we were treated worse than the Blacks."

Richard Anthony "Cheech" Marin. Born, 1946 in south Los Angeles to Mexican parents. His father was an LAPD officer, his mother a secretary. Attended Catholic grade school and high school. Graduated as English major from California State University, Northridge. Comedian, actor (movies, TV, voice), musician, activist, art collector, museum developer, author. Became famous as part of a comedy act, Cheech and Chong, with Tommy Chong both on the stage and in films. Does not speak Spanish fluently but has used a strong Chicano accent in films and voice acting. Dedicated marijuana user and businessman for cannabis products. Founded the Cheech Marin Center for Chicano Art in Riverside, California.

Lydia Mendoza. 1916–2007. Born Houston, Texas, Mother of Tejano Music (Tejano Music Hall of Fame), National Medal of the Arts (President Clinton). Recorded at least two hundred different Spanish songs on fifty plus albums. Spoke only Spanish. Played at Carter inauguration. Immigrant parents who returned to San Luis Potosí when Lydia was two. Upon returning to the United States she and her family were immersed in gasoline to kill any possible lice infestations, as were many Mexican immigrants to Texas.

Ricardo Montalban (Ricardo Gonzalo Pedro Montalbán y Merino). Actor (films and TV) spanning seven decades; *Fantasy Island, Star Trek, Star Trek II* (Kahn), *The Naked Gun*. Emmy Award. Many other awards, including Screen Actors Guild Lifetime Achievement. Star on the Hollywood Walk of Fame.

Edward James Olmos. Born in East Los Angeles, 1947. Actor, director, producer, political activist. Golden Globe, Emmy, Academy Award nominee (first native-born Chicano so honored, for *Stand and Deliver*), co-founder Latino Public Broadcasting, Executive Director, Lives in Hazard (gang prevention program). Starred in the TV series, *Miami Vice*. Star on the Hollywood Walk of Fame.

Lupe Ontiveros (Guadalupe Moreno). Actor. Born El Paso, Texas, 1942 to Mexican immigrants. BA Social Work Texas Woman's University Denton. Started as film extra in California then became a TV and movie actor in films such as "As Good as it Gets, The Goonies." Played many maid roles; played the woman who murdered Selena.

Jenna Marie Ortega. Born Palm Desert, California, 2002. Parents of Mexican descent. Maternal grandmother undocumented immigrant, Sinaloa, Mexico. As child actress-hopeful found few roles for Chicanas. Started with commercials. Dropped out of school in eighth grade to pursue acting. Entered Disney children's actor universe with TV and movie roles. Sitcom actress, "Stuck in the Middle." Nominated for three Imagen Awards for Best Young Actor, Television, winning in 2018. Garnered good reviews for the film "The Fallout" about a school shooting. Breakthrough again with a role in "Scream" and won the MTV Movie Award for Most Frightened Performance. Active philanthropist, supporting immigrant issues and working against discrimination, for AIDS care, bullying prevention. Her net worth is about five million dollars for the twenty-one-year-old.

Anthony Quinn (Manuel Antonio Rodolfo Quinn Oaxaca). Born Mexico City, 1920. Actor. Two Academy Awards (first Chicano to receive an Academy Award; only Chicano to receive two awards), Golden Globe. Author, artist, civil rights activist. His father fought with Pancho Villa and his mother helped feed the troops. Appeared in many classic films: "La Strada," "Blood and Sand," "The Guns of Navarone," "Lawrence of Arabia," "The Shoes of the Fisherman," "Lion of the Desert," "Zorba the Greek," "Lust for Life," "Viva Zapata," "Secret of Santa Vittoria." Honorary high school diploma from Tucson High. Star on the Hollywood Walk of Fame.

María Elena Salinas. News anchor, author, talk show host, political activist, reporter. Chicana, born Los Angeles, Mexican parents. UCLA degree. "Voice of Hispanic America." Co-anchors "Noticiero Univision" and other programs viewed in eighteen Latin American countries. Co-hosted presidential debates and has interviewed most major politicians and celebrities in a forty-year career. Retired from Univision, now contributor to CBS and ABC. Has worked for Latino voting rights. Peabody Award, Walter Cronkite Award, Gracie Award, Broadcast Legend Award, Emmy Award for Lifetime Achievement.

Selena Quintanilla-Perez (Selena). Singer (Queen of Tejano Music). Born, 1971, Lake Jackson, Texas, to a mother with a Cherokee background and a Mexican American musician father. Family Mexican restaurant failed, led to bankruptcy and loss of their home. Moved to Corpus Christi, Texas where she and her brothers formed a band. In early recordings she spoke Spanish only phonetically. Dad pulled Selena out of school in the eighth grade and bought an old touring bus and the family sang for food at restaurants as they toured. Discovered by founder of Tejano Music Awards (she won 10 consecutive awards as her career developed). Won Grammy Award for Best Mexican American Album (first female Tejano music star to do so). Her promising career ended in 1995 when she was murdered by her friend and former manager of her boutique stores, Yolanda Saldivar. A posthumous album topped the Billboard 200; first artist to accomplish this. Sold eighteen million records. Star on Hollywood Walk of Fame.

Robert Anthony Rodriguez. Born San Antonio., 1968. Filmmaker, director, composer, author. Launched TV Channel El Rey. The University of Texas at Austin, College of Communication. Has made many superhero movies as well as odd hits such as *El Mariachi*. Does everything on the set and has been known as the "one man film crew."

Gilbert Roland (Luis Antonio Damas de Alonso). Born Juarez, Mexico, 1905. Actor, film and TV. Fled Pancho Villa to U.S. Latin lover in films. U.S. Army Air Corps World War II. Starring role in many films. Played Cisco Kid in the movies of the 1940s. Two Golden Globe nominations. Star on the Hollywood Walk of Fame.

Linda Maria Ronstadt. Born, 1946 Tucson. Chicana singer, author, Queen of Country Rock and First Lady of Rock. Eleven Grammy Awards, three American Music Awards, two Academy of Country Music Awards, Emmy Award, American Latino Media Arts Award (ALMA), Latin Grammy Lifetime Achievement Award, Grammy Lifetime Achievement Award. Sold more than one hundred million records. Recorded songs in English and Spanish. Rock and Roll Hall of

Fame. National Medal of the Arts and Humanities (President Obama). Kennedy Center Honoree. Star on Hollywood Walk of Fame.

Carlos Humberto Santana Barragán. Born in Jalisco, Mexico. Rock guitarist, fused rock and roll with Latin American jazz. Has sold more than one hundred million records. Won ten Grammy Awards, three Latin American Grammy Awards, many others. Rock and Roll Hall of Fame. Kennedy Center Honoree. Star on the Hollywood Walk of Fame.

Ritchie Valens (Richard Steven Valenzuela). Rock and roll pioneer and forefather of Chicano Rock, among first Chicano rock stars. Singer, songwriter. Died in a plane crash at age seventeen along with Buddy Holly and the Big Bopper. *Donna*, side B of his million selling record, *La Bamba*, was about his girlfriend, Donna Ludwig, whose parents did not approve of Valens because of his ethnicity. Star on the Hollywood Walk of Fame.

Cecilia Marcellina Vega. Network news correspondent (ABC), White House correspondent (ABC), Weekend anchor World News Tonight, Good Morning America, 60 Minutes correspondent (first Chicana). Salesian High School, Richmond, California; American University. Emmy Award for newscasting.

Writers, Scholars, Academics, Social Activists, Sports, Business leaders, Others

Linda Martinez Alvarado. Born Albuquerque, New Mexico, 1952; lived in adobe home with no indoor plumbing. Pomona College, economics. Construction business owner, restaurant company owner, co-owner of Colorado Rockies baseball team. Started Alvarado Company at twenty-four, building sidewalks, then schools and stadiums. Built Mile High Stadium in Denver, two hundred fifty Taco Bell restaurants. Net worth of a quarter of a billion dollars. Quote: "I was told I was bound to fail because of the double whammy of being Hispanic and a woman. But I thought to myself, in math when you multiply two negatives, you get a positive."

Rudolfo Anaya. Author, educator, professor. Born in Santa Rosa, New Mexico. One of founders of Chicano literature. Book *Bless Me Ultima* also a 2012 film. BA and two MAs from University of New Mexico. Later was English professor at UNM. Thirty-nine books and anthologies published.

Elfego Baca. New Mexico lawman. One of the legendary lawmen of the west and the only Chicano so recognized. Books and films were made about his life, including the Disney classic, "The Nine Lives of Elfego Baca." Baca was also known as "The Man Who Couldn't Be Killed." Supposedly once told a client accused of murder in El Paso (while Baca was in Albuquerque): "Say nothing to anyone. I am on the way with two eye witnesses."

Albert Baez. 1912–2007. Mexican American physicist born in Puebla, Mexico. Moved to US at four, grew up in Brooklyn. Father Methodist minister, mother social worker at YWCA. BS (math and physics) Drew University; MS (math) Syracuse; PhD (physics) Stanford. Co-inventor of X-ray reflection microscope. Pacifist, refused to work in the defense industry. Professor at MIT. Developed optics for an X-ray telescope with Smithsonian Astrophysical Observatory. Director, Science Education Programs UNESCO Paris. President of Vivámos Mejor to help impoverished Mexican villages. Received the Hispanic Engineer National Achievement Award which was named in his honor. Father of singer Joan Baez.

Javier Becerra. Lawyer, politician. Born Sacramento, California, 1958. Working class Mexican American and Mexican parents. High school in Sacramento. University of Salamanca, Spain, BA (economics) Stanford (first in family to graduate from college). JD Stanford Law. Deputy Attorney General California, thirty-third Attorney General of California, California House of Representatives, U.S. House of Representatives (1993–2017), Chair Hispanic Caucus, Assistant to the Speaker of the House 110th Congress, twenty -fifth U.S. Secretary of Health and Human Services (under President Biden). Sued Trump Administration for building a wall on the Mexican border.

Martha E. Bernal. Born San Antonio, Texas, 1931, died, 2001. Parents Mexican immigrants. Father did not want her to go to school but her sister and mother won him over and she graduated high school and attended Texas Western College, Syracuse University and Indiana University Bloomington, where she received a PhD in clinical psychology, the first Chicana to do so. Universities would not hire Chicanas. She suffered greatly from sexism, racism and overall bias against Mexicans. It kept her from doing research for a time. Her high school would not let her speak Spanish and would not let her take advanced classes. She won a U.S. Public Health Service fellowship to UCLA where she conducted research for two years. Could not get hired by corporations or universities. Finally hired at Arizona State University. Studied ethnic identity of Mexican American children in classic research for its time. Developed Ethnic Identity Questionnaire for children and parents. Faculty member at UCLA Neuropsychiatric Institute and at the University of Denver. Influenced how Chicanos and other minorities are treated across the U.S. Worked to establish the National Hispanic Psychology Association, now known as the National Latino Psychological Association, and was its second president. Many awards from national psychological organizations.

Robert Leon Cardenas. Born, 1920, Mérida, Yucatan Peninsula, Mexico. Died, 2022 at age one hundred two. Brigadier General in the Air Force. Excelled in math and physics in high school and college (San Diego State University). World War II pilot, flew gliders and B-24 liberator bombers over Europe. Shot down and injured but worked his way to Swiss lines. Became chief test pilot for bombers at Edwards Air Force Base. He was the pilot who flew the B-29 that launched Chuck

Yeager's X-1 to break the sound barrier. Combat pilot in Korea and Viet Nam. As Chief of the National Strategic Target List Division, he was responsible for selecting targets across the globe should a nuclear war occur. After retirement, he became Chair of the California Veterans Board. Among many awards were the US Air Force Command Pilot badge, Distinguished Flying Cross, Purple Heart, Air Medal and Spain's Cross of Aeronautical Merit.

Tony Casillas. Born Tulsa, Oklahoma, Mexican and Cherokee descent. University of Oklahoma degree in Public Relations. College and Pro Football NFL defensive tackle. UPI Lineman of the Year. Lombardi Award, National Championship for OU, All American. Defensive Player of the Decade Award. College Football Hall of Fame (second Hispanic). Atlanta Falcons then Dallas Cowboys with back-to-back Super Bowl wins (XXVII, XXVIII).

Lauro Cavazos. Educator, politician. Born, 1927, King Ranch, Kingsville, Texas. Mother descended from Mexican Francita Alavez, Texas Revolution Heroine and "Angel of Mercy". Texas Tech University BA, MA zoology; PhD Iowa State (physiology). Professor at Tufts, Medical College of Virginia, Dean of Tufts School of Medicine. President Texas Tech University (first alumnus and first Hispanic president of Texas Tech University). U.S. Secretary of Education under Reagan and G.H.W Bush (1988–1990). Returned to Tufts as Professor of Public Health and Family Medicine. Distinguished Achievement Award, Iowa State's highest honor. Died at 95.

Angelico Chavez, Fray (O.F.M.) (Manuel Ezequiel Chavez). 1910–1996. Born in Wagon Mound, New Mexico, one of ten children; twelfth generation New Mexico family in New Mexico since 1598. Priest, scholar, author, poet. New Mexico's premier historian on New Mexico history, Chicano history, Church history. His family moved to San Diego in 1912 and Manuel wanted to follow in the footsteps of Junipero Serra. Attended Saint Francis Seminary in Ohio and worked hard to learn English, including writing and publishing fiction and essays.

First native New Mexican to become a Franciscan. Angelico was his pen name. He was a gifted painter and the friars gave him the name Angelico in honor of the painter Fra Angelico of Florence. Ordained in Saint Francis Cathedral in Santa Fe. Pioneer of Chicano literature.

César Chávez. Farm Workers Union, civil rights activist, manual laborer after two years in the Navy, various famous farm worker strikes (grapes, lettuce), battled for immigrant rights, fought against pesticides. Presidential Medal of Freedom (President Clinton). Considered a "folk saint" by Mexican Americans. Never invited to the White House but his bust is in Joe Biden's oval office.

Eric Cesar Chavez. Born Los Angeles, 1977 to Mexican father. Baseball player and coach, Oakland Athletics, NY Yankees, Arizona Diamondbacks. Third baseman. Six Gold Glove Awards (2001–2006), Silver Slugger Award (2002). 260 HRs, 902 RBIs. Coach for NY Mets. $66M contract with Athletics.

Denise Chávez. Born Las Cruces, New Mexico. Author, playwright, stage director, professor. New Mexico State (BA), Trinity University Massachusetts in Theater, University of New Mexico (MFA Creative Writing). Five books, eleven plays. Governor's Award in Literature (1995), Premio Aztlán Literary Prize, Hispanic Heritage Award for Literature, Lifetime Achievement Award, Paul Bartlett Ré Peace Prize, University of New Mexico.

Sandra Cisneros. Author, teacher. Chicana identity themes. One of the most famous Chicana writers. *House on Mango Street*. American Book Award, MacArthur Award. Loyola of Chicago BA, University of Iowa MFA.

Maria Contreras-Sweet. Guadalajara, Mexico. Grew up in California. California State at Los Angeles. Founded marketing research firm. District Manager U.S. Census Bureau. Cabinet Sec. California Transportation and Housing Agency. Former administrator of the Small Business Administration under President Obama; founder ProAmérica Bank. Founding director California Endowment Foundation.

France Córdoba. PhD Astrophysics Cal Tech. NASA Chief Scientist. Director National Science Foundation. She discovered soft X-rays from binary stars; a leader in multiwavelength astrophysics. NASA Distinguished Service Medal, National Science Board, American Academy of Arts and Sciences.

Oscar De La Joya. Boxer. Eleven world champion titles in six weight classes, Olympic Gold Medal. Born in East L.A. to Mexican parents. First Chicano to own a Boxing promotion company.

East L.A. Walkouts. Protesting Los Angeles high school students fighting racism in schools against Chicanos; first mass protest by Chicanos against racism. It was successful and changed how Chicanos were treated in high schools across the country. It led to a great increase in the number of Chicanos who went to college. Chronicled in the film *Walkout*.

Abe Espinosa. Monterey, California, 1889–1980. First Chicano to win a major golf tournament, Western Open, 1928. Became golf course architect.

Andre Ethier. Born Phoenix, Arizona. Major League Baseball player. Dodgers, 2006–2017. All Star, 2010–2011, Silver Slugger, 2009, Golden Glove Award, 2011. Grandfather and father were minor leaguers, brother a major leaguer. Played at Arizona State University. Drafted by Oakland Athletics, traded to LA Dodgers.

Patricio Fernandez Flores. Born Ganado, Texas to migrant worker parents. Janitor and other menial jobs. Catholic high school in Galveston, then two St. Mary's seminaries in Texas. Helped establish Hispanic rights in education and society. Worked in civil rights. Established Catholic Television in San Antonio. Archbishop of El Paso (1978), Archbishop of San Antonio (1979–2004). First Mexican American to become a bishop. Co-founder Hispanic Scholarship Fund. Documentary of his life on PBS: "A Migrant's Masterpiece." Quote: "I will work not for myself but for others."

Tom Flores. Born Sanger, California to very poor Mexican sharecroppers. No plumbing, slept in grape box with a blanket. Parents stressed education, though they never finished middle school. High school sports star. College of the Pacific scholarship and quarterback position. Quarterback (first Hispanic professional quarterback) with Oakland Raiders, Kansas City Chiefs (Super Bowl win). Quarterback coach Buffalo Bills. Oakland Raiders assistant coach to John Madden. When Madden retired, Flores became Head Coach for twelve years. First Hispanic head coach to win a Super Bowl. First Hispanic President and General Manager of a pro team (Seattle Seahawks). Not selected for Pro Football Hall of Fame, possibly due to his ethnicity.

Nasario García. Folklorist, author, historian, professor. Born, 1936 Bernalillo, New Mexico, grew up in Ojo del Padre, Guadalupe, Sandoval County. BA (Spanish), MA (Portuguese), University of New Mexico, PhD University of Pittsburgh (19th century Spanish literature). Has published thirty books in English and Spanish on New Mexico folklore and history. Dean of Arts and Sciences at University of Southern Colorado. First Lifetime Achievement Award from the Historical Society of New Mexico; his books have won dozens of national and regional awards.

Nomar Garciaparra. Mexican American, Whittier California. Outstanding major league baseball player. Six-time All-Star; American League Rookie of the Year; Silver Slugger Award; National League

Comeback Player of the Year (2006); two times American League Batting Champion. Boston Red Sox Hall of Fame.

Gustavo Garcia-Siller. Born San Luis Potosí, Mexico, oldest of fifteen siblings. Studied in Mexico, then sent to California. Seminary in California. Master of Divinity and Master of Theology degrees. Auxiliary Bishop Chicago, Bishop of San Antonio. One of very few Chicano Archbishops. Accused of ignoring sexual abuse in his diocese.

José Horacio Gómez. Born Monterrey, Mexico, 1951. Mexican American. BS Accounting University of Navarra; BA Philosophy, National Autonomous University of Mexico. Archbishop of Los Angeles, Archbishop of San Antonio, President U.S. Conference of Catholic Bishops. Only Latino Archbishop when first appointed.

Rodolfo "Corky" Gonzales. 1928–2005. Born Denver, Colorado. Father from Chihuahua, Mexico. Mother died when he was a baby. Political activist and organizer, boxer. Was a leader in the Crusade for Justice movement in Denver, supporting Chicano activism. Organized Chicano Youth Liberation conferences. Organized Chicanos in Denver to fight for their rights. Worked to start a Chicano third party for elections. Successful professional boxer considered fifth best boxer in the world on his retirement from the ring. Colorado Sports Hall of Fame.

Sidney McNeill "Sid" Gutierrez. Born June 27, 1951, Albuquerque, New Mexico. BS Aeronautical engineering Air Force Academy, MA (management) Webster University. Retired Colonel USAF. Fighter pilot (F-15 Eagle, F-16), T-38 instructor pilot, test pilot. NASA astronaut, 1984. Flew Shuttle simulators to test engines and software. Made two space flights as Shuttle pilot with four hundred eighty-eight hours in space. Served as Astronaut Office Branch Chief for Operations and Development of all Space Shuttle flights from takeoff to landing. Retired to work at Sandia National Laboratories. Member Experimental Test Pilots, Society of Space Explorers, NASA Outstanding Leadership

Medal, NASA Exceptional Achievement Medal, NASA Space Flight Medal (two), International Space Hall of Fame, Hispanic Engineer of the Year, many military medals.

José M. Hernandez. Born, 1962 Stockton, California. Engineer, astronaut, author, businessman. Parents Mexican immigrant fruit workers which José did as well. Learned English when he was twelve. In high school was in Upward Bound and Math, Science and Achievement Program (MESA) preparing for science and technology training (STEM). Infatuated by space flight. BS (electrical engineering) University of the Pacific; MS (computer and electrical engineering) UC Santa Barbara. Worked at Lawrence Livermore National Laboratory where he was co-developer of the digital mammography imaging system. Rejected eleven times for astronaut training. Finally accepted. Became a mission specialist on the Space Shuttle and was the first astronaut to tweet in Spanish from space. He played the first mariachi music from space to awaken the astronauts: José Alfredo Jimenez's *El Hijo del Pueblo*. Ran for Congress but lost in a contentious campaign. Won many awards, including a gold medal from the Society of Mexican American Engineers and Scientists, Outstanding Engineer Award, Lawrence Livermore Lab, National Hispanic Hero Award, U.S. Hispanic Leadership Institute. Movie, "A Million Miles Away," was made of his life.

Maria Hinojosa. Author, journalist, news anchor, television host, activist. Worked at CNN, CBS, NPR. Three times recognized as one of the one hundred most influential Hispanics. Barnard College, Latin American Studies. Born in Mexico City, 1962. Father a medical doctor descended from Conquistador Diego de Montemayor, founder of the city of Monterrey, Mexico. Father became surgeon at the University of Chicago, which is where Hinojosa grew up. Genes show an indigenous Mexican origin for Hinojosa on her mother's side. Won John Chancellor Award, Robert F. Kennedy Award for Journalism, National Association of Hispanic Journalists Award for Radio, Edward R. Murrow Award, Sidney Hillman Prize, National Council or La Raza Rubén Salazar Award. Honorary Doctorate from DePaul University in Chicago. Has won four Emmy Awards, a Pulitzer Prize and other honors.

Dolores Huerta. Dawson, New Mexico, 1930. Mexican immigrant coal miner family. Taken to Stockton California as a child. Suffered from racism in school. Became a teacher. Organized farm workers and taught them the importance of voting. With César Chavez, she founded the National Farm Workers Association. Arrested twenty-two times for her labor union activism. Contributed enormously to workers' and women's rights. Eugene V. Debs Foundation Outstanding American Award, U.S. Presidential Eleanor Roosevelt Award for Human Rights (first awardee), Presidential Medal of Freedom from President Obama. First Latina inducted into the National Women's Hall of Fame; fifteen honorary doctorates, Order of the Aztec Eagle, Mexico's highest honor. First used the phrase, *Si se puede*, later adopted by Barack Obama.

Jovita Idár. Born, 1885, Laredo, Texas. One of eight children. Her family were all political activists. Journalist, school teacher, political activist, civil rights worker. President League of Mexican Women, fought for free education for Chicano children in Laredo, Texas. When Nuevo Laredo attacked in Mexican Revolution, she became a volunteer nurse for the Cruz Blanca in Mexico. Her newspaper published articles opposing President Woodrow Wilson's plan to send troops and Texas Rangers to the border. Texas Rangers tried to enter her newspaper and she stopped them, something celebrated by Google Doodle in 2020 ("celebrating Jovita Idar"). Rangers finally destroyed her newspaper. Died, 1946, San Antonio.

Enrique La Madrid. Born Embudo, New Mexico. University of New Mexico (BA), University of Southern California (MA, PhD). Historian, author, poet, professor emeritus Portuguese, Chicano Studies University of New Mexico. Twenty-one books, authored/edited.

Evan Michael Longoria. Born Downey, California, father Mexican descent. College baseball Long Beach State, BA (criminal justice). Two years in minor leagues then Tampa Bay Rays. Major League baseball player. All Star, 2008, led Rays to playoffs and World Series. Rookie of the Year. In 2009, Player of Month, Player of Week, All Star Game.

Three-time All Star and three times Golden Glove awardee. Third base. One hundred-million-dollar contract extension in 2012. Traded to San Francisco Giants, 2018. Over long career: batting average .265; 1,895 hits; 334 HR; 1,137 RBI.

Nancy Lopez. Born Torrance, California. University of Tulsa (two years). One of greatest women golfers. World Golf Hall of Fame. Philanthropist. Eight amateur wins; forty-eight LGPA tour wins; Female Athlete of the Year (AP).

E. A. "Tony" Mares. 1938–2015. Born Albuquerque, New Mexico, Saint Mary High School, BA University of New Mexico, MA Florida State University, PhD University of New Mexico. University professor: University of Arkansas, University of North Texas Denton, University of New Mexico. Historian of New Mexico, Spain, Portugal. Professor, author, poet, playwright. Taught poetry to prisoners in the penitentiary in Santa Fe; developed poetry outreach website for University of New Mexico dedicated to high school students across the state. Studied healthcare availability for Chicanos in northern New Mexico. Scholar of Padre Martinez, the famous Taos priest and Mares' distant uncle, as well as the Spanish Civil War and the Abraham Lincoln Brigade.

Jennifer Martínez. Yale, Harvard education. Human rights lawyer, professor of law, Stanford University. Dean of Stanford Law School. Expert on international courts and tribunals and the laws of war.

Joe Louis Martinez Jr. 1944–2020. Mexican American, Albuquerque, New Mexico. Saint Mary High School; BA Psychology University of California San Diego; MS Experimental Psychology, New Mexico Highlands University; PhD Physiological Psychology, University of Delaware; postdoctoral work University of California Irvine and Salk Institute, University of California Berkeley. Professor retired; moved to University of Texas San Antonio where he founded and directed the Cajal Neuroscience Research Center. Then to University of Illinois as Chair of Department of Psychology. Worked with American Psychological Association to increase minorities in psychology. Published 200 papers and received numerous awards for psychological service and research. AAAS Fellow, AAAS Mentor Award. Founder of and leading researcher in modern Chicano psychology. He had a life of extraordinary contributions to psychology and service to minorities.

Antonio (Tony) Mendez. Mexican American, Nevada. Artist, author, spy. One of the greatest CIA undercover spies. Academy Award winning film *Argo* based on his exploits, with six-foot-four Ben Affleck playing five-foot-seven Tony Mendez. Father died when he was young. Never learned Spanish or felt Hispanic. Studied art in Colorado, became document forger for CIA. Was undercover spy throughout the world. CIA Medal of Merit, Intelligence Star, two Certificates of Distinction, Trailblazer Medallion.

Sylvia Mendez. Chicana from California. In 1946 at eight years old was part of case *Mendez v. Westminster* that ended segregation in California. Seven years later *Brown v. Board of Education* ended all school segregation. Before her case Chicanos could only attend Mexican schools. Became a nurse and lecturer on civil rights. Presidential Medal of Freedom from President Obama.

J. Mario Molina. California Chicano. Former CEO Molina Healthcare, Medical Medicare and Medicaid Health provider in more than a dozen states and the primary Medicaid plan in many states. Founding Dean Keck Graduate School, medical school (in progress). Fortune 500 company with many awards including the Padrino Award from Ohio Hispanic Coalition. Molina's net worth seventy-seven million.

Mario José Molina Henríquez. Mexican born U.S. citizen. University of Mexico (BA), University of Freiburg, Germany (MS), PhD Berkeley. Physical chemist. Taught at University of California Irvine, Cal Tech, MIT, Scripps Institute. Discovered ozone hole and developed a strategy to deal with it. CFCs (chlorofluorocarbon) research. Research on face masks during SARS-COV-2 pandemic. Nobel Prize for chemistry for ozone hole discovery and research. NASA Medal, UN Global 500 Award, Fellow AAAS, and many others. Awarded thirty honorary doctorates.

Richard Montañez. Frito Lay executive who began as a janitor for the company and worked his way up to senior management. One of ten siblings in a migrant labor camp in Los Angeles. Involved with the marketing of Flaming Hot Cheetos; his life was depicted in the movie "Flamin' Hot" directed by Eva Longoria.

G. Cristina Mora. Mexican American. Academic. University of California Berkeley, Princeton. Sociologist, Co-Director Institute of Governmental Studies, University of California Berkeley. Book: *Making Hispanics*. Studies Hispanics and other minorities.

Arturo "Arte" Moreno. Mexican American, Tucson, Arizona. Oldest of eleven children. Father owned a print shop. Grandfather owned first Spanish newspaper in Tucson. Vietnam War Veteran. University of Arizona degree in marketing. Officer in Outdoor Systems billboard company. Went public, purchased by Infiniti Broadcasting for eight billion dollars. Bought Los Angeles Angels baseball team (only Hispanic baseball team owner). Moreno Family Foundation supports youth programs. Net worth four billion. Endorsed Donald Trump.

Anthony Muñoz. Sports legend, actor, sports announcer. Mexican American from Ontario, California. Played football and baseball at University of Southern California. Won a bowl game in each of his seasons. Played tackle for Cincinnati Bengals and Tampa Bay Buccaneers. Offensive Lineman of the Year in, 1981 and 1988; NFL Players Association Lineman of Year in 1981, 1985, 1988, 1989. Considered one of the best football players of all time. Had a small but memorable performance as "Gonzalez" in the film, "The Right Stuff." Founded Anthony Muñoz Foundation to help young people in sports and beyond.

Ellen Ochoa. First Chicana astronaut in space, Astronaut Hall of Fame. Engineer. Flew four space shuttle missions and missions to Space Station (four flight medals); nine hundred fifty hours in outer space. Director Flight Operations at Johnson Space Center in Texas. PhD in Electrical Engineering. Member National Academy for Inventors. Flautist. First astronaut to play an instrument while floating in space. Quote: "Don't be afraid to reach for the stars. I believe a good education can take you anywhere on Earth and beyond."

John D. "Danny" Olivas. Born, 1966 North Hollywood, California, grew up in El Paso, Texas. His grandfather came to the U.S. from Mexico in 1894. BS Mechanical Engineering, The University of Texas at El Paso; MS Mechanical Engineering, University of Houston; PhD Mechanical Engineering and Materials Science, Rice University. NASA astronaut, 1998. Studied orbit shuttle repair and worked on *Aquarius* underwater laboratory. Was on Shuttle STS-117 *Atlantis* and STS-128 *Discovery* to the International Space Station. Had several space walks and was the first astronaut to repair the exterior of the Space Shuttle in outer space and the first Chicano to walk in space. After NASA he became a university director of The University of Texas at El Paso Center for the Advancement of Space Safety and then became a businessman.

Federico Fabian Peña. Politician, attorney. Born Laredo, Texas, 1947. BA and JD The University of Texas at Austin. Colorado House of Representatives, Mayor of Denver (first Hispanic mayor) 1980s–1990s, helped revitalize Denver's economy. Head U.S. Dept. of Transportation and Secretary of Energy (President Clinton).

Alonso S. Perales. Author, lawyer, diplomat, civil rights activist. Born in Alice, Texas, 1898; died, 1960. Orphaned at six. Founded LULAC (League of United Latin American Citizens). World War I clerk. Business college, then BA from National University School of Economics; law degree George Washington University Law School. One of the first Mexican Americans to practice law in the United States Helped create the U.N. Charter. Fought against discrimination of Mexicans.

Jim Plunkett. Born, 1947. Parents blind New Mexico Chicanos born in Albuquerque and Santa Fe. Family moved to California but were impoverished. Was outstanding at school sports. Stanford Scholarship for football. Set many league records. Won Rose Bowl. Heisman Trophy (first Hispanic winner). Maxwell Award for nation's best player. Outstanding NFL career with New England Patriots, San Francisco 49ers, Oakland Raiders, Kansas City Chiefs. Only Hispanic to win a Super Bowl as quarterback. Only one of four players to win the Heisman and be selected Super Bowl MVP. Retired, 1988 as only quarterback to win two Super Bowls with the same franchise in different cities (Oakland, Los Angeles). College Football Hall of Fame. Has never been selected to the Pro Football Hall of Fame. Ten concussions and many other injuries. Says his life "sucks" now due to so many injuries and constant pain.

Jorge Gilberto Ramos Ávalos. Born, 1958 Mexico City. Journalist, news anchor Univision. Won ten Emmy Awards. Immigrant at twenty-eight. Considered the most respected Latin American journalist.

Ernest Z. Robles. Born Pirtleville, Arizona, 1931; died, 2022, attended segregated schools. Led fight against segregation of Chicanos in California. U.S. Dept. of Education hired him to travel in the South presenting court orders to desegregate. Educator, Korean War Hero (Purple Heart, Bronze Star, Navy Commendation Medal of Valor, US Marine), established Hispanic Scholarship Fund helping tens of thousands of Hispanics attend college.

Alfonso John Romero. Designer, game developer, software engineer. Indo-Chicano from Colorado Springs, Colorado. Designed games *Wolfenstein 3D, Doom, Doom II, Hexen, Quake*, and many other games. Net worth of ten million dollars. Atheist.

Ruben Salazar. Chicano from Juarez (1928–1970). One of first Mexican American journalists. Texas Western College (The University of Texas at El Paso). Reporter for *LA Times*. Prominent in Chicano movement. First Chicano journalist to cover Chicanos in East L.A. News Director KMEX in Los Angeles. Twice winner of Greater Los Angeles Press Club Award, Posthumous winner of Robert F. Kennedy Journalism Award. Killed at age forty-two when, during a protest, police teargas grenade hit him in the head.

Robert Fortune Sanchez. Priest, Archbishop of the Diocese of Santa Fe. Born Socorro, New Mexico, 1934. Pastor, San Felipe de Neri Parish. Immaculate Heart Seminary, St. Michael's College, Santa Fe, Pontifical North American College in Rome. Teaching certificate University of New Mexico for teaching at St. Mary's High School Albuquerque. Degree in canon law from Catholic University of America in DC. Became first Hispanic to be named archbishop in the U.S. Worked closely with native Americans and Hispanics. Resigned in shame (the day before a "60 Minutes" exposé) for ignoring child abuse cases in his diocese and for having seduced young girls while at San Felipe Church. Died of Alzheimer's in Minnesota in 2012.

John Phillip Santos. Author, filmmaker, professor. Born San Antonio, Texas, 1957. More than forty documentary broadcasts in the social sciences, including culture, politics, religion, Chicano issues. Notre Dame BA Philosophy and Literature, MA English Literature Oxford. First Chicano Rhodes Scholar. Ford Foundation program officer providing forty million dollars in grant support to independent media networks throughout the world. Numerous awards including American Academy of Poets, Oxford Prize, Berlin Prize, Texas Medal for the Arts in Literature.

Lionel Sosa. San Antonio, Texas, 1939. Artist, advertising executive. Parents Mexican immigrants. Painted garbage cans in San Antonio for four years, before opening a graphic design agency. Worked successfully for several republican politicians increasing outreach to Mexican voters (John Tower, Ronald Reagan, George W. Bush). Many companies (Coors, Bacardi, Dr. Pepper) sought his services. Founded largest Hispanic ad agency in the world billing one hundred million dollars a year. Named one of twenty-five most influential Hispanics by *Time Magazine*.

Gary Soto. Author of forty-five books, poet. Hispanic Heritage Award for Literature, Academy of American Poets Prize, American Book Award. Farm worker laborer in his teens. MFA University of California, Irvine. Quote: "You can always spot bright people. They are reading a book."

Luis E. Tapia. Self-taught artist. Wood carver. Native New Mexican. Founded La Cofradia de Artes y Artesanos Hispanos with Federico Vigil. New Mexico Governor's Award for Excellence in the Arts (1996), Joan Mitchell Fellowship, National Heritage Fellowship.

Lee Trevino. One of the greatest golfers in history. "Supermex." Mexican ancestry, Texas born in 1939. Worked in cotton fields at age five when his father abandoned the family. Became a caddie, earned thirty dollars a week. Marine Corps machine gunner for four years. Won six major championships and twenty-nine PGA tours. World Golf Hall of Fame. Established many scholarships for Mexican Americans.

Solomon Dennis "Sol" Trujillo. Global businessman, media communications. Born Cheyenne, Wyoming, 1951 to Mexican American parents. Vice President Mountain Bell in New Mexico in 1974. President US West, 1996. President and CEO US West, 1998, first Chicano CEO of Fortune 200 company. In 2000 chairman and CEO of Graviton, wireless technology company. In 2003 CEO of Orange S. A., CAC 40 company (France). CEO Telstra (Australia). Honorary Doctorate, University of Wyoming, 2000, University of Colorado, 2002, Whittier College, 2017; National Hero of the Year award by U.S. Hispanic Leadership Institute; Ron H. Brown Corporate Bridge Builder Award by President Clinton.

Sara Martinez Tucker. Born, 1956 Laredo, Texas, The University of Texas at Austin (BA Journalism, Master of Business Administration). AT&T executive. CEO Hispanic Scholarship Fund. Board member of many companies. Hispanic of the Year 2000 for Hispanic One. 2005 *Time Magazine* twenty-five most influential Hispanics. Undersecretary Education US government, 2006 under George W. Bush. Chairman University of Texas Board of Regents.

Luis Valdez. Born in 1940 in California to Mexican migrant farm workers. Became farm laborer at the age of six. Playwright, actor, film director, screenwriter. Considered father of Chicano film and playwriting. Interested in theater from a young age; he graduated from San Jose State University in English. Worked with a mime troupe in San Francisco in guerilla theater. Made the film, *I am Joaquin* based on a poem by Corky Gonzales. Known for play and film *Zoot Suit*. First Chicano director to have a Broadway play. Directed the film *La Bamba*, about Ritchie Valens. Golden Globes for *Zoot Suit* and *La Bamba*. U.S. National Medal of Arts (2015).

Federico Vigil. Santa Fe *buon fresco* artist (a technique known from Italy in 16th century). Born, 1946. Founded La Cofradia de Artes y Artesanos Hispanos with Luis Tapia. Artist for restored churches in northern New Mexico.

Readings

"60 Minutes" report on Bishop Roberto Sanchez. YouTube, 1993.

Ackermann, C. *Historia Antigua de México: Facsimilar de la Edición de Ackerman 1826, Tomo II.* Government of the State of Puebla Secretary of Culture. 1826.

Adams, J. R. *Greasers and Gringos. The Historical Roots of Anglo-Hispanic Prejudice.* McFarland Publishing. Jefferson, North Carolina. 2006.

Alberts, D. E. *The Battle of Glorieta. Union Victory in the West.* Texas A&M Press, 1998.

Al Jazeera. Mexico's president slams calls for U.S. military to target cartels. *Al Jazeera.* March 9, 2023.

Allen, A. Credibility and Incredulity: A critique of Bartolomé de Las Casas' "A Short Account of the Destruction of the Indies." *The Gettysburg Historical Journal*: 9 (5).

Ambrose, S. *Crazy Horse and Custer: The Parallel Lives of Two American Warriors.* Doubleday Books, 1975.

Anaya, R. A. *Voces: An Anthology of Nuevo Mexicano Writers*. E. A. Mares. Once a Man Knew His Name (100-103). El Norte Publications/Academia, Albuquerque, 1987.

Anders, J. P. Something soft and wild and free. Willa Cather's sexual aesthetics. *Cather Studies*, Vol. 4. *Willa Cather's Canadian & Old World Connections*. R. Thacker, M. A. Peterman. U. Nebraska Press, Lincoln and London, 1999.

Associated Press. Professor predicts 'Hispanic Homeland.' *Citizen Review Online*, 2000.

Athearn, F. J. *A Forgotten Kingdom: The Spanish Frontier in Colorado and New Mexico,* 1540–1821. BLM Cultural Resources Series (Colorado 29), Chap. 2. The Reconquest of New Mexico, 1692–1704. 1979.

Athearn, F. J. *A Forgotten Kingdom: The Spanish Frontier in Colorado and New Mexico*, 1540–1821. BLM Cultural Resources Series (Colorado 29). Chap. 1. New Mexico, 1536–1680. 1989.

Attanasio, C., F. Fonseca. Protestors topple monument in Santa Fe Plaza, part of Indigenous Peoples Day Demonstration. *Las Cruces Sun News,* October 12, 2020.

Bailyn, B. *The Barbarous Years: The Peopling of British North America–The Conflict of Civilizations, 1600-1675*. Vintage Press, 2013.

Barbour, B. H. Kit Carson and the "Americanization" of New Mexico. *New Mexico Historical Review*, 77(2): 115-143, 2002.

Becerra-Valdivia, L., T. Higham. The timing and effect of the earliest human arrivals in North America. *Nature*, 584:93-97, July 22, 2020.

Beschloss, S. The sociopathy of Texas Governor. Greg Abbott. *America, America News*, 2021.

Bhole, A. Inside the Mexican drug labs that are "hidden in plain sight": Cartels flooding the U.S. with fentanyl and other drugs manufactured in pop-up Breaking Bad-style "factories" in homes, on farms and *piñata* stores. *Daily Mail*, March 11, 2023.

Bishop M., J. Shu. *The history of anti-Mexican violence and lynching*, 2016.

Blakemore, E. The largest mass deportation in American History. History Channel, March 23, updated June 18, 2019.

Blumenthal, R. The World: Revisiting World War II atrocities; comparing the unspeakable to the unthinkable. *The New York Times*, March 7, 1999.

Bogardus, E. S. Attitudes and the Mexican immigrant. In K. Young (ed). *Social Attitudes*, 291-327, Henry Holt, 1931.

Border police in drive on wetbacks. *Sarasota Journal*, Associated Press, June 17, 1954.

Bryan, H. *Incredible Elfego Baca: Good Man, Bad Man of the Old West*. Clear Light Publishers, Santa Fe, N. M., 1993.

Buchanan, R. *Don Diego de Vargas: The Peaceful Conquistador*. Hillside Education Publishers, 2016.

Buchholz, K. The countries most active in the Trans-Atlantic slave trade. *Statistica*, June 19, 2020.

Burrough, B., C. Tomlinson, J. Stanford. *Forget the Alamo*. Penguin Press, 2021.

Callaway, E. Genghis Kahn's genetic legacy has competition. *Nature,* 2015.

Candelaria, C. La Malinche, feminist prototype. *Frontiers: A Journal of Women Studies*, 5(2), *Chicanas en el Ambiente Nacional*/Chicanas in the National Landscape, Summer, 1980.

Canizales, S. L., Vallejo, J. A. Latinos and racism in the Trump Era. *Daedalus*, Spring, 2021.

Carlson, R. Don Juan de Oñate's prosecution for "crimes and excesses" in the Provinces of New Mexico, 1614. Senior Seminar, History Department Western Oregon University, 2008.

Carrigan W., C. Webb. The lynching of persons of Mexican origin or descent in the United States, 1848 to 1928. *Journal of Social History*, 37(2), 411-438, 2003.

Carrillo, L. *The California I Love*. Prentice Hall, Hoboken, N. J., 1961.

Carroll, P. J. *Felix Longoria's Wake. Bereavement, Racism, and the Rise of Mexican American Activism*. University of Texas Press, Austin, 2003.

Cather, W. *Death Comes for the Archbishop*. Knopf, 1927.

Cervantes, F. *Conquistadores: A New History*. Allen Lane Publishers, London, 2020.

Chamberlain, S. E. *My Confession: Recollections of a Rogue*, 1850. Texas State Historical Association, January 1, 1997.

Chamberlain, S. E. *My Confession*. Time, Inc., New York, 1956.

Chavez, A. *My Penitente Land: Reflections on Spanish New Mexico*. University of New Mexico Press. Albuquerque, 1974.

Cofield, C. Stephen Hawking: Intelligent aliens could destroy humanity, but let's search anyway. Space.com. 2015.

Colinvaux, P. *The Fates of Nations*. Penguin Books. New York, 1980.

CPTSD Foundation.org.

Critical Past. Video. American Marines World War II Japanese women jump cave entrances, 1944.

Curzio, L., J. L. Valdés-Ugalde. A reply to Samuel Huntington's "Hispanic Challenge." Voices of Mexico, 67: April-June, 2004. Cisan Unam (Centro de Investigaciones sobre América del Norte, Universidad Nacional Autónoma de México), Mexico.

Danel, C. Consecration of a bishop. *The Angelus*. January, 2019.

Davis-Undiano, R. C. *Mestizos Come Home! Making and Claiming Mexican American Identity*. University of Oklahoma Press, Norman, 2017.

Dawson, M. *Behind the Mule: Race and Class in African-American Politics.* Princeton University Press. Princeton, 1995.

De Aragon, R. J. *Padre Martinez and Bishop Lamy.* Pan American Publishing, California, 1978.

De Gree, A. (N.D.) *This Land is Your Land.* The CultureCrush.com.

Digital History. Bartolomé de las Casas, 1542. 2021.

Dumont, J. *El amanecer de los derechos del hombre: la controversia de Valladolid.* Madrid: Editorial Encuentro, 1997.

Ehlers, C., I. R. Gizer. Evidence for a genetic component for substance dependence in Native Americans. *American Journal of Psychiatry,* 170:154-164, 2013.

Eisenhower, D. D. Military-Industrial Complex Speech. 1961. Avalon Project, 2008.

Elving, R. Imagine another American Civil War, but this time in every state. National PR, January 11, 2022.

Espinosa, J. M. Crusaders of the Rio Grande, the story of Don Diego De Vargas and the Reconquest and Refounding of New Mexico. *Institute of Jesuit History*; First Edition, January 1, 1942.

Estrada, L. F., F. C. Garcia, R. F. Macías, L. Maldonado. Chicanos in the United States: A history of exploitation and resistance. Vol. 110, No. 2, *American Indians, Blacks, Chicanos, and Puerto Ricans.* Daedalus, MIT Press, American Academy of Arts and Sciences, 1981.

Farah, M. *JStor Daily Newsletter*, 2019.

Federation for American Immigration Reform. Chicano nationalism, Revanchism and the Aztlan Myth. 2022.

Fernandes, T., M. Liberato, C. Marques, E. Cunha. Three cases of feet and hand amputation from Medieval Estremoz, Portugal. *International Journal of Paleopathology*, 18:63-68, 2017.

Foster-Frau, S. Latinos are disproportionately killed by police but often left out of the debate about brutality, some advocates say. *Washington Post*, May 31, 2021.

Friede, J., B. Keen. (eds.). *Bartolome De Las Casas in History: Toward an Understanding of the Man and His Work*. Northern Illinois University Press. DeKalb, 1971.

Gabaldón, G. Voces Oral History Center, The University of Texas at Austin, Interviewer Maggie Rivas-Rodriguez, 2000.

García, U. J. State investigating claim that DPS Troopers were told to push migrants back in the Rio Grande and deny them water. *Texas Tribune*, July 18, 2023.

Gates, J. P., Marafioti, N. (eds). *Capital and Corporal Punishment in Anglo-Saxon England* (Anglo-Saxon Studies, 23). Boydell Press, Woodbridge, U.K., 2014.

Gilmore, N. Plan to rebuild obelisk will be withdrawn. *Santa Fe New Mexican*, March 15, 2023.

Glosser, D. S. Stephen Miller is an immigration hypocrite. I know because I'm his uncle. Politico.com, 2018.

Gonzales, M. G. *Mexicanos. A History of Mexicans in the United States.* Indiana University Press, Bloomington and Indianapolis, 1999.

Gregg II, G. L. (N.D.). George W. Bush: Foreign Affairs. Miller Center, University of Virginia.

Hall, R. E. They lynched Mexican Americans too: A question of Anglo Colorism. *Hispanic Journal of Behavioral Sciences*, 42(1):62-76, 2020.

Hallas, J. H. *Saipan: The Battle that Doomed Japan in World War II.* Stackpole Books, Lanham, Maryland, 2019.

Handel, G., J. Humphreys. The Phoenix Indian School Band, 1894-1930. *Journal Historical Research in Music Education*, 26(2):144-161, 2005.

Handwerk, B. Ancient DNA charts Native Americans' journeys to Asia thousands of years ago. *Smithsonian Magazine*: January 12, 2023.

Hedges, C. What every person should know about war. *The New York Times*, July 6, 2003.

Hernandez, R. D. Commentary: To be a Chicano is to inherit generations of resistance, defiance, resilience and dignity. *San Diego Union-Tribune*, December 31, 2020.

Hevesi, D. Archbishop Robert F. Sanchez, who fought discrimination, dies at 77. *The New York Times*, January 23, 2012.

Huntington, S. P. The Hispanic challenge. Foreign Policy, 141:30-45, March-April, 2004.

Irish Central Staff. Steve Bannon's Irish ancestors arrived to U.S. after Great Hunger, 2020.

Isaacson, W. *Steve Jobs*. Simon and Schuster, 2011.

Jones, O. L. *Pueblo Warriors and Spanish Conquest.* University of Oklahoma Press, Norman, 1966.

Kanellos, N. (ed.). *Herencia*. New York, Oxford University Press, 2002.

Kelly-Custer, G. *Princess Monahsetah: The Concealed Wife of General Custer*. Trafford Publishing, Bloomington, Indiana, 2008.

Kerby, R. L. *The Confederate Invasion of New Mexico and Arizona*, Westernlore Press, Los Angeles, 1958.

Kirkup, J. *A History of Limb Amputation*. Springer-Verlag, London, 2007.

Knowles, N. The torture of captives by the Indians of Eastern North America. *Proceedings of the American Philosophical Society*, 82:2, March, 1940.

KOAT-TV. Man arrested in protest shooting faces additional charges. June 17, 2020.

Lastres J. B. *Peruvian Aboriginal medicine*] [in Spanish]. *Revista del Museo Nacional*, Lima, Peru 1943.

LEAD. Latino Education and Advocacy Days. California State University at San Bernardino. 2021.

Léry, J. de. *History of a Voyage to the Land of Brazil, Otherwise Called America.* Janet Whatley (ed, trans). University of California Press, Berkeley, 1992.

Library of Congress. 2023. Voting rights for Native Americans.

Lozada, C. Samuel Huntington, a prophet for the Trump era. *Washington Post*, July 19, 2017.

Lincoln, A. 1848. Speech on War with Mexico. House Divided. Dickinson. edu.

Lubin, G. and V. Giang. The 17 jobs where you're most likely to become an alcoholic. *Business Insider*, October 25, 2011.

MacNeily, A. E. What's past is prologue. Canadian Urology Association. Journal. 14 (4):81. Published online April 1, 2020.

Mares, E. A. *In* Montiel, T., T. Atencio, and E. A. Mares. 2009. *Resolana: Emerging Chicano Dialogues on Community and Globalization.* The University of Arizona Press, Tucson, 2009a.

Mares, E. A. Padre Martinez and Mexican New Mexico. *In* Etulain, R. W. (ed.). *New Mexican Lives. Profiles and Historical Stories.* University *of New Mexico Press, Albuquerque, 2002.*

Mares, E. A. *Once A Man Knew His Name,* a poem by E.A. Mares about Po'pay, leader of the Pueblo Revolt of 1680. YouTube.com. 2009b.

Mares, E. A. *Astonishing Light. Conversations I never had with Patrociño Barela.* University of New Mexico Press, Albuquerque, 2010.

Mares, M. A. Mammal faunas of xeric habitats and the Great American Interchange. 489–520. In *The Great American Biotic Interchange.* F. Stehli, S. D. Webb (eds.). Plenum Press, New York, 1985.

Mares, M. A. (ed.). *Encyclopedia of Deserts.* University of Oklahoma Press, Norman, 1999.

Mares, M. A. Miracle on the prairie: The development of the Sam Noble Oklahoma Museum of Natural History. *Museologia* 2:31-50, 2000. *Museu de Ciência da Universidade de Lisboa.*

Mares, M. A. (ed) *A University Natural History Museum for the New Millennium.* Sam Noble Oklahoma Museum of Natural History, 2001.

Mares, M. A. *A Desert Calling: Life in a Forbidding Landscape.* Harvard University Press, 2002.

Marín, C. What is a Chicano? *HuffPost*, May 3, 2012, Updated July 3, 2012.

Martin, P. S. The discovery of America: The first Americans may have swept the Western Hemisphere and decimated its fauna within 1000 years. *Science* 179:969-974, 1973.

Martinez O. US-Mexico borderlands: The lynching of Mexicans in the Texas borderlands. *The Americas*, 75(4):792-793, 2018.

Masich, A. E. Civil War in the Southwest Borderlands, 1961–1867. University of Oklahoma Press, Norman, 2017.

Mavrofourou, A. Punitive limb amputation. *Clinical Orthopaedics and Related Research.* 472(10):3102-3106, 2014.

Mayell, H. Genghis Khan a prolific lover, DNA data implies. *National Geographic*, 2003.

McMurtrie, D. A. The history of early printing in New Mexico, with a bibliography of the known issues of the New Mexican Press, 1834–1860. *New Mexico Historical Review*, 4 (4):372-410, 1929.

Melzer, R. *Captain Maximiliano Luna: A New Mexico Rough Rider.* Rio Grande Books, Los Ranchos, New Mexico, 2017.

Michno, G. F. *Encyclopedia of Indian Wars: Western Battles and Skirmishes, 1850–1890.* Mountain Press, 2003.

Minge, W. A. *Acoma. Pueblo in the Sky.* University of New Mexico Press, Albuquerque, 2002.

Minnesota Historical Society. N.D. *Great Lakes Indigenous People and the French.* MNHS.org.

Montiel, T., T. Atencio, E. A. Mares. *Resolana: Emerging Chicano Dialogues on Community and Globalization.* The University of Arizona Press, Tucson, 2009.

Morgan, E. S. *American Heroes: Profiles of Men and Women who Shaped Early America.* Norton, 2009.

Morgan, E. S. Columbus' confusion about the New World. *Smithsonian Magazine*, October 2009.

Murillo, E. "America libre and Latinidades" as contestation to "The Hispanic Challenge." *Confluencia* 29 (2)121-135, 2013.

National Archives (U.S.). Japanese War Crimes. January 12, 2007.

National Guard Military. N.D. Gettysburg of the West, Glorieta Pass. National Guard.mil.

NDN Collective.org. N.D.

Noe-Bustamante, L., Gonzalez-Barrera, A., Khadijah, E., Mora, L., M. H. Lopez. Pew Research Center, November 2021.

O'Brien, C. Courageous explorer or bloodthirsty killer? The sobering truth about Kit Carson in Northern California. *ActiveNorCal* April 19, 2022.

Olivas, M. A. The "Trial of the Century" that never was: Staff Sgt. Macario Garcia, The Congressional Medal of Honor, and the Oasis Café. Maurer School of Law, *Indiana Law Journal: Indiana University*, 83 (4):1390-1403, 2008.

Pannier, B. Iran: Criminal loses hand and feet as Shari'a law is imposed. Rfer.org. January 7, 2008.

Passel, J., D. Cohn. U.S. Population Projections 2005–2050. Pew Research Center, February 11, 2008.

Patterson, M. R. Felix Z. Longoria, private, United States Army. Arlington National Cemetery, 2023.

Pimentel, O. R. Here's another statue that needs to come down. *Wisconsin Examiner* July 3, 2020.

Police Evidence Report. policeviolencereport.org. 2023.

Potter, B. A. *et al*. Current evidence allows multiple models for the peopling of the Americas. *Science Advances*, Vol. 4(8), 2018.

Price, M. Native Americans-and their genes-traveled back to Siberia, new genomes reveal. *Science*, January 12, 2023.

Quijano, A. Coloniality of power, eurocentrism, and Latin America. Nepantla 1 (3):533-580, 2000.

Rasmussen, M. *et al*. Ancient human genome sequence of an extinct Palaeo-Eskimo. *Nature* 463:757-762, February 11, 2010.

Rauch, S. K. *Shattered Faith*. Pantheon Publishers, New York, 1997.

Reich, D. *et al*. Reconstructing Native American population history. *Nature*, 7411:370-374, 2012.

Rincon, P. "Tribe Challenges American Origins." *BBC News Online*, September 7, 2004.

Rogers, R. *"The San Fernando Valley. 1944."* YouTube.com.

Rollings, W. H. "Citizenship and Suffrage: The Native American Struggle for Civil Rights in the American West, 1830–1965." *Nevada Law Journal* 126(5), 2004.

Romero, S. "New Mexico Grapples with Its Version of Confederate Tributes: A Celebration of Spanish Conquest." *The New York Times*, September. 8, 2018.

Romero, S. "Man is Shot at Protest Over Statue of New Mexico's Conquistador." *The New York Times*, June 15, 2020.

Ronstadt, L. *Simple Dreams*. Simon and Schuster, 2014.

Rosales, F. A. *Chicano! The History of the Mexican American Civil Rights Movement*. Arte Público Press, University of Houston, 1996.

Rubin, A. *Axios*, April 1, 2024.

Sagan, S. D. "The Face of Battle Without Rules of the War: Lessons from Red Horse and the Battle of the Little Bighorn." *Dædalus*, 24-43, Winter 2017.

Salazar, R. "Who is a Chicano? And What is it the Chicanos Want?" *Los Angeles Times*, February 6, 1970.

Sallust. "Letter of Mithridates on Roman Expansion. 66 BC." The Latin Library.com.

Sanchez, J. P., R. L. Spude, A. Gómez. *New Mexico: A History*. University of Oklahoma Press, Norman, 2013.

Schmal, J. P. *The History of Zacatecas*. Houston, Texas, Houston Institute for Culture, 2004.

Schüren, U., W. Gabbert. *Human Sacrifice and Ritualized Violence in the*

Americas Before the European Conquest." *Part IV–Religious, Sacred and Ritualised Violence*. Cambridge, England, The Cambridge World History of Violence, 2020.

Segale, S. B. *At the End of the Santa Fe Trail*. Bruce Publishing Company, Milwaukee, Wisconsin, 1948.

SF Gate News. "Urban Legends, the Smoky Satan." 2001.

Shelton, D., H. Adelman (eds). *Encyclopedia of Genocide and Crimes Against Humanity*. Macmillan Reference, New York, 2005.

Sides, H. *Blood and Thunder: The Epic Story of Kit Carson and the Conquest of the American West*. Anchor Books, New York, 2006.

Simmons, M. *The Last Conquistador: Juan de Oñate and the Settling of the Far Southwest*. Norman, Oklahoma, University of Oklahoma Press, 1991.

Sisak, M. R. "Bannon Charged in New York with Laundering Money Raised to Build Border Wall." *PBS News*, September. 8, 2022.

Skoglund, P. *et al*. "Genetic Evidence for Two Founding Populations of the Americas." *Nature* 525:104-108, 2015.

Stanley-Becker, I. "When McCain's Anti-Asian Slur Stalled His 'Straight Talk Express,' He Doubled Down. Then, He Apologized." *Washington Post*, August 27, 2018.

Steil, M. and T. Post. "Hundreds of Settlers Killed in Attacks." Minnesota Public Radio, September 26, 2002.

Steinfels, P. "Kennedy Blessing Raises Questions for Catholics." *New York Times*, January 28, 1995.

The Scalp Industry. University of Virginia.edu.

Trump, M. L. *Too Much and Never Enough: How My Family Created the World's Most Dangerous Man*. Simon and Schuster, 2020.

Truxillo, C. "El República del Norte–The Next American Nation?" B. Nelson, *The Social Contract Press*, 11 (1):42-45, Fall, 2000.

Truxillo, C. *The Sword and the Cross: The Historical Evolution of the Catholic World Monarchy in Spain and the New World, 1492–1825*. Praeger Publishing, 2001.

U.S. Census. 1940 population. New Mexico.gov.

U.S. Department of Commerce, Thirteenth Census of the United States Taken in the Year 1910. Statistics for New Mexico. U.S. Government Printing Office, 1913.

Valdéz, L. *La Conquista de México. Actos y el Teatro Campesino*. Fresno, California, Cucaracha Publications, 1971.

Vargas Journal. *In* Espinosa, J. M. *Crusaders of the Rio Grande*. Institute of Jesuit History; First Edition, 108-110, January 1, 1942.

Verano J. W., Anderson L. S., Franco, R. "Foot Amputation by the Moche of Ancient Peru: Osteological Evidence and Archaeological Context." *International. Journal of Osteoarchaeology*, 10: 77-88, 2000.

Villagrá, G. P. de. *Historia de la Nueva Mexico.* 1610a. Miguel Encinias, Alfred Rodriguez and Joseph P. Sanchez (trans, eds), Albuquerque, University of New Mexico Press, 1992.

Villagrá, G. P. de. *Historia de la Nueva Mexico.* 1610b. Excerpt and translation, Kanellos, N., *et al.* (eds), *Herencia: The Anthology of Hispanic Literature in the United States*, 47-56, Oxford Press, New York 2002.

Wagner, H. R. "New Mexico Spanish Press." *New Mexico Historical Review*, 12 (1):1-40, 1937.

Watson Institute. "Costs of War. Iraqi Civilians." Providence, Rhode Island, Brown University, 2021.

Warner, D. 1945. "Jap Soldiers Impale Baby on Bayonet." *News Adelaide*, November 1, 1945.

Weber, J. *From South Texas to the Nation: The Exploitation of Mexican Labor in the Twentieth Century.* University of North Carolina Press, Chapel Hill, 2018.

Weber, D. J. *On the Edge of Empire: The Taos Hacienda of Los Martinez.* Museum of New Mexico Press, Santa Fe, 1996.

Westermeier, C. P. "Teddy's Terrors. The New Mexican Volunteers of 1898." *New Mexico Historical Review*, 27 (2), 3:107-136, 1952.

Wike, R., L. Silver, S. Schumacher, A. Connaughton. "Many in the US, Western Europe Say Their Political System Needs Major Reform." *Pew Research Report*, March 31, 2021.

Yardley, J. "A Salute to Bravery: Medal of Honor Heroes Meet." *The New York Times,* June 7, 1998.

YouTube. "Largest Mass Execution in Recent Memory: Saudi Arabia Executes 81 Men in One Day." 2022.

YouTube. "Texas Installing Buoys in Rio Grande." *CBS Streaming News,* 2023.

Yuen Yiu. "The Fear of Setting the Planet on Fire with a Nuclear Weapon." *Discover Magazine*, July 17, 2020.

Zerjal, T. *et al*. "The Genetic Legacy of the Mongols." *American Journal of Human Genetics,* 72:717-721, 2003.

Zuehlke, E. "Immigrants Work in Riskier and More Dangerous Jobs in the United States." *Population Reference Bureau (PRB),* October 30, 2009.

Zuo, L., *et al*. "Sex Chromosome–Wide Association Analysis Suggested Male-specific Risk Genes for Alcohol Dependence." *Psychiatric Genetics,* (6):233-238, December 23, 2013.

Fig. 62. Spanish flag 1760–1785. Wiki Commons.

Fig. 63. The flag of the great state of New Mexico. Wikipedia, Creative Commons.

www.ingramcontent.com/pod-product-compliance
Lightning Source LLC
Chambersburg PA
CBHW061341300426
44116CB00011B/1938